THE SUMMER SHACK COOKBOOK

Also by Jasper White

COOKING FROM NEW ENGLAND

LOBSTER AT HOME

50 CHOWDERS

THE SUMMER SHACK COOKBOOK

THE COMPLETE GUIDE TO SHORE FOOD

JASPER WHITE

Illustrations by Ann Wood
Color Photography by Kate Sears/Sublime

W. W. Norton & Company

NEW YORK · LONDON

For information about permission to reproduce selections from this book,
write to permissions, W. W. Norton & Company, Inc., 500 Fifth Avenue, New York, NY 10110

Manufacturing by RR Donnelley, Harrisonburg
Book design by Chalkley Calderwood
Production manager: Andrew Marasia

Library of Congress Cataloging-in-Publication Data

White, Jasper.
    The summer shack cookbook : the complete guide to shore food / by Jasper White ;
    color photography by Kate Sears ; illustrations by Ann Wood.
        p. cm.
    Includes index.
    ISBN 978-0-393-05238-1 (hardcover)
1. Cookery (Seafood) I. Title.
    TX747.W445 2007
    641.6'92—dc22

WHITE   2007001284

W. W. Norton & Company, Inc., 500 Fifth Avenue, New York, N.Y. 10110
www.wwnorton.com

W. W. Norton & Company Ltd., Castle House, 75/76 Wells Street, London W1T 3QT

1 2 3 4 5 6 7 8 9 0

To my customers, staff, partners, and investors at Summer Shack

TABLE OF CONTENTS

ACKNOWLEDGMENTS 9

INTRODUCTION 13

CHAPTER ONE
SHACK FOODS AT HOME:
THE SHORE KITCHEN 16

CHAPTER TWO
EAT IT RAW! 44

CHAPTER THREE
KETTLE COOKING PART I: 66
STEAMING AND BOILING

CHAPTER FOUR
KETTLE COOKING PART II: 92
SOUPS, CHOWDERS, AND STEWS

CHAPTER FIVE
FROM THE ICEBOX: CHILLED
SEAFOOD AND SALADS 116

CHAPTER SIX
HOT OFF THE GRILL 144

CHAPTER SEVEN
FLASH IN THE PAN:
INDOOR COOKING 204

CHAPTER EIGHT
BOARDWALK AND SHACK
FAVORITES: CRISPY FRIED
FOODS AND OTHER
FUN STUFF 246

CHAPTER NINE
THE MORNING OVEN 288

CHAPTER TEN
REFRESHMENTS 320

CHAPTER ELEVEN
BASIC RECIPES 340

INDEX 359

ACKNOWLEDGMENTS

Opening a restaurant requires a leap of faith—you can only hope the people you hired will absorb what you teach them, understand the concept, and execute the game plan. Most of them do, a few of them get lost, and some go above and beyond—their contributions become part of the infrastructure of the restaurant. It is the same with a cookbook, it is the collaboration that defines it.

My heartfelt thanks go to all of the people on my restaurant and cookbook team, especially to:

Jeff Dugan, my right-hand man and partner, who keeps the ship on course.

Patrick Lyons and Ed Sparks, my partners, who helped to create and launch Summer Shack.

David Parr and Brian Flagg, executive chefs at Summer Shack, and their sous-chefs—Tim Willis, Mike Libby, and Henning Vagtborg.

Sidnei Felipe, Ben Korman, Michelle Boucher, and Tom Browne, general managers of our restaurants, and Dan Redfern, our financial guru.

My wonderful staff of dining room managers, waiters, bartenders, prep cooks, line cooks, bakers, busboys (and girls), runners, shuckers, dishwashers, and hostesses.

Max Harvey and Dave Forcinito, our "fish guys." Max and Dave can be found at the Boston Fish Pier, where they hand select, process, and deliver the fabulous fresh seafood we use at our restaurants. I would also like to acknowledge the fisherman and their families for the sacrifices they make to bring healthful and beautiful seafood to market.

Kay Rentschler, who worked with me on the original recipes and then meticulously retested and transcribed them. Katie Sherry, our Pastry Chef, and Frank Reardon, our bartender and expert mixologist, were of great help and assisted in developing some of the pastry and cocktail recipes.

Ann Wood, the painter and art director who makes the Summer Shack come to life. She has done it again with her illustrations for this cookbook.

Kate Sears, who did a beautiful job of photographing our simple food, and Michael Peterson, my favorite food stylist in the world.

Doe Coover, literary agent par excellence, who has shown the same amount of enthusiasm for this book as she does the Pearl hot dogs at Summer Shack—and that's a lot!

Maria Guarnaschelli, who always brings the best out in her authors; her passion is unparalleled. This is our third book together, and I'm grateful for all she has taught me.

Julia Child, our most famous "regular" at Summer Shack in Cambridge. She often came in after the movies for oysters and a lobster roll. I miss her dearly.

Chef Lydia Shire, who has been my cooking partner, valued confidant, and dear friend for many years.

Sally Jackson, my publicist, who only lets them say good things about me and who always finds a way to make me laugh.

Judith Sutton, this book's talented copyeditor; Chalkley Calderwood Pratt, whose design captured the spirit of Summer Shack, and the team at W. W. Norton: Star Lawrence, Jeannie

Luciano, Drake McFeely, Andrew Marasia, Debra Morton-Hoyt, Nancy Palmquist, Susan Sanfrey, Sue Carlson, and Sarah Rothbard.

Lastly, I send my love and gratitude to my family: Nancy, J.P., Mariel, Hayley, Mom, Dad, Trevor, Julie, Michael, Matt, Jamie, Matthew, Kristen, Elaine, Tom, and all my cousins, nieces, and nephews.

THE
SUMMER
SHACK
COOKBOOK

INTRODUCTION

As a kid growing up in Freehold, New Jersey, about ten miles from the ocean, I spent many happy days with my family and friends swimming and soaking up the sun at the beach, fishing in the surf, crabbing in the bays, and hanging out at the boardwalks in Asbury Park, Seaside Heights, and Wildwood. The boardwalk was the most fun of all because, in addition to the amusing rides, we kids could eat things we didn't usually get at home, like hot funnel cakes, sausage sandwiches, fried clams, pizza, and big crispy French fries—it was nirvana. The food obviously wasn't heart healthy, but it was heart happy—it added to the joy of being at the shore.

My family was Roman Catholic, so we ate seafood every Friday. But my mom, dad, brothers, and sister all enjoyed seafood, and it was often inexpensive or even free (when we caught our own or if a friend dropped some off) so we ate fish or shellfish more often than just on Fridays. My favorites, in no particular order, were blue crabs, steamers, blowfish tails, fluke, shrimp, striped bass, and lobster. Whatever type we had for dinner, my mom always prepared it simply. It gave me an appreciation and love for the pure flavor of unadulterated food fresh from the ocean. But when I pursued my career as a professional chef in upscale restaurants and then went on to become an entrepreneur, my personal favorites from my past were left in limbo.

Years ago, I owned and operated a very high-end dining establishment in Boston called Jasper's. My wife, Nancy, and I worked and lived in the city. To escape from the rat race, we bought a little camp house on Sawyer's Island in Maine. During those years, I avoided the "real" (sit-down) restaurants in the region and, when we didn't cook at home, we ate most of our meals at roadside clam shacks, waterfront lobster joints, diners, and festivals or fairs. Those were the places where I felt most comfortable, and I developed a burning desire to create a shack of my own, where this kid from the Jersey Shore could cook very simple foods and show his true identity. That desire remained with me for many years and was the inspiration for my Summer Shack restaurants, which I started in the year 2000.

Summer Shack is not just a "restaurant concept"—it is an expression of who I am and what I really like. The menu and now this cookbook tell the story of a chef who believes that great food is as much as or more about ingredients and where they come from than cooking techniques and creativity. This book is not just a collection of restaurant recipes—these are *my* recipes, and they are close to my heart. They evolved from a lifetime spent living near the shore and a cooking career focused on seafood. Some of the recipes were created by or have been adapted from cooks who have worked for me; I've cherry-picked those recipes over the years, and they have become a part of the restaurant's repertoire.

From its inception, Summer Shack has always been focused on serving groups of families, friends, and others who are comfortable being part of a group and who are out to enjoy each other's company and feast on fresh seafood and other summer delights. There is no question that seafood can be very elegant, but the essence of great seafood is not elegance, it is flavor—and that often calls for cooking and serving lobster, crab, and fish whole and clams, shrimp, and mussels in their shells. The flavor is elegant, but you need to roll up your sleeves and get a little messy to truly appreciate and enjoy this food. That is why I chose the word "shack" for the restaurant's name. It's not really a shack, it's a real restaurant, but you can eat as if you're at a clam shack or at a picnic table at the shore. The menu changes four times a year, featuring our seasonal, and signature offerings such as steamers, calamari, fried fish, shrimp, crab, and lobster. Large blackboards list the day's varieties of oysters, along with seafood appetizers, grilled fish, fresh-baked pies, and other daily specials, and these items account for almost half of our business. Being flexible with our menu and blackboard offerings is part of what defines our operation. In addition to our restaurants, Summer Shack also has a space on the Boston Fish Pier, where our seafood manager, Max Harvey, and his crew select and process the freshest and most interesting seafood available on the East Coast every day. Max works closely with our chefs, helping them to take advantage of what's best each day. Cooking seafood successfully at home requires the same mentality. You can plan your Thanksgiving menu a month in advance, but for great seafood dinners, you need to write your menu in pencil (or on a blackboard). The recipes in this cookbook reflect the flexibility needed to cook seafood successfully, and I give you options that will make it easy to change your dinner menu when you were planning on swordfish but the striped bass looks much better at the market.

The food served at Summer Shack is what I call "shore food." The shore is a region that includes towns, highways, marinas, boardwalks, farms, shops, bars, restaurants, food shacks, and, of course, beaches. Transcending simple definition, the shore comes complete with its own culture. Shore town communities have their own identities and idiosyncrasies, yet there is a common thread linking them so that they are more similar than they are different. Food is one of the defining characteristics of life at the shore, and "shore food" is a style of planning, preparing, cooking, and eating foods that are enjoyed along the Atlantic Coast from Canada to the Caribbean. Whether it is a Maine lobster bake, a Maryland crab dinner, a Carolina oyster roast, or a Key West shrimp boil, there is a commonality and sensibility that is the same up and down the coast. At the shore, we all can eat like kings.

The menu at Summer Shack is based largely on seafood—a combination of the traditional items such as fried clams, fritters, steamers, fish cakes, and fish and chips that you would expect at a "shack" blended with a raw bar and more innovative, contemporary preparations of grilled, sautéed, roasted, and even stir-fried fish and shellfish. We also serve fried chicken, steak tips, meat loaf, and "boardwalk foods" like corn dogs, snow cones, and big crispy French fries. Because we are located in New England, our offerings are largely reflective of this region, but we are by no means limited to it. We fly fresh shrimp and other Southern seafood up from the Carolinas and Florida almost every week. We make an authentic Jamaican jerk rub for fish, and we use Old Bay seasoning for our crabs, just as they do on the Chesapeake. Our inspiration may come from the Mediterranean, Asia, Middle East, or South America—we are not chauvinistic. But that inspiration needs to fit into our shore-food style: It can't be too fussy, and it can't overwhelm the natural flavors of the seafood.

Like most people who grew up near the ocean,

I find it difficult being away from it. With the exception of a summer I spent working in Montana, I have always lived within a half hour of the ocean. I have a need to be near it and to see it, even if for just a moment's fleeting glance. Whether I'm in Nova Scotia or Florida, I know the water—the Atlantic—and it is my home. Being involved in the seafood industry and having consulted for lobster companies in Canada, I've spent a good amount of time in maritime Canada, which is one of the world's richest regions for both wild and cultivated seafood. I have fond memories of eating just-landed snow crabs up in Shediack, New Brunswick, and of braising fresh halibut with local chanterelles in Nova Scotia. I have spent years summering up in Maine, where I explored the local foods on a daily basis. But I've lived the biggest part of my life in the Boston area and I'm very familiar with the coastal towns of Massachusetts, from Cape Ann and Cape Cod to the "South Coast," where the large Portuguese culture has influenced the way I cook seafood. My favorite place on the New England coast is Little Compton, Rhode Island, where my wife and her sister own a summer house right on the water at Warren's Point. Since opening a restaurant in southwest Connecticut (at Mohegan Sun Resort and Casino), I have gotten to know the Mystic Seaport area and now buy a lot of seafood from Stonington, Connecticut. As I mentioned earlier, I grew up on the Jersey Shore, where most of the species and preparations of seafood are similar to those of the Chesapeake region. I also spent time with a good friend who lived on Tilghman's Island on the Maryland side of Chesapeake Bay. Some of my family has lived in Flagler Beach, in northeastern Florida, for the last sixty years, so I have enjoyed the local seafood there for my entire life. My brother still lives there, and I always look forward to eating fresh shrimp and beautiful produce from the local farms when we visit each spring. I've also spent a lot of time in the Caribbean, both as a tourist and as a chef. I have a great fondness for the island cooks and their cuisine. I understand and love all the shore food from the "Atlantic Rim," and I want to share what I have learned about it with you in this book.

At Summer Shack, we believe that "Food Is Love." A slogan that I trademarked, it is a simple message that says it all. Food comes from the ocean and the land, and people work very hard, sometimes even risking their lives, in order to put that food on our table. I truly appreciate the efforts of the fishermen and farmers who make so many great meals possible. That is where the love begins—and it is up to all of us to keep that goodness going by treating the ingredients with great respect and cooking in a way that lets them taste the way nature created them. When we share the food with family and friends, when we gather together to partake, to roll up our sleeves and eat that food with passion and joy, we allow that food to fulfill its destiny and we complete the cycle of love.

INSIDE THIS CHAPTER

Strategies for Staying Cool and Making Great Meals   20

The Morning and Evening Kitchen   22

Finding Fresh Ingredients at the Source   24

Kitchen Equipment, Shack-Style   26

The Basic Pantry at the Beach   32

Seafood Tips, Notes, and How-To   36

-1-

THE SHORE KITCHEN

SHACK FOODS AT HOME

This book is chock-full of recipes that I have developed over the years, some at home and many in my restaurants. Each recipe is complete in itself, so if you only use this cookbook for the occasional recipe and don't read it from cover to cover, you won't be disappointed—but, as with everything else in life, there are layers here. The deeper you probe, the more you will learn. Many of my recipes have connections to each other because they were born from or inspired by my experience with foods that come from the sea or grow close to the shore. Some recipes were inspired by the many terrific (and some classic) seafood shacks and restaurants I have visited from Nova Scotia to the Caribbean. Although a lot of the dishes that make up the "shore food" genre were created in homes along the coast, even more were developed in shacks and restaurants and then translated into home cooking. Together they meld into more that just recipes—they form a foundation for a style of cooking that is driven by fresh ingredients, with lots of built-in flexibility. The shore kitchen is a very casual and fun place, and the cook doesn't have to be fussy to create spectacular dinners.

Whether you live along the East Coast or in the Midwest, you can create your own shore kitchen. Although it is certainly easier to find great seafood along the coast, air transport has made it possible for just about everyone to access good seafood. Any kitchen can be a shore kitchen–it's a state of mind.

Just for this moment, imagine that you are at Cape Cod, Martha's Vineyard, the Jersey Shore, the Chesapeake, the Carolinas, Florida, the Bahamas, or whatever your favorite coastal place is. (By the way, you don't have to work today.) It is eight a.m., and the sun is bright after burning off the early morning mist. It is a beautiful day, offering you a world of possibilities from going to the beach or fishing or clam digging to walking or biking to playing tennis, golf, or ball with the kids, and more. Of course,

you and your family and/or friends will enjoy a meal or two in between all the fun. But making delicious food doesn't have to take away from your day—it can become an enjoyable part of it. Dinner can even unfold along with your day, especially if you are fishing or gathering shellfish. The trick to making great shore meals is to have ready-to-eat and/or easy-to-make foods on hand as a supplement to the wonderful seafood, vegetables, and other fresh ingredients that are abundant in most seaside locations.

Relax. Forget the traditional concept of meal planning: it's different at the shore. Let the place, and all the food that happens around that place, seep into your subconscious. Keep a road map in your head of the sources for the best ingredients. Chances are that you will be passing at least one of these places while you are out and about. Let the day's market determine the night's menu. Even for serious cooks, the focus of the shore kitchen is not technique or artistry—it is the ingredients. And because the indigenous foods you'll find at the shore (especially in summer) are so excellent, the simplest of recipes and techniques are all that is needed to make the ingredients taste their absolute best.

Don't think of your kitchen as a production facility or an art studio. Think of it is a transfer station, where food is made ready to eat with as little fussing as possible. In this chapter, I give you my best advice on how to approach cooking at the shore, whether you live there or not. I share my ideas in cooking techniques, equipment, shopping, and lifestyle strategies that will enable you to make supreme meals without sacrificing precious hours of your time. Feeding friends and family doesn't have to be an obstacle to your pursuit of happiness. Instead, it can be a source of happiness, a meaningful experience that brings everyone closer.

STRATEGIES FOR STAYING COOL AND MAKING GREAT MEALS

When I go to the shore, I bring shorts, T-shirts, a bathing suit, and stuff for fishing, golf, and tennis. What I don't bring—dress clothes or any dark-colored clothing, chef's uniforms, socks, and hard shoes—is even more important. And this relates to shore food as well. To understand shore foods and to prepare them, you also have to "pack light." Leave your year-round habits behind, along with most of your recipes. Replace the things that you didn't bring with a new viewpoint, an expanded notion of the kitchen itself, as well as of ways to shop and cook.

Let's start with four concepts that will help to get you into the Summer Shack groove.

1. **The shore kitchen is not merely the room that holds the refrigerator and stove.** It is your deck, porch, or patio where the green beans are snapped, the grill outside the door, the bench or dock where you fillet fish, and the spot out back where the corn is shucked. It is the stone-lined pit you made for clambakes, the picnic table where you shuck clams and oysters, and the bonfire where you roast hot dogs and marshmallows. It's the special outdoor propane burner (see page 31) that you use on occasion for outdoor fish fries or for a shrimp boil (and for deep-fried turkey on Thanksgiving). Many shore kitchens start with a fairly humble room, often very dated. If you happen to have a large kitchen, it will be easier to work in. If you have a large kitchen with modern amenities, that's even better. But if you have only an average place or a small kitchen, it will have little or no bearing on the quality of the food you cook,

serve, and eat. Lobsters don't taste any better steamed on a Viking range then cooked outdoors over that propane burner.

2. **Shopping at the shore is more than a trip to the supermarket.** Try replacing some of your supermarket shopping with a stop at the nearby farm stand, fish market, bakery, and/or the local docks. Or fish first, shop later. Look. Food is all around you. It can be found at the rocky beach where you can pick mussels or periwinkles, the mud flats where you can rake clams, the inlet where you catch crabs, as well as the berry patch and the pot of herbs outside your door. The concept of gathering is at the heart and soul of the shore kitchen.

3. **Remember that you are not the only cook.** If you are usually the primary cook in your family, break away from that role and become the conductor instead. Delegate. Include everybody. Kids are great at shucking corn, snapping peas or beans, peeling potatoes, and many other simple tasks (and simple tasks are the bulk of the work). Helping with the family meal gives everyone a sense of connection and accomplishment.

4. **Make a suitable amount of food ahead of time and let the preparation time fit into your schedule.** There are many terrific one-pot meals, as well as side dishes, snacks, and desserts, that can be made ahead; many of them are actually better when prepared in advance. Time improves the flavor of slow-cooked foods like baked beans and chowders. Dishes like Creamy Potato Salad (page 141), Succotash Salad (page 138), and

Summer Shack Coleslaw (page 140) also improve if made a day ahead. Many of the recipes in this book can be made in stages. You can prepare these dishes up to a point earlier in the day, then finish them at dinner time. And doubling a recipe doesn't take double the time—often it takes only minutes longer. This is an economy of scale that works in your favor when making dishes that you would love to eat more than once over of a couple of days. "Make ahead and make a lot" is a mantra for the shore kitchen.

Armed with these concepts, let's now take a fresh look at the actual workings and organization of a shore kitchen. Basic tools and equip-

ment combined with beautiful, fresh local ingredients and top-quality staple items are all that you really need. If you are well organized and use your time in the kitchen wisely, you will be ready to let the meals happen. That is the Zen of making shack foods at home.

One last tip: many of the recipes in this book are very simple. The beauty in the presentation of shack foods or shore dinners is not in arranging them elaborately on individual plates or a platter, it is in the overall effect of several simple dishes set out together, family-style—their good looks are cumulative.

THE MORNING AND EVENING KITCHEN:

Managing Your Time to Keep the Living Easy

Years ago, I worked as a consulting chef at a small resort called Petite St. Vincent, one of the Grenadine Islands, down in the peaceful and beautiful "windward islands" of the Caribbean. To avoid the midday heat, which could be especially brutal near the stoves, the kitchen was closed from noon to six o'clock. We served three meals a day, feeding fifty to a hundred guests in addition to a large staff. The service was brilliantly organized, the menu and work schedule flowed beautifully. I thoroughly enjoyed this stint. I would work from six in the morning to noon, then return at six p.m. for just a few more hours. Here's how it played out: In the morning, the kitchen was all abuzz. It was the liveliest time of day, with eggs being cooked for breakfast, breads and desserts being baked for lunch and dinner, and soups, sauces, vegetables, and other dishes being prepped as much as possible without sacrificing quality. The cooks worked on breakfast, picnic lunches, the lunch buffet, and dinner all at the same time. By nine or ten a.m., the fishermen who lived on the island would bring their catch right to our door. We bought fresh conch, live rock lobsters, and three or four varieties of fish each day. Before noon, the seafood was filleted or prepped and chilled, ready to become the evening special. That island kitchen was the quintessential shore kitchen, where the cooks (well, all but the one or two who worked the lunch buffet) rested during the hottest time of the day.

The concept of the morning and evening kitchen can be a template for your summer kitchen. You can choose the time of day to prep and then divide the work to fit your schedule. It allows you to enjoy the process instead of becoming overwhelmed. The first stage is to bring the ingredients to the point that only minimal cooking and assembling will be needed to complete the dinner. The second stage is simply a matter of finishing the work started earlier. I have indicated the natural break in each recipe when applicable (see "Working Ahead"). Because most seafood requires last-minute cooking, the object is to balance the grilled fish, steamed lobster, or whatever main dish you've chosen with side dishes that are made ahead, or are partially prepared ahead and require only last-minute preparation, or are quick and easy, like steamed rice or Corn on the Cob (page 90). For example, you have two beautiful fillets of bass that a friend dropped off the night before. In the morning, you cut the bass into portions and whip up a Cold Cucumber Sauce (page 180) to serve with it. You might also parboil some potatoes so they can be grilled along with the bass. You stop at the farm stand on the way home from the beach for some local corn, tomatoes, and melon. At dinner, you only need to fire up the grill (or ask someone else to), pull out the fish and potatoes, season them, and grill them. You boil water for the corn (which was shucked by someone else) and make a salad of the sliced tomatoes. After dinner, you simply cut up some wedges of ripe melon.

A very fine shore dinner, indeed, and it took less than an hour of your time in the evening kitchen.

Remember the mantra "Make ahead, make a lot!" In order to do this efficiently, you need to consider several things. Some of the items you

DINNER TONIGHT

Grilled Striped Bass with Cold Cucumber Sauce

Grilled Potatoes

Sliced Tomato Salad

Corn on the Cob

Chilled Fresh Melon

will be preparing are desserts, salads, and side dishes that will eventually be served with a main dish you haven't always decided on yet. Recipes like Summer Shack Coleslaw (page 140), Succotash Salad (page 138), Home Fries (page 221), and All-Purpose Vinaigrette (page 342) are not neutral in flavor, by any means—they are bursting with flavor—but they complement many different foods. I am a big fan of multipurpose recipes. For example, the vinaigrette can be used as a marinade for fish or chicken, or it can be quickly modified to become a Tomato Vinaigrette (see page 342) for a salad to be served with grilled steak. A side dish of coleslaw lends itself to a wide variety of menus, whether it's seafood for dinner or sandwiches for lunch.

FINDING FRESH INGREDIENTS AT THE SOURCE

Shopping for groceries at a supermarket or wholesale club is not my idea of a good time. But shopping at the shore is a very different experience. Because it can include farm stands, farmers' markets, fish markets, general stores, docks, fishing boats, and even private homes, it's fun.

Dockside and Roadside Seafood

If you live near a coastal region where people make a living from commercial fishing or harvesting shellfish, you can buy seafood that has been out of the water for only hours. That is a luxury worth taking advantage of. Large seaports often have a specific area for commercial fishing vessels; smaller ones may serve a mixture of recreational and working boats. It is unlikely that the captain of a large commercial boat, with a crew of three or more, will give you the time of day, so look for the small "day boats." It's pretty easy to spot a commercial boat, because commercial fishermen take very good care of the engine, fishing gear, and other workings of their boats, but day boat crews don't often fuss over appearances. If you happen to catch a boat that is off

loading and you see a fish you would like to buy, pull out your wad of cash, so it is visible, and ask them, "How much?" Money talks.

If you take a drive along an Atlantic coast road, you are likely to pass a house with a handmade sign offering lobsters, crabs, or other fresh seafood. These places often sell only one kind of fish, but what you buy could be the freshest of the fresh. In many places, small fishermen will take their catch, or part of it, out to the road and sell it right out of the back of their truck, in a stripped-down version of a farm stand. I have bought fabulous fresh *borealis* red (Maine) shrimp up on Route 1, north of Wiscasset, Maine; soft-shell crabs roadside near Tilghman's Island on the Chesapeake; and freshly harvested cherrystone clams near St. Augustine, Florida. Since this seafood is freshly caught or harvested, the issue is proper storage and handling. I'm not at all afraid to stop and make this kind of purchase, and you shouldn't be either, especially if the seller shows up at the same spot frequently.

Just remember, when you head out to the docks or to a roadside stand, to bring an insulated cooler with you—temperature control is paramount with freshly caught finfish and shellfish.

Farm Stands, Roadside Stands, and Farmers' Markets

Farm stands and farmers' markets are places of pure inspiration. The ingredients speak to me as I stop at the different tables or stalls. The zucchini and eggplant remind me to make ratatouille, the tomatoes and basil beg me to slice them for a salad, and the tiny new potatoes ask to be steamed and dressed with a vinaigrette. There is no need to plan before going to a farm stand or market—in fact, planning is counterproductive. Just bring a large shopping basket, and let the fresh fruits and vegetables write your menu.

Because so many of us are acclimated to one-stop supermarkets, some people will not go out of their way to detour to a farm stand to buy local tomatoes. But some local farmers, who depend on their farm stand rather than commercial customers, have learned to supplement their own homegrown foods with an array of other fruits and vegetables for the convenience of their customers. That means that, at times, not all produce at the farm stand is equal. If the produce is not clearly labeled "our peppers," "just-picked," or something to that effect, you should ask questions. After all, the superior flavor and goodness of fresh local produce is the reason you went to the stand in the first place. It's fine to buy a few lemons that were obviously grown elsewhere, but you don't want to go home with California broccoli when you could be eating local green beans.

Much of what I have learned about cooking and ingredients over the years is the result of conversations I had with farmers, fishermen, and other people who grow or gather the food we eat. Occasionally they even pass on cooking advice. Some of it is not always sound, but it provides a window for me into regional cooking. Farm stands are important. They connect us to the farmer, to the seasons, and to the land, and they give us easy access to first-class ingredients.

In addition to the fresh fruits, vegetables, meats, and dairy products you will find at farmers' markets, many of these also serve as outlets for small artisan producers. From the handmade sheep's milk cheese I bought at the farmers' market in Damariscotta, Maine, to the fresh hopper shrimp I bought at the market in Flagler Beach, Florida, I've always been pleasantly surprised at the many options. At the shore and in the country, most farmers' markets are only open one or two days (usually mornings) a week. Find out the day for your local market and put it on your schedule. Then you can base the rest of your shopping on what you don't buy at the farmers' market.

KITCHEN EQUIPMENT, SHACK-STYLE

Shore food is all about simplicity, so it should follow that the equipment used for shack-style cooking would be equally simple. However, having the right knives, tools, and other equipment is very important and, ironically, some of these are more exotic then those used in a traditional kitchen. For example, you may not use a fish fillet knife often in your daily cooking, but in your shore kitchen it can be extremely useful, even essential. An outdoor propane burner can take the big mess of steaming seafood outdoors, where it becomes a fun event. An oversized steam pot guarantees perfectly steamed clams and lobsters. You can't open an oyster easily without a good oyster knife.

That being said, let's get our priorities straight: the equipment I talk about here makes cooking easier, not more complex. Note that my list is not complete—I don't feel compelled to discuss potato peelers, although you will probably want one. Here are some of the tools I consider uniquely important for making Summer Shack–style food.

Cooking Utensils, Pots, and Pans

Wooden Spoons

I love wooden spoons—solid or slotted, in any shape or size. I like the way they feel in my hand. I like the way they feel against the inside of the pot. I like them because they are gentle: metal against metal is harsh.

Wooden citrus reamer

Wooden Citrus Reamer

This two-dollar tool is indispensable for juicing all the lemons and lime you will need for seviches and other seafood recipes. It is also invaluable for making fresh juices for mixing cocktails.

Chef's knife

French Knife, Chef's Knife, or Japanese-Style Knife

This is the all-purpose knife every cook should own. Depending on your stature and style of cutting, you may use a knife that is heavier or lighter, shorter or longer—it is really a matter of personal taste. If you live very close to the water, avoid knives that are 100 percent carbon steel, as they will rust very quickly; stainless steel, or stainless–carbon steel (which are easier to sharpen), knives are a must. Or you might want to try the expensive new ceramic knives, which are quite excellent.

Chinese cleaver

Chinese Cleaver

A medium-sized Chinese cleaver can be used for many tasks, from cutting up chickens to cutting through fish bones (for fish steaks) to, most important, cutting up lobsters and crabs.

Chinese wire-mesh skimmer

Chinese Wire-Mesh Skimmer

An inexpensive wooden-handled mesh skimmer, which can be found in specialty cookware shops and Asian markets, is excellent for all kinds of jobs, particularly for lifting foods out of boiling water or hot oil. I highly recommend this tool.

Fish fillet knife

Fish Fillet Knife

A fish knife with a long, thin, flexible blade allows you to cut around the bones of the fish while pressing against them, taking as much meat as possible away from the bones. With a stiff knife, your yield is likely to be less.

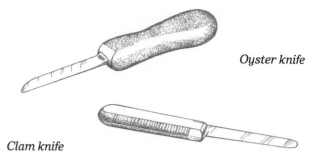
Oyster knife

Clam knife

Oyster and Clam Knives

These specialty knives are inexpensive but irreplaceable. An oyster knife has a very sturdy blade for leverage and a sharp point for minimum resistance upon entering the oyster. A clam knife is more like a dull paring knife, just sharp enough to slide in between the two half shells.

Japanese fish tweezers

Japanese Fish Tweezers or Needle-Nose Pliers

Japanese fish tweezers are not easy to find, so if you do come across this very special tool, buy a few. I have seen them in specialty equipment shops, seafood markets, and Asian markets. They are designed perfectly for pulling the pin bones from fish fillets, so they don't break the bones. If you can't find the tweezers needle-nose pliers work pretty well.

Sauté Pan

A medium-weight 9- to 12-inch slope-sided sauté pan is essential for quickly sautéing seafood and vegetables that benefit from fast cooking over high heat.

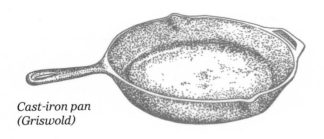

*Cast-iron pan
(Griswold)*

Cast-Iron Pan (Griswold)

These big (10- to 14-inch and even larger) black pans that you may see at the hardware store are reasonably priced and multipurposed. If you use one for cooking pancakes, eggs, or other breakfast items, you may wish to reserve it exclusively for this purpose, in which case you should never scrub it with an abrasive object—just wipe it clean with a rag. It will become seasoned and keep improving with age. Then have a second one as an-all purpose pan for searing fish, pan-frying potatoes, and many other uses. Lightly oil the pan before storing to prevent rust and maintain a smooth surface.

Dutch oven

Dutch Oven or Other Large Heavy Pot with a Tight-Fitting Lid

This is the pot for making stews, chowders, and soups. Every shore kitchen needs a heavy pot (at least 4 to 5 quarts) with a lid that can be used both on top of the stove and in the oven. It is essential for baked beans and terrific for deep-frying. The weight of the pot and the material will determine the expense, cast iron being the least expensive and more than adequate.

Porcelain-lined iron, stainless, or copper Dutch ovens are expensive but excellent.

Deep Fryer

To set up a simple deep fryer at home, choose a simple large high-sided heavy pot, such as a Dutch oven, between 4 and 6 quarts. You will need a deep-fry thermometer and a basket or wire-mesh skimmer for removing the fried items. For a large outdoor fish fry, use a large (3- to 4-gallon) heavy pot set on top of a propane burner (see page 31).

Steamer pot

Big Pot for Boiling and Steaming

This all-important pot can take many forms, from a fairly light, tall, narrow pot designated for corn on the cob to pots designed for boiling and steaming shellfish. The pot should be 12 to 14 inches across, whichever fits on your largest burner. The height will determine the capacity, but 4 to 6 gallons is ideal. It must have a tight-fitting lid. For steaming, you can set the pot up with a rack, or simply use rockweed to create a steamer (see page 71). There is also a special pot made just for steamers (soft-shell clams) that is also good for steaming lobsters and other shellfish; see page 70.

Roasting Pans

Try to get the biggest roasting pan that will fit into your oven, allowing a few inches all around for heat circulation. That way, when you catch an eight-pound fish, you can roast it whole and create a meal that just might be the defining one of your summer (see page 238). It's good to have other sizes of roasting pans around too. They can double as storage containers for items like fish or shellfish that you don't want dripping inside your refrigerator.

Long and short tongs

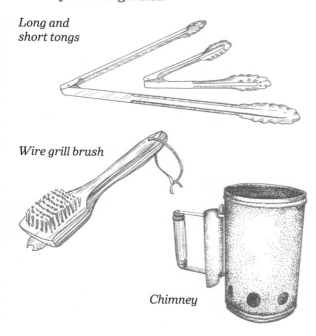

Wire grill brush

Chimney

Grilling Tools

You will need long-handled tongs and a long-handled spatula, a wire brush, and a chimney for starting your fire.

Pie Pans

I recommend the glass pie plates sold in most stores. They are inexpensive, they don't rust, they allow you to see the bottom crust to determine doneness, and the pies look nice served in the pans. I also think that pies bake more evenly in glass than in metal pans.

Rolling Pins

I recommend a solid wooden rolling pin (pins with ball bearings can rust out quickly near the shore). I prefer the long tapered (French) rolling pin over the old-fashioned ones that have handles, but that is up to you.

Salad Spinner

Salad is an essential food, and the salad spinner is an essential tool. There is no better, easier way to dry lettuce and other greens. Dry lettuce is crucial for a great salad.

Mason jars

Jars or Plastic Ware with Tight-Fitting Lids (for storage)

If you are near the shore, you cannot exist without different sizes and shapes of jars (canning jars work well) or plastic containers (such as Tupperware) with tight-fitting lids. Use these to store your spice mixes and pantry items like flour, sugar, and, especially, salt. Almost everything is more perishable at the shore.

Large and Plugged-in Equipment

Blender

"Don't leave home without it!" my buddies used to say when we would all head to the shore for our wild weekends, before life got too serious. There are important things that only a blender can make, like Watermelon Margaritas (page 336) and frozen daiquiris.

Food Processor or Handheld Blender

The food processor can save a lot of time, chopping ingredients and making purees or sauces, among other tasks. A handheld blender, also called a stick or immersion blender, can turn any bowl into a food processor.

Handheld blender

Electric Deep-Fat Fryer

Most people love fried foods but they don't make them at home because they are intimidated by the process. A Fry Daddy or other electric deep fryer solves many of the potential difficulties, particularly keeping an even regulated temperature. One of these is a terrific addition to any shore kitchen.

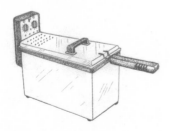

Electric deep-fat fryer

Fry Daddy electric deep-fat fryer

Outdoor Grill

I recommend you get the biggest charcoal grill you can find. You can always build a small fire on a large grill, but you can't do the opposite. I use a 48-inch round Weber. I build my fire in the middle so I can control the intensity of the heat by moving the food closer or farther from the center, as needed (see page 147). Gas grills may be convenient (as long as you don't run out of fuel), but they are inferior to charcoal grills because they can never deliver the intense heat and tasty smoke of a real wood fire.

Oven and Range

At the shore, you can make do with almost any range and oven; in the summer heat, it is ventilation that is most important—make sure your hood is performing at its best. If you own your shore home, upgrading your kitchen ventilation system can be an excellent investment. If you do not have "make-up air," then keep a nearby window open. Electric or gas? If you have a choice, go for gas or propane. You have more control over the heat with an open flame. Also, you can roast peppers and peel tomatoes by holding them over an open flame until they blister.

Test your oven temperature periodically with an oven thermometer. If you don't want to pay for calibration, if necessary, simply adjust the oven up or down to attain the desired temperature (mark the gauge accordingly).

Outdoor Propane Burner

This is a portable low-standing, single large gas burner. It is also called an outdoor propane stove or a candy cooker, a name that refers to its use in bakeries (where burners are not otherwise in high demand). A propane burner can be purchased at restaurant supply stores or some hardware stores. Although a propane burner is not a necessity by any stretch of the imagination, it

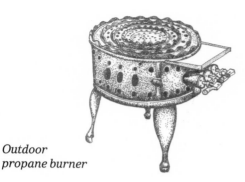

*Outdoor
propane burner*

costs less then a good gas grill and can become a focal point for large gatherings: whether it's a Key West Shrimp Boil (page 79), Lobster in the Rough (page 71), or Smashing Crabs (page 76), it can move the party outdoors. The mess and the heat move outside as well.

Thermal Coolers and Boxes

You might not think of coolers as kitchen equipment, but these can be invaluable when cooking for a lot of people because they increase your ability to keep cold foods cold and hot foods hot. Other than the obvious and important use of chilling beverages, thermal boxes can be used to keep cooked lobster and crab hot when you are serving more than your kettle can handle. Conversely, they are handy for chilling whole cooked lobsters and crabs and keeping them chilled so they don't take up space in your refrigerator. And you can use a cooler to supplement your refrigerator, especially for big items like watermelon. It is also smart to keep a smaller cooler in your car when you are shopping for seafood.

THE BASIC PANTRY AT THE BEACH

In the next few pages, I talk about some of the "support" ingredients needed to cook many of the recipes in this book and some of the issues that make storing and cooking them a little different at the beach, where humidity and dampness can wreak havoc with certain foods. I believe that a dish can only be as good as the worst ingredient, and therefore every ingredient you use in your kitchen is equally important.

Fresh Herbs

Fresh herbs are available at farmers' markets, farm stands, and most supermarkets these days, but you can easily grow herbs in pots or in the soil at home. In fact, many herbs, such as rosemary and cilantro, don't need rich soil and do very well in the sandy soil near the shore. Many farm stands and most nurseries sell potted herbs—all you need to give them is water and sunlight. Store fresh herbs in plastic bags in your refrigerater. Thyme, parsley, mint, basil, cilantro, and chives are the herbs that I find absolutely essential for creating summer flavors. Thyme and parsley are especially important in seafood preparations. Dill, tarragon, summer savory, rosemary, and lavender will add variety and great flavor to your summer dishes.

Dried Spices and Herbs

When you live close to the water, the humidity can ruin your dried spices and herbs because they soak up the moisture and become rehydrated, releasing flavors that should be going into the dishes you cook them in. Buy the small-est amount possible of your favorite seasonings, and be sure to keep the lids tightly sealed.

The dried spices and herbs that I keep on hand are: whole black peppercorns, cayenne pepper, crushed red pepper, bay leaves, whole nutmeg, ground cinnamon, whole cloves, cumin seeds, oregano, chili powder, Hungarian paprika, Colman's mustard, celery seeds, fennel seeds, and saffron threads.

Spice Mixes

Commercial and homemade spice mixtures are especially useful at the shore because they can be used to put together dishes like Smashing Crabs (page 76), where the spice mix—in this case Old Bay seasoning—is the flavor that defines the dish. You just sprinkle these seasonings on finfish or shellfish before steaming, grilling, or frying (and in some cases afterwards as well) and they are transformed—very easy, very in keeping with the notion of the laid-back shore kitchen. You will find recipes here for two easy-to-assemble homemade spice mixes, Spiced Seafood Salt (page 168) and Caribbean Spiced Salt (page 169).

Old Bay seasoning, originally developed in the Chesapeake region, is an essential ingredient in any East Coast seafood kitchen. You will find it used in several of my recipes for seafood and even for a great Bloody Mary. Zatarain's from New Orleans makes a wonderful seafood spice mix, and so does my friend Paul Prudhomme (Magic Seasonings). Other spice mixes that I keep on hand are Bell's poultry seasoning, Madras curry powder, and lemon pepper.

Whether they are store-bought or homemade,

keep these mixtures sealed tightly to avoid rehydration and clumping.

Salt and Sugar

Salt and sugar present a special problem near the water, because humidity and dampness cause them to lump up very quickly and become very difficult to use. As soon as you open a package of fine sea salt, kosher salt, or table salt, divide it among small jars with lids that create a very tight seal. Then pour out only a small amount at a time. Fine table salt is important for baking recipes because it can be measured with greater accuracy then larger-grain salts, but I don't think it is needed at the table. A small open bowl of a couple of tablespoons of kosher or sea salt with a demitasse spoon is much handier to use than a shaker that is clogged with table salt. Although it has more limited uses, coarse sea salt holds up very well in humidity. Use it when grilling meat, fish, or vegetables; it's also terrific sprinkled on ripe tomatoes.

Confectioners', granulated, brown, and other types of sugar should all be stored tightly sealed.

Flours and Grains

Flours of all types, cornstarch, cornmeal, and rice and other grains are also affected by the humidity near the shore, which can cause them to get lumpy or moldy. I recommend you keep them tightly wrapped in plastic wrap in your freezer or refrigerator. When using them in baking and other recipes, take them out and measure them early, then let them come to room temperature, as the cold temperature may have adverse effects on the recipe. Flours and grains that have taken on moisture will react differently in recipes and will often throw off the balance of dry to wet ingredients. For most of the recipes in this book, I use all-purpose flour,

preferably unbleached. King Arthur is my favorite.

Vegetable Oils

Canola, grapeseed, olive, peanut, and other vegetable oils should be stored in a cool, dark place in your pantry, but not the refrigerator. High temperatures or sunlight can cause the oils to change flavor or turn rancid. Grapeseed oil is a clean, neutral-flavored oil with a high burning point, which makes it ideal both for cooking and in cold preparations, like vinaigrettes. Of the neutral oils, grapeseed is my first choice, peanut or canola my second. (If you use peanut oil, you should inform anyone who might be eating the dish, in case they have a peanut allergy.) Olive oil is not neutral—it has a unique fruity flavor that often blends beautifully with seafood, but not in every dish. However, olive oil is an essential ingredient for enhancing the flavors of summer. I like to keep a rich, fruity cold-pressed extra virgin olive oil on hand for drizzling on tomatoes and other foods, but I don't often cook with it. I use less-expensive, mild-tasting olive oils for sautéing or panfrying. Vegetable oil sprays are convenient for baking, but they really earn their keep when used for "seasoning" your grill before you place the food on the grates.

Mayonnaise

Unless you can get fresh locally farmed, preferably organic, eggs, I recommend you don't use raw eggs for homemade mayonnaise, especially in the summer. It is safer to buy a good-quality manufactured product (keep it cold at all times); I am a big fan of Hellmann's.

Condiments and Other Refrigerated Items

Keep a supply of condiments and pickles in your refrigerator for impromptu shore meals. (In the city, some of these items can be stored at room temperature, but near the shore, where temperatures change more drastically, it's safer to keep them in the refrigerator.) Sometimes a simple condiment, like Worcestershire sauce on a steak or a drizzle of maple syrup on a pork chop, can make a big taste difference. I keep these items on hand: Tabasco sauce (and other hot sauces), soy sauce, Worcestershire sauce, Dijon mustard, grainy mustard, yellow mustard (for hot dogs), prepared horseradish, Heinz chili sauce, ketchup, barbecue sauce, molasses, maple syrup, and honey. I also like to have a good supply of olives, dill pickles, bread-and-butter pickles, pickled hot cherry peppers, and peperoncini. I use them in sauces and other recipes, and I serve olives with wine and pickles and hot peppers with sandwiches. Allow olives to come to room temperature before you snack on them.

Stocks and Broths

The liquid essence of fish, shellfish, poultry, and meat, stocks and broths greatly enhance the flavor and texture of many soups, stews, and sauces. Instructions for making a few of the most useful stocks are on pages 353–57. Making stock, however, isn't mandatory—for each recipe that calls for stock, I give substitutions, such as low-sodium canned chicken broth or bottled clam juice.

Dairy Products

Butter is essential at the shore: think corn on the cob, steamers, and lobster. So don't run out—keep some in the freezer, and move it to the refrigerator as needed. I always buy unsalted butter—I think it tastes better than salted butter. Sour cream and yogurt are good for quick sauces and dips. A high-quality cheddar for melting and Parmigiano-Reggiano for seasoning are the cheeses that I consider staples. Blue cheese, feta, and fresh goat cheeses add richness and protein to a main-course salad. Soft ripened and other eating cheeses are always handy for a snack or for lunch with bread and fruit. Keep milk, cream, and other dairy products tightly sealed and in the coldest part of the refrigerator. Take cheeses out and bring to room temperature before serving.

Canned, Cured, Dried, and Smoked Seafood

The art and industry of preserving seafood is alive and well despite the fact that our excellent refrigeration and freezing technologies have eliminated most of the necessity for canning, curing or smoking fish and shellfish. Worldwide, people are very fond of the unique flavors that are created through the various techniques used for preserving seafood, some of which date back thousands of years.

Canned anchovies are used in great abundance as a flavoring ingredient; I consider them an essential condiment. Cold-smoked salmon (cured and smoked but not cooked) not only tastes unlike cooked fresh salmon, but offers a very different textural experience. And dried salt cod is a different thing altogether from fresh cod. I really like canned sardines on toast with thinly sliced onion and roast pepper; fresh sardines are also excellent, but the taste and texture are not the same. I love grilled rare tuna, but I prefer canned tuna for my tuna salad sandwich. Even at the shore, where you can eat fresh fish everyday, preserved fish of various types provide variety and their own unique flavors.

Although canning and drying fish are not techniques most people would attempt at home, smoking and curing fish is not out of the question. For this book, however, in which I put a high value on managing your time, the processes are too involved—too much work for the shore kitchen, especially when you consider the excellent commercial products available.

If you enjoy preserved seafood, stock up on canned tuna, sardines, anchovies, smoked oysters, and whatever else you like. In a pinch, these shelf-stable (unrefrigerated) foods will provide you with a satisfying snack or small meal, or quick hors d'oeuvres for company. (Cover and refrigerate them after you open them.) All you need is a few pieces of toast or a few crackers, a little mayonnaise or aïoli, and maybe a few olives or roasted peppers. I like to have a jar of pickled herring in the refrigerator (where it keeps very well); it makes a delicious sandwich on rye or pumpernickel toast with thinly sliced apples and some of the onions it is packed with.

Tomatoes

Tomatoes are such an important ingredient for so many types of dishes that I consider them a defining food. You can judge a restaurant—or home kitchen—by the tomatoes it serves. So if you intend to serve tomatoes, be sure to stop at a farm stand where you can get sun-ripened local tomatoes. I use ripe plum (Roma) tomatoes in most dishes where the tomatoes are cooked. I also used canned plum tomatoes when I can't find fresh that are good. For salads and other cold preparations, there are myriad varieties available these days, and some, of course, are better than others. Experiment with different tomatoes to find the ones you like best.

Lemons and Limes

Because of their affinity with seafood and vegetables, not to mention cocktails, lemons and limes are essential to the shore kitchen. Always keep a couple or more on hand; you never want to be out of them—it's like running out of salt.

For some reason, many people trim the ends off lemons and limes before they cut them into wedges. This seems silly. I think that these fruits should be cut from end to end into wedges without losing their natural half-moon shape, which I find aesthetically pleasing.

Summer Fruits

Melons, berries, tree fruits, and vine fruits are the greatest gift of the long, hot, sunny days of summer. They are the essence of summer, like eating the sun. That big yellow circle of energy reaches down to us and finds its destiny in a peach, a plum, a strawberry, a cantaloupe. I can't think of any candy that is better than ripe cherries. The juiciness of a ripe peach or plum is rivaled only by that of ripe mangoes. Fruits are such a big part of summer that they have a place at every meal and in between. In my family, we bake a pie or other fruit dessert every now and then, but most often we eat fruit unadorned or with just a little enhancer, such as a very light sprinkle of salt on melon (it makes it taste sweeter) or a little cream or crème fraîche and a sprinkle of sugar with berries or sliced peaches or nectarines. Chilled watermelon is very special. Refreshing, messy, light, delicious, and gorgeous, it is a symbol of summer. With so much fruit around, we often put several of them together, especially if we have a lot of odds and ends, and make a fresh fruit salad with just a splash of Grand Marnier and a sprinkle of sugar.

SEAFOOD TIPS, NOTES, AND HOW-TO

Seafood is a vast and wonderful subject. I have been purchasing and cooking seafood professionally for more than thirty years, and I have been crabbing, clamming, and fishing since I was a small child. I know I have learned a lot, but I am still continually inspired by what I haven't learned yet. You can only learn this complex subject by doing. If you cooked every seafood recipe in this book, you would learn enough to become the best seafood cook in your circle of friends and family. To help you get started, I will review some important basics regarding fish and shellfish. More details and subtleties can be found in the individual recipes.

Purchasing Seafood

If you are not a fisherman, a clam digger, a mussel picker, a chicken necker (Chesapeake-speak for an amateur crabber), or a friend of someone who is, then, like most people, you will have to purchase your seafood. If you live near an area where people fish and harvest seafood for a living, try to buy directly from the fishermen or from a market that is tied into the local seafood trade. Find a reputable market where you can establish a relationship with someone who is willing to share his knowledge about the seafood in your region. Eventually he will come to know your likes and dislikes. If you have a choice of markets, play the field at first to see who does the best job. Usually the best markets are the busiest ones. As simple as it sounds, that is the surest sign of quality. Busy markets move their products quickly, which ensures that what you buy is as fresh as possible. And freshness is the most important factor in regard to seafood.

When you are buying a whole fish, it is easy to judge the quality. If by chance the fish is stiff, look no further. When a fish dies, it quickly goes into rigor mortis, meaning it becomes stiff as a board—rigor is a sure sign that the fish is only hours out of the water. Otherwise, look for clarity in the eyes, fresh-smelling and bright-colored gills, and shiny or even slimy skin. The slime is a sign of freshness, not of deterioration, as you might think.

When you are buying fillets, the meat should have clarity and it should look moist and shiny. The color should be brilliant, no matter what the species. The meat should be firm and smooth with a clean aroma reminiscent of the sea. Good fish never smells "fishy."

The freshness of shellfish is harder to judge. Live lobsters and crabs should be just that—lively. Clams should display a steely gray color, not chalky white. Mussels should be closed, not gaping. They should all feel heavy for their size. If you cook with shellfish often, you will acquire a sense of what is fresh.

Gathering Shellfish

Gathering mussels or digging for clams is good for the soul. It's primal, especially when the experience is shared with loved ones. It puts us in touch with our food as well as with our past. It reminds us of how complicated we have let our lives become and how simple life can be. It is the classic shore experience, and it creates lifelong memories, particularly for children. Before you even think about attempting to dig for clams, however, it is important that you check with your local authorities about whether you need to obtain permits and which places are allowed. There are no regulations, as far as I know, concerning harvesting mussels, but you should check with the Coast Guard to be sure there is no "red tide" or other reason it is safe not to do so.

Find out the time of low tide. Clams live in the wet sand or mud flats below the high-tide mark; at low tide, you can go out and dig them easily. Mussels are found on rocky beaches, and it is nearly impossible to pick them when they are covered by water. Usually the farther out you go, the larger the clams and mussels will be. If you have never clammed or gathered mussels, it will help if you can learn how from someone local, preferably a maven who has done it for years and knows the best places to go.

will have to go. If you are in an area that has a lot of clams, you don't have to feel them out with your feet: you can just "scratch" them out. You can use a hoe or garden rake to dig hard-shell clams, but the best tool is a quahog scratcher; it's like a rake with a wire mesh net attached. Bring a bucket too. After you locate the clams, pull them to the surface and put them in your bucket. Wash the clams well in saltwater before you take them home, and refrigerate them as soon as you get home. They will keep for upwards of a week, but the sooner you eat them, the better they will taste.

How to Dig Soft-Shell Clams

Soft-shell clams (steamers) are harder to dig up than hard-shell clams because they are smaller, they live deeper in the sand or mud, and they are very fragile. They live in the flats between the

Clam hoe

How to Dig Hard-Shell Clams

Quahogs, cherry-stones, top necks, and little necks are all the same species of hard-shell clam: their names indicate their size (see the chart on page 57). Because they live only inches below the surface of the sand, they are easy to locate by feeling around with your bare feet. They feel like smooth round rocks. You can find them anywhere below the high-tide mark, but the more popular your spot is, the farther out you

Quahog scratcher

high- and low-tide marks, usually in protected tidal estuaries. To find them, look for little holes in the sand or mud; when you step near them, you will see the spray from their siphons come up from the holes. For tools, you need both a clam hoe and a shovel or spade. You can find a clam hoe at local fishing supply and some hardware stores. Don't forget your bucket or basket. Start by digging out the sand or mud 8 to 10 inches deep, about a foot in front of the clam holes. This allows you to loosen the sand or mud around the clams so the pressure of pulling them out won't crack their shells. Next, stick the clam hoe straight down and lift the clams gently up toward the area you dug out. Pick them up gently and put them in your bucket. Wash them well in saltwater before you take them home, and refrigerate them as soon as you get home. They will keep for a couple of days, but the sooner you eat them, the better they will taste.

How to Pick Mussels

Mussels grow on rocky beaches, attaching themselves to the rocks below the high-tide mark. Wait until the tide is at its lowest point and walk out as far as you can. The mussels from the deepest areas, which are submerged almost all the time, are the plumpest and tastiest. Avoid those that grow close to the high-tide mark. For picking mussels, you only need a bucket and a strong back. Stoop over, pick the biggest ones (leave the babies alone) with your hands and put them in your bucket. If you have tender hands, you may want to wear a pair of cloth gardening gloves. As soon as you have finished harvesting the mussels, rush them home and refrigerate them. It is a real treat to eat them immediately, but they will keep for up to three days or even longer.

The Proper Handling of Seafood

Once you catch, gather, or purchase, beautiful fresh seafood, you have to take a few important steps to ensure that it reaches the plate in first-class condition. There are some basic procedures that will make a big difference in the final product.

There is no substitute for freshness. Whenever possible, purchase seafood the day you will be eating it. At worst, set a 36-hour limit. At the shore, this is easy to accomplish.

Temperature control is probably the single most important variable in the handling of seafood. It is imperative that from the time the seafood leaves its habitat until minutes before it is cooked, it is kept chilled at all times. Commercially, seafood is always kept on ice or under refrigeration, even during processing. A good seafood market will display its products on ice and, if you ask, will give you some ice to keep it chilled while traveling home. Once you purchase seafood, you must make it a priority to keep it chilled. I carry a small cooler with me when I'm shopping for seafood. If you can't do that, purchase the seafood last and rush it home. One hour at room temperature (or warmer) is equivalent to adding a full day to the age of the fish.

If you are a sports fisherman, try to maintain commercial standards or better. If your boat isn't equipped with a live well, gut the fish immediately after catching it and pack it in a cooler with ice. For many species, especially the fast swimmers like bluefish and tuna, you should cut the vein behind the gill and bleed the fish. It will have a milder flavor when you cook it. Never leave fish out in the sun for an extended period. It could cause the growth of histamines and bacteria to accelerate, making it dangerous to consume.

Once you get seafood home, you should put it in the coldest part of your refrigerator (usually the bottom shelf), preferably on ice.

Ice is all-important, but it must be used properly. Shaved or crushed ice is better, because ice cubes can dent the flesh of a fish. That being said, just enough ice cubes to cover the fish are better than no ice. If the fish is whole, you can put the ice directly on it; the same is true for skin-on fillets, if you put the ice on the skin. Ice is good, water is bad: be sure that the fish is set above a pan that water from the melting ice can drip into; otherwise, the fish will absorb water and become soggy, and the texture will be ruined. When storing skinless fish fillets, wrap them tightly in plastic wrap and then cover them gently with ice, again in a pan where the water can drain.

🐟 Bivalves like mussels, clams, and oysters also need to be chilled. Put them in a mesh bag (an onion bag will do) and seal the bag very tightly. This will prevent them from gaping and losing a lot of their natural juices. It is fine to ice the bag, as long as the melting ice can drain so water doesn't touch the shellfish. Fresh water will literally kill bivalves. If your refrigerator is running consistently at 38°F or lower, it is not as important to ice shellfish as it is with finfish.

🐟 Keep live lobsters and crabs chilled but never iced. The best way to store them is to wrap them in damp newspaper and keep them in the coldest part of your refrigerator. Remember to be cautious when you unwrap them, as they might get you with a claw if a band has come loose.

🐟 If you have extra fish from a good day of fishing and you want to freeze it, keep in mind that the goal is to freeze it as quickly as possible. That means that your freezer should have enough room for cold air to circulate around the fish. Most freezers are not capable of freezing whole fish unless they are small (1 pound and under), so it is best to fillet them first. Wrap fillets in flat, even packages, never layered. The thinner the packages are, the faster the fish will freeze. Use frozen fish as quickly as possible, ideally within 3 weeks. Pull your fish out of the freezer the day before or early in the morning of

the day you will be cooking it and put it on a plate in the refrigerator. A long defrosting period will cause less damage to the flesh, preserving its texture.

🐟 Do not try to freeze bivalves like clams, oysters, or mussels in their raw state: it doesn't work. You can try cooking them and freezing the meat, but I have had only minimal success with this—nothing I would serve to guests. Scallops are the exception. They do freeze fairly well in their raw state. Just pack them in a single layer so they freeze very quickly.

🐟 Fresh raw shrimp spoil quickly. If you see black spots forming on the shells, cook them as soon as possible—they are too expensive to waste. Cooked crabs and lobster will also get spots on their shells after a day or two; if you see this beginning, remove all the meat from the shells and use it that day.

🐟 Understand that there are species that are acceptable and delicious when eaten raw or cooked to only rare or medium and those that should be fully cooked. Oysters, clams, conch, and scallops are good raw, so it follows that when you cook them, you can cook them lightly—it's okay if they are a little underdone. Other shellfish, like mussels, squid, shrimp, and even lobster, are safe to eat raw, but their flavor is better when cooked. With fish, it is different. Many fish are suitable for raw preparations, but many others are not. Stick to tuna, salmon, striped bass, herring, mackerel, sardines, and other small fish for raw or partially cooked preparations. Always cook "ground fish," like cod, hake, monkfish, halibut, flounder, tautog, and other white-fleshed fish, all the way through in order to kill any parasites (visible or invisible). Swordfish is another fish that should never be eaten raw. In my recipes, I tell you the proper doneness of each species.

🐟 If you are working on a preparation that takes more than a few minutes, such as stuffing flounder or cutting squid, take the fish or shellfish out of the refrigerator a few pieces at a time and return the prepared seafood to the refrigerator as quickly as possible.

🐟 If you are afraid of or squeamish about handling live lobsters, they will become dormant and easy to handle after a few minutes in the freezer. When splitting a live lobster, cut through the head first—that will kill it instantly. Crabs are nasty and mean and will try to pinch you every chance they get. Hold them by the body and be careful of their claws. Rubber or thick cloth gloves come in handy when handling crabs.

🐟 Finally, when cutting fish, peeling shrimp, or handling crab, lobster, and other seafood, be careful not to nick, scrape, or cut yourself on the creature you are handling. The levels of bacteria and contaminants on the outside of seafood are considerably higher than inside and can cause a bad infection. If you do get a scrape or cut, wash it quickly with an antibacterial soap or rinse it out and apply antibacterial lotion. One way to minimize these kinds of infections is to wear protective gloves. Disposable surgical gloves are light enough to wear while doing dexterous jobs like peeling shrimp yet offer fairly good protection.

How to Gut a Fish

Start at the soft part of the belly, near the tail: You will see a hole there (where the fish excretes). Place a sharp knife at the hole and insert the knife, with the blade facing the head, just deep enough to cut through the skin. If you go in too deep, the job will be messier than necessary. Cut straight up through the belly until you reach the head. The entrails will fall out, and you can pull them out with a little tug. Rinse the cavity of the fish well.

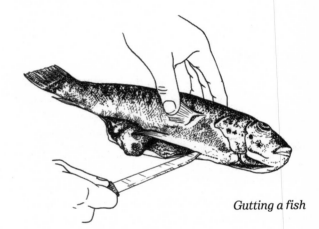

Gutting a fish

How to Scale a Fish

If you scale fish often, there are a couple different types of scaling tools you might want to try; any of them works fairly well. They are available in some gourmet shops; or ask your fish market to order one for you. Otherwise, the job can be done using an old dull knife or the back of your fish fillet knife or chef's knife. Most important, you need a good place to do it. Many fishermen gut and scale their fish on the dock and then hose it down afterward. If you don't have a dock, choose (or build) a small wooden table and place it somewhere away from your house, but close to running water. Ideally, the table should have a hole in it with a garbage can underneath it to catch the entrails and scales. Scaling a fish is easy. Just hold onto the tail and use one of the above-mentioned tools to scrape toward the head. Keep scraping the fish on both sides until all the scales are removed. Scale all your fish at one time. Rinse them well, and then wash down your table before you begin filleting. If at all possible, learn filleting by watching someone who is practiced at the art, such as a cutter at the market.

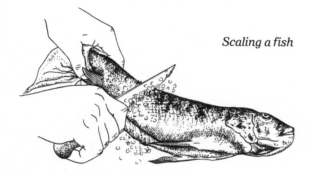

Scaling a fish

Filleting Fish

Each fish is a little different, and only experience can teach you the subtle differences of each species. However, as it is unlikely that you will be cutting large fish like tuna or swordfish, you really only need to know the techniques for cutting the two basic categories of fish, flatfish and round fish. "Flats" include all varieties of flounder and sole, as well as fluke (summer flounder), dabs, and halibut. Round fish include bass, snapper, bluefish, and just about all the other fish used in this book.

How to Skin and Fillet Flatfish

For small flatfish (under 5 pounds) like flounder, it is best to skin the fish before you fillet it; the opposite is true for large flatfish like halibut and "doormat" fluke and flounder. To skin the fish first, make a little V-shaped incision near the tail and loosen enough skin with your knife to get a firm grip on it. With one hand holding the tail and the other holding the skin, pull the skin toward the head in one fast, strong motion. It will come off in one piece. Flip the fish over and repeat. Although avid fishermen and professional cutters can easily fillet flatfish into two larger fillets, there is an easier cut for novices called quarter-filleting. This technique can be done whether the fish has been skinned or not, so it is good for flatfish of any size. Make a lengthwise incision straight down the backbone (center) of the fish from the head to the tail. Use a fillet knife or other flexible knife with a thin blade and work from the head down. Lean your knife at about a 15- to 20-degree angle against the backbone. Keeping your knife in this position, press gently against the bones, separating the meat from the bones as you cut your way down. Fold the fillet over as you cut so you can see what you are doing. Remove the two top fillets, and then repeat on the other side.

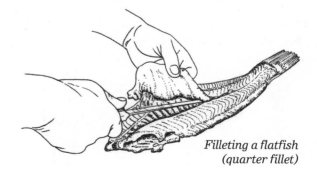

Filleting a flatfish (quarter fillet)

How to Fillet and Skin Round Fish

Round fish are usually filleted with the skin on, and then the skin is removed afterwards, if desired. Make an incision behind the head of the fish, then feel around with your knife and locate the backbone. Keep the tip of the knife pressed firmly against that bone, without letting it extend past it into the other side of the fillet, and hold the knife almost flat against the bones as you cut down the first side of the fish. Fold the fillet up as you work your way down to the tail so you can see where you are. Starting from the head again, hold the knife at a more of an angle, keeping it pressed gently on the rib bones, and cut the fillet away from those bones. Remove any pin bones from the fillet with a pair of surgical tweezers or a pair of needle-nose pliers. Even better is a Japanese tool made especially for pin-boning fish, which you may be able to purchase from your local fish market or an Asian specialty store; see page 27.

If you want to skin the fillets, place each one skin side down on your cutting board. Make a cut near the tail, positioning your knife between the skin and the meat at a very slight angle. Hold the skin firmly with one hand as you slide the knife toward the head end, using a slight sawing motion as you separate the fillet from the skin.

Removing the skin from a fish fillet

Cutting and Portioning Fish

Once a fish is filleted, the way you portion the fish will depend on your recipe. But first you must decide whether or not you want to remove the skin. Always remove the skin from flatfish (either before or after filleting). With round fish, I usually leave the skin on if I am grilling. The skin helps to hold the fish together and, with many species, it gets crispy and tasty on the grill. For other cooking techniques, it is usually best to remove the skin. There are two basic ways to cut portions from a side or other large fillet of fish. For grilling, poaching, steaming, and roasting, you should cut straight down across the fillet in order to obtain the thickest cut possible. For panfrying, sautéing, or deep-frying, slice the fillet on a bias to obtain your desired thickness. The wider the bias, the thinner your portion will be.

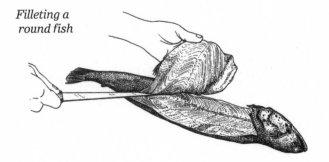

Filleting a round fish

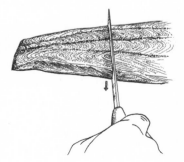

Portioning a fillet using a straight cut

Now you are armed with a few general strategies and rules to help you get started. Of course, there are many subtle differences in the best ways of handling and cooking the dozens of varieties of seafood found here on the East Coast. It is a lifelong study and passion of mine, and I hope that as you explore the pages that follow, your understanding of handling and cooking seafood will enhance your appreciation of the wonderful and unique flavor experiences these magnificent creatures offer.

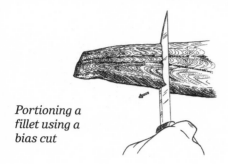

Portioning a fillet using a bias cut

INSIDE THIS CHAPTER

Box: Health Concerns about Raw Seafood 47

Oysters on the Half-Shell 48

Box: Competitive Oyster Shucking 51

Mignonette Sauce 53

Fresh Horseradish Sauce 54

Oyster Shooters 55

Box: Freezing Vodka 55

Hard-Shell Clams 56

Clams on the Half-Shell 58

Wasabi, Lime, and Soy Dipping Sauce 59

Cherrystone Seviche 60

Seafood Seviche with Citrus 61

Conch Salad Bahamian-Style 62

Variation: Scorch 63

Box: How to Crack Conch 63

Tuna (or Salmon) Tartare 64

-2-

EAT IT RAW!

*S*ome varieties of seafood are absolutely perfect in their natural uncooked state. This is especially true of shellfish including oysters, hard-shell clams, scallops, and conch, as well as certain finfish, particularly tuna. At their freshest, they possess nuances of flavor so sublime that exposing them to heat can only alter them.

What's more, raw seafood is sensual. Besides purity of flavor, freshly shucked bivalves and uncooked finfish offer a textural experience that excites the taste buds as well as the imagination. Served chilled, these precious morsels of almost pure protein are true "appetizers"—they stimulate the appetite. Another part of the sensuality of raw seafood dishes is their lightness. Most of the recipes in this chapter have no added fat and the few that do use only minimal amounts.

In addition to being high-quality protein (without saturated fat), the seafood choices in this chapter also have substantial amounts of beneficial omega-3 fatty acids. They provide healthful eating and are at the same time sophisticated.

If you buy high-quality seafood from a reputable retailer and make it clear when purchasing it that you intend to eat it raw, the risk will be small and the reward will be great. If you are buying finfish, ask for sushi or sashimi grade. You may have seen the sign "Eat sushi, live longer." I believe that it is true. My children have grown up watching my wife, Nancy, and me eat raw shellfish and fish since they were very young, and today, I am happy to say, as teenagers they enjoy eating raw oysters, clams, and other seafood.

From the traditional New England raw bar to new-wave sashimi bars to Latino seviche bars, raw and partially cooked or cured seafood is on its way to becoming mainstream in America. This is no surprise to anyone familiar with early American history, when raw oysters were the rage and most cities on the East Coast had dozens of oyster bars. Making this kind of food at home, however, is something that many home cooks do not feel comfortable attempting. I love to shuck oysters and clams for my friends and family, and they love to eat them. What a wonderful surprise it is when someone serves you light, refreshing, luscious, and tasty chilled raw seafood. If you have been reluctant to shuck oysters and clams at home, don't worry—I'll teach you how. And there are other options too in this chapter, such as preparing a spicy Conch Salad Bahamian-Style (page 62) or a beautiful Cherrystone Seviche (page 60). There is no better way to start a meal.

Health Concerns about Raw Seafood

As with any raw or partially cooked food, there are some health issues associated with eating seafood this way. With clams and oysters, there are concerns about infectious disease and bacteria, often related to human waste and pollution. At our raw bars at Summer Shack, we serve only oysters and clams that have been raised in nonindustrial areas of New England, Maritime Canada, and the Pacific Northwest, where the clean cold waters inhibit bacterial growth. In my thirty-plus years in the restaurant business, I have never had a problem related to raw shellfish. With scallops and conch, the part we eat is the muscle, not the entire body, so they are effectively void of risk. With raw fish, there can be issues similar to those of shellfish, but the biggest concern is parasites. With the protection of marine mammals, such as harbor seals, along our coastline (these are the source of many of the parasites), the incidence of parasites has increased over the last twenty years. There are very few fish native to our Atlantic Coast that I recommend eating raw or even partially cooked or cured. I would not hesitate to eat uncooked tuna (all species), salmon, mackerel, and bass (both striped and black sea); I have never seen a parasite in any of these species. Nor have I ever seen parasites in bluefish, but I don't think their flavor is well suited for raw preparations. If you want to try other species, then I advise you to be exceedingly cautious and to freeze the fish you buy until it is almost frozen solid before using it in a raw preparation. Freezing will kill most parasites. Pregnant women should, of course, avoid eating raw seafood entirely.

OYSTERS ON THE HALF-SHELL

Men have enjoyed eating oysters since they were not much more than monkeys.
—M. F. K. Fisher, *Consider the Oyster*

It isn't easy to describe the experience of eating a beautiful fresh oyster. Oyster fanatics and devotees such as myself are aware that the ritual of eating an oyster and slurping its liquor transcends almost any other food experience. Chilled freshly shucked raw oysters offer us a pure taste of the sea, a reminder of the first time we swallowed the salty ocean or maybe even a more primal memory that is stored in our DNA. Oysters are exquisitely delicious, and each has its own particular flavor, texture, and brininess.

Oysters are living creatures. The act of eating an oyster combines sacrifice and pleasure (the oysters' sacrifice, our pleasure). Eating oysters, like drinking wine, can be a simple sensory experience, but this simple ritual becomes more profound when you understand how to properly taste them.

Oysters 101

Oysters are bivalves (creatures that have two shells attached with a hinge, like clams and mussels) that strain the water they live in, sifting out nutrients; in effect, they are filters of the ocean, bay, or estuary they grow in. Their size, shape, color, flavor, and brininess reflect that place. Cultivated oysters are grown in a variety of ways, usually in the same places where wild oysters grow. Their feed is all natural, so the only difference between cultivated and wild oysters is that the former tend to be more pristine and uniform in size. Wild oysters attach themselves to rocks or any hard material, including the shells of dead oysters. In the wild, they grow in clusters, and because they often have no room to grow sideways, they become elongated or take on other weird shapes. In the profession, we call the long ones "bananas." Wild oysters that are harvested by skipjacks, draggers, and other commercial methods are usually shucked and sold for frying. Wild oysters that are harvested manually are usually better quality and are mostly sold for consumption on the half-shell.

At our raw bars, we may offer over fifty different oysters over the course of a year. Just about all of the oysters on the East Coast, both wild and cultivated are of the same species: *Crassotoa virginicus*. There is one exception: the European Flat oyster, sometimes falsely referred to as Belon, which was transplanted to this side of the Atlantic more than thirty years ago. You may be wondering why, if most oysters are the same species, they are so different? Oysters are like wine. Chardonnay grapes can be used to make a wide variety of white wines, from a modest table wine to the majestic Chassagne Montrachet, a white Burgundy. What distinguishes one from the other is the earth the grapes grow in. The French call this phenomenon *terroir*. With oysters, it is the same. Oysters are affected by the microorganisms that grow in certain bodies of water, the tides that wash the feed in, the brackishness of the water, and the time of year they are harvested. The more you eat them, the more you will be able to differentiate the characteristics of a Wellfleet oyster from Cape Cod from those of a St. Anne oyster from Nova Scotia. For most oyster lovers, the goal isn't to find the "best" oyster—it is to delight in the variations that nature has provided.

Tasting and Eating Oysters

Let's start with a plate of six perfectly shucked oysters (shucking instructions follow): three Island Creeks from Duxbury, Massachusetts, and three Malpeques from Prince Edward Island in Canada. These perfectly shucked oysters are sitting level on a bed of crushed ice. Their flesh is a shiny mixture of beige and gray with a tinge of green. They are whole, smooth, unadulterated. The shells are full of their natural juices. First look at the shapes and identify the two types (ask the person who shucked them if you aren't sure). Now pick up an oyster, being careful to keep it level so you don't spill any of the precious juice. Never pick an oyster up out of the shell with a fork—that is blasphemy. I recommend that you always eat the first oyster (of each variety) unadorned. You can play with the condiments later, but first you need to experience the oyster *au naturel*. Pass it under your nose and give it a whiff. You should get a clean ocean scent, a delightful preview of the oyster to come. (If by any chance the oyster smells unusual or unpleasant, don't eat it.) Next slide the oyster and all of its juices, or "liquor," as it is often called, into your mouth. Feel the cold temperature. Taste the salt on your tongue. Is it very salty or only mildly so? Let the juices trickle down your throat. You should start to taste the ocean. Now bite into the oyster and chew it a few times, letting the flavor explode in your mouth. Is it a clean, bright flavor? Is it mild or robust? Does it remind you of cucumbers or another food? Does it have a slightly bitter flavor, or is it sweet? Does it have a faintly metallic flavor or an herbaceous one? Is the texture firm and chewy, or is it more meaty and soft? After you swallow the oyster, savor the aftertaste. Does it linger? Is it similar to the way the oyster tasted in your mouth? There is a lot going on here, but this is not work—it's fun! Growing and harvesting oysters is work. Good-quality oysters are expensive, and the best way to get your money's worth is to fully appreciate all their subtleties.

Purchasing and Storing Oysters

If you are experienced enough to know which varieties of oysters to buy and how they should look or how they should feel in terms of their individual weights (oysters should feel heavy for their size), then you already know where to purchase them. If you are in an area that has oyster aquaculture, then, by all means, go to the source if you can and buy them from the grower. The fresher the oyster, the juicier and more flavorful it will be. Some types of oysters, especially those with deep bottom shells (cups), are naturally juicier than others, but freshness is the greatest factor in this department. If you can't buy directly from the aquaculture farm, the next best place is a busy reputable seafood market. Ask them for their recommendations. Or, if you have a first-rate oyster bar in your area, find out what they are serving (the chefs know which purveyors and which varieties are best). When you have guests, I think it is fun to serve at least two different types of oysters.

Once you've purchased the oysters, it is best to keep them wrapped tightly in a mesh bag. Ask your market to pack them that way. (An onion bag also works.) Twist the bag so the oysters become scrunched tightly together—this keeps them from opening up and losing their precious juices. If you don't have a cooler in your car, rush them home as quickly as possible. Store in the coldest part of your refrigerator (usually the bottom). You can put ice on top of them, as long as you set them on a rack in a pan that drains. Never let oysters become submerged in fresh water; it will kill them. Do not wash them until shortly before you intend to shuck them.

Cleaning Oysters

About an hour before you are ready to shuck, you should wash the oysters. The reason you want to wash them ahead of time is that while you are cleaning the oysters, they will become tense, making them harder to open. Gently scrub both sides of each oyster shell with a soft brush, rinsing them in a bowl of cold water or under cold running water. Place them in a pan with the flat side up and the cup side down—this is how you will open and serve them. Allow the oysters to drain, and cover with a damp towel. Place them back in the refrigerator, and in an hour they will be relaxed and ready to be shucked.

Oysters, cup side down

Serving Oysters

Before you shuck the oysters, chill a deep platter or plates that will hold the crushed ice. The cold platter will prevent the ice from melting too quickly. You can buy crushed ice or make it with a food grinder. Another way to make crushed ice

is to put the ice in a towel and smash it against the floor. In any event, crushed ice is a must. It keeps the oysters cold, yes, but even more important, it keeps them level so the juices don't escape. I think oysters should always be served plain, with the condiments put out as an option. The condiments are up to you. Lemon wedges; Mignonette Sauce (page 53); Cocktail Sauce (page 347); Fresh Horseradish Sauce (page 54); grated fresh or prepared horseradish; Tabasco or other hot sauce; black pepper; and Wasabi, Lime, and Soy Dipping Sauce (page 59) are all good, but there is no need to offer all of them. Only lemon is mandatory.

In Ireland and England, oysters are served with buttered brown bread, a lovely touch. I recommend it. Toasted common crackers (see page 98) or store-bought oyster crackers also make fine accompaniments. For beverages, Champagne, sparkling wine, and dry acidic white wines like Sancerre or Chablis are all wonderful. So are ale, beer, and Guinness. Chilled vodka can be quite elegant, especially if you place a small dollop of caviar on each oyster.

Shucking Oysters

Opening oysters is more a matter of leverage than of brute strength. When shucking at home, the trick is to maintain a nice steady pace while focusing on opening the oysters properly. The more force you exert, the greater the likelihood of having an accident. Remember that the oysters are alive and will clamp more tightly shut when disturbed. So your best chance of opening them easily is to not disrupt them. Start by gently placing the oyster in front of you, cup side down, in a cloth or towel, pressed firmly against the work surface. Although it is a standard technique for professional shuckers, I do not recommend opening oysters in midair, as you would clams. Keep your hand away from the area into which the knife might slip. It is not uncommon for an oyster knife to go into or through the palm of someone's hand. (I still have a scar as a souvenir from learning to shuck.) Place the tip of the knife in place near the pointy tip of the oyster (see illustration 1 below) where the top and bottom shells meet. I call this place the "Achille's heel." Turn your hand, as if you were turning the throttle of a motorcycle, while pushing in with steady pressure until you feel a slight snap or pop. That was the hard part—the rest is easy. Now give a full twist to make enough of an opening to slide the knife along the top of the shell, severing the abductor muscle (see illustration 2 below). Once the top of the shell is off, all that is left to do is to cut the bottom of the same muscle and place the oyster in its half-shell in the crushed ice. Keep the oyster level at all times so you don't lose any of the precious juice.

1. Shucking an oyster

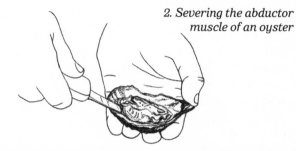

2. Severing the abductor muscle of an oyster

Competitive Oyster Shucking

Oyster shucking is serious business for some people, including me. In certain circles, it is a spectator sport: there are sanctioned events all along the East Coast (from Wellfleet, Massachusetts, to Block Island to Mohegan Sun, Connecticut, to St. Mary's, Maryland) where shuckers compete according to very strict rules and high standards for the "look" of the finished oyster—the competitions are based on speed, but seconds are deducted for oysters that are not opened properly. Competitive shucking requires a combination of dexterity, hand-eye coordination, and arm strength. At Summer Shack, we employ more than a dozen shuckers, six of them who are skilled enough to compete in regional and national tournaments. Champion shuckers can open twenty-four perfect oysters in about two minutes! It is a thing of beauty to watch a great shucker perform, and then you are rewarded by eating the oysters as well.

Oyster Varieties

I don't eat raw oysters from south of Long Island; cooked, I'll take my chances. So if this list seems incomplete, it is. These are just some of the favorite oysters that we serve at Summer Shack.

All oysters are cultivated unless otherwise noted.

CANADA

PETITE ST. SIMON *New Brunswick*
Small triangular shells with plump meats; heavy brine with fruity undertones and a sweet finish.

MALPEQUE *Prince Edward Island*
Medium sized; delicate texture, and very briny throughout.

CONWAY CUP *Prince Edward Island*
Medium sized; delicate texture, briny with hints of seaweed at the finish.

ST. ANNE'S *Nova Scotia*
Emerald-green shells with plump, robust meats; earthy flavor with a sweet ending.

SALTAIRE *Prince Edward Island*
Small with deep cups; delicate and briny all the way through.

FOX ISLAND *Nova Scotia*
Small to medium; delicate and very briny.

SUMMERSIDES *Prince Edward Island*
Small; very briny from start to finish, with nice plump meats and some fruity undertones.

CAPE BRETON *Nova Scotia*
Smooth pearly shells with dark, plump meats; moderate brine with a seaweed finish.

NEW ENGLAND

ISLAND CREEK *Duxbury, Massachusetts*
Medium sized; available year-round; salty and sweet.

WELLFLEET–EAST SIDE *Massachusetts*
Wild or farm-raised. Medium-sized with stone-like shells; meaty texture, mild start, and a sweet finish. Cultivated Wellfleet oysters are excellent.

BLUEPOINT *Long Island, New York, and Connecticut*
Wild or farm-raised. Medium to large with flat shells; mild flavor, moderate brine, and a sweet finish.

BARNSTABLE *Massachusetts*
White and green shells with a medium cup; mild brine, fruity seaweed finish.

KATAMA BAY *Martha's Vineyard, Massachusetts*
Small to medium-sized with fluted tan shells; plump meats, mild and sweet.

MOONSTONE *Point Judith Pond, Rhode Island*
Large tapered cups; very delicate meats with moderate to heavy brine.

SUNKEN MEADOW *Massachusetts*
Small and pearly with deep cups; plump meats with a distinct sweet seaweed-like finish.

FALMOUTH *Buzzards Bay, Massachusetts*
Wild oysters with unique green, spiked shells; very meaty, with a sweet scallopy flavor.

BREWSTER CUP *Cape Cod Bay, Massachusetts*
Light-colored with medium cups; medium to heavy brine with a fruity finish.

PEMAQUID *Maine*
Medium to large; distinctive, meaty, and briny. Very special.

NEWPORT CUP *Rhode Island*
Dark-shelled with deep cups; very earthy, with plump meats and moderate brine.

NINIGRET CUP *Rhode Island*
Medium-sized and tan in color; delicate meats with a strong brine, slight vegetable finish.

WAREHAM *Buzzard's Bay, Massachusetts*
Hearty wild oysters. Green shells; medium brine, and a sweet scallopy finish. One of the best.

MARTHA'S VINEYARD *Massachusetts*
Medium to large, green, pearly shells; very meaty but quite mild, with a hint of seaweed.

WINTER POINT *Maine*
Medium to large with deep cups; meaty with a heavy brine and a crisp finish.

PLEASANT BAY *Massachusetts*
Medium-sized with triangular shells and deep cups; delicate meats with sweet fruity undertones.

Condiments for Oysters on the Half-Shell

Lemon and Pepper
One of the very best ways to eat oysters is to squeeze fresh lemon over them, then top them with a little grind of black pepper from a mill. Very simple, but all that a great oyster needs.

MIGNONETTE SAUCE

The word *mignonette* indicates crushed black pepper here. This simple sauce is wonderful on oysters. You can make it with a good-quality champagne, white wine, or red wine vinegar. If the vinegar has over 5 percent acidity, you might want to replace 1 tablespoon of it with water. Make sure to crack the peppercorns yourself—grinding them in a mill won't yield the same results. Serve the sauce with a small spoon and remind everyone that only a drop or so is needed (about 1/8 teaspoon per oyster).

1   **large shallot (2 ounces), finely minced**
1   **tablespoon whole black peppercorns, crushed with a small heavy skillet**
1/4   **cup champagne, white wine, or red wine vinegar**

1. Combine all the ingredients in a small bowl. Cover and refrigerate until ready to use.

MAKES 1/4 CUP, ENOUGH FOR ABOUT 8 DOZEN OYSTERS

FRESH HORSERADISH SAUCE

Fresh horseradish is very strong and sometimes bitter. I use this recipe to soften the flavor, making it more suitable for oysters and clams. The mixture is fairly dry; if you want to make it into a sauce for roasted meats or grilled fish, add another 1/4 cup sour cream and a squeeze or two more lemon juice.

One 4-ounce knob fresh horseradish
2 tablespoons fresh lemon juice
2 tablespoons sour cream
1/2 teaspoon sugar
1/2 teaspoon kosher or sea salt

WORKING AHEAD
Make this sauce a day ahead so the flavors come out nicely.

1. Peel the horseradish and finely grate it on a box grater (there should be about 3/4 cup). Place the horseradish in a small bowl.

2. Add the remaining ingredients and stir well to combine. Cover with plastic wrap flush against the surface and chill for at least 1 hour, or, preferably, overnight.

MAKES 1/2 CUP

OYSTER SHOOTERS

This recipe is a sure way to get a party started. It may not be the ideal way to savor a raw oyster, but it is certainly one of the best shots you will ever drink. Don't use fancy oysters here—a common wild oyster like a bluepoint will suffice. The daikon batonnets serve as stirrers and then provide a spicy and refreshing crunch after the shot goes down. If you don't want leftover daikon (you only need a 3-inch piece here) or if it is not available, you can substitute a few small celery stalks.

Freeze the vodka for at least several hours beforehand, and put four tall 2-ounce shot glasses in the freezer as well. This recipe can be doubled, tripled, whatever—but don't try to operate a vehicle or other heavy equipment afterwards.

One 3-inch piece daikon radish, peeled
1   tablespoon Cocktail Sauce (page 347)
1   teaspoon Fresh Horseradish Sauce (page 54) or prepared horseradish
4   medium or large oysters
12 dashes Tabasco sauce
1/2 cup plain Stolichnaya or other good-quality vodka, frozen for several hours

1. Square the rounded sides of the daikon with a chef's knife to create a rectangle. Slice the daikon lengthwise into 1/3-inch-thick planks, and cut each plank lengthwise into 1/3-inch-wide batonnets. Place the batonnets in a small bowl, cover with plastic wrap, and refrigerate until ready to use. (If you are substituting celery, cut the stalks into wide 3-inch-long pieces.)

2. Mix the cocktail sauce and horseradish together, and chill.

3. Shuck each oyster and slide it, along with its juice, directly into a chilled shot glass. Top each one with 3/4 teaspoon of the cocktail sauce mixture, followed by 3 dashes of Tabasco. Place a daikon batonnet in each glass, like a cocktail stirrer (reserve the remaining batonnets if you are making another round). Carefully fill the shot glasses with the frozen vodka and serve at once.

SERVES 4 AS AN APPETIZER

Freezing Vodka

The simplest way to freeze vodka is to put the bottle in your freezer. But if you want to be really festive, find a bucket or similar container (we use large—#10—tomato cans in the restaurant) that is large enough to hold the bottle of vodka with about 1 1/2 to 2 1/2 inches of space all around it. Put the bottle in the middle of the bucket and fill the bucket with water. Place the bucket in your freezer; it will take at least 8 hours to freeze thoroughly.

Before you serve the vodka, run cold water around the outside of the bucket and remove the bottle with the ice attached. Because of the alcohol, vodka doesn't ever really freeze, but it becomes cloudy and more viscous, making it pour a little more slowly than when at room temperature.

HARD-SHELL CLAMS

All commercially available East Coast hard-shell clams from north of Virginia are the same species: *Mercenaria mercenaria*. South of Virginia to the Gulf of Mexico there is a similar clam, *M. campechiensis*. Since the slightly thicker shell of the latter is the only distinguishing difference, the two species are sold by their size, not species. Unfortunately for the consumer, regional sizes and names vary, causing much confusion. In this book, I use the New England names when I refer to different-sized clams. The accompanying chart lists the regional differences and, I hope, makes the topic less confusing. Note that there is a range in sizes within each category, so some recipes call for "small cherrystones," for example, or "large top necks."

Two last points that need clarifying: First, in New England, all hard-shell clams are referred to as quahogs (pronounced "*co*-hog"): commercially, however, only the largest clams are classified as quahogs. Also in New England, where clams are taken very seriously, for commercial purposes, there are five different sizes instead of only four, as in other regions. Second, "Little neck" (two words) is East Coast terminology, not to be confused with "littleneck" (one word), a variety of clam from the West Coast.

REGIONAL CLAMS

New England
Maine, New Hampshire, Massachusetts, Rhode Island

Name	Weight	Width
Count Neck	1 1/4 to 1 1/2 ounces	1 to 1 1/2 inches
Little Neck	1 1/2 to 3 ounces	1 1/2 to 2 inches
Top Neck	3 to 4 ounces	2 to 2 1/2 inches
Cherrystone	4 to 7 ounces	2 1/2 to 3 inches
Quahog	8 to 16 ounces	3 inches plus

New York
(Fulton Market) U.S. Department of Commerce

Name	Weight	Width
Count Neck	1 3/4 to 2 1/4 ounces	1 to 2 inches
Top Neck	2 1/4 to 4 ounces	2 to 2 1/2 inches
Cherrystone	4 to 8 ounces	2 1/2 to 3 inches
Chowder	8 to 16 ounces	3 inches plus

North Carolina
consistent with other southern states

Name	Weight	Width
Little Neck	1 1/2 to 2 1/4 ounces	1 to 2 inches
Middle Neck	2 1/4 to 4 ounces	2 to 2 1/2 inches
Top Neck	4 to 8 ounces	2 1/2 to 3 inches
Chowder	8 to 16 ounces	3 inches plus

CLAMS ON THE HALF-SHELL

Small little necks (also called "special count" or "count necks"), regular little necks, top necks, and cherrystone clams are all delicious eaten raw on the half-shell. Larger clams (quahogs, aka chowder or sea clams) are not very appealing raw. The size of clam you serve is a subjective choice. Bostonians prefer smaller clams, like little necks and top necks. In Connecticut, my customers prefer cherrystones. Cherrystones are sometimes difficult to open, so if you are just beginning to learn to shuck, you might want to start with small clams. Ironically, the smaller the clam, the more it costs per piece. This is because smaller clams are considered fancier and are in greater demand.

Although I adore clams, both raw and cooked, they are not as delicate as oysters—their flavor is stronger, more briny, herbaceous, and straightforward. Although clams do taste slightly different from place to place, the difference is not as pronounced as with oysters. Therefore, clams on the half-shell don't stimulate as much conversation as oysters do. But hard-shell clams share many characteristics with oysters. They are briny—they taste of the ocean. They are refreshing and sensual, and they are a true appetizer, meaning they stimulate the appetite, making us hungrier than we were before we ate them. Because the flavor of clams is more assertive, they can stand up to very strong flavors like chiles, hot sauce, onions, cilantro, soy sauce, and ginger, as well as horseradish.

Most of my advice for oysters (see pages 49–50) applies to clams. They should be purchased from a reputable purveyor. As clams age out of the water, their shells change from steely gray to chalky white, so clams that are pure white are not as fresh as they could be. Clams should be stored, tightly wrapped in a mesh bag, in the coldest part of your refrigerator. They should be kept iced only if they are placed on a rack or in a perforated pan that allows the water to drain; clams will die if they become submerged in water. Finally, they should be rinsed and scrubbed about an hour before shucking so these living creatures have a chance to relax after being banged around during cleaning.

How to Open a Clam

The technique for shucking any hard-shell clam, from the smallest little neck to the largest cherrystone, is the same; it just requires more strength as the size increases. If you look closely and use a bit of imagination, you will see that the shape of a clam resembles a harp. Hold the clam upright firmly positioned in the palm of your hand, with the hinge at the top. Hold the clam knife with your other hand. This hand only holds and glides the knife; the hand that is holding the clam does most of the work. Line up the blade of the knife with the upper right-hand corner of the clam, parallel to the edge where the two shells meet. Curl the fingers of the hand holding the clam around the dull edge of the knife and exert steady pressure until the knife slides in. Now turn the clam so it is level, to prevent the juices from spilling out. Twist the wrist of your knife hand to make an opening wide enough to slip the knife in along the top of the shell, and cut the top muscle, keeping the blade of the knife above the clam to avoid cutting into the body of the clam. Break off the top shell and cut the bottom muscle, still keeping the clam as level as possible to avoid spilling the juices. Place the shucked clams on crushed ice to keep them level and well chilled.

Shucking a hard-shell clam (little neck)

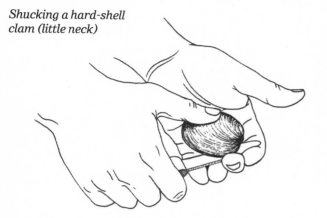

How to Eat Clams on the Half-Shell

Eating raw iced clams on the half-shell is similar to eating oysters. Lift the first one up and wave it under your nose—smell the sea. Slide it into your mouth with all its salty, delicious juices. Chew it a little and enjoy the flavor as it explodes on your palate. Swallow the clam and take time to appreciate its lingering aftertaste. However, unlike oysters, you won't have different types of clams to compare, so the tasting is more one-dimensional. I do recommend you eat at least one clam with no accompaniments to experience the pure herbaceous and briny flavor.

WASABI, LIME, AND SOY DIPPING SAUCE

This quick and tasty sauce for raw shellfish can be served with grilled fish as well. We started making the sauce for our raw bars at Summer Shack in response to requests from many of our Asian customers. Now it has become a standard accompaniment with oysters and clams; I prefer it on clams. It is best to serve the sauce the same day that you make it because otherwise the wasabi will lose its potency.

2   tablespoons wasabi powder
Juice of 1 lime (3 to 4 teaspoons)
1   teaspoon sugar
3   tablespoons water
3   tablespoons soy sauce
1   small scallion, trimmed and finely minced
A thumb-sized piece of fresh ginger, peeled and finely minced (1 tablespoon)

1. Mix the wasabi powder with the lime, sugar, and water in a small bowl. Slowly whisk in the soy sauce, and then the minced scallion and ginger.

2. Cover and refrigerate for at least 1 hour before serving. Serve chilled.

MAKES 2/3 CUP, ENOUGH FOR 3 DOZEN OYSTERS

CHERRYSTONE SEVICHE

Seviche is a Latin American dish (actually a category of dishes) of raw seafood cured in juice from limes, lemons, and/or other citrus, then flavored with onions, chiles, and other ingredients. Although seviche is usually made with fish or scallops (recipes follow), I started making this version with cherrystone clams more than twenty years ago, an improvisation based on my love of clams. Seviche has been a popular appetizer for many years, but in the hands of a new generation of creative young Latino chefs, it has become a craze. It is wonderful food for our times, bursting with flavor, high in protein, low in fat, and very refreshing. In this recipe, the flavor of the ocean comes from the juice of the fresh clams and blends beautifully with the chopped jalapeños, onions, cilantro, tomatoes, and lime juice. The colorful mixture is stuffed back into the clam shells and presented on a bed of sparkling crushed ice, as beautiful and dramatic as it is delicious and healthful. Crushed ice (see Serving Oysters, page 50) is essential because it keeps the clams both cold and level, so their juices don't escape. This seviche is perfect with a pitcher of margaritas at cocktail hour.

Cherrystone seviche is ideal for practicing your shucking skills with no one watching, because the clams need to be shucked ahead.

Although hard-shell clams are named according to their size (see page 57), their size can vary with the given name. Cherrystone clams, which are medium size, can range from 4 to 7 ounces. The best cherrystones for this seviche are small—4 to 5 ounces. You can use smaller top neck clams if you wish; choose large top necks, which are 3 1/2 to 4 ounces. They are especially good if passing this around.

WORKING AHEAD

The seviche mixture can be made several hours in advance, but don't add the clams until 2 hours before you will serve the dish.

12 small cherrystone clams (or 16 large top-neck clams), shucked and cut into small dice, juices strained and reserved, 12 or 16 (well-scrubbed) shells reserved (12 if serving as an appetizer, 16 for an hors d'oeuvre)

Juice of 3 large limes, or more to taste

2 jalapeño chiles, seeded and finely diced

1 medium ripe tomato, seeded and cut into small dice

1/2 medium red onion, cut into small dice

8 sprigs fresh cilantro, leaves removed and coarsely chopped, plus a few sprigs for garnish

Freshly ground black pepper

Hot sauce (optional)

Lime wedges for garnish

1. Combine the clams, lime juice, jalapeños, tomato, onion, and chopped cilantro in a glass bowl. Add half of the reserved clam juices. If the seviche isn't moist enough (there should be enough liquid to cover the ingredients), add a little more of the juices. Season to taste with black pepper. Cover and refrigerate for 2 hours. (Refrigerate the remaining clam juices.)

2. Check the seasoning—if you want the seviche spicier, add a little hot sauce. If you want it more acidic, add a little more lime. If the seviche seems dry, add a little more clam juice.

3. To serve, place the clam shells on a platter or plates lined with crushed ice. Fill each one with seviche and as much juice as it will hold. Garnish with wedges of lime and cilantro sprigs.

MAKES 16 PIECES FOR AN HORS D'OEUVRE; SERVES 4 AS AN APPETIZER

SEAFOOD SEVICHE WITH CITRUS

Oranges and grapefruit give this seviche a familiar yet exotic flavor. Because the milder citrus juices are not as powerful as pure lime or lemon juice, this seviche takes a little longer to "cure" than the traditional seviche in the preceding recipe.

If you live on the East Coast, some of the best fish to cure for seviche are striped bass and black sea bass. If you live in the South, go with snapper, yellowtail, Spanish mackerel, or grouper. Tuna and salmon, available in most markets, can also be used. Avoid any ground fish such as cod or flounder, which may contain parasites. You can also substitute sliced scallops, or use half scallops and half fish.

12 **ounces skinless fish fillets (see headnote), blood line trimmed, or 12 ounces medium (20–30 per pound) dry sea scallops, sliced 1/3 inch thick**
2 **medium navel oranges**
1 **medium grapefruit**
Juice of 2 limes
1 **small red onion (4 ounces), halved lengthwise and very thinly sliced**
1/2 **habanero chile, seeded and minced (1/2 teaspoon)**
8 to 10 **sprigs fresh cilantro, leaves removed and coarsely chopped (1/4 cup), plus 4 big sprigs for garnish**
1 **teaspoon kosher or sea salt**
1/2 **teaspoon freshly ground black pepper**
4 **Boston lettuce leaves**
4 **lime wedges**

1. If using fish, slice the fillets crosswise into rectangles 1 inch wide and 1/3 inch thick and place in a large glass bowl. (Or place the sliced scallops in the bowl.)

2. Slice 1/2 inch from the top and bottom of each orange. One at a time, stand each orange on a cutting board, slice the skin and white pith from the orange, and discard. Use a sharp thin knife to release the segments from the mem-

branes of the fruit, and toss the segments into the bowl with the fish. Squeeze the juice from the membranes into the bowl, and discard the membranes. Slice off the top and bottom of the grapefruit, and remove the segments in the same way, adding them to the bowl with the fish. Squeeze the juice from the membranes into the bowl, and discard the membranes.

3. Add the lime juice, onion, chile, and chopped cilantro and toss gently to combine. Season with the salt and pepper. Cover with plastic wrap placed flush against the surface, making sure the fish is submerged in citrus juice. Refrigerate for 3 hours, tossing the fish three times.

4. Line four small glass bowls or plates with the lettuce leaves, and spoon in the seviche with the juices. Garnish with the lime wedges and cilantro sprigs.

SERVES 4 AS AN APPETIZER

CONCH SALAD BAHAMIAN-STYLE

In Florida and the Bahamas, as well as most of the Caribbean, conch is abundant, free to divers and affordable for most people, and it is often served raw. This salad and many different variations on it are common throughout the Caribbean, where *lambis* (Creole for conch) is prized both for its sweet flavor and for its power as an aphrodisiac. Many places in the Bahamas make this salad to order, cracking the conch when you ask for it.

Conch has become more widely available now that it is farm-raised, a fairly recent development. One pound of conch meat will make a hearty appetizer for 4 to 6 people. If you are starting with conch in the shell, you will need 3 large or 4 medium conch to yield one pound of conch meat. Sea salt is very important to this dish. In the Bahamas they use a moist sea salt from the island of Abaco, which is similar to the French fleur de sel. There is no black pepper or oil in this salad.

1 **pound conch meat (from 3 large or 4 medium conch)**
Juice of 1 small juicy orange
Juice of 1 juicy lime
Juice of 1/2 juicy lemon
1 **small onion (4 ounces), cut into 1/4-inch dice**
1 **small tomato, cut into small dice**
1/2 **red or green bell pepper, cut into small dice**
1/2 **teaspoon minced habanero chile**
1 **Caribbean bird chile (or Thai chile), seeded and minced**
1/2 **teaspoon sea salt, or more to taste**

WORKING AHEAD

You can prepare the ingredients for this salad a couple of hours before you plan to eat it, but don't combine them until 1 hour before serving. This salad is best eaten very fresh.

1. Slice the thin side of the conch meat from the fatter trunk and cut it into 1/4-inch dice. Slice the trunk into strips, cut the strips in half, and

cut into 1/4-inch dice. Place the conch (there should be about 3 cups) in a large glass bowl.

2. Add the citrus juices, onion, tomato, bell pepper, chiles, and salt and toss to combine. Cover with plastic wrap placed flush against the surface and chill for 1 hour before serving.

SERVES 4 TO 6 (GENEROUSLY) AS AN APPETIZER

Variation: Scorch

If you go under the bridge that takes you from Nassau to Paradise Island, on the Nassau side, you will encounter many vendors selling fruits, vegetables, and seafood. Some are set up in little shacks where they cook local foods and sell beer. Each little restaurant can seat no more than ten or twelve people, making eating there a fun and intimate experience. I have tried a few of the places, but my favorite is #8, also known as The Burning Spot. You can get a beautiful conch salad there, but nine out of ten patrons (almost all local) sit down and order a beer and "scorch": similar to conch salad but simpler—no tomatoes or peppers, just conch, onion, juices, salt, and hot chiles—lots of hot chiles. This dish definitely falls into the "hotter than hell" category.

To make Scorch, omit the tomatoes and bell peppers from the salad and double the amount of habanero and bird chiles.

How to Crack Conch

To crack conch, you will need a small hammer and a small sharp knife. Find the spot where the abductor mussel is fastened to the shell almost directly behind the opening, and tap with the hammer to crack a hole there. Insert the knife and cut the conch away from the shell. It will slide right out. Cut away the soft viscera and discard. Wash the meaty part of the conch in saltwater or salted water. Drain well.

TUNA (OR SALMON) TARTARE

If you are lucky enough to know a tuna fisherman, keep this recipe handy for the next tuna he lands. Because the meat is chopped, this is a great way to use odd pieces of tuna that cannot be cut into steaks. However, do not use pieces with sinew—remove any sinew before chopping. Tuna is the very best fish for tartare, but fresh salmon will stand in very nicely. A mixture of diced and finely minced fish provides a great texture and flavor contrast. This makes an excellent passed hors d'oeuvre or plated appetizer.

12 ounces tuna or skinless salmon fillet, any blood line removed
8   slices white or pumpernickel bread

FOR THE VINAIGRETTE

1   tablespoon Dijon mustard
3   anchovy fillets, minced
2   teaspoons cognac
1/2 teaspoon Tabasco sauce
1/2 cup olive oil
2   teaspoons fresh lemon juice
2   tablespoons capers, rinsed and finely chopped
1   tablespoon chopped fresh Italian parsley
1/4 cup minced onion
1/4 teaspoon freshly ground black pepper
Kosher or sea salt to taste

MAKING AHEAD

The tuna can be diced a couple of hours ahead. The vinaigrette can be mixed ahead, but do not add the salt until ready to serve. Just before serving, add the tuna and season the tartare. The toast points can also be made ahead.

1. With a large chef's knife, cut three-quarters of the fish into 1/4-inch dice. Mince the remaining tuna. Place the fish in a bowl, cover with plastic wrap placed flush against the surface, and refrigerate until ready to use.

2. To make toast points, preheat the oven to 400°F. Trim the crusts from the bread and cut each slice into 4 triangles. Place on a baking sheet and bake for 6 to 8 minutes, until crisp. Set aside.

3. To make the vinaigrette: Combine the mustard, anchovies, cognac, and Tabasco in a large bowl and whisk vigorously. Add half the olive oil 1 tablespoon at a time, whisking constantly until the sauce emulsifies. Whisk in the lemon juice, then whisk in the remaining oil 1 tablespoon at a time. Whisk in the capers, parsley, onion, and black pepper. Refrigerate until ready to use.

4. Add the fish to the vinaigrette and mix it vigorously until the fish absorbs the dressing. Season with salt to taste. Serve with the toast points.

MAKES A GENEROUS 2 CUPS, ENOUGH FOR 20 CANAPÉS; SERVES 4 AS AN APPETIZER.

INSIDE THIS CHAPTER

Box: The Steamer Pot 70

Lobster in the Rough 71

Drawn Butter 75

Smashing Crabs 76

Indoor Clambake 77

Key West Shrimp Boil 79

Steamers with Drawn Butter 80

Variation: Little Neck Steamers 81

Box: How to Eat Steamers 81

Steamers Cooked in Beer 82

Wild Mussels Cooked like Steamers 84

Box: Preparing Mussels for Cooking 85

Mussels with White Wine, Garlic, and Herbs 86

Mussels in Spicy Red Sauce 87

Steamed Black Sea Bass with Ginger and Scallions 88

Corn on the Cob 90

3

STEAMING AND BOILING

KETTLE COOKING PART I

For shore cooks, the kettle is a vital piece of equipment, where many magnificent shellfish feasts begin. Steaming or boiling lobsters, crabs, soft-shell clams, shrimp, mussels, and other seafood in a kettle preserves their pure flavor. When the shellfish is impeccably fresh, fine distinctions, such as the herbaceous scent of soft-shell clams or the distinct aroma of steamed lobster as it is released from its shell, emerge. Add herbs, spices, and vegetables to the kettle, and other magical things happen: the marriage of blue crabs and Old Bay seasoning, for example (see page 76), or the mix of spices and shrimp in a Key West Shrimp Boil (page 79). Kettle cooking is big cooking, serious stuff, but meant only for the most casual of gatherings. It is eat-with-your-hands kind of food, and it is deliciously messy.

Steaming and boiling may appear to be similar techniques, but they accomplish different things. Steaming is the more gentle cooking method. It preserves the natural flavors of foods, frequently cooked on their own, resulting in a more singular flavor. Boiling is more often used to combine different ingredients and seasonings to create a flavor that is the sum of many parts. Both require a good strong kettle or pot that has a heavy bottom to conduct heat efficiently and is large enough for the size of your tribe. Boiling requires high heat. If you use a kettle often, you may want to consider investing in a portable propane burner (see page 31) and move the entire affair outdoors.

The next time you want to have a special dinner of lobster, crab, shrimp, clams, or mussels, or a combination, go to the docks or the fish market, load up a big pile of sea creatures, fire up the kettle, and let the good times roll. Don't forget to chill the beer and melt the butter.

STEAMING TIMES
Lobsters

Weight	Males	June, July, August, and September Females *	July, August, September, and October New-Shell **
1 pound	10 minutes	12 minutes	8-9 minutes
1 1/4 pounds	12 minutes	14 minutes	10 minutes
1 1/2 pounds	14 minutes	16 minutes	12 minutes
1 3/4 pounds	16 minutes	18 minutes	
2 pounds	18 minutes	20 minutes	
2 1/4 pounds	20 minutes	22 minutes	
2 1/2 pounds	22 minutes	24 minutes	
2 3/4 pounds	24 minutes	26 minutes	
3 pounds	25-30 minutes	25-30 minutes	

* Females contain roe in these months and therefore require extra time to steam. Cook them for the same time as the males the rest of the year.

** New-Shell (soft-shell) lobsters have less meat inside and therefore require less time to steam.

East Coast Crabs

Species	Weight	Cooking Time
Jonah	1 pound	20 minutes
Rock (Maine)	12 ounces	18 minutes
Blue	12 ounces	18 minutes
Blue, Jumbo	1 pound	25 minutes
Snow	1 1/2 pounds	20 minutes
Snow	2 pounds	25 minutes

East Coast Shrimp

Species	Per Pound	Cooking Time
Maine (Aboreal Red)	40+	2-3 minutes
Stonington Red (CT)	20-25	5-6 minutes
Stonington Red (CT)	16-20	7-8 minutes
White, Pink, Hopper, and Brown	30-40	3-4 minutes
	20-25	5-6 minutes
	16-20	7-8 minutes

The Steamer Pot

For most of the recipes in this chapter, you will need a large pot (4-gallon or bigger) with a steamer rack and a tight-fitting lid (also see page 28). If you really enjoy steamers and other steamed seafood, you may want to consider buying a special steamer pot. They are sometimes available in fish markets or hardware stores. They are all constructed similarly, consisting of three pieces: a wide (usually enamel) pot that has a spigot, a perforated insert (steam rack) that fits inside the pot, and a lid. The spigot is situated so that it doesn't drain the liquid from the very bottom of the pot, so the sand that settles at the bottom will not be mixed into the broth you serve. Although these pots are designed for cooking steamers (soft-shell clams), they are also useful for cooking lobster, crab, shrimp, and even fish. A good investment.

LOBSTER IN THE ROUGH

When people ask me what the best way to cook lobster is, my reply is that it depends how often you eat them. If you don't eat lobster often, I think it should be eaten "in the rough." To truly experience all the nuances of lobster, such as the different textures and flavors from different parts, you must keep the lobster plain: steamed whole.

If you are near the ocean and can boil lobsters in ocean water, by all means do so. Otherwise, steaming is a far superior technique for cooking lobster. Steaming is less messy and safer than boiling and, because it cooks the lobsters more gently, it results in more tender meat, especially with larger specimens. And steaming captures the natural flavors of the lobster. Boiling a lobster in tap water dilutes its salty, sweet, wonderful flavor.

As you plan your lobster dinner, remember that, when the lobster is served, the importance of everything else on the table diminishes. So keep the menu simple: a couple of salads, some boiled or steamed new potatoes, bread, and drawn butter. If you are serving corn on the cob, you might want to serve it before the lobster.

Plan on 1 1/2 to 2 pounds of lobster per person. A hard-shell lobster weighing 1 1/2 pounds is an ample serving. In the late spring and summer, as lobsters molt and the season of new-shell lobsters begins, you might consider serving lobsters closer to 2 pounds, because soft-shell lobsters contain less meat. Serving 2 chicken (1-pound) lobsters to each person gives the appearance of abundance, and they will probably cost less than a 1 1/2-pound hard-shell lobster for each guest. If you are serving chicken lobsters, you can steam them in two batches, so the second batch of lobsters is hot when you eat them.

If you do not have a special steamer pot (see page 28), you will need a large pot with a tight-fitting lid. My rule of thumb is to allow about 3 to 4 cubic quarts per 1 1/2-pound lobster; e.g., for four 1 1/2-pound lobsters, you should use a 12-quart (3-gallon) or larger pot. Place about an inch of ocean water or salted tap water in the steamer or other pot. If you are improvising a steamer pot, use a wire rack to elevate the lobsters above the water; the steamer pot has a built-in rack. You could also use rockweed, a seaweed available from most stores that sell lobster, to make a wonderful natural steaming rack. Bring the water to a boil, and when the pot fills up with steam, put in the live lobsters one by one: Hold each lobster with your thumb and fingers on the carapace (the body shell), and arrange them in different directions in a stack on top of each other so the steam can circulate all around them. Cover the pot and wait until the pot is full of steam again; once you see steam escape when you crack the lid a little, begin timing the lobsters according to the chart on page 69. The "recovery time" of the steam filling the pot will vary with different pots and different ranges, but once the steam is going full blast, the timing will be the same. Halfway through the cooking, use a pair of tongs to quickly rearrange the lobsters in different positions and directions, so they cook evenly. Cover again and continue timing the lobsters. When they are cooked, remove them with your tongs. Although it isn't at all necessary, I usually punch a little hole in the top of each lobster's head after they have cooked, using the tip of my chef's knife, and allow the liquid from the body to drain. I also split the tail lengthwise from the top, using a sharp chef's knife to cut right through the shell. Then I crack the claws. It makes eating the lobster much easier for everyone, especially children or people who don't eat lobster often.

Serve the lobsters with drawn butter (page 75) in small bowls, lobster crackers, and long thin picks (forks) for getting all the precious meat out of every nook and cranny. Place a large empty bowl in the center of the table for shells. Side dishes should be served on separate plates, because the lobster plates will be full of water and juice.

Cooking Lobsters for a Large Group

If you need to cook more lobsters than you can fit in your kettle, you will have to cook them in batches. The best way to keep the cooked lobsters hot is in a thermal box or cooler. Simply transfer the cooked lobsters from the steaming kettle to the cooler, ladle a few cups of the steaming liquid over them and put the lid on. They will stay hot remarkably well and won't become overcooked.

How to Eat a Lobster

Eating a whole "lobster in the rough" is a ritual that is best done in a casual setting where you can roll up your sleeves and get messy. A lobster bib might come in handy, but very often these only transfer the juices from your chest to your lap.

Hard-shell lobsters and native new-shell lobsters are eaten in the same way, but because hard-shells are chock-full of meat, they contain less liquid and are a little less messy. New-shell lobsters have softer shells and are therefore easier to crack and eat. Personally, I prefer the new-shell lobsters for this "ripping and dipping" ritual; their flavor is a little more salty-sweet than that of hard-shells.

I think it is a good idea to eat the largest pieces of lobster first—the tail—so that you get the most lobster meat while it is still hot.

Snap off the tail by twisting it sideways, then put your hand over the tail fins and pull them straight off in one piece. Pick the meat from the tail fins. As you separate the tail from the carcass, juices will come out. The green stuff (tomalley) and the red stuff (roe, from females only) are very tasty. I like to stir a little bit of the tomalley into the drawn butter I dip the lobster meat in, but most people don't eat the tomalley because the color turns them off. The roe is dense and a little goes a long way. Most people who like it dip it in butter and eat it a little bit at a time.

1. Removing a lobster tail

Using a fork or your index finger, push the tail meat from the opening where the tail fins were toward the large opening at the other end. The meat should come out easily in one large piece. Pick over the tail fins by squeezing the meat out with your fingers—there are small but tasty morsels within.

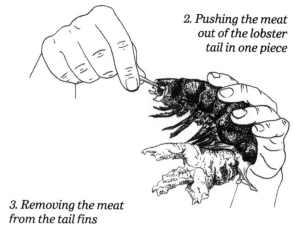

2. Pushing the meat out of the lobster tail in one piece

3. Removing the meat from the tail fins

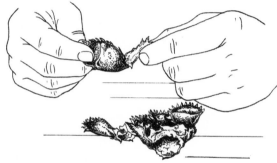

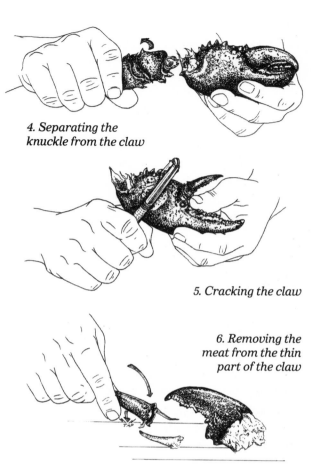

4. Separating the knuckle from the claw

5. Cracking the claw

6. Removing the meat from the thin part of the claw

Next, pull off the claws and separate the knuckles from the claws, keeping in mind that the claws are often full of liquid and this is where you might get wet. Use your lobster crackers to split the thickest part of each claw in half and remove the meat with a fork. If the meat from the skinny part of the claw doesn't come right out, just tap it on the table, and it will. Crack the knuckles and use a small fork or a pick to extract the meat. Take time to savor the meat from the knuckles, which I believe are the tastiest morsels in the lobster.

Snap off the eight walking legs with your hands and break the legs in half at the joint. To extract the meat, put the piece of leg right in your mouth and use your teeth to push the meat out as you suck on it. (Because of the technique needed for this process, no butter is eaten with the walking legs.)

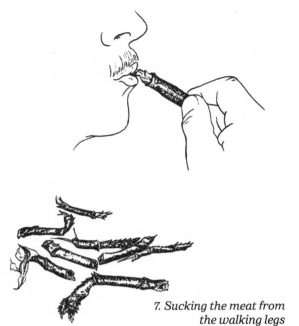

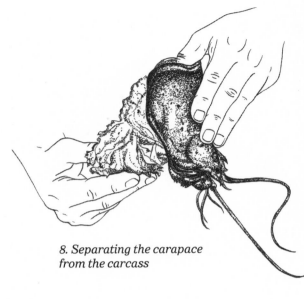

8. Separating the carapace
from the carcass

7. Sucking the meat from
the walking legs

Now that you have eaten the big meat from the lobster, it is time to tackle the body. Most people don't even try, and that's too bad, because there are succulent rewards within. Remove the carapace (top shell) from the body by lifting it up and pulling down on the carcass. Hold the carcass in both hands with your thumbs in the center and pull it apart into two halves. Now use your fingers to remove the delicious white meat from between the gills. This meat is soft and tender, like crabmeat, and although there isn't much, it is well worth the effort.

9. Pulling apart the
lobster carcass

DRAWN BUTTER

Drawn butter is the classic accompaniment to many plain steamed seafood dishes, such as lobster and steamers. It is surprising how many people, especially restaurant chefs, overcomplicate this simple preparation. Stir the butter often while it melts to prevent it from separating. Don't use clarified butter as a substitute—because the milk solids have been removed, it has much less flavor.

2 tablespoons (1 ounce) unsalted butter per person

Kosher or sea salt

1. Put the butter in a small pot and place over a medium heat. Stir the butter often as it melts. Before the melted butter comes to a boil, season to taste with salt. Then keep stirring until it boils—it should be cloudy, almost emulsified. Divide among small bowls and serve at once.

SMASHING CRABS

In Baltimore especially but throughout the entire Chesapeake area of Maryland and Virginia, there is a ritual that includes blue crabs steamed or boiled with Old Bay seasoning. The cooked crabs are dumped into the middle of a newspaper-lined table, then little wooden mallets, small forks, pitchers of beer, and lots of napkins are set down. You sit and pick and drink and pick, until the crabs are gone or you are full. It is a fabulous affair, communal, tasty, fun. (see the color photo). Accompaniments might include corn on the cob, corn fritters or hush puppies, Summer Shack Coleslaw (page 140), and other salads, but, as with a lobster feast, once the crabs arrive, everything else is secondary.

In New England, we have trouble getting lively blue crabs, but we have an abundance of rock crab and Jonah crab and we use them for our own version of the Chesapeake ritual, which I have dubbed as "smashing crabs" (double entendre intended). Before you start, line your table with a cheap plastic tablecloth, then cover the entire table with newspapers. Pour the hot crabs into the middle of the table and serve with wooden crab mallets (available in many retail fish markets) and empty bowls or buckets for the shells.

For equipment, you will need a steamer pot (see page 70) or a large pot with a tight-fitting lid and a pair of long tongs.

24 big blue crabs (jimmies) or 18 rock or Jonah crabs
Two 12-ounce bottles beer
1   cup apple cider vinegar (or distilled white vinegar)
1   cup Old Bay seasoning

1. Rinse the crabs well under cold water and drain.

2. Place the beer and vinegar in the kettle and bring to a boil. Quickly arrange the crabs in layers, generously sprinkling each layer with Old Bay, using about 3/4 cup in all.

3. Cover the pot and, once you have seen a little steam escape from the sides of the pot, steam the crabs for about 20 minutes (see the chart on page 69).

4. Using a pair of tongs (rubber gloves also work well), transfer the crabs to a large bowl or pot, and sprinkle them with the remaining Old Bay seasoning. Dump onto the table and grab a mallet.

SERVES 4 TO 6 AS A MAIN COURSE (THOUGH SOME PEOPLE CAN EAT A DOZEN CRABS AT A SITTING)

INDOOR CLAMBAKE

A true clambake (called a lobster bake in Maine) isn't just a dish—it is an all-day event at the shore. Family and friends share the work, of which there is no shortage: building the fire, preparing the different foods, layering the bake, cooking, unveiling, and serving, then cleaning up. It is a glorious cookout, maybe the finest of America's many outdoor cooking traditions.

Clambakes vary up and down the coast. Although they all start with steamers and lobsters, in Maine you might find chicken and hot dogs; on Cape Cod, whole fish; and, in other places, crabs. A famous clambake that has been held each summer for more than a hundred years by the Friends (Quakers) of Allen's Neck in Westport, Massachusetts, features tripe that is braised and wrapped in little foil packages. In my clambakes, I include Portuguese sausage (chouriço or linguiça), an addition that is common around the "South Coast" area of Massachusetts and Rhode Island.

I have written extensively about clambakes in my other books (*Lobster at Home* and *Cooking From New England*), and I encourage anyone so inclined to make a true clambake, but in this book I will share with you a simple, easy way to imitate the clambake indoors. Although the beauty and drama of unveiling a clambake cannot be duplicated inside, the traditional ingredients can easily be assembled and cooked in your own kitchen. At Summer Shack, we sell thousands of these indoor clambakes each month. I invented and patented a cooking system for our restaurants that allows us to cook 100 clambakes at a time. We purchase special custom yellow mesh bags for cooking the clambakes, so all the ingredients cook together. You can make a clambake in the same style at home by saving the mesh bags that onions (5 or 10 pounds) are sold in.

When you make a true outdoor clambake, the food is layered, with the ingredients that require the longest cooking times on the bottom and those with the shortest cooking times on top. For an indoor clambake, all the ingredients must cook in the same length of time, so the potatoes, or any other food that needs to steam for more than twenty minutes, must be partially or fully cooked in advance. The eggs in this recipe are a nod to my old friend and bake master Johnny Stevens, from Boothbay Harbor, Maine, who taught me to hide an egg in the clambake and then crack it open before unveiling the bake— if the egg is hard-boiled, the lobsters will be cooked through as well.

Choose lobsters that weigh 1 to 1 1/4 pounds each. Larger lobsters require more cooking time, and that would cause the steamers and mussels to overcook.

For equipment, you will need a 4-gallon or larger kettle with a tight-fitting lid, along with 4 mesh bags. The bags should be about 12 inches square (about the size of a 5-pound onion bag). If you can't find suitable mesh bags, you can improvise them by bundling the clambakes in fishnet or even cheesecloth.

8 **medium new potatoes, red or white**

1/4 **cup Spiced Seafood Salt (page 168)**

4 **ears corn, shucked**

1 1/2 **pounds mussels, scrubbed, debearded, and rinsed**

2 **pounds steamers, scrubbed well**

1 **pound chouriço or linguiça (andouille or kielbasa can be substituted), cut into 4 pieces**

4 **live lobsters, 1 to 1 1/4 pounds each**

5 **extra-large eggs in the shell**

1 **lemon, cut into 4 wedges**

4 **ounces or more unsalted butter, prepared as Drawn Butter (page 75)**

1. Boil or steam the potatoes until fully cooked, about 20 minutes. Cool, then refrigerate.

2. Place your large pot on the stove and add 1 inch of salted water. Use a rack to elevate the clambakes above the water (rockweed makes a great natural steam rack). Cover and bring the water to a boil. When the pot fills up with steam, add 2 tablespoons of the spiced salt to the water. Bring to a rolling boil and cover tightly.

3. Meanwhile, divide the potatoes, corn, mussels, steamers, and sausage among the mesh bags. Place the lobsters in the bags (take off the rubber bands carefully—or wait until they are cooked if you aren't confident). Right before you add the lobsters to the pot, add 1 egg to each bag.

4. Seal the bags, then gently place them in the pot. Place the extra egg in the center, where you can easily retrieve it. Cover the pot tightly and steam the "bakes" for about 20 minutes. Remove the egg and crack it open—if it is hard-boiled, the clambakes are cooked!

5. Put each bag on a large plate and use a knife or scissors to cut it open through the center. Spread out the food and sprinkle lightly with the remaining 2 tablespoons spiced salt. Serve with the lemon wedges, with the drawn butter and some of the broth from the pot in separate cups.

SERVES 4 AS A MAIN COURSE

KEY WEST SHRIMP BOIL

The smell of shrimp—they're beginning
to boil . . .

—*Margaritaville*, Jimmy Buffet

Boiled shrimp are most popular in places where shrimp are abundant, so logic follows that it is a great way to eat shrimp. It is! This aromatic dish is meant for a casual, roll-up-your-sleeves occasion. You could serve these "peel 'n' eat" shrimp as a starter, a snack, or as a main course (double the recipe) with cold beer and/or margaritas. If you have a portable propane burner (see page 31), by all means cook this outdoors. Serve plain or with Drawn Butter (page 75), Cocktail Sauce (page 347), or Summer Shack Rémoulade (page 345).

For equipment, you will need a 4-quart saucepan and a Chinese wire-mesh skimmer.

1   **small yellow onion (3 to 4 ounces),**
    thinly sliced
1   **lemon, thinly sliced**
4   **sprigs fresh thyme**
2   **teaspoons crushed red pepper flakes**
1   **tablespoon whole black peppercorns**
4   **small dried bay leaves, broken into pieces**
1/2 **teaspoon celery seeds**
1/2 **teaspoon mustard seeds**
1/2 **teaspoon coriander seeds**
1   **tablespoon Hungarian paprika**
1   **teaspoon freshly ground black pepper**
3   **tablespoons kosher salt**
4   **cups water**
Cajun or Creole shrimp or crawfish spice
    (optional)
1   **pound shrimp (21–25 per pound)**
    in the shell

1. Combine the onion, lemon, thyme, red pepper flakes, black peppercorns, bay leaves, celery seeds, mustard seeds, coriander seeds, paprika, black pepper, salt, and water in large saucepan and bring to a boil over high heat. If you like it really spicy, add 1 to 2 tablespoons Cajun or Creole spices, swirling the spices in the water with a spoon to prevent them from sticking to the sides of the pot. Cover, reduce the heat to a simmer, and simmer for 5 minutes.

2. Add the shrimp and stir well. Poach, uncovered until the shrimp begin to curl into a U-shape, about 3 minutes.

3. Remove the pan from the heat. Using a Chinese wire-mesh skimmer, lift the shrimp out of the boil and transfer them to a large bowl. Moisten the shrimp with some of the broth. If desired, sprinkle some more Cajun or Creole spices over the shrimp. Serve warm.

SERVES 4 AS AN APPETIZER

STEAMERS WITH DRAWN BUTTER

Soft-shell clams are usually called steamers when they are sold whole for steaming and fryers or belly clams when they are sold shucked (with siphon removed) for frying. I have been eating steamers my whole life, and I adore them. When I was a kid growing up on the Jersey Shore, steamers were abundant and cheap, so we ate them often. Nowadays steamers are very expensive, especially in the summer, when the demand outstrips the supply. Up in Maine, the steamers are especially sweet and are often held in lobster tanks (without lobsters, of course), where the flowing saltwater purges most of their sand or grit. Steamers are usually harvested from sand or mud tidal flats. I prefer the "mudders," from mud flats. They have the most pungent flavor and they are not sandy. You may not have a choice at the market, but if you do, ask for mudders.

Make sure to put a bowl on the table to accommodate the shells. Serve the hot broth and drawn butter in small individual bowls. For equipment, you will need a large steamer pot (see page 70) or a large pot with a steamer rack and a tight-fitting lid and a Chinese wire-mesh skimmer. If not using a steamer pot, you will need a fine strainer.

Steamers (soft-shell clams)

3   **pounds medium (1 1/2 to 2 inches in diameter) steamers (soft-shell clams)**
2   **cups water**
1   **large stalk celery, thinly sliced on a diagonal**
1/2 **onion, thinly sliced**
1/4 **teaspoon freshly ground black pepper**
8   **tablespoons (1 stick) unsalted butter**
Lemon wedges

1. Fill two large pots (or two sinks) with cold water. Gently place the clams in one pot, discarding any dead clams or clams with cracked shells. If a clam looks shriveled up, poke the siphon; if it doesn't retract into the shell, the clam is dead. Swish the clams gently in the water and let soak for a few minutes, then lift them out with a wire-mesh skimmer and place them in the other pot of cold water. Rinse out the first pot and fill it again. Swish the clams around again and let soak briefly, then transfer them to the clean pot. Swish and repeat with successive batches of clean water until the water is perfectly clear (4 or 5 soakings). Drain the clams and set them aside.

2. Set up your steamer pot. Add the water, celery, onion, and pepper, cover, and turn the heat on high. When the pot has a full head of steam, add the steamers and replace the lid. Steam (the water should be at a rolling boil) for 4 minutes. Uncover the pot and stir once gently. Cover and continue to steam until the clams are completely open and somewhat firm, 4 to 5 minutes more (5 to 6 minutes more for large steamers).

3. Meanwhile, melt the butter to make drawn butter (see page 75).

4. Remove the pot from the heat and gently transfer the steamers to a large bowl with the wire-mesh skimmer. Drain the broth through the spigot or strain through a fine strainer into four small bowls.

5. Serve the steamers with the bowls of broth, drawn butter, and lemon wedges.

SERVES 4 AS AN APPETIZER

Variation: Little Neck Steamers

Where I come from, steamers always mean soft-shell clams, but I have learned that some people (especially from the West Coast) call steamed little necks steamers. Although I prefer to eat little necks raw or grilled, they are quite tasty when steamed and dipped in broth and butter.

Substitute 4 to 5 pounds of little necks, scrubbed, rinsed, and drained. Increase the total cooking time to 10 to 12 minutes. As soon as the clams open, they are ready.

How to Eat Steamers

Steamers are fragile, so handle them gingerly. The proper way to eat a steamer is to pick it up with your fingers and carefully pry the clam from the shell. (If it does not come out easily, it means the clams are undercooked.) Toss the shells into a bowl or bucket. Place your thumb and forefinger (left hand if you are a right-hander and vice versa) on the bottom of the siphon and use the thumb and forefinger of your other hand to peel away the protective (inedible) membrane from the siphon.

Double-dipping: Holding the siphon at the top, dip the belly of the clam into the hot broth for a few seconds, then transfer it into the drawn butter and into your mouth in one graceful motion. To fully appreciate the uniquely rich, low-tide flavor of the clam, chew it a few times and let the flavor expand. The siphons of soft-shell clams are chewy but worth eating unless the clams are quite large.

Since steamers are usually served in a communal bowl, it is important that you become adept at the double-dipping technique if you want to eat your fair share. When you are finished with the steamers, feel free to drink the broth. It is wonderful and healthful. Just sip the broth from the top of the bowl, and don't stir it. Leave the bottom quarter of the broth—it can be gritty.

Removing the protective membrane from the siphon of a cooked steamer (soft-shell clam)

STEAMERS COOKED IN BEER

If you eat steamers often, you might want to mix it up once in a while and try this recipe. I recommend that you buy a six-pack (or more) of a lager beer or light ale that you really enjoy and use the same beer or ale to steam open the clams. This recipe is for 4 starters, but you can double the recipe and make a meal out of it. Try an American (steamer) version of the Belgian tradition of serving mussels with a big basket of Boardwalk French Fries (page 268). These are great with one of Belgium's hundreds of excellent beers and ales.

For equipment you will need a large steamer pot (see page 70) or a large pot with a steamer rack and a tight-fitting lid and a Chinese wire-mesh skimmer. If not using a steamer pot, you will need a fine strainer.

3   pounds medium (1 1/2 to 2 inches in diameter) steamers (soft-shell clams)
2   cups lager beer or light ale
4   cloves garlic, thinly sliced
1   large stalk celery, thinly sliced on the diagonal
1/2 yellow onion, thinly sliced
1   dried bay leaf
4   sprigs fresh thyme
1/4 teaspoon freshly ground black pepper
8   tablespoons (1 stick) unsalted butter
Lemon wedges

1. Fill two large pots (or two sinks) with cold water. Gently place the clams in one pot of water, discarding any dead clams or clams with cracked shells. If a clam looks shriveled up, poke the siphon: if it doesn't retract into the shell, the clam is dead. Swish the clams gently in the water and let soak for a few minutes, then lift them out with a Chinese wire-mesh skimmer and place them in the other pot of cold water. Rinse out the first pot and fill it again. Swish the clams around again and let soak briefly, then transfer them to the clean pot. Swish and repeat with successive batches of clean water until the water is perfectly clear (4 or 5 soakings). Drain the clams and set them aside.

2. Set up your steamer pot. Add the beer, garlic, celery, onion, bay leaf, thyme, and pepper, cover, and turn the heat on high. When the pot has a full head of steam, add the steamers and replace the lid. Steam (the beer should be at a rolling boil) for 4 minutes. Uncover the pot and stir once gently. Cover and continue to steam until the clams are completely open and somewhat

firm, 4 to 5 minutes longer (6 to 7 minutes more for large steamers).

3. Meanwhile, melt the butter to make drawn butter (see page 75).

4. Remove the pot from the heat and gently transfer the steamers to a large bowl with the wire-mesh skimmer. Drain the broth through the spigot or strain through a fine strainer into four small bowls.

5. Serve the steamers with the broth, drawn butter, and lemon wedges.

SERVES 4 AS AN APPETIZER

WILD MUSSELS COOKED LIKE STEAMERS

This is how I cook mussels when we (usually my kids) pick them wild off the rocks at Warren's Point, in front of my wife's family home in Little Compton, Rhode Island. The small wild mussels are big in flavor and you just can't get them any fresher. They stand alone just fine without any wine or herbs, so we steam them open like steamers and serve them with the mussel broth and drawn butter.

Make sure to put an empty bowl on the table to accommodate the shells. For equipment, you will need a large steamer pot (see page 70) or a large pot with a steamer rack and a tight-fitting lid and a Chinese wire-mesh skimmer. If not using a steamer pot, you will need a fine strainer.

2   **cups water**
1   **large stalk celery, thinly sliced on the diagonal**
1/2 **onion, cut into thin slices**
1/4 **teaspoon freshly ground black pepper, or more to taste**
3   **pounds medium mussels, scrubbed, debearded, and rinsed**
8   **tablespoons (1 stick) unsalted butter**
Lemon wedges

1. Set up your steamer pot. Add the water, celery, onion, and pepper, cover, and turn the heat on high. When the pot has a full head of steam, add the mussels and replace the lid. Steam (the water should be at a rolling boil) for 3 minutes. Remove the lid and stir once gently. Continue to steam until the mussels are completely open and firmly cooked, 3 to 4 minutes more.

2. Meanwhile, melt the butter to make drawn butter (see page 75).

3. Remove the pot from the heat and gently transfer the mussels to a large bowl with a Chinese wire-mesh skimmer. Drain the broth through the spigot or strain through a fine strainer into four small bowls.

4. Serve the mussels with the broth, drawn butter, and lemon wedges.

SERVES 4 AS AN APPETIZER OR 2 AS A MAIN COURSE

Preparing Mussels for Cooking

Wild mussels take more time to clean and debeard than cultivated mussels, which are cleaned and usually debearded before being sent to market. Start by rinsing the mussels in a colander under cold water; don't let them sit in water. Use a small scrub brush or rag to scrub each mussel individually. The "beard" consists of the inedible fibers in the center of the shell that the mussel uses to attach itself to rocks. When you scrub the mussel, debeard it by pinching the fibers and pulling them away from the shell.

Rinse the mussel and put in the colander to drain. Try to work quickly so the mussels are not at room temperature for more than 10 to 15 minutes. Once the mussels have drained, cover and refrigerate.

Removing the beard from a mussel

MUSSELS WITH WHITE WINE, GARLIC, AND HERBS

This is a classic and very tasty way to cook mussels. The broth is so divine that the mussels almost become an excuse to drink it. Use wild or cultivated mussels for this recipe, and drink the same wine you use to cook the mussels. A medium-bodied Sauvignon Blanc, Pinot Gris, Vidal Blanc, or other crisp, somewhat acidic white wine will serve you well. Serve the mussels in soup plates, with crusty bread on the table.

Make sure to put bowl on the table to accommodate the empty shells. You can use a shell, instead of a spoon, to drink the broth. For equipment, you will need a 10- to 12-inch deep sauté pan (sauteuse) or a 4- to 6-quart pot with a tight-fitting lid and a Chinese wire-mesh skimmer.

- **2 tablespoons olive oil**
- **1 dried bay leaf**
- **1/8 teaspoon crushed red pepper flakes**
- **2 tablespoons minced shallots (2 large)**
- **1 tablespoon minced garlic**
- **2 tablespoons minced fresh thyme**
- **2 tablespoons minced fresh tarragon**
- **2 cups dry white wine**
- **3 pounds medium mussels, scrubbed, debearded, and rinsed**
- **4 tablespoons cold unsalted butter, cut into tablespoons**
- **2 tablespoons chopped fresh Italian parsley**
- **2 tablespoons chopped fresh chives**

1. Heat the olive oil in a large deep sauté pan or a medium pot over medium heat. Add the bay leaf and red pepper and sauté until they sizzle, about 30 seconds. Add the shallots, garlic, thyme, and tarragon and sauté until fragrant, about 1 minute. Add the white wine, increase the heat to high, cover, and bring to a boil.

2. Add the mussels, replace the lid, and cook for 3 minutes. Remove the lid and stir once gently. Cover and cook until the mussels are completely open and firm, about 3 to 4 minutes more.

3. Remove the pan from the heat and gently transfer the mussels to a large bowl with a Chinese wire-mesh skimmer or a slotted spoon. Return the pan to the heat and bring back to a boil. When the sauce is at a rolling boil, add the butter piece by piece. Off the heat, stir in parsley and chives.

4. Pour the sauce over the mussels and serve immediately.

SERVES 4 AS AN APPETIZER

MUSSELS IN SPICY RED SAUCE

I love this dish, which is also called mussels fra diavolo, because my Italian grandmother made it often, especially around the holidays. It's Italian-American comfort food: the lusty combination of mussels and spicy red sauce is irresistible. But forget about serving it with pasta—you absolutely must have a loaf of crusty, chewy Italian or French bread to dip in the sauce.

Make sure to put a bowl on the table to accommodate the shells. For equipment, you will need a 10- to 12-inch deep sauté pan (sauteuse) or a 4- to 6-quart pot with a tight-fitting lid and a Chinese wire-mesh skimmer.

2 tablespoons olive oil
1 tablespoon minced garlic
1 to 2 teaspoons crushed red pepper flakes
1 cup dry white wine
2 cups Red Sauce (page 349)
3 pounds medium mussels, scrubbed, debearded, and rinsed
2 tablespoons chopped fresh Italian parsley

1. Heat the olive oil in a large deep sauté pan or a medium pot over medium heat. Add the garlic and red pepper and sauté until fragrant, about 30 seconds. Add the white wine and red sauce, increase the heat to high, cover, and bring to a boil.

2. Add the mussels, replace the lid, and cook for 3 minutes. Remove the lid and stir once gently. Cover and cook until the mussels are completely open and firmly cooked, about 4 minutes more.

3. Remove the pan from the heat and gently transfer the mussels to a large bowl with a Chinese wire-mesh skimmer or a slotted spoon. Return the pan to the heat and bring to a boil. Boil for a minute or two, until the sauce is thick enough to coat a spoon.

4. Pour the sauce over the mussels and serve immediately.

SERVES 4 AS AN APPETIZER

STEAMED BLACK SEA BASS WITH GINGER AND SCALLIONS

Black sea bass is a spectacular fish, one of my very favorites. It is a small fish, usually in the 1 1/2- to 2-pound range, with beautiful rich but flaky white meat and a delicious flavor. Black sea bass ranges from Cape Cod to the Carolinas and in recent years has been fairly abundant. My daughter, Hayley, holds the Rhode Island state record for the summer of 2003, when she landed a 4.6-pound black sea bass off Newport.

Black sea bass is very versatile. Filleted, it can be panfried or grilled. Whole, it can be roasted or deep-fried, but my favorite way to cook it is in the Chinese style—steamed whole with ginger and scallions. (Black sea bass has long been a favorite of the Chinese.) You will need about a pound of whole fish, or even a little more, per person. If you steam an odd number of fish, say three fish for four people, it doesn't matter, because the fish are whole on a platter, family-style. A bowl of plain rice is a perfect accompaniment. It is customary in China to serve the head of the fish to the most important guest, because the sweetest, most tender meat is contained in the fish cheeks.

For equipment, you will need a large steamer pot (see page 70) or a fish poacher and a large spatula to transfer the fish to a platter. Although it isn't completely necessary, pieces of parchment paper cut to fit under each fish will make the process of transferring the fish easier.

2 or 3 whole black sea bass, 1 1/2 to 2 pounds each, gutted and scaled
A large thumb-sized piece of fresh ginger
6 scallions, trimmed
1/4 cup vegetable oil
Kosher or sea salt
1 cup Soy-Ginger Sauce (page 348)

WORKING AHEAD

You can trim the fish and set it up with the ginger and scallions early in the day. Keep refrigerated until ready to steam.

1. Using a sharp knife or scissors, trim the fins off the fish. Make 2 diagonal incisions on each side of each bass.

2. Peel the ginger and slice it as thin as possible into long wide slivers. Cut 3 of the scallions into 1-inch pieces, then cut the white parts lengthwise in half. Thinly slice the remaining 3 scallions for garnish.

3. Place a thin sliver of ginger, a piece of scallion green, and a piece of scallion white inside each slit in the fish. Place the remaining slivers of ginger and cut scallions in the cavities of the fish. Refrigerate the fish if you are not cooking it right away; remove it from the refrigerator about 20 minutes before you want to steam it.

4. Set up the steamer or fish poacher; it should hold the fish with ample room for the steam to circulate. Fill the bottom of the steamer with

water (it should not touch the steamer rack), salt the water, and bring it to a boil. Cover the steamer.

5. Meanwhile, rub the skin of the fish with the vegetable oil and sprinkle it lightly with salt. If you have parchment paper, put a small piece, cut to the same size as the fish, under each fish. Place the fish in the steamer and cover the steamer. Once you see steam escaping from the pot, note the time: it will take about 20 minutes for 1 1/2-pound fish, or 30 minutes for 2-pound fish. To check for doneness, carefully remove one fish from the steamer and take a peek inside the cavity. If you see white spots of protein forming inside close to the head, it is ready. You can always cut into the meat (bottom side, so your guests won't see it) near the head—if the meat is pure white, the bass is cooked.

6. Transfer the bass to a large serving platter. Generously spoon about half the soy-ginger sauce over the fish, and serve the remaining sauce on the side.

SERVES 4 AS A MAIN COURSE

CORN ON THE COB

Sweet corn on the cob is such an important part of my family's summer (and yours too, I bet) that it often becomes a point of reference that defines a certain summer. Almost every summer, the local lobsters taste sweet, the melons and berries are juicy, the Boston Red Sox get our hopes up, and the corn is good—but some summers, the corn is spectacular! Yesterday I had the best corn in recent memory, maybe in my life. Cole Walker from Little Compton, Rhode Island, is a farmer I admire greatly. For twenty-five summers, I have enjoyed his corn, tomatoes, and other produce. He is a genius with sweet corn, and we will long remember this year as the year of the best corn ever.

The Silver Queen, which is quite common in the Northeast, peaked in the last week of August. It was the plumpest, sweetest, juiciest, creamiest corn imaginable. In fact, on the day of this writing, I was disappointed because we had a commitment to go out in the evening and I just wanted to stay home and eat more of Walker's Silver Queen corn. To remedy the situation, I went out and bought several ears, cooked them, and served them to my gang at four in the afternoon. During summer at the shore, that afternoon ritual is much more appropriate than tea and scones.

When I was growing up in New Jersey during the '50s and '60s, summer marked the time that we ate corn from the local fields almost every night, especially the years when we grew our own. Our "Jersey corn," a variety that I know only by that name, was small (6 to 8 inches long), light yellow in color, and very sweet, provided it was cooked shortly after picking. Today the "super-sweet" hybrid corns don't convert the sugar to starch the way the old-fashioned varieties did, so it is often not an issue, but, as a rule, true summer corn on the cob requires local corn, picked the same day, preferably within hours of the time you are going to eat it.

Shucking Corn

During corn season, we shuck hundreds of ears for our family of six (five plus Granddad), so throwing the husks in the garbage is not an option. We have a special compost place where we leave the husks; if possible, you should too. After you remove the husks, use a clean towel to rub the silks off—it is very effective.

Boiling Corn on the Cob

Use a pot that is at least 12 inches wide and then figure on 1-quart capacity per ear of corn (e.g., a 12-quart [3-gallon] pot is ample for 12 ears of corn). Fill the pot two-thirds full with water and bring to a boil. Add a small amount of salt (2 teaspoons per gallon) and bring to a boil. Take a taste of the corn that you are about to cook, which will be a good indicator of how long it will take to cook. If the corn is delicate—clean and sweet tasting, with a light texture (wet, not starchy)—you only need to heat it through. Add it to the pot (with the water boiling vigorously) and cook for about 3 to 4 minutes. Corn that is starchy or not very fresh has a thick gummy texture and tastes less sweet; it will take 6 to 8 minutes to cook. I call that kind of corn "chowder corn" because, although it is not ideal for eating, it does produce very good corn chowder or creamed corn.

Serving Corn

The idea of serving corn as a separate course may seem somewhat obsessive, but it's an idea that I have tried to push for years. It doesn't make a lot of sense to put corn out with the other food at dinner. The corn is at its best as soon as it is cool enough to eat (about 2 minutes out of the pot) and it requires immediate attention. Unlike other vegetables and side dishes, you don't want to eat just a bite, then put it down and taste something else—corn on the cob is a start-to-finish endeavor. So why not serve it first? I'm not saying it's an appetizer. Of course you may have appetizers and cocktails before dinner, but try my suggestion and serve the corn when you first sit down. Then serve the rest of the meal. The corn becomes an event in itself, a prelude to a great shore dinner.

Corn Etiquette

Is it proper to roll your corn sideways over a stick of sweet butter? My answer is a resounding yes—as long as you dedicate that stick of butter to the corn and you don't "double-dip" (no rolling after you've started eating the ear). The butter should be a little cool (20 minutes out of the fridge) and the corn rolled while it is still quite hot. It is nice to serve the corn on special corn plates, but not mandatory. Corn holders are okay, but I like to eat corn with my hands. Lastly, I prefer to put the salt in a small bowl to pinch and sprinkle, because at the shore, salt-shakers always get clogged and pour unevenly.

INSIDE THIS CHAPTER

Clam Soup That Cures 95

Creamy Cape Cod Clam Chowder 97

Box: Toasted Common Crackers 98

Coney Island Red Clam Chowder 99

Cataplana—Portuguese-Style Clam Stew 101

Variation: Cataplana with Mussels 102

Quick and Tasty Oyster Stew 103

Home-Style Lobster Stew 104

Crab, Tomato, and Vegetable Soup 106

Callaloo 108

Portuguese Fisherman's Stew 109

Pork Stew with Clams and Garlic Sauce 111

Shack Bouillabaisse 113

Croûtes 115

Red Pepper Aïoli (Rouille) 115

4

SOUPS, CHOWDERS, AND STEWS

KETTLE COOKING PART II

Boiling or simmering foods in broth or other liquid is a timeless technique. Until the mid-1800s, the vast majority of kitchens in America featured an open hearth with a large kettle suspended over an open fire with an iron tripod. Making soups, chowders, and stews was a natural and necessary solution to this limited technology. Although the advent of the kitchen stove freed the cook from the necessity of making these kinds of preparation as a staple, it didn't put an end to them. On the contrary, the greater flexibility and temperature control offered by the stove gave the cook an opportunity to improve on many time-honored recipes for soups and stews.

Braises, chowders, soups, and other slow-cooked dishes have recently come up against a different kind of challenge—very few people have time to prepare them these days. Ironically, these dishes, which were always considered to be in the realm of the home cook, are becoming restaurant fare, because professional chefs do have the time to do it right.

The recipes in this chapter are, without a doubt, the most time-consuming and complex dishes in this book. I don't expect that you will use them frequently during the dog days of summer, but as the nights turn cold and the summer has passed, you'll want to make a meal out of any of them. So break out your soup kettle or Dutch oven and wooden spoon and let the recipes that follow fill your afternoon or morning with pleasant preparation time, fill your home with wonderful rich aromas and at meal time, and fill your belly with goodness.

CLAM SOUP THAT CURES

This is the seafood version of Jewish penicillin, chicken soup, a simple broth served with lots of love. It is my version of an old James Beard recipe, made with soft-shell clams (Beard used razor clams). I loved the name and the concept of a clam broth with minimum fat and maximum flavor served as a restorative. I have always felt that shellfish has the ability to give strength, so whether you need it or not, try this wonderful light soup. It makes an excellent starter to almost any meal.

For equipment, you will need a steamer pot (see page 70) or a large pot with a steamer rack and a tight-fitting lid, a Chinese wire-mesh skimmer, a fine strainer (if not using a steamer pot), and a heavy 3-quart stainless steel saucepan.

3   pounds medium (1 1/2 to 2 inches in diameter) steamers (soft-shell clams)
2   cups water
Clam juice if needed
2   tablespoons unsalted butter
1   medium leek, well washed and finely diced or 2 large shallots, finely diced
1   clove garlic, minced
1   stalk celery, finely diced
1/2 teaspoon minced fresh thyme
1   tablespoon finely chopped fresh Italian parsley
1   tablespoon finely minced fresh chives
Freshly ground black pepper

WORKING AHEAD

The clams can be steamed, shelled, and trimmed the morning of the day you're planning to make the soup. Cover and refrigerate the clam broth separately.

1. Fill two large pots (or two sinks) with cold water. Gently place the clams in one pot of water, discarding any obviously dead clams or clams with cracked shells. If a clam looks shriveled up, poke the siphon; if it doesn't retract into the shell, the clam is dead. Swish the clams gently in the water and let soak for a few minutes, then lift them out with a wire-mesh skimmer and place them in the other pot of cold water. Rinse out the first pot and fill it again. Swish the clams around again and let soak briefly, then transfer them to the clean pot. Swish and repeat with successive batches of clean water until the water is perfectly clear (4

or 5 soakings). Drain the clams and set them aside.

2. Set up your steamer pot. Add the water, cover, and turn the heat on high. When the pot has a full head of steam, add the steamers and replace the lid. Steam (the water should be at a rolling boil) for 4 minutes. Uncover the pot and stir once gently. Cover and continue to steam until the clams are completely open and firm, 4 to 5 minutes more.

3. Remove the pot from the heat and gently transfer the steamers to a large shallow dish with the wire-mesh skimmer. Let the steamers cool slightly. Drain the broth through the spigot or strain through a fine strainer into a large glass measure. There should be 3 cups of broth. If not, compensate with bottled clam juice—the broth should be as strong as possible. Set aside.

4. Shell the clams while they are still warm. Trim off the siphons (black necks) and discard. Place the clams in a small bowl and refrigerate until ready to use.

5. Heat the butter in a heavy 3-quart stainless steel saucepan over medium heat until foaming. Add the leek, garlic, celery, and thyme and sauté, stirring frequently, until the vegetables are thoroughly softened but not browned, about 10 minutes.

6. Add the reserved clam broth, increase the heat to medium-high, and bring the broth to a boil. Reduce the heat to very low. Add the clams, parsley, chives, and pepper to taste. Let the soup sit over low heat for 5 to 10 minutes before serving. As it sits, the flavors will expand.

MAKES 4 TO 5 CUPS; SERVES 4 AS AN APPETIZER OR A LIGHT MEAL

Wellfleet Oysters
on the Half-Shell,
page 48

The Raw Bar at
Summer Shack

Conch Salad Bahamian-Style,
page 62

Smashing Crabs,
page 76

Indoor Clambake,
page 77

Creamy Cape Cod Clam Chowder (foreground), page 97, and Coney Island Red Clam Chowder, page 99, with Toasted Common Crackers, page 98

**Chilled Maine Shrimp with Cabbage
and Peanuts, Vietnamese-Style,
page 121**

Cataplana with Mussels (shown here in an authentic cataplana pot)
page 102

CREAMY CAPE COD CLAM CHOWDER

On Cape Cod, clam chowder means quahog chowder. Quahogs are large hard-shell clams (see the chart on page 57), also known as chowder clams, and they are abundant on the Cape. Quahogs have a wonderful flavor that makes a distinctive chowder. Chowder is a dish of humble origins and it often relies on "found foods" like fish you catch yourself or clams you dig. Clam chowder is like apple pie in that everyone has his or her concept of what it should be like (usually people like their mother's version best). In the spirit of true home-style chowder making, this recipe depends on potatoes to lightly thicken the chowder; no other starch is added. I use salt pork, which imparts a mild richness to the chowder; you can substitute bacon for a smokier flavor. This chowder can be served in small cups as a starter or in larger bowls as a main course. Serve toasted common crackers (see the box on page 98), Pilot crackers, oyster crackers, or saltines on the side for a little crunch.

For equipment, you will need a 4- to 6-quart pot with a tight-fitting lid and a fine strainer.

10 **pounds small quahogs or large cherry-stone clams**

2 **cups water**

4 **ounces meaty salt pork, rind removed and cut into small (1/3-inch) dice**

2 **tablespoons unsalted butter**

2 **medium yellow onions (about 12 ounces), cut into 1/2-inch dice**

2 **cloves garlic, finely chopped**

2 **stalks celery (4 ounces), cut into 1/3-inch dice**

5 to 6 **sprigs fresh thyme, leaves removed and chopped (1 tablespoon)**

1 **large dried bay leaf**

2 **pounds Yukon Gold, Maine, PEI, or other all-purpose potatoes, peeled and cut into 1/2- to 3/4-inch dice**

2 **cups heavy cream**

Freshly ground black pepper

Kosher or sea salt if needed

1/4 cup chopped fresh Italian parsley

WORKING AHEAD

All chowders improve after they are made, so allow at least an hour from the time the chowder is cooked until it is served. You can make the chowder 1 or 2 days in advance. Reheat it slowly; never let it boil.

1. Scrub the clams and rinse well. Place them in a large pot, add the water, cover, and turn the heat to high. Once you see a little steam escape from the pot, let the clams cook for about 5 minutes. Remove the lid and quickly move the clams around in the pot so they will cook evenly, then cover and cook for 5 minutes more, or until the clams open.

2. Pour off the broth and reserve. After it has settled a bit, strain the broth, leaving the bottom 1/2 inch of broth (and sediment) in the container. You should have about 4 cups. Remove the clams from the shells, place in a bowl, and refrigerate until cold.

3. Dice the clams into small (1/3- to 1/2-inch) pieces. Cover and refrigerate.

4. Rinse and dry the pot and heat over low heat. Add the salt pork and cook until crispy and brown. Add the butter, onions, garlic, celery, thyme, and bay leaf and sauté, stirring occasionally with a wooden spoon, for about 10 minutes, until the onions are softened but not browned.

5. Add the potatoes and 4 cups reserved clam broth. The broth should just barely cover the potatoes; if it doesn't, add more broth or water. Turn the heat to high, cover the pot, and boil vigorously for about 10 minutes, until the potatoes are soft on the outside but still firm in the center. Smash a few potatoes against the side of the pot and stir them into the chowder to lightly thicken it.

6. Remove the pot from the heat and stir in the cream and diced clams. Season with black pepper; you may not need salt (the clams usually add enough of their own). If you are serving the chowder within the hour, just let it sit and "cure." Otherwise, let cool to room temperature and refrigerate it; cover it after it has chilled.

7. When ready to serve, reheat the chowder slowly over medium heat; do not let it boil. Ladle into cups or bowls and sprinkle with the parsley.

MAKES 3 QUARTS; SERVES 12 AS AN APPETIZER OR 6 TO 8 AS A MAIN COURSE

Toasted Common Crackers

Common crackers are small round crackers (1 to 2 inches in diameter) made with a yeast dough, which gives them a rich flavor and a hollow center. Traditionally they are split open with a fork or knife and the halves are then buttered and toasted in the oven (about 15 minutes at 350°F). They are served as a side to chowder, adding a much needed crunch. These crackers have been made commercially for more than two hundred years, so nobody really makes them at home anymore. Common crackers, along with the famous Pilot cracker (Nabisco) and "hard bread" of Maritime Canada, are deeply rooted in the history of chowder making. They are the descendants of hardtack, or ship's biscuits, which were nothing more than baked bricks made of flour and water. Hardtack was a necessity, because it was the only way that flour would keep from rotting on ships or in damp coastal areas. In early days, crackers were added right into the chowder; as potatoes became popular, the crackers worked their way out of the bowl and onto the side, where they are still served as a crispy garnish for chowders and soups.

Common crackers

CONEY ISLAND RED CLAM CHOWDER

I don't buy the whole Manhattan-versus-New England clam chowder rivalry. No one other than food writers really talks about it. I have long believed the white and red chowder rivalry was just a metaphor for the Red Sox and Yankee rivalry, which is far more real. I don't even believe that Manhattan clam chowder is really from Manhattan, although some food historians theorize that it was created by Neapolitan immigrants in New York's Little Italy. Chowder isn't a dish that is ever created, it just kind of happens. It traditionally originated in the same place the defining ingredients come from. Long Island, a pristine farming community at the turn of the nineteenth century, was a major producer of both tomatoes and clams, so it seems most likely to me that red chowder probably was popularized in that area. There were also restaurants on Coney Island during that era that were called chowder mills. The chowder mills had easy access to the clams and tomatoes of Long Island. This type of red chowder resembles a clam and vegetable soup. It has so many vegetables that you need to add more broth than the clams will make, either bottled clam broth or other broth or stock.

The chowder can be served in small cups as a starter or in larger bowls as a main course. Serve toasted common crackers (see box), Pilot crackers, oyster crackers, or saltines on the side for a little crunch.

For equipment, you will need a 4- to 6-quart pot with a tight-fitting lid and a fine strainer.

10 pounds small quahogs or large cherry-stone clams
2 cups water
4 ounces slab bacon, rind removed and cut into small (1/3-inch) dice
2 tablespoons olive oil
1 large onion (8 to 10 ounces), cut into 1/2-inch dice
4 cloves garlic, finely chopped
2 stalks celery (4 ounces), cut into 1/3-inch dice
1 medium green bell pepper (6 ounces), cored, seeded, and cut into 1/2-inch dice
2 medium carrots (4 ounces), peeled and cut into 1/2-inch dice
1 tablespoon dried oregano
2 dried bay leaves
1/2 teaspoon crushed red pepper flakes
1 1/2 pounds Yukon Gold, Maine, PEI, or other all-purpose potatoes, peeled and cut into 1/2- to 3/4-inch dice
One 28-ounce can whole tomatoes in juice, drained, juice reserved, and cut into 1/2-inch dice
1 cup bottled clam juice, clam broth, Fish Stock (page 354), Chicken Stock (page 356), or canned low-sodium chicken broth, or more if needed
Freshly ground black pepper
Kosher or sea salt if needed
2 tablespoons chopped fresh Italian parsley
2 tablespoons minced fresh chives

WORKING AHEAD

All chowders improve after they are made, so allow at least an hour from the time the chowder is cooked until it is served. You can make the chowder 1 or 2 days in advance. Reheat it slowly; never let it boil.

1. Scrub the clams and rinse well. Place them in a large pot, add the water, cover, and turn the heat to high. Once you see a little steam escape from the pot, cook the clams for about 5 minutes. Remove the lid and quickly move the clams around in the pot so they will cook evenly, then cover and cook for 5 minutes more, or until the clams open.

2. Pour off the broth and reserve. After it has settled a bit, strain the broth, leaving the bottom 1/2 inch of broth (and sediment) in the container. You should have about 4 cups. Remove the clams from the shells, place in a bowl, and refrigerate until cold.

3. Dice the clams into small (1/3- to 1/2-inch) pieces. Cover and refrigerate.

4. Rinse and dry the pot and heat over low heat. Add the bacon and cook until it is golden brown and has rendered most of the fat. Add the oil, onion, garlic, celery, bell pepper, carrots, oregano, and bay leaves and sauté, stirring occasionally with a wooden spoon, for about 10 minutes, until the onions are softened but not browned.

5. Add the potatoes and 4 cups reserved clam broth. The broth should just barely cover the potatoes; if it doesn't, add more broth or water. Turn the heat to high, cover the pot, and boil vigorously for about 10 minutes, until the potatoes are soft on the outside but still firm in the center. Smash a few potatoes against the side of the pot and stir them into the chowder to lightly thicken it. Add the tomatoes, with their juices, and the 1 cup clam broth and simmer, uncovered, for 5 minutes.

6. Remove the pot from the heat and stir in the diced clams. Season with black pepper; you may not need salt (the clams usually add enough of their own). If you are serving the chowder within the hour, just let it sit and "cure." Otherwise, let cool to room temperature, then refrigerate it. Cover it after it has chilled.

7. When ready to serve, reheat the chowder slowly over medium heat; do not let it boil. Ladle into cups or bowls and sprinkle with the parsley and chives.

MAKES 10 CUPS; SERVES 10 AS AN APPETIZER OR 6 AS A MAIN COURSE

CATAPLANA
Portuguese-Style Clam Stew

cataplana is a special hinged cooking pot used in Portugal for cooking clams and other shellfish. Whatever is cooked in the cataplana is called by that name. I'm not sure if my recipe is authentic, but this is how it is served in Portuguese fish houses along the East Coast. I have made it for years to nothing but rave reviews. The strong acidic flavor of wine and tomatoes balances the assertive flavors of the garlic and Portuguese sausage. I love the way the little droplets of fat from the chouriço dot the broth and the clams. Use one of the clam shells to drink the broth after you have eaten all the clams. Don't forget to serve a good crusty bread to dunk in the broth and to set out a bowl for the empty shells. Following this recipe is a simple variation substituting mussels for the clams.

For equipment, look for a cataplana in specialty and ethnic markets (see the color photo). If you use one, you can bring the cataplana to the table. Or you can make the dish in a large (12-inch) sauté pan with a lid.

8   whole allspice berries
3   tablespoons olive oil
2   large or 4 small dried bay leaves
1/2 teaspoon crushed red pepper flakes
6   cloves garlic, sliced
1   small onion (3 to 4 ounces), cut into 1/4-inch dice
1   small to medium green bell pepper, cored, seeded, and cut into 1/4-inch dice
One 6-ounce piece chouriço, cut into 16 slices
One 14-ounce can whole tomatoes in juice, drained, juice reserved, and diced
1   cup dry white wine
1/4 teaspoon freshly ground black pepper
3 1/2 pounds small little neck clams (about 32 clams), scrubbed
2   tablespoons chopped fresh Italian parsley

WORKING AHEAD
The stew can be made completely ahead to the point where the clams go in; chill it quickly in a sink of ice water, then cover and refrigerate. To finish, bring the stew base up to a boil over medium heat, add the clams and proceed with the recipe.

1. Crack the allspice berries by gently crushing them under a small frying pan. Heat the oil in a cataplana or large sauté pan over medium heat. Add the allspice berries, bay leaves, and crushed red pepper and cook, stirring constantly, until the bay leaves turn dark olive, about 1 minute.

2. Add the garlic and swirl it in the oil until golden brown on the edges, about 1 minute. Stir in the onion and bell pepper, increase the heat to

medium-high, and sauté, stirring frequently, until the bell pepper begins to lose its vibrant color, about 4 minutes.

3. Add the chouriço and sauté until it begins to tint the vegetables brownish-red, about another minute. Stir in the tomatoes, with their juice, the wine, and black pepper and let the stew come to a boil at a leisurely pace. (No salt will be needed because of the natural salinity of the clams.)

4. Add the clams, cover tightly, and steam them for 5 minutes. Stir them quickly, cover the pot again, and steam for another 4 to 5 minutes, until all the clams are open. Stir in the chopped parsley and serve family-style in the cataplana or divide among four soup plates.

SERVES 4 AS A MAIN COURSE

Variation: Cataplana with Mussels

Substitute 3 pounds of mussels for the little neck clams. After adding the mussels, cook for only 4 minutes before stirring, and then for another 3 to 4 minutes to finish the cooking.

QUICK AND TASTY OYSTER STEW

This is a timeless creation, a milky broth permeated with the flavor of plump, briny oysters. It may be of New England origins, but it has found its way into kitchens up and down the East Coast and is as popular today as it has been since the early 1900s. Some people add sherry to oyster stew; I prefer to serve the sherry in small glasses and give my guests the option to put a little in their stew or just drink it on the side. The flavors are beautiful together.

You can buy shucked oysters at most seafood markets; if you want to shuck fresh oysters for your stew, you will need about 2 dozen to make a pint. Serve the stew with common crackers, oyster crackers, or croutons on the side for a crunchy option.

This recipe can easily be doubled.

For equipment, you will need a fine strainer and a heavy 3-quart stainless steel saucepan.

1 **pint oysters, with their juice**
2 **tablespoons unsalted butter**
1 **small leek, well washed and finely diced, or 1/2 small yellow onion, finely diced**
2 **small stalks celery, finely diced**
1 1/2 **cups milk**
1/2 **cup heavy cream**
Kosher or sea salt and freshly ground black pepper
1 **tablespoon chopped fresh chives**
1 1/2 **cups fino (dry) or amontillado (medium-dry) sherry (optional)**

1. Pick over the oysters, looking for any pieces of broken shell. Strain the oyster liquid into a separate container, and keep both refrigerated until ready to use.

2. Heat the butter in a heavy 3-quart saucepan over medium heat until foaming. Add the leek or onion and celery and cook, stirring frequently, until the vegetables are thoroughly softened but not browned, 8 to 10 minutes. (The idea is to extract the maximum amount of flavor from the vegetables.)

3. Stir in the milk, cream, and oyster liquid and heat until hot; do not allow the liquid to boil. Reduce the heat, add the oysters, and poach them gently until the oysters begin to shrink and curl at the edges, about 2 minutes. Season the stew with salt and pepper to taste. Remove the stew from the heat and allow the flavors to meld for a few minutes.

4. Reheat the stew if necessary, but do not boil. Divide it among four bowls and sprinkle with the chopped chives. Serve with four small glasses of the sherry.

SERVES 4 AS AN APPETIZER

HOME-STYLE LOBSTER STEW

*L*ike oyster stew, this venerable dish is as popular today as ever. I think the simplicity of the dish and the purity of its flavor is the reason for its longevity. Once you cook the lobster and remove the meat, the stew takes only minutes to prepare. You could make the recipe with purchased lobster meat, but it really is better if you cook the lobsters yourself, because you want to undercook them slightly; the meat will finish cooking in the stew. Small chicken lobsters are perfect for this dish—no need to spend money on the more expensive larger sizes.

For equipment, you will need a large steamer pot (see page 70) or a pot with a steamer rack and a tight-fitting lid, a deep 10- or 12-inch skillet, and a pair of tongs.

3 **live hard-shell or 4 live new-shell 1-pound chicken lobsters or about 14 ounces cooked lobster meat**
4 **tablespoons unsalted butter**
1 **teaspoon sweet Hungarian paprika**
Freshly ground black pepper
4 **cups whole milk**
1/2 **cup heavy cream**
Kosher or sea salt if needed
1 **tablespoon chopped fresh chives**
1 **tablespoon chopped fresh chervil or Italian parsley**

WORKING AHEAD

Since once the lobster meat is cooked, the dish literally takes minutes, the only thing you really need to prepare ahead is the lobster. The stew should be allowed to stand for at least 30 minutes once made, to allow the flavors to expand. Although it is best the day it is made, the stew can be kept refrigerated for up to 2 days.

1. If using live lobsters, steam them following the instructions on page 71, but reduce the cooking time by 2 minutes (8 minutes total). Using tongs, remove the lobsters to a pan or platter and let cool to room temperature.

2. When the lobsters are cool enough to handle, remove the meat from the tails, knuckles, and claws, reserving any juices. Cut the meat into 3/4-inch chunks. Remove any roe from female lobsters, coarsely chop it, and add it to the lobster meat. You can also pick the meat

from the carcasses and the walking legs; otherwise, wrap and freeze them for later use in a stock or broth. Or cut the store-bought lobster meat into chunks. Cover and refrigerate until ready to use.

3. About an hour before serving the stew, drain the chunks of lobster so that they are somewhat dry; reserve the juice. Heat a 10- or 12-inch deep skillet (you want plenty of surface area) over medium heat, and melt the butter. When it is foamy, add the lobster meat, with any roe, and sizzle it gently for about 1 minute. Turn the pieces with tongs and cook 1 minute more; the butter will have turned a pale red-orange color. Sprinkle with the paprika and grind a little fresh pepper over the lobster meat. Reduce the heat to low and cook for 1 minute more.

4. Pour the milk and cream over the lobster and let it heat slowly until the stew is hot but not quite simmering, about 5 minutes. Do not boil. Remove from the heat and let the stew sit for at least 30 minutes. The sitting time is crucial, for it allows the flavors to expand and the stew to transform itself from good to great. If the stew isn't to be eaten within an hour, refrigerate it after it has cooled to room temperature; cover it after it is chilled.

5. To serve, return the stew to low heat. Season again with pepper and a little salt, if needed. When the stew is very hot but not boiling, ladle it into warmed cups or bowls and sprinkle with the chopped chives and chervil. Serve immediately.

MAKES ABOUT 7 CUPS; SERVES 8 AS AN APPETIZER OR 4 AS A MAIN COURSE

CRAB, TOMATO, AND VEGETABLE SOUP

This superb summer soup combines fresh crab with vegetables straight from the garden or farm. It has layers of flavors that come from the contrast of the deep rich crab stock and the bright flavor of fresh vegetables. It's a bit of work, because you have to make a crab stock, but it will make you a hero with your friends and family. If you can buy soup crabs, you will save yourself a lot of trouble: make the stock with them, and purchase 6 ounces of crabmeat for garnish. This is a big recipe—because it features so many delicious vegetables, it is almost impossible to make a smaller batch.

For equipment, you will need a 4-quart heavy stainless steel saucepan.

2   pounds live rock, Jonah, or blue crabs
4   tablespoons unsalted butter
4   cloves garlic, minced
1   tablespoon minced fresh ginger
2   small onions, cut into medium dice
3   small stalks celery, cut into medium dice
1   medium green bell pepper, cored, seeded, and cut into medium dice
1   medium carrot, peeled and cut into medium dice
2   dried bay leaves
2   cups Chicken Stock (page 356) or canned low-sodium chicken broth
2   tablespoons Old Bay seasoning
One 12-ounce can diced tomatoes, with their juice
One 8-ounce potato, peeled and cut into small dice
1   large ear of corn, shucked, silk removed, and kernels cut from cob
3   ounces Savoy cabbage, shredded or thinly sliced (1 1/2 cups)
1   cup green beans cut into 1/2-inch lengths or 1 cup shucked fresh or frozen peas
A small handful of chopped celery leaves
3   scallions, trimmed and finely chopped
Kosher or sea salt and freshly ground black pepper

WORKING AHEAD

The crab stock and crabmeat can be prepared up to a day in advance. The vegetables can also be prepped well in advance. I think the flavor of the soup is best when it is made shortly before serving, but you could make it ahead if you need to: Transfer to a bowl, chill in a sink of ice water so it cools rapidly, and refrigerate. Reheat gently to serve.

1. Cook the crabs according to the method described on page 76. Pick the meat from the claws and body. You should have 5 or 6 ounces. Cover and refrigerate. Make a crab stock with the carcasses and shells, following the instructions on page 355. Cool, then cover and refrigerate.

2. Heat the butter in a 4-quart heavy saucepan over medium heat until foaming. Add the garlic, ginger, onions, celery, bell pepper, carrot, and bay leaves. Sauté, stirring frequently, until the vegetables are thoroughly softened but not browned, 10 to 12 minutes.

3. Meanwhile, heat the chicken stock and 6 cups of the reserved crab stock until hot.

4. Stir the Old Bay, tomatoes, chicken and crab stock, and potato into the vegetables. Bring to a simmer over medium-high heat and simmer for 10 minutes. Add the corn, cabbage, and green beans, if using, and simmer 5 minutes more. If using peas, add them about 3 minutes before the soup is done.

5. Stir in the celery leaves, cooked crab, and scallions. Seasoning to taste with salt and pepper. Remove the pan from the heat and let the flavors infuse for 10 minutes.

6. Ladle the soup into bowls and serve piping hot.

MAKES 3 QUARTS; SERVES 12 OR MORE AS AN APPETIZER

CALLALOO

Callaloo is a large, leafy, richly flavored green, also called dasheen, grown throughout the Caribbean. It is often used in soup and when it is, the soup is also called callaloo. I am not one hundred percent sure that every green in the Caribbean called callaloo or dasheen is exactly the same species, and the dish is also different on different islands. It ranges from a simple green soup of callaloo and chicken broth to much more elaborate chowder-like concoctions. I favor the more elaborate version. Since callaloo (the green) is not readily available, I substitute spinach, and it's terrific. If you can find callaloo, substitute it for the spinach, but cook it for 10 minutes after adding it.

Chiffonade is a term used to describe lettuces, herbs, and fine greens cut into thin strips. The spinach in this recipe is cut into chiffonade.

For equipment, you will need a 4- to 6-quart pot.

3 ounces slab bacon, cut into very small dice
2 tablespoons unsalted butter
3 cloves garlic, chopped (1 tablespoon)
2 jalapeño chiles, finely diced (1 1/2 to 2 tablespoons)
4 sprigs fresh thyme, leaves removed and chopped (1 tablespoon)
1 tablespoon Jamaican curry powder or Curry Paste (page 171)
5 cups Chicken Stock (page 356) or canned low-sodium chicken broth
1 1/2 cups unsweetened coconut milk
1 tablespoon kosher or sea salt
1/2 teaspoon freshly ground black pepper
12 ounces okra, trimmed and cut into 1/2-inch pieces
10 ounces spinach, trimmed and cut into thin slivers (chiffonade)
4 scallions, trimmed and thinly sliced
8 to 12 ounces crabmeat, picked over for fragments of shell or cartilage.

WORKING AHEAD

Although this soup is best served shortly after it is made, it can be made ahead and refrigerated for 2 or 3 days. The color will not be as brilliantly green when it is reheated.

1. Cook the bacon in a large heavy pot over medium heat until it has rendered most of its fat and is crisp. Pour off about half of the fat and add the butter, garlic, jalapeños, and thyme. Cook for about 1 minute, then add the curry powder and cook for 1 more minute.

2. Add the chicken stock, coconut milk, salt, pepper, and okra and bring to a boil. Turn down the heat and simmer for 10 minutes.

3. Add the spinach and stir it into the hot broth until it is wilted. Remove from the heat and add the chopped scallions and crabmeat. Let the soup sit for at least 30 minutes to let the flavors blend. If the callaloo isn't to be eaten within an hour, refrigerate it after it has cooled to room temperature; cover it after it is chilled.

4. To serve, reheat the soup. Season again with salt if needed.

MAKES ABOUT 10 CUPS; SERVES 10 AS AN APPETIZER OR 6 AS A LIGHT MAIN COURSE

PORTUGUESE FISHERMAN'S STEW

This is one of the most popular dishes served at our Summer Shack restaurants, and it is a great dish to make at home. Robustly flavored with garlic, tomatoes, saffron, and spicy sausage, the stew is very satisfying without being heavy. It is a perfect dish in which to use full-flavored fish such as bluefish or mackerel. In the Portuguese tradition, these fatty fish are balanced with an equal amount of lean fish like hake, cod, or bass. The Portuguese community on the East Coast plays a major role in the fishing industry; it is no surprise that they are wonderful seafood cooks.

Serve this dish with a side of plain white or brown rice.

For equipment, you will need a 6- to 8-quart Dutch oven or braising pot (a heavy stockpot will work, but it won't look good at the table) and a pair of tongs.

1/4 cup olive oil
4 small dried bay leaves
1/2 teaspoon crushed red pepper flakes
1 tablespoon minced garlic
1 medium onion (5 ounces), thinly sliced
1 medium red or green bell pepper (6 ounces), cored, seeded, and thinly sliced
4 sprigs fresh thyme, leaves removed and chopped (1 tablespoon)
1 teaspoon saffron threads, chopped
One 14-ounce can whole tomatoes in juice, drained, juice reserved, and cut into strips
1 cup dry white wine
2 cups Fish Stock (page 354), clam juice, Chicken Stock (page 356) or canned low-sodium chicken broth, or water
4 ounces chouriço or linguiça sausage, casings peeled off and sliced 1/2 inch thick
8 littleneck clams, scrubbed and rinsed
8 ounces fatty fish fillets, such as bluefish or mackerel, with skin, any blood line removed and cut into 4 pieces
8 ounces lean fish fillets, such as hake, cod, halibut, or striped bass, cut into 4 pieces
10 ounces mussels, scrubbed, debearded, and rinsed
4 ounces cleaned squid, including tentacles, bodies cut into 1/2-inch-wide rings

Kosher or sea salt and freshly ground black pepper

2 tablespoons chopped fresh Italian parsley

2 tablespoons chopped fresh cilantro

WORKING AHEAD

The stew itself can be made ahead through Step 2. Chill it quickly in a sink of ice water, then cover and refrigerate. To finish, bring the stew base to a boil over medium heat, add the chouriço and clams, and proceed with the recipe.

1. Heat the olive oil in a 6- to 8-quart Dutch oven or pot over medium heat. Add the bay leaves and red pepper flakes and sauté until they sizzle and the bay leaves begin to turn brown. Add the garlic, onion, bell pepper, and thyme and sauté, stirring frequently, until the vegetables begin to soften but not brown, about 5 minutes. Stir in the saffron and sauté for 1 minute more.

2. Add the tomatoes, with their juices, the white wine, and fish stock, increase the heat to medium-high, and bring to a boil, stirring once or twice.

3. Stir in the chouriço and clams and simmer, uncovered, for 2 minutes. Add both kinds of fish and stir to submerge them. Simmer slowly for 5 minutes (reduce the heat if the stew is boiling too fast). Add the mussels and squid, leaving them on top of the stew, without trying to submerge them (the steam will cook them), and simmer for 3 minutes more. Remove the pot from the heat and allow the stew to sit for about 10 minutes to allow the flavors to blend.

4. Using tongs, distribute the fish and shellfish evenly among four soup plates. Return the broth to the stove, add salt and pepper to taste, and stir in the parsley and cilantro. Ladle the broth into each bowl of fish. Or, if you are using a Dutch oven or other pot that would look good on the table, you can serve the dish family-style, seasoning the stew and stirring in the parsley and cilantro, then ladling it from the pot into large soup plates.

SERVES 4 AS A MAIN COURSE

PORK STEW WITH CLAMS AND GARLIC SAUCE

This famous pork stew from the Alentejo region of Portugal, known as *porco à alentejana*, is my favorite of the many Portuguese dishes I have learned to cook over the years. Chunks of pork shoulder are first marinated in a chile-garlic paste, then braised with even more garlic, along with onions and tomatoes, in wine. The stew is finished with little neck clams, which add their wonderful briny and herbaceous flavor to the sauce. Finally, the stew is topped with pickled vegetables, which contrast with the rich pork. The best accompaniment for this dish is home-fried potatoes or plain rice. Portuguese restaurants in the Northeast usually serve both potatoes and rice with many traditional dishes.

For equipment, you will need a 5- or 6-quart Dutch oven or other heavy pot with a lid, a slotted spoon, and a pair of tongs.

3 **pounds boneless pork shoulder, cut into 1 1/2-inch cubes**
1/4 **cup Portuguese red chile paste or Vietnamese chile paste (sambal olek), or 1 tablespoon chopped garlic mixed with 1 tablespoon crushed red pepper flakes**
2 **tablespoons sweet Hungarian paprika**
2 **teaspoons freshly ground black pepper, or to taste**
1/4 **cup olive oil**
3 **medium onions (6 ounces each), thinly sliced**
1 **head garlic, cloves separated, peeled, and thinly sliced**
1 **tablespoon kosher or sea salt, or to taste**
3 **cups water**
2 **cups dry white wine**
One 14-ounce **can whole tomatoes in juice, coarsely chopped**
30 **littleneck clams, scrubbed**
1/4 **cup coarsely chopped fresh Italian parsley**
One 16-ounce **jar pickled vegetables (such as Pastene giardinera), at room temperature**

WORKING AHEAD

The stew meat benefits greatly from a full overnight in the refrigerator to absorb the flavors of the marinade. The stew itself can be made ahead up through Step 3. Chill it quickly in a sink full of ice water, then cover and refrigerate until ready to proceed. Bring it back to a simmer before continuing with the recipe.

1. Combine the cubes of pork with the chile paste (or garlic and pepper flakes), paprika, and black pepper in a large bowl, tossing to coat. Cover and marinate in the refrigerator for at least 6 hours; overnight is ideal.

2. Heat a 6-quart Dutch oven or other heavy pot over high heat for 5 minutes. Add the olive oil and pork and sear the meat on one side only to brown it, about 2 minutes. Turn the meat and push it to the edges of the pot. Add the onions and garlic to the center of the pot, lower the heat to medium-high, and sauté, stirring frequently, until they are soft, about 10 minutes. Sprinkle the meat and vegetables with the salt.

3. Stir in the water, white wine, and tomatoes and bring to a boil. Reduce the heat to low, cover, and simmer until the meat is tender, about 1 1/2 hours. Stir occasionally.

4. Preheat the oven to 200°F.

5. Remove the lid from the stew and simmer uncovered for 10 or 15 minutes. Remove the pot from the heat and, with a slotted spoon, transfer the meat to the center of a large ovenproof platter. Put the platter in the oven to keep the meat warm.

6. Add the clams to the pot, increase the heat to high, and bring to a boil. Cook the clams for about 8 minutes, until they open. Using tongs, arrange the clams around the outside of the platter of pork.

7. Return the pot to the stove and simmer over high heat until the broth is reduced and coats the back of a spoon. Taste and adjust the seasoning with salt and pepper if needed. Stir in the parsley and ladle the broth over the pork and clams. Arrange the pickled vegetables over the stew, and serve immediately.

SERVES 6 AS A MAIN COURSE

SHACK BOUILLABAISSE

The classic bouillabaisse from the South of France is made with seven or more different types of fish, most of which are not available in the United States. At Summer Shack, our bouillabaisse uses the classic flavors that you would find in Marseilles—saffron, orange, fennel, tomato, and fish stock—but we make our version with all shellfish. It is far from authentic, but it is exquisitely delicious.

The recipe starts by making a flavorful broth. Meanwhile, the seafood is prepped. The lobsters and clams are cooked in the broth first, and the shrimp, mussels, and scallops are added later so that each type of shellfish is cooked just right. If you have a decorative pot, you can serve the bouillabaisse family-style at the table. Otherwise, divide the shellfish and broth among individual soup plates or pasta bowls. Toasted baguette slices (croûtes) on the side, along with rouille, a red pepper aïoli, are traditional. Your guests can spread the aïoli on the croûtes and dip them in the broth as they enjoy the shellfish.

For equipment, you will need a 4- to 6-quart Dutch oven or other heavy pot with a lid, saucepan, and a pair of tongs.

1/4 cup olive oil

3 cloves garlic, minced (about 1 tablespoon)

1 medium leek, white and light green part only, cut lengthwise in half and then across in 1/2-inch slices, washed well

1 small fennel bulb (6 ounces), stalks removed (save a few fronds for garnish), quartered, cored, and thinly sliced

1 stalk celery, thinly sliced on a diagonal

1 medium onion (6 ounces), thinly sliced

1 dried bay leaf

1 teaspoon saffron threads

1/2 teaspoon fennel seeds, crushed

2 cups Fish Stock (page 354) or Lobster Stock (page 356)

1 cup acidic dry white wine

One 14.5-ounce can whole tomatoes, drained, juice reserved, and cut into thin strips (julienne)

Freshly ground black pepper

1/4 teaspoon cayenne pepper

1 tablespoon very finely sliced orange zest (remove the zest with a vegetable peeler, and remove any white pith)

Two 1- to 1-1/4 pound live hard-shell lobsters

12 littleneck clams, scrubbed

8 large shrimp (16 to 20 per pound), peeled (leave the tail fin attached) and deveined

16 to 20 mussels, scrubbed, debearded, and rinsed

Kosher or sea salt

12 medium sea scallops (20–30 per pound), "strap" (side muscle) removed

Kosher or sea salt if needed

Croûtes (recipe follows)

Red Pepper Aïoli (recipe follows)

The broth and vegetable mixture can be made as early as a day in advance. Chill it quickly in a sink of ice water, then refrigerate covered. Reheat before proceeding with the recipe. The croûtes and aïoli can also be made a day ahead.

1. Heat 2 tablespoons of the olive oil in a Dutch oven or other large heavy pot over medium heat. Add the garlic, leek, fennel, celery, onion, bay leaf, saffron, and fennel seeds, cover, and cook for about 12 minutes, stirring occasionally, until the vegetables are soft but not brown.

2. Add the fish stock, wine, and tomatoes, with their juice, and bring to a boil. Season with black pepper to taste and add the cayenne and orange zest. (Because of the natural salinity of the seafood, no salt will be added until the very end of cooking.) Reduce the heat and simmer for 15 minutes.

3. Transfer the vegetable and broth mixture to a medium saucepan, cover, and keep warm over medium heat while you prepare the seafood. Clean and dry the large pot—you will need it for the final cooking.

4. Cut the lobsters into 6 pieces each, as you would for pan-roasted lobster (see page 226).

5. Place the large pot over medium-high heat. Add the remaining 2 tablespoons olive oil to the pot, and when it smokes, add the lobster claws and body (not the tails), along with the clams, and cook, stirring occasionally, for about 2 minutes, until the shells turn red. Add the broth and vegetable mixture and bring to a boil, then turn the heat down to a simmer. Cover and cook for 3 minutes. Add the lobster tails and cook, covered, for 1 minute. Add the shrimp and mussels, cover, and cook for 1 minute. Add the scallops, cover, and cook for 1 minute.

6. Remove the pot from the heat and let the bouillabaisse sit for 2 minutes before serving. Season with a little salt and pepper, if needed. Serve the bouillabaisse family-style, directly from the pot, or use your tongs to divide the shellfish evenly among four soup plates and ladle the broth and vegetables over the shellfish. Garnish with the reserved fennel fronds, and serve the croûtes and aïoli on the side.

SERVES 4 AS A MAIN COURSE

CROÛTES

Preheat the oven to 350°F. Slice a baguette on the bias into long 1/3-inch-thick pieces. Arrange the slices on a cookie sheet and bake for 15 to 20 minutes, until the croûtes are golden brown and dry. Let cool, then store airtight.

RED PEPPER AÏOLI (ROUILLE)

2   large egg yolks

2   cloves garlic

2   medium red bell peppers, roasted (see page 136), peeled, and seeded

Juice of 1/2 lemon

1 1/2 cups extra virgin olive oil

Kosher or sea salt and freshly ground black pepper

Tabasco sauce

1. Place the egg yolks, garlic, roasted peppers, and lemon juice in the bowl of a food processor and puree for about 2 minutes, until the mixture is very smooth. With the machine running, slowly pour the oil through the feed tube until a creamy emulsion has formed. Season with salt, pepper, and Tabasco to taste. Transfer to a bowl, cover, and refrigerate until ready to use.

MAKES ABOUT 2 CUPS

INSIDE THIS CHAPTER

Fabulous Retro Shrimp Cocktail 119

Chilled Maine Shrimp with Cabbage and Peanuts, Vietnamese-Style 121

Chilled Crab: Whole, Claws, and Crabmeat Cocktail 122

Chilled Whole Crab 125

Chilled Crab Claws 125

Crabmeat Cocktail 126

Creamy Mustard Sauce 127

Soy-Mirin Dipping Sauce 127

Split Chilled Lobster 128

Lobster Salad 130

Shrimp Salad 131

Chilled Mussels with Curry Mayonnaise 132

Curry Mayonnaise 133

Cold Poached Salmon 134

Portuguese Salad 135

Green Beans, Red Onions, Black Olives, and Blue Cheese with Romaine 137

Succotash Salad 138

Parsley Salad 139

Summer Shack Coleslaw 140

Creamy Potato Salad 141

New Potato Salad Vinaigrette 142

Variation: Warm or Hot Potato Salad 143

-5-

CHILLED SEAFOOD AND SALADS

FROM THE ICEBOX

believe that when you entertain, the goal should be to spend as much time with your friends and family as possible, with minimal time in the kitchen. One of the easiest (although not the most economical) ways to accomplish this is to serve a variety of chilled seafood and salads, with a few simple grilled or other hot dishes for contrast. This requires dedicating time early in the day to prepare the different dishes, but the reward comes later when you present a sumptuous spread and make it look easy. I strive to keep each dish simple and true to the flavor of the main ingredient, remembering that a family-style meal is the total of its parts. If you serve multiple dishes that are complicated, it makes the meal confusing and ultimately less memorable. Remember, great seafood is as much about the quality of the fish and shellfish as it is about the artistry of the cook.

The recipes I use for chilled seafood are straightforward—crab, lobster, and shrimp in their most unadulterated form with one or two sauces, made optional by serving them on the side. These are expensive ingredients, and they should be celebrated by serving them simply. If your budget does not allow for lobster or crab, Cold Poached Salmon (page 134) is a seafood classic, perfect for a light summer meal. Chilled cooked mussels are also wonderful, served with a drop of curry mayonnaise (see page 132).

When you are deciding on which salad or salads to prepare, consider the moment. If you are entertaining a crowd and making lots of dishes, choose salads that feature just a couple of ingredients. Complicated composed salads are better served at a traditional meal or as a light main course on their own, especially during the dog days of summer.

The nature of simple chilled salads and vegetable dishes calls for an awareness of the seasons and of your locality. When you have beautiful fresh ingredients, you hardly need a recipe. You can blanch fresh broccoli or other green vegetables, chill them, and toss them at the last minute with All-Purpose Vinaigrette (page 342). Or grill zucchini, summer squash, eggplant, or even potatoes and do the same. When tomatoes come into season, all I do is slice them, drizzle them with a fruity olive oil, and sprinkle with coarse sea salt, black pepper, and a chiffonade (thin strips) of basil leaves. That's all a fresh ripe garden tomato needs, and that's all you need. Don't be intimidated into thinking more is better—let the food tell you what to do.

FABULOUS RETRO SHRIMP COCKTAIL

Shrimp cocktail may be the single most popular seafood dish in America—Americans love shrimp. Yes, we all know it is overdone, and too often the shrimp served are inferior, but when you use large wild shrimp, fresh or frozen, and cook them properly, it is hard to resist the merits of this classic preparation. It makes a refreshing and delicious start to almost any meal. These poached shrimp can also be used in salads or as part of a larger platter of chilled shellfish. I like cocktail sauce with shrimp, but only a little bit. If you use too much, it overpowers the shrimp. Or, for a change of pace, serve Summer Shack Rémoulade (page 345) instead. This recipe calls for 2 teaspoons of Tabasco sauce, but if you want more zing, double that amount.

This recipe calls for 16–20 size shrimp (meaning 16 to 20 shrimp per pound). I don't recommend using smaller shrimp, but if you do, be sure to lessen the poaching time. If you want to use larger shrimp (U-12s, under 12 per pound), add an extra minute. Don't buy tiger shrimp. These farm-raised imports have an inferior taste and texture compared to our own East Coast and Gulf of Mexico "white, brown, and pink" shrimp, which are substantially more expensive but worth the price because they are superior in every way.

For equipment, you will need a 4-quart saucepan with a lid, a Chinese wire-mesh skimmer, and a fine strainer.

1 stalk celery (2 ounces), thinly sliced
1 lemon, thinly sliced
1 small onion (3 to 4 ounces), thinly sliced
1 tablespoon whole black peppercorns
4 small or 2 large dried bay leaves
3 tablespoons kosher or sea salt
2 teaspoons Tabasco sauce, or more to taste
4 sprigs fresh thyme
4 cups water
1 pound shrimp (16–20 per pound) in the shell
4 lemon wedges
4 sprigs fresh Italian parsley, watercress, or other fresh herb
1/2 cup Cocktail Sauce (page 347)

WORKING AHEAD
You can prepare the shrimp early in the day and keep them chilled in the poaching liquid until a few minutes before you serve them.

1. Combine the celery, lemon slices, onion, peppercorns, bay leaves, salt, Tabasco, thyme, and water in a large saucepan. Bring to a boil over high heat, then lower the heat, cover, and simmer for 10 minutes.

2. Add the shrimp and poach for 3 to 3 1/2 minutes, stirring once each minute, until the shrimp begin to curl into a U-shape; don't wait until they curl around completely. Remove from the heat. Using a wire-mesh skimmer, lift out the shrimp, drain them briefly, and transfer to a shallow pan. Let them cool for about 10 minutes. Strain the liquid through a fine strainer and allow it to cool down as well. (If you are in a

hurry, place the liquid in a stainless steel bowl on ice.)

3. While they are still warm, peel the shrimp, leaving the tail section intact. Make a small (1/8-inch-deep) incision down the back of the shrimp to the tail, and pull out the intestinal tract (it should pull out in one piece).

1. Peeling a shrimp

2. Making a small incision down the back of the shrimp

3. Pulling out the intestinal tract of the shrimp

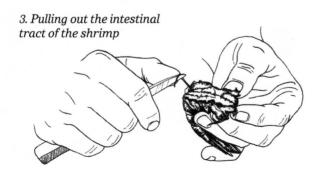

4. As soon as the poaching liquid is cooled to lukewarm or room temperature, pour it over the shrimp. Cover the pan with plastic wrap and chill the shrimp in the liquid.

5. Find four beautiful martini glasses or other glasses and, if desired, put a few shells or sea glass from the beach in the bottom of each one. Chill the glasses well.

6. When ready to serve, fill the glasses about three-quarters full with crushed ice. Drain shrimp well and arrange them around the rims of the glasses, using the ice to stabilize them; the tails will hang over the sides slightly. Put a lemon wedge and an herb sprig in the center of each glass. Serve the cocktail sauce in a small chilled bowl with a small serving spoon. The idea is to put a small dollop on each shrimp—dunking them in the sauce is common, but it is not a good thing to do because it coats them with too much sauce.

SERVES 4 AS AN APPETIZER

CHILLED MAINE SHRIMP WITH CABBAGE AND PEANUTS, VIETNAMESE-STYLE

At Summer Shack we love to mix chilled Maine shrimp, crisp Chinese or Napa cabbage, carrots, scallions, cilantro, and chopped peanuts with a spicy Vietnamese dressing. The salad is refreshingly tart and crunchy, a perfect foil for soft and sweet Maine shrimp. Serve this as an appetizer, a light main-course salad, or even as a side dish with grilled tuna or other seafood.

Maine shrimp are often sold cooked and peeled, but if you want to use a different type of shrimp, you can substitute any peeled cooked shrimp; if they are large shrimp, they should be deveined. Cut larger shrimp on a bias into long thin (1/4-inch-thick) slices. Asian chile paste, sambal olek, can be found in upscale food markets—Tuong ot Toi Viet-nam from California (not Vietnam) is an excellent brand.

FOR THE SALAD

12   ounces chilled cooked and peeled Maine shrimp
1/2   small head Chinese or Napa cabbage (about 12 ounces)
20   sprigs (1/2 bunch) fresh cilantro
1   small head Boston lettuce
1   small carrot (2 ounces), peeled and grated
1/2   cup roasted unsalted peanuts, coarsely chopped

FOR THE DRESSING

1/3   cup rice vinegar
2   tablespoons fish sauce
3   tablespoons peanut oil
2   tablespoons Asian chile paste (sambal olek)
1   teaspoon finely chopped fresh ginger
1   tablespoon sugar

1. Pick over the shrimp, discarding any pieces of shell. Cover and refrigerate.

2. Slice the cabbage into chiffonade (very thin strips) about 1 to 2 inches long. Slice 12 of the cilantro sprigs (stems and leaves) very thin; reserve the remainder for garnish. Separate and wash the Boston lettuce leaves. Keep everything well chilled until ready to mix the salad.

3. To make the dressing: Mix the vinegar, fish sauce, peanut oil, chile paste, ginger, and sugar in a small bowl. Set aside at room temperature.

4. When ready to serve the salad, combine the shrimp, cabbage, carrot, sliced cilantro, and two-thirds of the chopped peanuts with the dressing and toss well. Line four small soup plates or salad plates with the tender leaves of lettuce and divide the shrimp and cabbage mixture evenly among them, mounding it in the center. Sprinkle the remaining chopped nuts over the salad and garnish with the cilantro sprigs.

SERVES 4 AS A HEARTY APPETIZER OR LIGHT MAIN COURSE

CHILLED CRAB: WHOLE, CLAWS, AND CRABMEAT COCKTAIL

Chilled freshly cooked crab, unembellished, is a symbol of gracious hospitality and understated elegance. Regarding preparation, it requires more money than time. But it is perfect on so many levels—taste, texture, appearance, and the impression of generosity it makes—that it is an investment that you won't ever regret. Certainly your guests won't.

I have fond memories of eating cooked and chilled snow crabs right off the boat in Shediac, New Brunswick; of jumbo lump crab cocktail at Commander's Palace in New Orleans; and of ice-cold fresh stone crabs served on sultry Florida nights. I would also be remiss, even in this East Coast cookbook, not to mention my passion for Dungeness crab from the West Coast; they are very special. But our East Coast crabs, and we have several varieties, can be divine—equal to those from any region in the world. Here they are, from north to south.

Whole Snow Crabs

These large spider-like crabs from Maritime Canada are much maligned because the majority of the catch is frozen. Although the commercial product can be quite good, it is often sold in second-rate restaurants as clusters (4 legs). After improper defrosting and overcooking, they don't stand a chance. Snow crabs have a soft shell, not as soft as in blue crabs that have just shed their shell (see Soft-Shell Crabs, page 209), but soft—meaning that the shells, which are not edible, are very thin and pliable. Snow crabs, which are more abundant in the Pacific, are highly prized by the Japanese. Indeed, most of the catch of Atlantic snow crab is shipped to Japan. When purchased live and cooked fresh, they have a meaty texture and sweet flavor that is excellent—absolutely wonderful when served chilled.

Snow Crabmeat

Because the majority of the meat in a snow crab is in the legs, it is very easy to pick. The long red pieces of meat can make a dramatic presentation for a crab cocktail. You can use the meat in any recipe that calls for crabmeat.

Maine Rock Crabmeat (Peekytoe)

Rock crabs or sand crabs, also called Maine crabs because they live north of Cape Cod and are abundant in the Gulf of Maine, are a close cousin of the West Coast Dungeness crab. Like that of their cousin, their meat is very sweet and has an appealing orange-red color. Rock crabs can be served hot and picked like blue crabs, but they are a lot of work, so most often they are sold as picked meat. This hand-picked product is very fancy and makes a beautiful crab cocktail. Rock crabs are in essence a by-product of lobstering and much of the picking is done by the wives of lobstermen. It is common to see roadside signs offering crabmeat in front of homes in Maine, and I recommend that you stop if the opportunity presents itself. Because it is highly perishable, you will rarely find fresh rock crabmeat outside of the Northeast. In a stroke of genius, my friend Rod Mitchell, from Browne Trading in Portland, Maine, popularized the name "peekytoe" (Mainespeak for "picked toe") years ago. His customers, who include many of the best chefs in America, have made this once-common Maine product into one of the most prestigious names in seafood.

Jonah Crab Claws

Jonah crabs are found in deep waters in the Gulf of Maine. Large and meaty, they are a good substitute for blue crabs for a Chesapeake-style crab feast. Chinese restaurants often serve Jonah crabs. The meat is pretty good for most hot crab dishes. The body meat, however, is a bit stringy and is not suitable for crab cocktail. The claws are available cooked and chilled, often "saw-cut," making them easy to crack open and eat. The crab claws are very nice served on ice with a little Creamy Mustard Sauce (page 127) for dipping. They are fairly uniform in size. For an appetizer, serve 3 or 4 claws per person.

Blue Crabmeat

The meat from blue crabs has long been the gold standard for crab cocktail. For crab cocktails, purchase fresh or pasteurized crabmeat, not frozen. "Jumbo lump backfin" is the fanciest blue crabmeat, large white chunks of body meat with very little cartilage; it is the best choice for crab cocktail, but it is very expensive. "Backfin," also called "lump backfin," has smaller chunks, but it can be used for crab cocktail if you pick through it for cartilage.

Stone Crab Claws

Stone crabs are caught off the coast of Florida in the fall and winter. This highly regulated fishery allows only one claw to be taken from the crabs that are caught. The crabs are returned to sea to regenerate their lost claws and the harvested claws are cooked and chilled immediately, on the boat. With their black tips and orange-and-white markings, they are very beautiful. Stone crab claws are as delicious as any chilled crab you will ever eat. They are highly perishable and should be eaten within a day or two off the boat. Serve the claws on ice with Creamy Mustard Sauce (page 127). People cannot get enough of these fabulous claws, so the portions you serve will depend on your budget.

Cooking and Chilling Crabs

In most cases, you will buy crab claws and crabmeat already cooked. If you find yourself in a position where you need to cook and chill whole crabs, rest assured that it is a simple and easy task. Directions for steaming crabs are given in the Smashing Crab recipe (page 76). Cooking times for the different varieties are listed on the Steaming Chart on page 69. When you chill cooked crabs yourself, the trick is to get them as cold as possible as quickly as possible. Most home refrigerators are not up to the task, so I recommend a thermal cooler that has a drain. Take the hot crabs from the steamer and place in your sink, allowing them to cool a bit as they drain. After 10 minutes, place them in the cooler and cover them with ice cubes. Let the uncovered cooler drain into your sink (or take it outside). After 10 minutes, rearrange the crabs (gently, so you don't break off their legs) while adding more ice. Put the lid on the cooler and let them chill for another 30 minutes. By now they should be almost completely chilled. Add ice one more time, and you are all set until you are ready to prepare them for serving. Check the cooler every 2 hours and add more ice as needed.

Cleaning Whole Crabs

Once the crabs are completely chilled, you can clean them up for serving. The technique is the same for any species of crab.

Pry the carapace away from the crab. Remove the tomalley (crab butter) from the body and the inside of the carapace; place it in a small bowl, cover, and keep refrigerated. Set the carapace aside.

Prying the carapace from a crab

Using a paring knife, trim the feathery gills away from the body of the crab.

Trimming the gills from a crab

Give the crab a quick gentle rinse under cold water. Place the carapace back on the body and wrap the entire crab loosely in plastic wrap, tucking in and protecting the legs. Put back in the cooler and keep chilled on ice until ready to serve.

Storing Cooked Crabmeat

Crabmeat is usually sold in airtight containers. To keep them at their best, pack the containers in ice in the refrigerator. Don't let the containers get submerged in water—change the ice when it melts to the point that any water might slip in.

CHILLED WHOLE CRAB

You can serve any crab chilled, although smaller crabs like rock crab and blue crab are a lot of work to eat and require some expertise. Fresh snow crabs still aren't very common south of the Canadian border, but I am beginning to see them more frequently. I think they are a marvelous treat, and it is only a matter of time before the fresh supply increase.

Now that you know how to cook, chill, and clean crabs, you need only portion the whole crabs and give the big claws a little crack to help everyone out. For an appetizer, figure on about 12 ounces to 1 pound of whole crab per person; double that if you want to serve whole crabs as the main course. Remove the carapace, and you will see four legs on each side. Using a cleaver or heavy chef's knife, cut the crab right down the middle. There is no need to break down rock or blue crabs more than in half; for snow crabs or other very large crabs, cut each half across the center, dividing the crab into four clusters of two legs each. Line a platter with crushed ice and arrange the crab pieces on the ice. Put the carapaces back on the crabs.

If you would like to try something different, use the reserved crab tomalley in a Soy-Mirin Dipping Sauce (page 127); the recipe is especially well suited for snow crabs. Otherwise, find an attractive ramekin or bowl for the crab tomalley and place it on the platter. Many people love to eat it, even cold. Serve the crab with lemon wedges, Creamy Mustard Sauce (page 127), and sprigs of parsley, chervil, or cilantro. Also provide lobster crackers (or a crab mallet), small picks, and a bowl for the empty shells.

CHILLED CRAB CLAWS

Dishes that make people ooh and aah usually require some effort. Crab claws, especially stone crab claws, are dramatic—they make people swoon in anticipation—but they are almost effortless. If you want to be a most generous host, you can give each claw a little crack, using a crab mallet or the back of a heavy knife, but it is not really necessary. Many crab claws are sold "saw-cut," which is a fancy way to crack the claws. Line a platter with crushed ice, arrange the chilled crab claws in an attractive pattern, and garnish with lemon wedges and sprigs of parsley, chervil, or cilantro. Serve with Creamy Mustard Sauce (page 127), allowing about a scant 1/4 cup for each person. Provide lobster crackers (or a crab mallet), small picks, and a bowl for the empty shells.

CRABMEAT COCKTAIL

Back when I started cooking more than thirty years ago, most formal dining rooms, especially in hotels, used "supremes" for serving seafood cocktails and other foods that were best presented at the table on crushed ice—even for fresh-squeezed orange juice. The supreme had a silver base for holding the crushed ice, a glass bowl that fit into the base, and a silver top that fit around the perimeter of the base, leaving the glass bowl exposed in the center. Back then, it seemed stogy to me, but now I see the purity in that design, because the elaborate serving vessel allowed the crab, shrimp, or lobster to be served very simply and very cold.

Keeping silver supreme bowls on hand (I think they still make them) is not really practical, but the idea of having a cup or bowl inside another filled with ice is a winner. So be creative, and think of the cups and bowls that you already have that can be adapted to this concept. You might come up with something special.

WORKING AHEAD
Carefully pick over the crabmeat, pulling out any particles of shell or cartilage without shredding the crabmeat. Try to keep the pieces as large as possible. Repack the crabmeat in its original container and keep chilled until time to serve.

- **1 pound rock crabmeat (peekytoe) or blue crabmeat—either jumbo backfin lump or smaller backfin lump, picked over for shells and cartilage**
- **1/2 cup Creamy Mustard Sauce (recipe follows)**
- **4 lemon wedges**
- **4 sprigs fresh Italian parsley or other leafy herb, such as chervil, cilantro, or mint**

1. Chill the bowls (see headnote above) you will be using for the crab cocktail.

2. Fill the chilled bottom bowls with crushed ice and place the smaller cups or bowls in the ice. Divide the crabmeat among the cups a little at a time, placing it in the center and allowing it to fall to the side—this will keep it light and airy, making a better presentation. Put a small dollop of mustard sauce on top of each serving. Place the lemon and parsley toward the side, on the ice if possible. Serve the remaining sauce on the side.

SERVES 4 AS AN APPETIZER

CREAMY MUSTARD SAUCE

The classic combination of chilled crab (of any kind) with a creamy mustard sauce is perfection. There is no substitute.

1/2 cup sour cream
1/2 cup Homemade Mayonnaise (page 343) or Hellmann's mayonnaise
1/4 cup Dijon mustard
1 tablespoon fresh lemon juice
Pinch of freshly ground black pepper

1. Combine the sour cream, mayonnaise, mustard, and lemon juice in a bowl and whisk vigorously.

2. Season the sauce to taste with black pepper and a little more lemon juice if you wish. Salt is not needed. Cover with plastic wrap and refrigerate until ready to use. The sauce will keep well for several days in the refrigerator.

MAKES ABOUT 1 1/4 CUPS

SOY-MIRIN DIPPING SAUCE

In Japan, this sauce is often served at restaurants that specialize in crab. I make it when we cook fresh Canadian snow crabs, because they are especially full of tomalley, or crab butter, as it is sometimes called. The tomalley, which is essential to this sauce, echoes some of the flavor of the crab. The sauce can be served warm with steamed crab or cold with chilled crab. It is best made right before the crabs are served.

For equipment, you will need a coarse strainer or a colander and a whisk.

1 cup cooked crab tomalley (crab butter)
1/3 cup light soy sauce
1/3 cup mirin
1/3 cup water
1 1/2 teaspoon minced fresh ginger
4 scallions, trimmed, finely chopped

1. Push the tomalley through a coarse strainer (or colander) into a deep bowl. The strainer will catch any pieces of cartilage or gills and make it easier to emulsify the tomalley in the sauce. Add the soy sauce, mirin, water, ginger, and scallions and whisk well. (If making the sauce in advance, cover and refrigerate.)

2. If you are serving the sauce with steamed crab, simply heat it very slowly in a saucepan until it is warm, then turn off the heat. Do not let it get hot to the touch, or the tomalley will separate out of the sauce.

MAKES ABOUT 2 CUPS, ENOUGH FOR 4 JUMBO CRABS

SPLIT CHILLED LOBSTER

Most people eat lobster whole and hot, or cold in lobster salad. A third way to enjoy lobster is chilling the cooked lobster and then splitting it. Chilled lobster meat is fantastic; it is dense, luscious, and sweet right out of the shell. A platter of lobster halves with the body cavities stuffed with the meat from the claws and knuckles makes a beautiful presentation.

This recipe can easily be doubled. Half of a chicken lobster (1 pound) or of a quarter lobster (1 1/4 pounds) can be served as an appetizer. For a cold main dish, serve two halves of a smaller lobster or half of a lobster weighing 1 3/4 to 2 1/4 pounds. Chilled lobster is delicious with Jasper's Lobster Mayonnaise or my avocado-based Green Goddess Dressing.

It is important to chill the lobsters as quickly as possible after they are cooked. Most home refrigerators are not up to the task, so I recommend a thermal cooler that has a drain. Take the hot lobsters from the steamer and place them in your sink, allowing them to cool a bit as they drain. After 10 minutes, place them in the cooler and cover them with ice cubes. Leave them to drain in the cooler in your sink (or take it outside). After 10 minutes, rearrange the lobsters as you add more ice. Put the lid on the cooler and let them chill for another 30 minutes. By now the lobsters should be well chilled. Add ice one more time, and now you are all set until you are ready to prepare them for serving. Check the cooler every 2 hours and add more ice as needed.

For equipment, you will need a steamer pot (see page 70) or a pot with a steamer rack and a tight-fitting lid and a pair of long tongs.

2 live hard-shell lobsters, 1 to 1 1/4 pounds each
1/2 cup Jasper's Lobster Mayonnaise (page 344) or 1/2 cup Green Goddess Dressing (page 346)
4 lemon wedges
4 sprigs fresh Italian parsley or chervil

WORKING AHEAD

The lobster can be prepared and the sauce made early in the day you will serve them.

1. Place about an inch of ocean water or salted tap water in the steamer pot. Use a rack to elevate the lobsters over the water (rockweed makes a great natural steam rack). Bring the water to a boil, and when the pot fills up with steam, add the lobsters. Try to arrange them in a way that the steam can circulate all around them. Cover the pot and wait until the pot is full of steam again; if you see the steam escape when you crack the lid a little, begin timing the lobsters according to the chart on page 000. The "recovery time" of the steam filling the pot will vary with different pots and different ranges, but once the steam is going full blast, the timing will be the same. Halfway through the cooking, using a pair of tongs, quickly rearrange the lobsters so they will cook evenly. Cover again and continue timing the lobsters.

2. When they are cooked, remove the lobsters with your tongs and place them in the sink to cool for 10 minutes. Chill the lobsters, using the cooler method described above or by putting them in the coldest part of your refrigerator.

3. Once the lobsters are completely chilled, you may prepare them any time before serving. Start by breaking off the claw and knuckle section from both sides of each lobster—hold the lobster in one hand and gently twist the claw; it should snap right off. Then split the lobster lengthwise in half, trying to be exact. Remove the head sac (at the top of the head, near the eyes). Remove the intestinal tract that runs the length of the tail.

4. Remove the meat from the claws, leaving it whole if possible. The best way to do this is to snap off the thin bottom part of the claw; sometimes the meat will stay attached to the claw.

Crack the big claw gently and try to pry the meat out. Shuck the knuckles; the meat should come out in 2 pieces each. Place the meat from the knuckles and claws into the cavity of each lobster. Wrap in plastic wrap and chill until ready to serve.

5. To serve, line a platter or individual plates with crushed ice. Place the lobster halves on the ice and nap a small amount of sauce over each claw. Serve the remaining sauce on the side, and garnish the lobsters with lemon wedges and sprigs of parsley.

SERVES 4 AS AN APPETIZER

LOBSTER SALAD

In New England, tastes for lobster salad are highly individual. Some people like only mayonnaise, others want onions and celery added. Some dice the meat small, others prefer huge chunks. My version uses a special mayonnaise with a small dice of cucumber and scallion. The cucumber is crunchy and its mild flavor complements the lobster. I have served hundreds of thousands of lobster rolls at Summer Shack using this recipe, and people love it. In addition to providing the filling for the venerable lobster roll, you can use this salad to stuff a ripe tomato or papaya for a delicious cold plate, layer it between slices of almost any kind of bread to make a great sandwich, or roll it up to make a wrap.

If you buy cooked lobster meat from a good-quality market, it can be a fair deal. If the meat looks dull in color or has reddish stains, that means it isn't very fresh. In that case, cook your own lobster and remove the meat as described on page 71.

WORKING AHEAD

You can make the salad a few hours before you serve it, but in that case, don't add the scallions until half an hour before serving.

1   **pound cooked lobster meat or 5 pounds live lobsters**
1   **small to medium cucumber (4 to 5 ounces), peeled, seeded, and cut into 1/4-inch dice**
1/2   **cup Jasper's Lobster Mayonnaise (page 344) or Hellmann's mayonnaise**
2 or 3 **small scallions, trimmed and thinly sliced**
Freshly ground black pepper
Kosher or sea salt if needed

1. If you are using live lobsters, steam them (see page 71) until fully cooked and allow to cool to room temperature. Crack and remove the meat from the claws, knuckles, and tails (see page 72). Remove any cartilage from the claws and the intestine from the tails.

2. Cut the lobster meat into 1/2- to 3/4-inch dice. If using whole lobsters, you can pick all the meat from the carcasses and add it to the meat, or freeze the carcasses for soup or stock.

3. Place the diced cucumber in a colander and let stand for at least 5 minutes to drain the excess liquid.

4. Combine the lobster, cucumber, mayonnaise, and scallions in a bowl. Season with a bit of pepper if needed; it is unlikely that salt will be needed. Cover with plastic wrap and chill for at least 30 minutes before serving.

MAKES 2 CUPS, ENOUGH FOR 4 OR 5 SANDWICHES OR TO SERVE 4 OR 5 AS A LIGHT MAIN COURSE

SHRIMP SALAD

Shrimp salad can be transformed into a delicious shrimp salad roll (the lobster roll's poor cousin) by serving it in a buttered and griddled bun. For that matter, it will turn almost any type of bread into a tasty sandwich or roll-up. You can also serve shrimp salad as part of a family-style lunch or dinner with an array of other salads and side dishes, or as part of a cold plate.

Maine shrimp (also called popcorn shrimp, see page 261) are small and sweet, with a soft texture that is perfect for shrimp salad. These red shrimp are abundant off the coast of Maine in the winter, when you can purchase them fresh for about $2 per pound. Most of the harvest is processed and frozen. Frozen cooked and peeled Maine shrimp are usually about 1/2 the price of larger commercial shrimp.

If you are using frozen shrimp, pull them from the freezer the day before and defrost them slowly in your refrigerator. For this recipe, you can use any type or size of peeled cooked shrimp. When I'm using Maine shrimp, I divide the shrimp into thirds and leave one-third whole, then coarsely chop another third and finely chop the rest. The different sizes create a wonderful contrast while enhancing the overall flavor of the salad. If you are using larger shrimp, cut one-third into 3/4-inch chunks, one-third into pieces half that size, and finely chop, almost shred, the remainder.

1 **pound peeled cooked Maine shrimp or other shrimp**
1 **stalk celery, finely diced (1/3 cup)**
2 **teaspoons fresh lemon juice**
2 **teaspoons finely chopped onion**
1 **tablespoon minced fresh chives**
1/2 **cup Hellmann's mayonnaise**
1/2 **teaspoon kosher or sea salt, or to taste**
1/2 **teaspoon freshly ground black pepper, or to taste**

WORKING AHEAD

You can make the shrimp salad a day in advance, but in that case don't add the onion and chives until an hour before serving. Leftover salad will keep for 2 or 3 days.

1. Place the shrimp in a colander set over a bowl in your refrigerator to drain very well.

2. Divide the shrimp into three piles and cut them as described above. Place in a mixing bowl and add the celery, lemon juice, onion, chives, mayonnaise, salt, and pepper and stir to combine. Taste for seasoning. Transfer the salad to a plastic container with a lid and chill thoroughly before serving.

MAKES 2 CUPS, ENOUGH FOR 4 SHRIMP ROLLS OR SANDWICHES

CHILLED MUSSELS WITH CURRY MAYONNAISE

Although chilled mussels are not found on many menus, they are refreshing and very flavorful. This unusual dish may seem a bit fussy, but it is a great idea for an appetizer or hors d'oeuvre. Mussels have an affinity for white wine. In this dish, the mussels are steamed in a small bit of wine and then the broth is used to flavor and thin down the sauce. A mix of crunchy cucumbers and cabbage is placed in the mussel shells, the cooked chilled mussels placed over it, and the whole topped with a dollop of spicy curry mayonnaise with the essence of mussel broth. The black shells with the yellow orange centers are striking against the glimmering crushed ice.

For equipment, you will need a 10- to 12-inch deep sauté pan (sauteuse), a Chinese wire-mesh skimmer, and a fine strainer.

1 1/2 pounds blue mussels, scrubbed, debearded, and rinsed
1/4 cup dry white wine
1 small cucumber
1 teaspoon kosher or sea salt
1 cup finely chopped cabbage
10 sprigs fresh cilantro, chopped, plus small leaves for garnish
Freshly ground black pepper
1 cup Curry Mayonnaise (recipe follows)

WORKING AHEAD
You can steam open and chill the mussels early in the day you serve them. The cucumber mixture can also be made early in the day.

1. Place the mussels and wine in a 10- to 12-inch deep sauté pan with a tight-fitting lid. Cover and steam the mussels over medium heat for 3 minutes. Stir the mussels quickly, cover again, and cook for another 3 to 5 minutes. The mussels should all be open and the meat should be firm to the touch. Remove the mussels from the pan and allow them to cool. Strain the liquid and reserve for the curry sauce.

2. Remove the mussels from the shells and save a half-shell for each mussel. Put the mussels in a bowl, cover, and refrigerate. Keep the reserve shells chilled as well.

3. Peel the cucumber, cut it lengthwise in half, and remove the seeds with a spoon. Grate the cucumber on the medium holes of a box grater.

Toss the grated cucumber with the salt in a colander or strainer. Allow to drain for 15 minutes.

4. Squeeze any excess liquid from the cucumber, and mix it with the cabbage and cilantro in a bowl. Season with pepper and with a bit more salt if needed.

5. Arrange the mussel shells on a tray. Place about a teaspoon of the cucumber mix in the bottom of each mussel shell, making a little nest for the meat. Place the mussels in the center. Cover and keep chilled until ready to serve.

6. When ready to serve the mussels, line a platter or individual plates with crushed ice. Use a spoon to nap each mussel with enough of the curry mayonnaise to cover the center, leaving a little of mussel and the chopped cucumber mix showing. Place a tiny cilantro leaf on each one as a garnish. As you finish each mussel, place it on the platter or individual plates. Serve right away.

MAKES ABOUT 30 HORS D'OEUVRES; SERVES 4 TO 6 AS AN APPETIZER

CURRY MAYONNAISE

You can make this tasty sauce quickly and easily with store-bought mayonnaise and curry powder, but it is much more special made with homemade mayonnaise and curry paste. Clam broth can be substituted for the mussel broth if you are making this for another dish.

- 4 teaspoons Curry Paste (page 171) or 2 teaspoons Madras curry powder
- 1/4 cup broth from steamed mussels, or as needed
- 3/4 cup Homemade Mayonnaise (page 343) or Hellmann's mayonnaise
- 1/4 teaspoon cayenne pepper

1. Combine the curry paste or powder with the mussel broth in a small saucepan and bring to a boil over low heat, stirring often to make a smooth mixture. When the mixture boils, transfer it to a small bowl to cool.

2. Once the curry mixture has cooled to room temperature, add the mayonnaise and cayenne pepper and whisk until smooth. The sauce should coat a spoon but still be thin enough that it is easy to nap over the mussels; if it is too thick, thin it with a little more mussel juice. The sauce can be refrigerated for up to 3 days.

MAKES ABOUT 1 CUP

COLD POACHED SALMON

ate spring and summer is the best time for wild salmon from the West Coast, and it is readily available in most markets then. I prefer it over farmed Atlantic salmon, which has become a subject of controversy. What's more, it has a bland taste compared to its wild cousin. You could substitute striped bass or halibut for the salmon in this recipe.

Poaching fish in a court bouillon and then cooling it in the poaching liquid creates a delicious, moist, and elegant cold entrée. Serve it with chilled hard-boiled eggs, sliced tomatoes, potato salad, and/or one of the salads that follow this recipe. I always enjoy a fresh squeeze of lemon and a small dollop of Fresh Horseradish Sauce with poached salmon, but you might prefer something creamier like Jasper's Lobster Mayonnaise (page 344), Green Goddess Dressing (page 346), or Summer Shack Rémoulade (page 345).

For equipment, you will need a fish poacher or a large deep skillet or a straight-sided sauté pan (sauteuse), a fine strainer, and a slotted spatula or a Chinese wire-mesh skimmer.

FOR THE COURT BOUILLON

- 1 1/2 **cups dry white wine**
- 5 1/2 **cups water**
- 1 **tablespoon fresh lemon juice**
- 1 **medium onion (6 ounces), thinly sliced, or 1 medium leek, white and light green parts only, well washed and chopped**
- 1 **medium carrot, peeled and thinly sliced**
- 1 **stalk celery, chopped**
- 1 **small bay leaf**
- 1 **teaspoon whole black peppercorns**
- 4 **sprigs fresh thyme**
- 10 **fresh parsley stems**

- 2 **teaspoons kosher or sea salt**
- One 1 1/2-pound **skinless salmon fillet cut from the thickest part of the fillet, pin bones removed and cut into four 6-ounce portions**
- 1 **cup Fresh Horseradish Sauce (page 54)**

WORKING AHEAD

This dish is best made well ahead, as much as a day; it will keep for 3 days.

1. To make the court bouillon: Place a fish poacher or other pan able to accommodate the fillets on the stove, add the wine, water, lemon juice, onion, carrot, celery, bay leaf, peppercorns, thyme, and parsley stems, and bring to a simmer over medium heat. Reduce the heat and simmer until the court bouillon is straw-colored and fragrant, about 15 minutes.

2. Strain the broth into a bowl and then return it to the poaching pan and add the salt. Submerge the salmon completely in the court bouil-

lon, cover, and bring to a simmer. Reduce the heat to hold the court bouillon at just under a simmer, cover, and poach the salmon until the flesh turns opaque and begins to firm up, about 5 minutes (125°F internal temperature). Remove the pan from the heat and cool the salmon in the court bouillon for 30 minutes. The fish will finish cooking in the liquid.

3. Using a slotted spatula or a wire-mesh strainer, transfer the salmon to a shallow plastic container or glass baking dish and strain the liquid over the fish. Cover and refrigerate until ready to serve.

4. To serve, drain the salmon well and arrange on a platter or individual plates. Serve the horseradish sauce in a small bowl on the side.

SERVES 4 AS A MAIN COURSE

PORTUGUESE SALAD

This scrumptious summer salad, made with roasted tomatoes and bell peppers along with crispy salted cucumbers, is more evidence that Portuguese food is the most underrated of all European cuisines. Because of the large Portuguese population (including many fishermen), we in New England are lucky to have a lot of exposure to wonderful flavor combinations originating in Portugal.

This colorful and boldly flavored salad is terrific as an accompaniment to grilled fish, chicken, or pork. When serving it with fish, there is no need for a sauce: serve the salad on the same plate as the fish, and spoon a little of the dressing right over the fish.

It is essential to cut the cucumbers thick and then salt them and drain them on a rack or in a colander. It is an easy extra step that makes the cucumbers very crisp. If you can locate Portuguese olive oil, you will not be disappointed. It is usually very reasonably priced yet tastes as fruity as other oils that cost two or three times as much. Another flavor that contributes to this salad's taste is Portuguese red chile paste; if you can't find it, you can substitute Vietnamese chile paste (sambal olek) or 1 teaspoon chopped garlic plus 1 teaspoon of crushed red pepper.

For equipment, you will need a pair of long tongs, and a rack set over a baking sheet or a colander.

3   **medium green bell peppers (5 to 6 ounces each)**

6   **ripe plum tomatoes (or 3 large ripe tomatoes—1 1/4 to 1 1/2 pounds)**

1/2 **cup extra virgin olive oil, preferably Portuguese**

2   **medium cucumbers, peeled and sliced 1/2 inch thick**

Kosher or sea salt

12 **sprigs fresh cilantro, leaves and stems, coarsely chopped (2/3 cup)**

1/4 **cup red wine vinegar (5 to 6 percent acidity)**

2   **teaspoons Portuguese or Vietnamese chile-garlic paste**

Freshly ground black pepper

Because this recipe is somewhat involved for a salad, I have made it into a large batch so you can serve it twice. Before you add the cucumbers, divide the salad in half and refrigerate half the salad and half the cucumbers in separate containers. Without the cucumbers, the salad will keep well for up to 3 days. Add the cucumbers the day you will be serving the salad.

1. To roast the bell peppers and tomatoes, you can use one or more gas burners, a broiler, or a grill, whichever is most convenient. Place the peppers directly on the burner grates, on a baking sheet under the broiler, or on the grill and roast, turning occasionally with tongs, until the skin is blistered and blackened all over. Place in a bowl, cover tightly with plastic wrap, and set aside. Brush the tomatoes on all sides with about 1 tablespoon of the olive oil. Place them as close to the heat or flame as possible and roast, turning them as the skin blisters until blistered all over, about 3 minutes—it's okay if the skin is charred or blackened, but roast them as quickly as possible so the flesh doesn't become overcooked. Set the tomatoes on a pan and let them cool.

2. After the bell peppers have cooled, peel off the skins, remove the core and seeds, and cut them into pieces that are about 1 inch square (or cut into triangles). Peel the tomatoes and cut them into pieces about the same size as the peppers.

3. Meanwhile, place the cucumber slices on a rack set over a baking sheet or in a colander and sprinkle them lightly with salt on both sides. Allow them to stand for 20 minutes to release their juices, then pat dry with paper towels.

4. Combine the roast peppers, tomatoes, and cucumbers in a large salad bowl and sprinkle with the chopped cilantro. Stir in the remaining olive oil, the red wine vinegar, and chile paste and toss to combine. Season with salt and pepper. If you are not serving the salad right away, cover and refrigerate, but pull out the salad and let it stand at room temperature for 30 minutes before serving.

SERVES 8 TO 10 AS A SIDE DISH

GREEN BEANS, RED ONIONS, BLACK OLIVES, AND BLUE CHEESE WITH ROMAINE

This is a wonderful old-fashioned salad that features the strong flavors of onions, blue cheese, and olives in contrast with the milder flavors of green beans and crunchy romaine. It is a knockout served as a side with a juicy grilled steak, pork, or chicken—you will want to make it time and time again. The salad is also hearty enough to be eaten as a main dish at lunch or for a light supper. At Summer Shack, we use the local Great Hill blue cheese, which is one of the very best blue cheeses in America.

For equipment, you will need a 3-quart saucepan and a colander.

8   **ounces green beans, trimmed**
4   **ounces blue cheese, such as Great Hill Blue, Maytag Blue, Stilton, or Roquefort**
3/4 **cup All-Purpose Vinaigrette (page 342)**
1   **medium red onion (3 ounces), thinly sliced into rings**
1   **head romaine, washed, dried, and torn into bite-sized pieces (6 generous loosely packed cups)**
Kosher or sea salt and freshly ground black pepper
1/2 **cup pitted Calamata olives, drained and chopped**

WORKING AHEAD

You can blanch the green beans, make the vinaigrette, and prepare the other ingredients earlier in the day. Toss the salad right before you serve it.

1. Bring 6 cups of heavily salted water to a boil in a medium saucepan. Add the green beans and cook until tender, 5 to 7 minutes. Drain the beans in a colander and chill thoroughly under cold running water.

2. Break up 1 ounce of the cheese in a small bowl with a fork. Pour the vinaigrette over and stir well to combine.

3. Combine the green beans and red onion in a large bowl, pour the vinaigrette over, and toss to coat. Add the romaine and toss gently. Season with salt and pepper.

4. Serve the salad on individual plates, loosely arranging most of the green beans on top so they are visible. Garnish with the olives and crumble the remaining blue cheese over the top.

SERVES 4 AS A LIGHT MAIN COURSE OR 6 AS A SALAD OR SIDE DISH

SUCCOTASH SALAD

This is my chilled version of the classic Native American stew, made with tender sweet corn and soft cooked beans tossed in a light dressing. It is as versatile as potato salad and coleslaw, maybe more so. Succotash salad is the ultimate side dish for any summer spread because it goes well with a variety of seafood, poultry, or meats. During the dog days of July and August, if you make this salad in the morning, you can just fire up the grill at dinner and you'll have no reason to cook indoors.

You can use several different types of beans for this recipe as long as you end up with 3 cups of cooked beans. My first choice would be fresh shell beans: cranberry beans (horticultural beans) or lima beans (butter beans). Otherwise, most other tasty, tender cooked bean will taste fine.

For equipment, you will need a 2 large pots (or a large saucepan and a large pot if using dried beans), a colander, and a Chinese wire-mesh skimmer.

1   **pound fresh cranberry or lima beans, shelled, or 8 ounces dried cranberry, yellow-eye, lima, or cannellini beans, soaked overnight in water to cover (or 3 cups canned beans, rinsed and drained)**
8   **ounces green beans**
2   **medium or 3 small ears sweet corn, husks and silks removed**
10   **large sprigs fresh cilantro, chopped (1/4 cup)**
1   **small red onion, finely diced (1/2 cup)**
1/4 **cup grapeseed, canola, or vegetable oil**
Juice of 1 lime (2 tablespoons)
Kosher or sea salt and freshly ground black pepper

1. If you are using fresh beans, boil them in a large pot of unsalted water until they are tender, about 15 minutes. Drain in a colander and then rinse under cold water until they are cool. If you are using dried beans, pick through them, removing any rocks or bad beans, and place them in a large saucepan. Cover the beans with cold unsalted water; the water should come at least an inch over the beans. Bring to a boil, then skim the foam that comes to the top. Turn down the heat and simmer until the beans are very tender but not breaking open. The length of time will be determined by the type of bean, but count on about 25 to 30 minutes.

2. Meanwhile, put another large pot of heavily salted water on to boil. Trim the green beans, cut diagonally into 1-inch lengths, and add to the boiling water. Cook until tender, about 5 to 6 minutes. Use a Chinese wire-mesh skimmer to

remove the beans from the pot and place them in a colander in the sink. Run cold water over them until they are cooled. Drain well.

3. Add the corn to the water you cooked the beans in and boil for 3 to 4 minutes, until tender. Remove the corn and let cool to room temperature.

4. Slice the kernels from one ear of corn at a time: Hold a sharp paring knife in one hand, stand the ear upright in a large bowl with the other hand, and use long downward strokes to cut the kernels from the cob into the bowl.

5. Add the cooked green beans and shell beans and stir gently. Add the cilantro, onion, oil, and lime juice and toss to combine. Season to your liking with salt and pepper. Cover with plastic wrap and chill for at least 2 hours before serving.

SERVES 6 TO 8 AS A SIDE DISH

PARSLEY SALAD

Parsley is an important and useful ingredient in seafood preparations, but because it is sold in large bunches, you will inevitably find yourself with an overabundance of the stuff. Here is a recipe that solves the problem by turning parsley into a very tart and refreshing salad that complements most grilled fish, shellfish, and even chicken. I especially love it with grilled sardines (see page 154). The recipe is best made with Italian flat-leaf parsley, but curly parsley is also acceptable. Serve it in small portions.

1/2 bunch Italian parsley, leaves removed (about 2 cups loosely packed)
1 lemon
2 tablespoons extra virgin olive oil
1 shallot, finely diced
Kosher or sea salt and freshly ground black pepper

1. Wash the parsley and dry it very well. Put it in a medium bowl.

2. Using a rasp grater or the fine side of a box grater, grate the zest of half the lemon into a small bowl. Cut the lemon in half and squeeze the juice from one half over the zest; pick out the seeds. Add the olive oil and shallot and whisk well.

3. Drizzle the lemon and oil mix over the parsley, tossing to coat. Season to taste with salt, pepper, and more lemon juice if needed. The salad should be very acidic.

SERVES 4 AS A SIDE DISH

SUMMER SHACK COLESLAW

Coleslaw is not just a dish, it is a phenomenon. This enormously popular salad of shredded cabbage has a place of importance at tables in every region of America. Because it is a near perfect accompaniment to fried seafood, almost every good fish house has its own version. For restaurants and clam shacks, coleslaw can be a defining item, distinguishing them from their competitors. So when I opened Summer Shack, I wanted to create a coleslaw that was familiar yet had a bold and pronounced flavor. I wanted it to cut through to the taste buds, clear the palate and sinuses, and complement whatever seafood it was served with. The small amount of chopped pickles and horseradish in this recipe imparts a nice kick.

Coleslaw is great with fried fish or shellfish and fish cakes, but it is also sensational with grilled fish and meats, roast or barbecued pork or other meats, and sandwiches. Since it is so versatile and keeps well, my recipe makes enough slaw for two meals, but it can be cut in half easily.

2   **pounds white cabbage, tough outer leaves and core removed**
1   **small white onion, peeled**
2   **whole kosher dill pickles**
1   **pound carrots, peeled**
1 1/4 **cups Homemade Mayonnaise (page 343) or Hellmann's mayonnaise**
2   **tablespoons prepared horseradish**
2   **tablespoons distilled white vinegar**
2   **tablespoons sugar**
1/2 **teaspoon ground celery seed**
1   **teaspoon paprika**
2   **teaspoons kosher or sea salt, or to taste**
1   **teaspoon freshly ground black pepper, or to taste**

1. Thinly slice the cabbage. Finely chop the onion and pickles. Shred the carrots on a box grater. Or put the onion, pickles, and carrots through the grating attachment of a food processor. Place all the vegetables and the pickles in a large bowl and toss well.

2. Combine the mayonnaise, horseradish, vinegar, sugar, celery seed, paprika, salt, and pepper in a medium bowl and whisk well.

3. Pour the dressing over the vegetables and toss to distribute. Cover and refrigerate for at least 1 hour, or up to 3 days. Adjust the salt and pepper to your liking before serving.

MAKES ABOUT 7 1/2 CUPS; SERVES 8 OR MORE WITH LEFTOVERS

CREAMY POTATO SALAD

almost everybody loves creamy potato salad—soft potatoes with no skins, chopped eggs, mayonnaise, and other choice ingredients. I have been making this recipe for years, and I haven't thought of a way to make it better. The richly flavored potato salad is a luscious side dish to cold meats, sandwiches, chilled seafood plates, and fried chicken (my favorite combination). Creamy potato salad is also an indispensable addition to a quick lunch or a packed lunch, especially for a picnic.

The trick to making a great creamy potato salad is to cook the potatoes whole, so the outsides are very soft by the time the centers are cooked through but still firm. When the potatoes are mixed with the other ingredients, the soft part melts, giving a creamy texture to the salad without having to add excessive amounts of mayonnaise. This technique also allows the flavor of the potatoes to dominate. Although distilled white vinegar is considered passé these days—most chefs and recipe writers would call for champagne or white wine vinegar for this salad (you may substitute it if you please)—the acute sharpness that makes the vinegar undesirable for most dishes, especially vinaigrettes, is what spikes the flavor perfectly in this dish. Make the salad well in advance, if you can—it is really at its best the second day.

The best potatoes for this salad are medium-sized all-purpose (medium-starch) potatoes such as PEIs, Kennebec, or California white chef's potatoes. Yukon Gold potatoes also work beautifully in this recipe.

For equipment, you will need a 4-quart pot and a colander.

4   **medium all-purpose potatoes (about 2 1/2 pounds)**
2   **tablespoons plus 1 teaspoon kosher or sea salt, or more to taste**
2   **hard-boiled eggs, roughly chopped**
1   **small onion (2 to 3 ounces), cut into 1/4-inch dice**
1   **large stalk celery, peeled and cut into 1/4-inch dice (1/2 cup)**
2   **scallions, trimmed and finely chopped**
1   **medium kosher dill pickle, finely chopped**
2   **tablespoons minced fresh Italian parsley**
1/4 **cup Hellmann's mayonnaise**
1/4 **cup vegetable oil**
2   **tablespoons distilled white vinegar**
2   **teaspoons Dijon mustard**
1/2 **teaspoon freshly ground black pepper, or more to taste**

1. Pour 2 quarts cold water into a 4-quart pot and add 2 tablespoons of the salt. Peel the potatoes one by one, adding them to the pot as you work. Cover the pot and bring to a boil over high heat. Immediately reduce the heat to medium and simmer until the potatoes are very tender, 25 to 30 minutes, depending on their size.

2. Drain the potatoes in a colander, transfer them to a baking sheet, and let cool until they can be handled.

3. Cut the potatoes into irregular 1-inch cubes, and place in a large bowl. Add the eggs, onion, celery, scallions, pickle, parsley, mayonnaise, oil, vinegar, and mustard and mix well with a rubber spatula. Season with the remaining 1 teaspoon

salt and the pepper. Cover with plastic wrap placed flush against the potatoes and chill for at least 2 hours, or preferably overnight. (The salad keeps for up to 3 days refrigerated.) Check the seasoning before serving, and add salt and pepper to taste if needed.

MAKES 4 CUPS

NEW POTATO SALAD VINAIGRETTE

Here is a very quick and simple potato salad that can be made well in advance and served chilled, at room temperature, or even warm (see the variation below). Because there are very few ingredients in the recipe, the quality of the potatoes is paramount to its success (kind of like many of my seafood preparations). That means late summer and autumn are the best times for this light potato salad.

Use any type, color (red or white), or size of new potato, but make sure they are uniform in size and shape so they cook evenly. Because the thin skin on this type of potato is tasty, healthful, and colorful if you use red-skins, the potatoes should be cooked in their jackets. They are easy to slice after they are well chilled. My All-Purpose Vinaigrette contains shallots and mustard, which are perfect with the sliced potatoes, but I like a little more onion flavor, so I add sliced scallions as well. I often add chopped fresh parsley, but I also substitute other more assertive herbs, such as basil, mint, thyme, savory, or tarragon, depending on the dish I am serving the potato salad with.

For equipment, you will need a 4-quart pot and a colander.

2 pounds new potatoes
1/2 cup All-Purpose Vinaigrette (page 342)
2 tablespoons chopped fresh Italian parsley or other fresh herb
3 scallions, trimmed and thinly sliced
Kosher or sea salt and freshly ground black pepper

1. Scrub the potatoes and rinse under cold water—remember, you will be eating the skins. Place them in a 4-quart pot, cover with water, and lightly salt the water. Quickly bring the potatoes to a boil, then turn down the heat and simmer until the potatoes are tender but still firm. Medium-sized potatoes will be cooked in 10 to 15 minutes; adjust the cooking time to the size of your potatoes. Drain the potatoes in a colander and run them under cold water to stop the cooking, then drain well and chill in the refrigerator.

2. Slice the cold potatoes about 1/3 inch thick and place in a medium bowl. Gently toss the potatoes with the vinaigrette, parsley, and scallions. If not serving within 1 hour, cover and refrigerate.

3. Right before serving, season the potato salad with salt and pepper to taste. Serve chilled or at room temperature.

MAKES ABOUT 3 CUPS

Variation: Warm or Hot Potato Salad

The best way to serve the salad warm or hot is to make it in advance and then heat it in the oven. Omit the scallions and parsley (or other herb) in the initial mixing, and add them right before serving. Preheat the oven to 300°F. Spread the potato salad in a glass or nonstick baking dish and cover tightly with aluminum foil. Bake for about 20 minutes, or until warm or hot. Toss with the scallions and parsley and season to taste with salt and pepper.

INSIDE THIS CHAPTER

Getting Started 147

Sea Scallops 152

Shrimp 153

Sardines 154

Mackerel 155

Striped Bass 157

Halibut 158

Swordfish 159

Tuna 160

Bluefish 161

Salmon 163

Tautog (Blackfish) 164

Red Snapper (and Other Snapper) 165

Mahimahi (Dolphinfish) 166

Seasoned Salts and Spice Rubs 167

Spiced Seafood Salt 168

Caribbean Spiced Salt 169

Jamaican Jerk Seasoning 170

Curry Paste 171

Sauces, Butters, Relishes, and More for Grilled Seafood 172

Lemon Herb Butter 172

Corn Relish 173

Tapenade 174

Roasted Garlic and Mustard Glaze 175

Saffron Stewed Tomatoes 176

Wasabi Lime Vinaigrette 177

Tropical Fruit Salsa 178

Maple Lemon Glaze 179

Cold Cucumber Sauce 180

Caribbean Hot Pepper Oil 181

Variation: Avocado or Papaya Hot Oil 181

Red Onion Vinaigrette 182

Brazilian Relish 183

Fennel Slaw 184

A Few Special Grilled Seafood Recipes 185

Grilled Oysters with Lemon Butter 185

Grilled Clams with Garlic Butter 186

Marinated and Grilled Calamari Accordion-Style 187

Grilled King Mackerel with Lime Marinade and Garlic Butter 188

Grilled Rock Lobster Tails with Ají Verde 190

Variation: Grilled American Lobster Tails 191

Ají Verde (Yucatán Green Sauce) 192

Grilling Poultry and Meat 193

Grilled Marinated Chicken 194

Grilled Long Burgers 195

Grilled Sausages 197

Grilled Steaks and Chops 198

Grilled Vegetables 201

-6-

HOT OFF THE GRILL

*G*rilling food over a wood fire is the oldest of all cooking techniques. It is simple, clean, and, because it takes the heat outdoors, a great way to cook in the summer. Grilling is ancient, yet it remains relevant, fitting into our modern lifestyles as suitably as it did for groups of nomad hunters. When I cook outdoors over a wood grill, I am often mesmerized by the fire, the scent of the smoke, the crackling sounds of the wood, and the sizzle of the fish or meat as it sears over the raging heat. It is all quite primal, and I enjoy the entire experience.

The reason this original cooking technique is still so popular is that the intense heat of a wood or charcoal fire creates a crispy smoke-flavored crust on the outside of the fish or meat that contrasts so nicely with the juicy center. An initial quick sear over intense heat makes grilling fish easier because that way the crust forms quickly preventing the fish from sticking to the grates and tearing when you turn it. Whether it is a thick chunk of fresh tuna, a small whole mackerel, a jumbo porterhouse steak, a hot dog, or an ear of corn, proper grilling techniques will always give you tasty results. If you build your fire correctly, you should be able to have full mastery and control over the grill. If you are using a gas grill, I give you the information you need to make this piece of equipment perform at its very best.

Over the years, Summer Shack has served a very large repertoire of grilled dishes, especially seafood, many of which I share with you in this chapter. Please understand, however, that no recipe can tell you the precise moment that a piece of fish or meat is just right, because there are so many variables. A wood or charcoal fire, or, for that matter, a gas grill, is not as accurate as an oven—temperatures can vary widely. The type of grill, the type of wood or charcoal, even the velocity of the wind on a particular day, can all affect the fire. And a piece of swordfish, for example, that weighs eight ounces can be three-quarters of an inch thick or two inches thick: the weight is the same, but the cooking time isn't. But don't worry—for every complexity presented by the technique of grilling, there is a simple solution.

GETTING STARTED

The Grill

I am not going to endorse any brand of grill, because I have seen a gamut of grills that range from funky homemade split oil drums to beautiful custom outdoor stone fire pits, and everything in between, with good and bad results regardless of the type. At home, I use a 48-inch-diameter round Weber; it is a beautiful machine, even if it does resemble a flying saucer. It's important that your grill is designed to allow air to flow all around the fuel—top and bottom. With most commercial grills, that isn't an issue. The shape, whether rectangular or circular, doesn't mean much either. It's really all a matter of what you get used to. So what is the defining issue with grills? It is size and bigger is better. You can build a small fire on a large grill, but you can't do the opposite.

An oversized grill is ideal because it allows you to build a big hot fire in one section while leaving space away from the direct heat of the flames, where food can cook more slowly. With ample space, you can move the food closer or away from the fire as needed. As simple as that sounds, it gives you control of the heat at all times, and that means great-tasting food. With a large grill set up as I have described, you can use the system I use for grilling most fish and meat: sear the food directly over the hot coals, then move it to a cooler spot (medium heat) to finish cooking. There are exceptions, such as cooking rare tuna (high heat all the way) or grilling shrimp (medium direct heat). Such exceptions will be noted when I discuss each type of seafood or meat.

Figure out the number of people you usually cook for and buy a grill that has about one square foot of surface per person. The recipes in this book are designed for a 22-inch or larger grill. Whatever the size, it is important to have a tight-fitting lid for cooking large pieces of fish or meat, for adding extra smoke when desired, and for controlling the fire at times.

Getting Set Up

In addition to the right grill, you should also have a chimney (fire starter, for charcoal grills), a wire grill brush, a long-handled spatula, long tongs, and a rag that you can soak in oil to brush on the grill grate. I also recommend a spray bottle filled with water to help control flare-ups. While it is not completely necessary, it is nice to have a work surface (a stand or table) on each side of the grill. That way you can have your uncooked food, along with the cooking oil and seasonings, on one side of the grill and a platter for the cooked foods on the other side.

Wood Charcoal and Charcoal Briquettes

Hardwood charcoal, sometimes call "cowboy" charcoal or "lump" charcoal, is preburned chunks of wood, and it is the first option for pure flavor and intensity of heat. Wood charcoal can be a mixture of different types of woods. It is interesting to hear someone cite the merits of different types of wood, such as apple, cherry, maple, grapevines, and the like, but frankly, I don't detect any real difference in most wood used for grilling—with the exception of hickory, which does impart a distinctive flavor, and mesquite, which cooks hotter than other wood charcoals. Charcoal briquettes are commercially produced from wood composite and are the second choice for grilling. (Wood chips for smoking are something else altogether.)

Building the Fire and Setting Up the Grill

Start by filling the bottom section of a chimney starter with crumpled newspaper, usually two sheets. Place the chimney on the bottom rack of the grill and fill the top of the chimney with charcoal. Light the paper in several spots around the bottom, and let the charcoal ignite and burn until it is covered with a layer of fine gray ash and flames are coming from the top of the chimney, about 20 minutes. The coals are now ready. If your grill is round, spread the coals in a single even layer in the center of the grill, so the heat is steady, leaving space around the periphery so the food can be moved to the outside as necessary to finish cooking. For a rectangular grill, I also recommend building the fire in the center—that gives you cooler spots on both sides of the fire for finishing the cooking.

If you are cooking a small amount of food, a chimneyful may be all the coals you need. If you are grilling a large amount of food, you may want to make the fire bigger, by layering more charcoal over the hot coals.

Set the grill rack on the grill and let it get very hot. Don't rush hardwood fires. After the grate is hot, clean it with a wire brush and wipe it with vegetable oil, using an oil-soaked rag. When the coals are white, you are ready to start grilling recipes that call for a very hot fire (500° to 600°F). For a medium fire (350° to 450°F), you will need to allow the coals to cook down for another 10 to 15 minutes.

Using a Gas Grill

The heat from most gas grills is comparable to a medium fire in a hardwood grill. Sometimes gas grills are even slower, making it difficult to sear the food as well as you can on a wood fire. Also, gas grills don't impart an authentic smoky flavor the way wood charcoal does. That said, gas grills can be used with great success—if you get to know them. Most gas grills have hot and cool spots. Once you find and remember those spots, they can be used to your advantage. The suggested cooking times in this chapter are for cooking over a charcoal fire, so if you are using a gas grill, the food will need extra time—somewhere in the range of 25 to 35 percent longer.

To prepare a gas grill for cooking, turn all the burners to high and ignite them. Lower the lid and heat the grill until it is very hot, about 15 minutes. After the grate is hot, clean it with a wire brush and wipe the grates with vegetable oil, using an oil-soaked rag. Unless you are cooking very thin steaks or tuna, turn down the heat on either side of the grill, leaving the heat high in the center, so you can move the seared food to a slightly cooler spot to finish cooking (if your grill has only two burners, turn one down).

Cooking Seafood on the Grill

Once your grill is ready, check the suggested cooking time for the fish or shellfish that you are preparing. Grilled food is best served as soon as it is cooked, so make sure everything else for the meal is ready before you start grilling.

I recommend that when cooking most fish fillets you leave some of the skin attached (exceptions will be noted in the following sections or individual recipes). The crispy skin has good flavor and helps hold the fish together. The species

I recommend for grilling are somewhat firm, tight-grained fish, such as swordfish, tuna, and bass (the list is actually quite long). Really flaky or delicate fish, like cod, haddock, and flounder, are poor candidates for grilling because they tend to fall apart as they cook through.

In general, most types of fish, especially the white-fleshed species (which are prone to parasites), are best cooked through, until all the flesh is hot but still juicy. Parasites are not easily detectable, and they are harmless if cooked, so a good rule of thumb is that if a species of fish isn't good to eat for sushi (raw), it should always be cooked through to the center. For fish that is good raw or partially cooked, such as tuna, salmon, and mackerel, there is no need to cook it all the way through. This is also true of shellfish like scallops, squid, oysters, and clams. The reason one grills these is to warm them and create a little smoky flavor—there is no reason to cook them well-done.

My Favorite Combinations

In order to give you lots of options for grilled seafood, I have organized the first section of this chapter into two parts. First I list the various species, giving you any specifics you might need to know as well as grilling suggestions and serving suggestions. Then I provide some of my favorite recipes for seasonings, sauces, flavored butters, relishes, and other accompaniments that are especially good with grilled seafood. Under each species, I list the accompaniments that I think are most enjoyable and complementary. However, although I wanted to give you many options, don't get carried away—stay close to my recommendations. Seafood is very versatile, but you must be careful not to mask the flavor of the fish. Always pair mild fish with more

delicate sauces; with fuller-flavored seafood, there is an opportunity to introduce more robust flavors.

Salt and Pepper Fish

Every spring when we get the first shipment of wild salmon from Alaska at Summer Shack, we offer it with salt and pepper and lemon for that first week, giving our customers a chance to enjoy the pure flavor of the fish. We also do that opening week of striped bass season and when we get a fabulous shipment of fresh hopper shrimp from Florida (another seasonal item). As enjoyable as it is to create wonderful flavor combinations with grilled seafood as a focal point, I also want you to realize that it is perfectly fine to serve grilled seafood plain, seasoned with only salt and pepper and finished with just a brush of olive oil or butter, with a lemon wedge on the side. In fact, when the seafood is very special—caught or harvested that day, bought right off the boat, or the first of the season—it is a smart thing to do. When the fish is the freshest it can be, I prefer to taste only the pure natural flavor of the food. It does mean you have to cook the fish just perfectly, because there is no sauce to add moisture or alter the flavor of the fish. When you do this, call it Salt and Pepper Salmon (or Striped Bass, etc), letting your guests know that you are purposely keeping the food simple (it's actually a quite sophisticated way to serve it).

Cold Seafood, Hot Grill

It is imperative that seafood be held at very cold temperatures at all times (see The Proper Handling of Seafood, page 38). And to grill fish correctly, the fish must be cold and the grill hot.

The recommended cooking times for my recipes are based on this premise, so be sure to keep your seafood as cold as possible right up until it hits the grill.

Ready, Set, Grill

So, your fire is ready, the grill rack is clean, hot, and oiled. The fish is chilled. The rest of the meal is almost ready to serve. Now brush the seafood with a little vegetable or olive oil and season with salt and pepper or a spice mix, depending on the preparation you have chosen. Place the fish directly over the hot coals, with the skin side up. Allow it to sear for about 2 minutes, without touching it. After 2 minutes, the fish will have begun to firm up. Gently loosen the fish from the grill with your spatula, trying not to let any flesh stick. Unless you are going to try to "cross-mark" the fillet (recommended only for species that are very firm, such as swordfish; see page 159), let it cook a little longer. If you look at the side of the fillet, you will see the flesh gradually turning from translucent to opaque. When the color change is about two-thirds of the way up the side of the fillet, flip it gently. Sear for 1 to 2 more minutes, trying to crisp the skin without burning it. Once the fillet is seared, move it to a cooler part of the grill to finish cooking slowly over medium heat. The time for finishing will vary according to the species and the thickness of the fillet. Even within certain species—such as bluefish, snapper, and striped bass—differences in size can be dramatic.

To test for doneness, you can feel the firmness of the fillet with your fingertip—once you become truly experienced, you will be able to tell by touch. But in the meanwhile, just pry open the center or thickest part of one piece and look: if the fish is a solid color and steaming hot, it is ready. If it looks a little translucent in the center, give it a little more time. But be sure to give it the finger test, even after prying open the fish—that is how you will learn to test for doneness by touch. Serve the fish as soon as it comes off the grill.

Grilled Seafood Cooking Times

Note: HSMF means hot sear (directly over coals) then finish on medium heat (away from hot coals). Unless otherwise noted, chart refers to fish fillets.

Species	Thickness or Size	Recommended Temperature	Cooks in Minutes	Comments
Sea Scallops	16/20	high	6-8	cook medium on skewer - HSMF
Sea Scallops	jumbo (U-10)	high	10-12	light sear; cook longer - medium
Shrimp	16/20	medium	3-4	cook directly over coals on skewer
Shrimp	jumbo	medium	5-7	cook gently over coals
Whole Sardines	3/4 - 1"	high	6-7	skin-on, head-on, whole - HSMF
Atlantic Mackeral	1/2 - 3/4"	medium	4-5	skin-on cook directly over coals
Whole Tinker Mac	1 - 1 1/4"	medium	8-10	skin-on, whole, cook gently over coals
Striped Bass	1 1/2 - 2"	high	11-13	skin-on, cover grill - HSMF
Halibut	1 - 1 1/2"	high	10-12	no-skin - HSMF
Swordfish	1 - 1/2"	high	9-11	remove skin after cooking - HSMF, cross-mark
Tuna: Yellowfin, Big Eye, and Bluefin	1 1/2 - 2"	very high	4 rare 5-6 mr	no-skin, cook directly over hot coals, cross-mark
Albacore	1 - 1 1/2"	high	8-10	no-skin - HSMF - cross-mark
Bluefish, Medium	1 - 1 1/2"	high	11-12	skin-on - HSMF
Bluefish, Snappers	1/2 - 3/4"	high	8-9	skin-on - HSMF
Salmon (fillets)	1 1/4"	high	6-8 mr 8-9 md	skin-on - HSMF
Salmon (steaks)	2"	high	12-14	skin-on, cover grill - HSMF
Tautog (Blackfish)	3/4 - 1"	high	7-8	no-skin - HSMF
Red Snapper	3/4 - 1"	high	7-8	skin-on - HSMF
Whole Snapper	2"	medium	14-16	skin-on, cover grill, grill gently
Mahi mahi	1"	high	9-10	no-skin, cross-mark - HSMF

SEA SCALLOPS

Specifics

Scallops come in a wide range of sizes. The best size for grilling is large (16–20 count—about 3/4 to 1 ounce each) or jumbo (U-10—about 2 ounces each). Smaller scallops are better broiled, sautéed, or deep-fried. Lately the term "diver scallop" has gained enormous popularity. Technically it refers to large scallops that divers harvest by hand, but the term has become a cliché, used on menus to describe any large sea scallop. Unless you see a guy in a wetsuit, don't assume that it's really a diver scallop. But as long as you buy fresh "dry" sea scallops, it doesn't really matter. The term "dry" refers to untreated fresh scallops; inferior-quality "soaked" or "treated" commercial scallops have been immersed in a solution that whitens the color and adds weight. It is easy to tell if a scallop has been treated, because it will always release the added liquid when you cook it, an especially undesirable result for food that is grilled.

For easy handling on the grill, it is best to skewer scallops. Be sure to soak wooden skewers in water for at least an hour before you use them; otherwise, they will burn on the grill. It is also wise to pick through scallops before you skewer them, removing the strap (side muscle) and any particles of shell. Line up the scallops in rows, as you will skewer them, on your work surface and push a skewer through the center of each row while they are still flat on the surface. This will create one even side that will mark nicely on your grill. When you grill the scallops, start with that side down (scallops vary in thickness, so the second side may not be even).

Grilling Suggestions

I like to grill scallops first over high heat and then briefly over lower heat, leaving them slightly undercooked in the center. Since they are perfectly safe to eat raw, there is no reason to overcook them. Their natural sugars caramelize on the grill, making them particularly delicious. Sea scallops require about 2 minutes searing on each side over high heat, and then they should be moved to lower heat to finish cooking slowly: 2 to 4 minutes longer will be about right for 1-ounce scallops; cook jumbo scallops for another 6 to 8 minutes after they are seared.

Serving Suggestions

Generally, I like to keep the seasoning for scallops very simple—salt and pepper. They are wonderful, however, brushed with Curry Paste (page 171) and served with rice. Another of my favorites is to skewer them with thick pieces of partially cooked bacon and brush them with Maple Lemon Glaze (page 179). For both of these preparations, brush the glaze or paste on the scallops during the last 2 minutes of grilling. Grilled scallops are also excellent with a simple White Wine Butter Sauce (page 351), Garlic Herb Butter Sauce (page 352), or Corn Relish (page 173) or served over Fennel Slaw (page 184).

SHRIMP

Specifics

There are basically three types of shrimp available to the consumer: frozen wild shrimp, frozen farmed tiger shrimp, and fresh shrimp. Most frozen wild shrimp are white shrimp (*penaeus setiferus*) from the Gulf of Mexico. They are a high-quality product and are expensive. Tiger shrimp are farm-raised in Asia and other places. They are an inferior product that I don't recommend. Ask your seafood market what you are buying, as most markets sell tiger shrimp as "shrimp" with no added information. Fresh shrimp can be tremendous, definitely my first choice, but they are not available in many places.

Commercially packed shrimp are sold by the number of headless shrimp per pound. For example, "16–20 shrimp" are 16 to 20 per pound, about an ounce each. The next smaller size is 21–25, and they are also suitable for grilling, but I don't recommend grilling anything smaller than that. Jumbo shrimp are labeled as U–16s or U–10s, meaning under 16 or under 10 per pound; they are excellent cooked on the grill. Fresh shrimp are sometimes sold head-on, and often you will find a wider range of sizes within one batch. Don't let that bother you—just buy the shrimp, peel them, leaving the last tail section of shell attached, and devein them, then match them up by size on skewers. Most often the large shrimp you buy fresh will be in the 16–20 range—they are a nice luxurious size. The smaller ones will take a little less time on the grill. Fresh shrimp are available along the Atlantic Coast from North Carolina to the Caribbean, and if you are lucky enough to be able to purchase large ones, you must try them on the grill.

Grilling Suggestions

You don't have to skewer shrimp, but it sure makes grilling them a lot easier. Remember to soak wooden skewers in water for at least an hour before you skewer the (peeled and deveined) shrimp. Because shrimp flesh is dense, they don't lose their juices during cooking, so a medium heat on the grill is fine. Cook them quickly, directly over the flames. In terms of timing, 16–20 count shrimp will take about 1 1/2 to 2 minutes on each side over medium heat. I look for the color change—the orange red color will become more intense (deeper) as the shrimp cook. If you are uncertain about doneness, grill one shrimp separately and cut into the thickest part (near the head end) to check the doneness. Ideally, the shrimp will be just slightly opaque in the very center. The shrimp will continue to cook a bit more off the grill, so if you remove them at this stage, they will be perfect when served. It is important not to overcook shrimp, or they will be very tough.

Serving Suggestions

Shrimp are one of the most versatile of all seafood. Used in most of the world's cuisines, they pair well with a wide array of flavors. My brother Mike, who lives in Flagler Beach, Florida (just south of St. Augustine), where there is a small but productive shrimping fleet, couldn't care less about all that: he thinks that the local shrimp he buys are so good that anything other than salt and pepper is an unnecessary distraction. And when I am with him, eating fresh hopper shrimp right off the boat, I agree.

I also know that most shrimp are not sold fresh and so are enhanced by added flavoring. One simple and tasty way to season grilled shrimp is to brush them with the All-Purpose Vinaigrette (page 342) while they are cooking and then one last time again after they come off the grill. If you want them garlicky, add some finely chopped garlic to the vinaigrette. Shrimp skewers can also be brushed with Curry Paste (page 171) or Jamaican Jerk Seasoning (page 170), Roasted Garlic and Mustard Glaze (page 175), or Maple Lemon Glaze (page 179) while they are on the grill. You can serve plain grilled shrimp, seasoned with salt and pepper only, with Tomato Vinaigrette (page 342), Tropical Fruit Salsa (page 178), Caribbean Hot Pepper Oil (page 181), Brazilian Relish (page 183), Saffron Stewed Tomatoes (page 176) or Ají Verde (page 192). A simple White Wine Butter Sauce (page 351) or Garlic Herb Butter sauce (page 352) is a richer accompaniment that is also good with grilled shrimp.

SARDINES

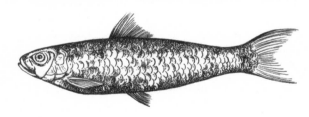

Specifics

These small, fatty fish are possibly the most full-flavored of all fish—either you love them or you don't. Sardines are members of the herring family and are very healthful, high in beneficial omega-3 fatty acids. Although we occasionally get local sardines in New England, most of the sardines that we eat, both fresh and frozen, are imported from the Mediterranean, particularly from Portugal and Spain. They are always sold whole with the head on and that is how they are usually cooked, guts and all. But I recommend gutting the sardines (see page 40)—it makes them more palatable to timid American tastes. Most sardines weigh about 1 1/2 to 2 ounces after they are gutted. In Europe, these small sardines are often eaten bones and all. Jumbo sardines, the largest size, weigh about 3 ounces, and they are my favorites. Since I don't eat the bones, I find it easier to pick over the meatier jumbos. The flavor of sardines of any size is equal.

Grilling Suggestions

Brush the sardines with a bit of olive or vegetable oil and season simply with salt and pepper. The goal when grilling sardines is to keep the skin intact. I like to start with a hard sear (1 minute or a little less per side) over high heat to get the skin to bubble–that will also greatly reduce the chance that the fish will stick to the grill. Then I move them to a cooler part of the grill and cook for 4 to 5 minutes more. Because sardines are very fatty, they are forgiving if you leave them on the grill a little too long. This is good because sardines are a fish you want to cook through—thorough cooking really helps develop their flavor.

Serving Suggestions

Because sardines taste so strong (a word I very seldom use to describe any fish), it's fun to serve them with assertive accompaniments like Tapenade (page 174), made with black olives, garlic, anchovies, capers, lemon, and olive oil. They are also delicious with Brazilian Relish (page 183), Tomato Vinaigrette (page 342), or Caribbean Hot Pepper Oil (page 181) or simply seasoned with salt and pepper and served with lemon wedges. I like to serve my lemony Parsley Salad (page 139) along with any of these sauces. It is a refreshing palate cleanser that is a nice finish after the robust flavors of the grilled sardines. You can make a meal of sardines, but I think they are best served as an appetizer—2 (large) per person.

MACKEREL

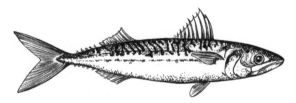

Specifics

Atlantic mackerel, with their beautiful iridescent blue-green markings, are, without a doubt, one of the most splendid-looking fish in the ocean. The smallest mackerel, less than 9 inches long, are referred to as "tinker mackerel," and they are terrific when cooked whole on the bone. Larger Atlantic mackerel, which don't get much bigger than 14 inches (1 1/2 pounds), can also be cooked whole, but for grilling they are better filleted and deboned.

Mackerel are fatty fish, high in beneficial omega-3 acids. Along with sardines, they are among the most healthful of all fish species. Unfortunately, because of their bold flavor, mackerel are not as popular in the United States as in other countries, such as Ireland, where they are beloved. Because they usually fetch a low price, they are not given the respect they deserve by commercial fishermen, who don't even bother to gut them before sending them to market. But when mackerel are handled properly—that is, gutted and iced shortly after they are caught—they are one of the tastiest fish I know. Mackerel are abundant, inexpensive, and delicious, and I believe they will become much more popular in the future. In addition to Atlantic mackerel, other members of the family, especially Spanish mackerel and king mackerel (better known as kingfish, see page 188), are also excellent grilling fish.

Grilling Suggestions

Although Atlantic mackerel have scales, they are so fine that they are almost nonexistent. When grilling fillets, I recommend that you leave the skin on to help hold the tiny fillets together. As you grill the mackerel, you will see the outer coating of skin melt and peel away—no scaling to worry about. Grill the fillets directly over high heat; they will only take about 2 minutes on each side to cook through.

To grill whole tinker mackerel, the size of the fish will determine how many you need. If the mackerel are 6 inches long, you might want 2 per person; if they are 9 inches long, one may suffice. Whole mackerel should be grilled at medium heat, not directly over the coals. Place the fish in a spot hot enough that the skin sizzles but doesn't burn. Grill 6- to 9-inch whole tinker mackerel for 3 to 5 minutes on each side.

Serving Suggestions

Mackerel have a bold flavor like that of sardines, just a bit milder and sweeter. They are delicious served plain with salt, pepper, and lemon, but they also hold up to big flavors like Tapenade (page 174), Wasabi Lime Vinaigrette (page 177), and Caribbean Hot Pepper Oil (page 181). My absolute favorite accompaniment for Mackerel is Soy-Ginger Sauce (page 348), which I use as both a marinade and a sauce. If you are grilling for 4 people, you will need a full cup of the sauce. Put the mackerel fillets in the marinade for just 5 minutes, then drain, pat dry, and finally brush with oil (to prevent sticking) right before grilling. No salt is necessary. If you are grilling whole tinker mackerel, remove the gills, or if you prefer, remove the entire heads. Make 2 or 3 shallow diagonal slits on each side of the fish to allow the marinade to flavor the fish; this will also help it to cook evenly. The slits should go through the thickest part of the fish, starting about halfway up from the tail. Serve extra soy-ginger sauce on the side to spoon over the fish as desired.

Since mackerel is such a healthful fish, stay in that mode and serve it with a light summer salad and plain steamed white or brown rice. I also recommend my lemony Parsley Salad (page 139) as a refreshing side dish. If you do not want to use the soy marinade, cook the mackerel plain (simply seasoned with salt and pepper) and glaze it with Roasted Garlic and Mustard Glaze (page 175) or top it with Tapenade (page 174) made with green or black olives. Tomato Vinaigrette (page 342) or Red Onion Vinaigrette (page 182) would also be a nice alternative.

STRIPED BASS

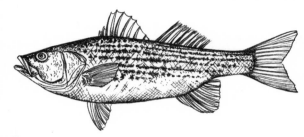

Specifics

Striped bass is in season in New England from June through September; farther down the East Coast (Mid-Atlantic to Florida), where it is also called rockfish, it is in season most of the year. Because striper, as many people affectionately call it, is a species recovering from overfishing, it is subject to many needed regulations. Sports fishermen can keep only stripers over a certain size (state regulations differ, but it is usually a 30-inch minimum). Commercially, the season is limited by how much fish has been previously caught. In Massachusetts, striped bass can only be fished commercially from Monday through Thursday, and the season ends abruptly each year when the authorities decide that the quotas have been filled. After having gone without striped bass for many years, I'm grateful for whatever we are allotted.

Stripers are exceptional fish in many ways. The big flaky, moist fillets are absolutely delicious. Striped bass is excellent on the grill, but it is versatile and can be poached, steamed, baked, sautéed, and even roasted whole.

Grilling Suggestions

Striped bass should be cooked through, as in "cooked but not overcooked," the way most peo-ple prefer to eat flaky white fish. Since small striped bass are not usually available (commercially or otherwise, except in the South) you will most likely be cooking fillets that are between 1 1/2 to 2 inches thick. After brushing them with oil and seasoning them lightly, sear the fillets over high heat, flesh side down, for 2 minutes, then skin side down for a minute. After the fish is seared, move it away to a medium-hot part of the grill. Covered with the lid of the grill, the fillets will take an additional 6 to 8 minutes after searing; uncovered, about 10 minutes more.

Serving Suggestions

The full clean flavor of striped bass is terrific when left to stand on its own with just a squeeze of lemon, but it is also excellent paired with light summer dishes like Saffron Stewed Tomatoes (page 176). Served next to grilled bass, this side dish works as both vegetable and sauce. Cold Cucumber Sauce (page 180), Tomato Vinaigrette (page 342), Red Onion Vinaigrette (page 182), Fennel Slaw (page 184), and Corn Relish (page 173) are a few of my other favorites because they don't overpower the bass. Rice or potatoes are also appropriate side dishes. For a light entrée, serve grilled striper over a tossed green salad.

HALIBUT

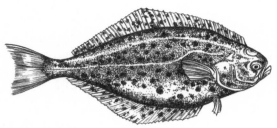

Specifics

Halibut is the largest and most highly prized of flatfish from the Atlantic. (Pacific halibut is for all intents and purposes identical to Atlantic.) It has firm, flaky, moist flesh that is mild and sweet. Unfortunately, East Coast halibut are not as abundant as they once were. The catch as of late has been spotty and the average size has decreased. I have seen a couple of big ones this summer (close to 200 pounds), but the average fish is usually about 20 to 30 pounds. Small halibut, under 10 pounds, called "chicken halibut," are good for sautéing or panfrying and they make superb Beer-Battered Fish and Chips (page 266), but they don't hold up very well on the grill. Halibut is sometimes cut straight across into true fish steaks, but these are difficult to grill. Fillets that are 1 to 1 1/2 inches thick are perfect for grilling. If you are cutting your own fish, you can determine the thickness by cutting them on a bias.

Grilling Suggestions

Halibut is delicate, so it requires extra attention when grilling because it will tend to stick to the grill more easily than most fish. It is very important that your grill be very clean, well oiled, and very hot. Place the chilled halibut fillets on a large plate or in a pan and brush them on both sides with oil. Sprinkle them generously with salt and pepper. Grill the fillets on the hottest part of the grill for 2 minutes, without moving them. Loosen gently with a spatula, turn, and grill for 2 more minutes. Move the fillets to the cooler (medium heat) periphery of the grill and cook them for 4 to 6 minutes more on each side. I don't recommend covering halibut when grilling, because too much smoke flavor will overpower the mild flavor.

Serving Suggestions

Halibut is versatile fish, good poached, braised, pan-roasted, sautéed, or grilled. But it is not as versatile in terms of flavor combinations—keep it simple. Complement the lovely flavor of halibut with similar mild flavors, like a simple White Wine Butter Sauce (page 351) finished with minced fresh chives. Other ideas for grilled halibut include Lemon Herb Butter (page 172), Green Goddess Dressing (page 346), Red Onion Vinaigrette (page 182), or Corn Relish (page 173). Serve with salad, potatoes, corn on the cob, or a green vegetable.

SWORDFISH

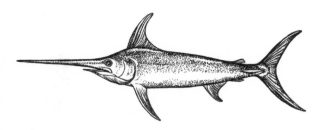

Specifics

Swordfish migrates from the Caribbean, and even South America, to Canada each summer, traveling up the East Coast, becoming a "local" fish in different places at different times of year. The season in New England and Maritime Canada is from July through October, making it a perennial summer favorite. Swordfish is one of the most popular fish in America, appealing to people who like its meaty texture and pronounced but clean flavor.

The average size of swordfish has decreased over the years. The 200- to 400-pound fish that used to be the mainstay of the swordfishing industry are no longer as common as 50- to 150-pounders. Small swordfish, weighing under 60 pounds, are called pups. We often buy these young fish at Summer Shack because they are less prone to a buildup of mercury than larger, older fish. I only serve swordfish during our local season, because out of season, when they are caught in much warmer waters, they are less fresh and more prone to parasites.

Grilling Suggestions

Because even a small swordfish is a big fish, the thickness of the steaks (which are not true fish steaks, because they are boneless) is determined by the fish cutter. Swordfish steaks should be a minimum of 1 inch thick; I recommend 1 1/2 inches. Although the skin is not edible, it is usually left on during grilling to help hold the shape. The skin should be peeled off the fish once it has been cooked.

Cooking swordfish on the grill is easy because it is so dense that it is like cooking a piece of meat. I think that this is probably why what are technically fillets are so often called swordfish steaks. You can sear swordfish on a hot fire and make cross marks with very little effort. However, cooking it just right—cooked through but still juicy in the center—requires attention. Swordfish must always be cooked through because it is prone to parasites, which are harmless when cooked. Brush the steaks on both sides with oil and sprinkle them generously with salt and pepper. Place them on the hottest part of the grill for 2 minutes, without moving them, or, if you are making cross marks, rotate them 90 degrees after 1 minute. Loosen them gently with a spatula, turn, and grill 2 minutes more. Transfer the fillets to the cooler part of the grill (medium heat) and cook for about 6 minutes more if 1 inch thick, 10 minutes more if 1 1/2 inches thick.

Serving Suggestions

The combination of hot grilled swordfish with creamy Cold Cucumber Sauce (page 180) is one of the greatest grilled seafood dishes that I know—you must try it. It was on the menu of the Café Plaza at the Copley Plaza Hotel in Boston when I became the chef there in 1979. Over the years, I have had a lot of fun by varying the flavors of the sauce—mild dill, spicy cilantro, mellow mint all work nicely—but the genius of this dish is the contrasting temperature of the cold, melting cucumber sauce on top of the hot swordfish steak.

Swordfish has a rich flavor that makes it enjoyable with many different flavors. The steak-like characteristic of the fish, along with a ten-dency toward dryness, make it especially suitable for pairing with compound butters like Lemon Herb Butter (page 172) or Garlic Herb Butter (page 352), dolloped on the hot fish. Grilled swordfish is also good with Caribbean Spiced Salt (page 169) and Tropical Fruit Salsa (page 178).

TUNA

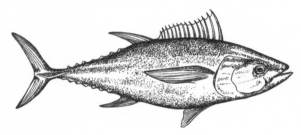

Specifics

There are several species of tuna caught in the Atlantic Ocean and consumed on the East Coast: yellowfin, bigeye, bluefin, and albacore. The flesh of the first three is deep red, with a mild but rich flavor and a meaty texture. These red-fleshed tunas are best enjoyed when cooked rare or medium-rare. Albacore tuna has very pale flesh that cooks up to an off-white color. I think the best way to cook albacore is medium, with the very center of the fish just slightly under-cooked; its flavors improve with this longer cooking. The fanciest yellowfin and bluefin tuna, sold as sushi-quality tuna (#1 tuna), are best reserved for a raw preparation (sushi-quality bigeye tuna is rarely available). For grilling, you can buy yellowfin, bigeye, or bluefin tuna that is less fancy (#2 tuna), usually cut from smaller, leaner fish. As with swordfish, tuna fillets are often marketed as steaks, although they are not true fish steaks, because they are boneless. Since tuna is so delicious rare, it is best if cut extra thick—I recommend that you ask for tuna that is 1 1/2 to 2 inches thick.

Grilling Suggestions

Rare tuna is so popular nowadays that before you cook it you only need to ask your guests if there is anyone who doesn't like it rare. The ideal grilled tuna fillet offers a transition between a crispy, charred, seasoned exterior and a cool, rare center. Unless you want to cook your tuna past medium-rare, tuna steaks of any size should be grilled on high heat, directly over the coals. For 1 1/2- to 2-inch-thick pieces, grill them about 2 minutes per side for rare. For medium-rare, allow an extra minute or two. If you look at the side of a piece of tuna, you can literally see the doneness. Because the flesh of tuna is dense and firm, it is easy to give the fish the traditional cross marks (see page 150). If you are grilling albacore tuna, sear the meat on high heat, directly over the coals, for about 2 minutes on each side before moving it to a cooler part of the grill (medium heat). It will take the albacore about 6 more minutes to finish cooking.

Serving Suggestions

Raw tuna is traditionally served with soy sauce, pickled ginger, and wasabi, which is sometimes called Japanese horseradish, although it is not actually in the same family. This combination can also be used with grilled rare tuna. One interesting variation on this idea is to serve the tuna with Wasabi Lime Vinaigrette (page 177); another is to serve it with Soy-Ginger Sauce (page 348). A simple green salad or Japanese seaweed salad (sold in many fish markets these days) along with plain steamed rice will go well with any of these Asian flavors.

Tuna is a staple worldwide and has long been important in many of the world's cuisines, especially those of the Mediterranean, Asia, and the Americas. It has a clean, meaty flavor that can be matched with a variety of other flavors, such as Tapenade (page 174), Brazilian Relish (page 183), Red Onion Vinaigrette (page 182), Saffron Stewed Tomatoes (page 176), and Ají Verde (page 192). Another idea is to make a Butter Sauce (page 351), but substitute red wine for the white wine and whip in a few finely chopped anchovies at the end.

BLUEFISH

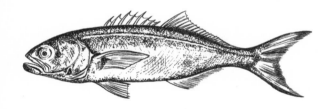

Specifics

From Florida to New Brunswick, the mysterious, migrating bluefish is abundant, inexpensive, and, best of all, healthful and delicious. Bluefish are ferocious fighters, making them a lot of fun to catch. To me, the bluefish is a true harbinger of summer. Sometimes called the piranhas of the Atlantic, bluefish are notorious eating and killing machines. Where we summer in Little Compton, Rhode Island, the fish will chase the bait in very close to shore; you can literally stand on the beach and watch hundreds of fish in a feeding frenzy. About once a year it gets so bad that the beaches have to be closed for swim-

ming. If you catch a bluefish, you must always be aware of its teeth, because these angry fish will bite you if they can.

When bluefish are handled properly, they are a beautiful-tasting fish—assertive but not at all "fishy." The proper way to handle bluefish is to kill them immediately once caught, then cut the vein behind the gill and bleed the fish. This will give the flesh a lighter color and milder flavor. After gutting the fish, pack it in ice and keep it on ice until it passes through rigor mortis. Then it can be filleted (leaving the skin on) and trimmed entirely of the dark blood line.

Grilling Suggestions

Fillets from large bluefish (10 to 15 pounds) are difficult to grill because they are delicate and soft; it is best to bake or stew them. Fillets from medium bluefish (5 to 8 pounds) are delicious on the grill but they require attention and a very hot fire so they don't stick. Small bluefish

(2 to 4 pounds), often called "schoolies" or "snapper blues," are less fatty and milder flavored than medium bluefish. The fillets are firm and easy to grill.

Brush the fillets on both sides with oil and sprinkle them generously with salt and pepper or seasoned salt (see below). Fillets from medium-sized bluefish will be about 1 to 1 1/4 inches thick. Grill them flesh side down on the hottest part of the grill for 2 minutes, without moving them. Loosen gently with a spatula, turn, and grill skin side down for 2 minutes. Transfer the fillets to the cooler part of the grill (medium heat) and grill 4 minutes more on each side. If you are adding a glaze or jerk seasoning (see below), brush it on the fish after the initial searing over the coals. Fillets from small bluefish (3/4 inch thick) should be seared over high heat for about 2 minutes per side and then moved to a cooler spot (medium heat) to finish cooking, 4 to 5 more minutes.

Serving Suggestions

Bluefish are quite fatty, especially in late summer and fall; they are very high in beneficial omega-3 fatty acids, making them an important source of protein. The high fat content gives them a soft, moist texture and an assertive big flavor that stands up well to equally assertive flavors such as garlic, ginger, onion, tomatoes, soy, mustard, exotic spices, and stronger herbs. The fish is great cooked with Jamaican Jerk Seasoning (page 170) or, for another Island inspiration, seasoned with Caribbean Spiced Salt (page 169) and served with Caribbean Hot Pepper Oil (page 181) or Tropical Fruit Salsa (page 178). It is also wonderful with Roasted Garlic and Mustard Glaze (page 175), Soy-Ginger Sauce (page 348), Tapenade (page 174), Saffron Stewed Tomatoes (page 176), Red Onion Vinaigrette (page 182), and even Wasabi Lime Vinaigrette (page 177). Small bluefish can be paired with the same assertive flavors, but they also go well with more subtle flavors, such as Lemon Herb Butter (page 172) or Cold Cucumber Sauce (page 180).

SALMON

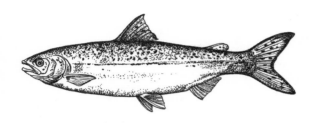

Specifics

Salmon is an anadromous fish, born in fresh water and then returning to its place of birth to spawn after living for years in the ocean. On the East Coast, the logging industry took its toll on wild Atlantic salmon before the end of the last century. Because of logjams, the salmon were unable to get back up the freshwater streams to spawn. Today almost all Atlantic salmon are farm-raised. Wild salmon from Alaska and the West Coast, which is available in the late spring, summer, and early fall, has a superior flavor to that of farm-raised salmon. Salmon is a very healthful fish, as all salmon are high in beneficial omega-3 fatty acids.

Salmon offers a range of eating experiences: When it is cooked medium-rare, the flavor will be mild. If it is cooked through, its flavor will develop and become more pronounced. Chinook and sockeye are two species of wild salmon that are lean and taste best when cooked only to medium-rare. King salmon, the most popular and abundant wild species, is best cooked medium or just barely through. Farm-raised Atlantic salmon are also best cooked medium or just barely through. Salmon is sold in fillets or steaks (true steaks—cut across the whole fish, with a center bone). Fillets from a 10-pound fish (average size) will be about 1 1/4 inches thick. Grilled salmon skin is particularly delicious; ask your market to sell you the fillets skin-on if possible. If you don't mind picking around a couple of bones, I recommend salmon steaks for grilling because, like a beefsteak, they will be crispy outside but juicy inside, both lean protein (center) and fatty, crispy belly section. Each bite is a little different, making them fun to eat.

Grilling Suggestions

To grill fillets, brush them on both sides with oil and sprinkle generously with salt and pepper or seasoned salt (page 167). Grill flesh side down on the hottest part of the grill for 2 minutes, without moving the fillets. Loosen them gently with a spatula, turn, and grill skin side down for 1 minute more. Now move the fillets to the cooler part of the grill (medium heat). If you want them medium-rare, cook them about 3 or 4 more minutes. To cook them through, allow about 3 or 4 minutes per side on medium heat, being careful to crisp up the skin without burning it.

To grill salmon steaks, brush them on both sides with oil and sprinkle them generously with salt and pepper or seasoned salt (page 167). Place the steaks on the grill directly over the hot coals and sear for 2 minutes on each side. After they are seared, move them to a cooler spot on the grill (medium heat). Salmon steaks must be cooked through so that the center bone can be pulled away after they are cooked. It is a good idea to cover the grill right after the salmon is seared. That creates an oven effect and helps the fish cook a little faster and more evenly. If the steaks are 2 inches thick (a good size), they will take about 8 to 10 minutes longer after they are seared with the grill covered. If the grill is uncovered, it will take a few minutes more. Be sure to turn the fish once during the final cooking. When the fish is cooked, pull the center bone away from the center (toward the belly) with your tongs; it will remove the rib bones at the same time. If the center bone doesn't pull away easily, the fish isn't cooked through—leave it on the grill until the bone does pull away.

Serving Suggestions

Salmon is one of the most popular fish in the United States, and that popularity is partly fueled by the cheap price of farm-raised fish from all over North and South America. If you want to be frugal, eat bluefish or mackerel—they are much tastier than farmed salmon. If you want to eat salmon, splurge for wild fish—you won't be disappointed. When wild salmon comes into season each spring, our restaurants offer it plain—salt, pepper, and lemon only—for the first week or two. You should eat it plain at least once in the beginning of the season, then start adding sauces as the season progresses. Salmon is often paired with dill, lemon, or cream and butter sauces that are mild, yet it has an assertive flavor that can hold its own with lots of different flavors. Salmon has an affinity for cucumbers, so it's fun to pair it with Cold Cucumber Sauce (page 180) or Brazilian Relish (page 183), made with cucumbers, peppers, tomatoes, and onions. If you want a milder sauce, try Lemon Herb Butter (page 172) or White Wine Butter Sauce (page 351) finished with chopped dill. For a surprisingly good combination, glaze the salmon during the last couple minutes on the grill with Maple Lemon Glaze (page 179). Boiled new potatoes are the perfect starch to serve with grilled salmon.

TAUTOG (BLACKFISH)

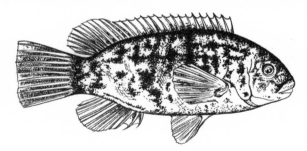

Specifics

Tautog, also called blackfish, is a native of the North Atlantic, most commonly found from the southern coast of New England to the New Jersey shore. In New England, tautog live along the rocky beaches close to shore, making them very popular with spear fishermen. The most common size at market is 3 to 5 pounds, but I've watched spear fishermen catch really big ones, over 20 pounds. Tautog is not a species that is specifically targeted by fishermen, but in the last few years, it has become more widely available. If you see tautog at the market, don't pass it over. It is a sweet, moist, and tender white-fleshed fish and a welcome addition to the summer repertoire.

Grilling Suggestions

Tautog fillets will be about 3/4 to 1 inch thick, so they cook quickly. It is not a dense fish—handle it gently while you are moving or turning it. The skin should always be removed before cooking, as it is thick and rubbery. Brush the fillets on both sides with oil and sprinkle them generously with salt and pepper or spiced salt (page 167). Grill the fillets on the hottest part of the grill for 2 minutes, without moving them. Loosen gently with a spatula, turn, and grill 2 minutes more. Transfer the fillets to the cooler part of the grill (medium heat) and grill 3 to 4 minutes more, turning once halfway through.

Serving Suggestions

Tautog has a pleasant sweetness and a clean flavor. It goes well with many simple summer flavors, like Corn Relish (page 173) or Tomato Vinaigrette (page 342), and it is good enough to eat plain with salt, pepper, and lemon. (It is also a wonderful fish for frying—it makes great Beer-Battered Fish and Chips, page 266—and for fish stews.) My favorite way to serve grilled tautog is to line the outside of a platter with sliced ripe tomatoes and then fill in the center with Fennel Slaw (page 184), at room temperature. After the fish is grilled, I place it on top of the slaw, where the juices will mingle with the liquid from the slaw, creating a wonderful flavor combination.

RED SNAPPER (AND OTHER SNAPPER)

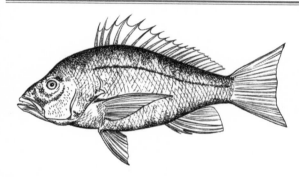

Specifics

There are about 250 species of snapper from the Gulf of Mexico, the Caribbean, and the southern Atlantic coast. Most snapper have a similar spectacular appearance, although size and coloration vary. True red snapper from the Gulf of Mexico are the most prized and fetch the highest price at market. They have a wonderful distinctive yet somewhat mild flavor, with moist white meat reminiscent of sea bass. Red snapper, silk snapper, and mutton snapper are similar in flavor, texture, and size (3 to 5 pounds are common, but they can reach over 10 pounds); I like to grill skin-on fillets from a 3- to 5-pound snapper. Yellowtail snapper and gray "mangrove" snapper are smaller (1 to 1 1/2 pounds are the most common) and can be cooked whole on the grill. Mangrove snapper can be found as far north as North Carolina.

Grilling Suggestions

To grill fillets (they will be 3/4 to 1 inch thick), brush on both sides with oil and sprinkle generously with salt and pepper or Caribbean Spiced Salt (page 169). Grill the fillets flesh side down on the hottest part of the grill for 2 minutes, without moving them. Loosen gently with a spatula, turn, and grill skin side down for 1 minute. Transfer the fillets to the cooler part of the grill (medium heat) and grill 4 to 5 minutes on the flesh side. Turn and grill skin side down for 2 minutes.

To grill small whole yellowtail or mangrove

snapper (1 to 1 1/4 pounds each), let the fire cook down to a medium heat. Brush the whole fish on both sides with oil and season generously with salt and pepper or Caribbean Spiced Salt (page 169). Start the fish over the coals and cook for 2 minutes on each side. Move the fish to the cooler part of the grill, cover the grill, and cook for about 5 to 6 minutes on each side.

Serving Suggestions

Whether whole or in fillets, all snappers are very tasty cooked on the grill, where they lend themselves to the intense tropical flavors of the Caribbean. Season the snapper with Caribbean Spiced Salt (page 169) and serve it with Caribbean Hot Pepper Oil (page 181) or Tropical Fruit Salsa (page 178). Snapper can also be cooked with Jamaican Jerk Seasoning (page 170). With these Caribbean-inspired preparations, I like to serve plain rice or, for a real treat, Black Beans and Rice (page 222). If you want to serve the snapper with more traditional American flavors, any of my recommendations for striped bass (page 157) will be suitable.

MAHIMAHI (DOLPHINFISH)

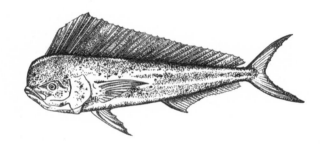

Specifics

When this fish was becoming a commercially viable species some twenty-five years ago, the name dolphinfish caused confusion among consumers—it is not a mammal. The solution was to adopt its Hawaiian name, mahimahi. They are caught in the Pacific and the Atlantic Ocean, where they range from South America up the Gulf Stream to as far north as New England. In the summer, mahimahi is commonly caught around Rhode Island and Cape Cod. This is a spectacular-looking fish with a big round forehead (which is why it was first called dolphinfish) and brilliant hues of green and golden. And it tastes pretty good too! Mahimahi has a full flavor and, because it is firm, the fillets are very good for grilling.

Grilling Suggestions

Most mahimahi fillets will be about 1 inch thick. The skin is very tough; it is not edible. Brush the fillets on both sides with oil and sprinkle them generously with salt and pepper or Caribbean Spiced Salt (page 169). Grill the fillets on the hottest part of the grill for 2 minutes. Because this fish is firm, you can make cross marks on the grill if you want to—just turn it 90 degrees after the first minute. Then turn and grill for 2 minutes more. Transfer the fillets to the cooler part of the grill (medium heat) and grill for another 5 or 6 minutes total, turning the fish once.

Serving Suggestions

This exotic-looking fish can be grilled plain and served with a wide range of flavors, but I like it best when sprinkled with Caribbean Spiced Salt (page 169) and served with Tropical Fruit Salsa (page 178) or Caribbean Hot Pepper Oil (page 181). For a wonderful sweet-hot combination, make a small dice of ripe papaya and mix it into the hot pepper oil. Mahimahi is also wonderful brushed with a little Curry Paste (page 171). Serve with steamed rice or Black Beans and Rice (page 222). For a simpler preparation, brush the mahimahi with All-Purpose Vinaigrette (page 342) during grilling or serve it topped with Lemon Herb Butter (page 172).

SEASONED SALTS AND SPICE RUBS

Seasoned salts and spice rubs are wonderful to keep around your kitchen because they can enhance, even alter, a simple dish with a minimum of effort. A plain piece of fish becomes "Jamaican Jerked" or "Curry Rubbed" or "Caribbean Spiced" in a matter of seconds. It's that easy. Rubs are usually (you guessed it) rubbed on the food, seasoned salts are usually sprinkled on the food.

Many celebrity chefs, food writers, and TV personalities have a line of seasoning mixes these days. Some of these are very good. My old friend Paul Prudhomme pioneered the trend with his Cajun Magic line of seasonings many years ago and they are still terrific; so are Emeril's and Wolfgang Puck's. I am also a big fan of some of the old-time mixtures, like (McCormick's) Old Bay seasoning, originally from the Chesapeake region, and Zatarain's Crab Boil and Cajun spices from Louisiana. You might be wondering, with all the spice mixes on the market, why make your own? For one, it takes five minutes to make a batch that will probably cost a quarter of the price of a commercial brand. And you get a chance to personalize the mix. Flavors are subjective—I like clove, you may not. I started fooling around with these mixes years ago, and, to be honest, I learned a lot from reading the labels of commercial mixtures, observing the order of the ingredients listed. Then I would try to copy them, adding ideas and preferences of my own.

Making seasoned salt is easy: combine all the ingredients and stir. The most important part of the operation is to secure a jar with a tight-fitting lid; humidity will ruin the mixture. You can keep these through the season and make new batches every few months. Store them in a cool, dry place; if you are near the shore, store rubs and seasoned salts in the refrigerator or freezer to keep out moisture, which would cause them to clump.

SPICED SEAFOOD SALT

If you catch or are given a lot of one type of fish, so you will be having it for a couple of days in a row, eat it plain (just salt, pepper, and lemon) the first night while it is extremely fresh, then try it the next day with a sauce or simply grilled with this spiced salt, or the one that follows. Lightly oil the fish and sprinkle it on both sides, using a bit more than you would use if you were sprinkling pure salt. This seasoning salt is good with any firm, full-flavored fish that is suitable for grilling, but it is especially good with bluefish and striped bass, which are the fish I catch most often in the summer. You can omit the granulated garlic if you are using this on milder white fish such as black sea bass or halibut. The salt can also be used to season fish and chips and other fried, broiled, or baked seafood.

2   tablespoons fresh thyme leaves, very finely chopped
1   tablespoon finely grated lemon zest
1/2 cup kosher salt
2   tablespoons brown sugar
1   tablespoon cracked black pepper
1/2 teaspoon cayenne pepper
2   tablespoons sweet Hungarian paprika
1   tablespoon fennel seeds, crushed or finely chopped
1   tablespoon dried dillweed
1   tablespoon granulated garlic (optional)

1. Place the thyme and lemon zest on a paper towel and let them sit out in the open air for about 30 minutes. (This step isn't absolutely necessary, but the fresh ingredients will blend better with the other dry ones if they are dried out a little first.)

2. Transfer the thyme and zest to a small bowl, add the salt, brown sugar, black pepper, cayenne pepper, paprika, fennel seeds, dill, and the optional garlic, and mix well.

3. Place the mixture in a sealed container and refrigerate or freeze until ready to use. This keeps for months.

MAKES 1 CUP

CARIBBEAN SPICED SALT

Nutmeg, clove, allspice, and cinnamon are grown throughout the Caribbean. In fact, Grenada is the second-largest spice producer in the world (Indonesia is the largest). It follows that spices are used generously in this region. Here is the seasoned salt recipe I developed with my Haitian friend Novillus Petit-Frère for grilled fish at a Caribbean restaurant we collaborated on called the C-Bar. It is good with snapper, grouper, bass, swordfish, mahimahi, and other firm full-flavored fish suitable for grilling, and it is especially delicious sprinkled on shrimp or lobster tails. Lightly oil the fish and sprinkle it on both sides, using a bit more than you would use if you were sprinkling pure salt.

1/2 cup kosher salt
1/4 cup packed brown sugar
1 tablespoon ground cinnamon
1 tablespoon chili powder
1 teaspoon ground allspice
1 teaspoon freshly grated nutmeg
1 teaspoon ground ginger
1/2 teaspoon ground cloves
1 teaspoon freshly ground black pepper
1 teaspoon cayenne pepper

1. Combine all the ingredients in a small bowl and mix well.

2. Place the mixture in a sealed container and refrigerate or freeze until ready to use. This keeps for months.

MAKES ABOUT 1 CUP

JAMAICAN JERK SEASONING

For those who can taste through the intense heat of Scotch bonnet peppers, this jerk rub has wonderful nuances of roasted allspice, cinnamon, and nutmeg. Because jerk seasoning is a wet rub, it is not meant for grilling on high heat; it is best for food that is cooked over a low wood fire, so the smokiness of the grill is a desired effect. Jerk seasoning is most widely used for chicken and pork, but it is also excellent for grilled seafood. Full-flavored seafood like shrimp, king mackerel, mahimahi, red snapper, swordfish, and bluefish are my recommendations for jerk seasoning.

I learned to make this from my friend Jessica Harris, who is an expert on Caribbean and Afro-centric cuisine. The rich flavor comes from roasting the allspice and grating the nutmeg fresh. Jessica uses dark rum in her seasoning, but I have switched to fresh lime juice because my seasoning is especially intended for seafood. Making jerk seasoning requires lots of chopping. When working with Scotch bonnets or other fiery chile peppers, I wear disposable plastic gloves. Some chiles are so hot that you could burn your eyes or other body parts if you touch them even hours after you chop the chiles.

If you want to keep the entire process of jerking seafood in the realm of easy, I recommend Busha Browne's or Walkerswood jerk seasoning; they are both authentic and very good. If you can't find these at Caribbean or Spanish markets, you can order them direct from Busha Browne's (www.bushabrowne.com; 845-246-0194) or Walkerswood (www.walkerswood.com; 800-827-0769).

Cooking jerked fish is easy. Mix 1 part vegetable oil into 2 parts jerk seasoning; you will need about 1 tablespoon for each portion of fish. Build a medium fire as instructed on page 148. Let it burn down so it is even cooler than medium and place the jerk-rubbed seafood on the grill over the coals. Cover the grill and let the seafood take on some smokiness. Flip the fish once during the cooking. If you "jerk" the fish just right, it will take about 20 minutes to cook. Any faster, and the fire is too hot. Serve with lime wedges and some sort of rice dish.

For equipment, you will need a mortar and pestle or spice grinder.

1/3 cup whole allspice berries
2   teaspoons ground cinnamon
2   teaspoons freshly grated nutmeg
4   sprigs fresh thyme, leaves removed and chopped
4   Scotch bonnet (or habanero) chiles, seeded and minced
2   bunches large scallions (10 to 12), trimmed and minced
Juice of 4 limes
About 2 teaspoons kosher or sea salt
About 1 teaspoon freshly ground black pepper

1. Preheat the oven to 350°F.

2. Place the allspice berries on a small baking sheet or in a pie pan and toast them in the oven for 5 to 6 minutes, or until fragrant.

3. Combine the allspice berries with the cinnamon and nutmeg in a mortar or spice grinder and grind until fine.

4. Combine the ground spices with the thyme, chiles, and scallions in a food processor and pulse to mix. Add the lime juice and process to a fine paste. Season with salt and pepper to taste. Cover the mixture tightly and keep in the refrigerator, for up to 1 month, until ready to use.

MAKES ABOUT 1 1/2 CUPS

CURRY PASTE

This is a flavorful multipurpose condiment made with garlic, ginger, chile peppers, onions, apples, and spices. It can be brushed on seafood, shellfish, poultry, or lamb as it is grilled over a wood fire to create deep, rich flavors. I love this paste on grilled shrimp, scallops, and firm fish like mahimahi. The curry paste can also be used in place of curry powder in stews and sauces, but use two or three times as much paste as you would powder. A few tablespoons stirred into Homemade Mayonnaise (page 343) makes an aromatic dip for fried fish or fritters or chilled poached shrimp or mussels. It can also be added to dishes such as stir-fried or sautéed vegetables. Serve white rice with curried dishes, preferably basmati or jasmine.

For equipment, you will need a 10-inch skillet.

1 1/2 cups vegetable oil
One 1 1/2-ounce piece fresh ginger, peeled and coarsely chopped (about 1/4 cup)
4   garlic cloves
1   large jalapeño pepper (1 ounce), seeded and coarsely chopped
1   small onion (4 to 6 ounces), coarsely chopped
1   medium apple, peeled, cored, and coarsely chopped
1/4 cup Madras curry powder
2   teaspoons kosher or sea salt

1. Set a 10-inch skillet over low heat, add 1/2 cup of the oil, the ginger, garlic, chile, and onions, and sauté until the vegetables begin to soften, about 5 minutes. Add the apple and continue to sauté, stirring occasionally, until softened, about 5 minutes.

2. Stir in the curry powder and cook until fragrant, about 2 minutes. Remove from heat and let cool until lukewarm, about 20 minutes.

3. Transfer the mixture to a food processor, add the salt, and process briefly to combine. With the processor running, add the remaining 1 cup oil in a steady stream. Transfer the curry paste to a covered container and refrigerate until ready to use. The paste keeps for 1 month.

MAKES ABOUT 2 CUPS

SAUCES, BUTTERS, RELISHES, AND MORE FOR GRILLED SEAFOOD

Grilling food outdoors isn't serious stuff—it is fun. I think the sauces, garnishes, and other foods served with grilled seafood should also be fun—nothing overly complex, just clean flavors that are bold enough to complement it. Many of the sauces, relishes, and accompaniments I make go well with more than one type of seafood. That is why I organized the beginning of this chapter into species, with recommendations for grilling and serving; the following recipes are referred to there within the individual species. For the recipes here, I suggest the grilled seafood that I like to serve each one with. You can stray a bit from my suggestions, but I do hope you will try some of them. All are tried and true and have been served to the thousands of our customers at Summer Shack who eat our grilled seafood specials listed on the blackboard every day.

LEMON HERB BUTTER

This is a delicately flavored compound butter that is used similarly to Garlic Herb Butter (page 352) but is best paired with milder fish, like halibut, haddock, swordfish, snapper, and mahimahi. It is also good melted over grilled salmon steaks.

Because this butter is versatile and can be kept in tiptop condition in the freezer for over a month there is no reason not to make a big batch. This recipe uses half a pound of butter; you can easily double the recipe.

For equipment, you will need a standing or hand electric mixer or a food processor (you can mix the herb butter by hand in a large bowl, but it won't be as fluffy and light).

1/2 pound (2 sticks) unsalted butter, softened
1 tablespoon fresh lemon juice
1 teaspoon Worcestershire sauce
6 large sprigs fresh Italian parsley, leaves removed and finely chopped
1/2 cup plus 2 tablespoons minced fresh chives
3/4 teaspoon kosher or sea salt
1/4 teaspoon freshly ground black pepper

1. Using a standing mixer fitted with the paddle attachment (or a handheld mixer), or a food processor, beat or pulse the butter until fluffy, about 2 minutes. Scrape down the sides of the bowl with a rubber spatula and add the lemon juice, Worcestershire, parsley, chives, salt, and pepper. Mix until all the ingredients are thoroughly blended.

2. Place a strip of parchment paper or plastic wrap about 14 inches long on the counter with a long side parallel to the counter edge. Using a rubber spatula, transfer the butter to the paper or wrap, forming a log across the end toward you, ending 2 inches short of each end. Roll the butter up into a tight cylinder about 10 inches long and 1 1/4 inches in diameter, and twist the ends in opposite directions to secure. Roll the cylinder up in aluminum foil and refrigerate.

3. After the butter is thoroughly chilled, you can cut the log into smaller sections, if desired, then rewrap. Refrigerate for immediate use or freeze for future use; the butter can be frozen for 1 month.

4. To serve, take the butter out of the refrigerator and let it soften for 10 minutes. Slice the butter into rounds and place on top of hot fish.

MAKES ABOUT 8 OUNCES, ENOUGH FOR 12 SERVINGS

CORN RELISH

This is an old-fashioned corn relish that I adapted from my grandmother's recipe. Modern corn relishes are more like corn salad, so easy to make that you don't really even need a recipe. This relish is like a pickle and sauce combined, perfect for grilled seafood like scallops, striped bass, halibut, and tautog. It's a useful staple that also pairs well with grilled poultry and meats, as well as barbecued and cold roasted meats.

This recipe calls for raw corn, but if you happen to have a lot of leftover cooked corn, you can use it. If you are buying corn especially for the relish, choose a hearty yellow or bi-color variety; tender sweet white corn doesn't make the best relish.

For equipment, you will need a 2- or 3-quart saucepan.

8   ears corn, husks and silk removed
1   cup apple cider vinegar
1/2 cup water
1/3 cup sugar
2   teaspoons kosher or sea salt
1/2 teaspoon crushed red pepper flakes
2   teaspoons turmeric
2   teaspoons mustard seeds
1/2 teaspoon celery seeds
1/2 teaspoon ground ginger
1/2 teaspoon ground allspice
1   tablespoon Colman's dry mustard
1   teaspoon cornstarch
1   medium red bell pepper (6 ounces), cored, seeded, and cut into 1/4-inch dice
1   medium green bell pepper (6 ounces), cored, seeded, and cut into 1/4-inch dice
1   medium onion (6 ounces), cut into 1/4-inch dice

1. Place a large bowl in the sink. With a sharp knife, slice the kernels from one ear of corn at a time into the bowl, holding the ear upright in the bowl and using long downward strokes of the knife. Then use the back of the knife to scrape the pulp from the corncobs. Discard the cobs and set the corn aside.

2. In a heavy medium saucepan, combine the vinegar, water, sugar, salt, red pepper flakes, turmeric, mustard seeds, celery seeds, ginger, allspice, dry mustard, and cornstarch and bring to a boil over medium heat. Add the diced pep-

pers and onion, reduce the heat, and simmer until tender, about 10 minutes.

3. Add the corn and cook until tender, about 5 minutes. Allow to cool completely, then divide among small jars with tight-fitting lids. The relish keeps refrigerated for up to 1 month.

MAKES ABOUT 5 CUPS

TAPENADE

Tapenade is a Provençal olive relish that is often served on toasts (*croustades*), but it is wonderful with sardines and other strong-flavored fish like tuna, mackerel, and bluefish. You can substitute flavorful green olives, such as Sicilian olives, for the black olives in this recipe to make Green Olive Tapenade. This recipe makes about 1 1/2 cups, enough for a grilled fish dinner one night and snacks or hors d'oeuvres later in the week. It keeps well for up to a week in the refrigerator.

For equipment, you will need a food processor. (You can make this recipe by finely chopping all the ingredients, but that is a lot of work; with a food processor, it takes minutes.)

2   **cloves garlic, halved**
1   **large shallot, quartered**
2   **anchovy fillets**
1   **cup (8 ounces) Calamata, Niçoise, or Moroccan olives, pitted and roughly chopped**
2   **teaspoons capers, rinsed and chopped**
1   **red bell pepper, roasted (see page 136), peeled, seeded, and chopped**
2   **tablespoons chopped fresh Italian parsley**
1/3 **cup extra virgin olive oil**
1   **tablespoon fresh lemon juice**
1/4 **teaspoon freshly ground black pepper**

1. Combine the garlic, shallot, and anchovies in a food processor and pulse until finely chopped. Add the olives, capers, and roasted pepper and pulse for 1-second intervals until the mixture is finely chopped (1/4 inch or less) and spreadable but not pureed. Use a rubber spatula to scrape down the bowl several times so the ingredients are evenly chopped. Add the olive oil, lemon juice, and pepper and pulse for a few seconds to mix. Transfer the tapenade to a container, cover tightly, and refrigerate. The tapenade should be served at room temperature; remove from the refrigerator 1 hour before serving.

MAKES 1 1/2 CUPS

ROASTED GARLIC AND MUSTARD GLAZE

The sweet mellow flavor of roasted garlic combines with Dijon mustard to make a glaze that is perfect with grilled bluefish, mackerel, and even shrimp. It is also quite good with pork chops.

1 **small head garlic (1 1/2 ounces)**
2 **tablespoons vegetable oil**
1 **tablespoon Dijon mustard**
2 **teaspoons fresh lemon juice**
1/4 cup olive oil
Pinch of kosher or sea salt
Freshly ground black pepper

1. Preheat the oven to 325°F.

2. Place the garlic in the center of a doubled sheet of aluminum foil that is large enough to enclose the garlic. Rub the head of garlic with a little of the oil to lightly coat it. Wrap it loosely in the foil and roast for 1 hour, or until very soft.

3. Remove the garlic from the oven and allow it to cool. Separate the garlic cloves and squeeze the pulp into a small mixing bowl. Mash the pulp with a fork; you will have about 2 tablespoons of puree. Whisk in the mustard and lemon juice. Slowly drizzle in the olive oil, whisking all the while, until all the oil is incorporated and you have a smooth paste. Season with the salt (just a pinch) and pepper to taste. Place in a small bowl or container, cover, and keep refrigerated. This keeps for 5 days.

MAKES 1/2 CUP

SAFFRON STEWED TOMATOES

This saucy dish of stewed fresh tomatoes does double duty with grilled fish—it serves as both a vegetable and a sauce. It complements nearly any grilled seafood, but my favorite pairings are with striped bass, tuna, tautog, or shrimp.

For equipment, you will need a 6-quart pot, a Chinese wire-mesh skimmer or a slotted spoon, a coarse strainer, and a deep 10- or 12-inch sauté pan.

3 **pounds ripe plum tomatoes**
2 **tablespoons olive oil**
1 **medium onion (4 ounces), thinly sliced**
1/2 **teaspoon saffron threads**
1 **tablespoon tomato paste**
1 **teaspoon kosher or sea salt**
1/2 **teaspoon freshly ground black pepper**
4 **tablespoons cold unsalted butter, cut into chunks**

WORKING AHEAD
The stewed tomatoes keep well for 3 days, so you can make the dish well in advance. Reheat slowly and gently before serving.

1. Bring 4 quarts of water to a boil in a 6-quart pot over high heat. Score a small X in the base of each tomato with a paring knife. Fill a large bowl with ice cubes and water and place it near the stove. When the water boils, add the tomatoes, in batches, to the boiling water and blanch them until the skin curls back at the X marks, 30 to 45 seconds. With a wire-mesh skimmer or a slotted spoon, immediately transfer the tomatoes to the ice water. Let them chill thoroughly before removing from the ice bath.

2. Remove the tomato skins with a small paring knife. Cut out the cores and slice the tomatoes lengthwise in half. Using a small spoon, remove the pulp and seeds from each tomato half, and transfer the pulp to a coarse strainer set over a small bowl. Use a ladle or a spoon to push the tomato juices through the strainer, leaving the seeds behind. Discard the seeds, and set the juice aside.

3. Combine the olive oil and onion in a 10- or 12-inch deep sauté pan and cook over medium-low heat, stirring frequently with a wooden spoon, until the onion is very soft and golden brown, about 15 minutes. Add the saffron threads and sauté for 1 minute. Stir in the tomatoes and their juices, along with the tomato paste, increase the heat to medium-high, and bring to a simmer. Cook for about 8 minutes, until the tomatoes soften and the sauce thickens slightly. Season with the salt and pepper, then stir in the butter piece by piece as the sauce simmers. Serve hot.

MAKES 4 CUPS

WASABI LIME VINAIGRETTE

This tasty vinaigrette is terrific on tuna, albacore, bluefish, and mackerel (it is not intended for dressing salad). And it is very quick and easy to make.

1/3 **cup wasabi powder**
1/3 **cup water**
1/3 **rice vinegar**
1/3 **cup fresh lime juice**
 2 **teaspoons sugar**
 1 **teaspoon kosher or sea salt**
 1 **teaspoon minced fresh ginger**
 4 **scallions, trimmed and finely chopped**
1 1/2 **cups vegetable oil**

1. Place the wasabi powder in a medium bowl, add the water, and whisk to a smooth paste. Add the rice vinegar, lime juice, sugar, and salt and whisk until well combined. Add the ginger and scallions. Whisk in the oil in a slow, steady stream. Transfer to a jar with a tight-fitting lid and refrigerate until ready to use. The vinaigrette keeps, refrigerated, for 1 month.

MAKES ABOUT 2 1/2 CUPS

TROPICAL FRUIT SALSA

a wonderful salad-like concoction that is sweet, spicy, and savory all at once, this pairs beautifully with mahimahi, snapper, grouper, and other southern (tropical) fish. It is also good with bluefish and swordfish. You can serve it with plain (salt-and-pepper) grilled fish or, even better, with fish that has been seasoned with Caribbean Spiced Salt (page 169). We use tomatoes a lot in the summer, so I have not included them in this salsa, but my friend Novillus Petit-Frère, a Caribbean native who taught me the dish, had a little in his recipe. Add 1 small tomato, cut into 1/2-inch dice, if you like.

This recipe makes 4 cups, which might seem like a lot, but it should be served in generous portions (1/2 cup per person). It is as much a side dish as a sauce. If you have some left over, you can put it out the next day as a snack with tortilla chips.

1/2 **pineapple, trimmed, cored, and cut into 1/2-inch dice (2 cups)**

1 **papaya, peeled, seeded, and cut into 1/2-inch dice (1 cup)**

1/2 **red bell pepper (2 to 3 ounces), cut into thin 1-inch-long strips**

1/2 **small red onion (2 to 3 ounces), cut into thin 1-inch-long strips**

3 **jalapeño chiles or 1 Scotch bonnet chile, finely diced, or more to taste**

10 **sprigs fresh cilantro, stems finely chopped, leaves coarsely chopped**

3 to 4 **scallions, trimmed and thinly sliced**

3/4 **cup orange juice**

1/4 **cup fresh lime juice (2 limes)**

1 **teaspoon kosher or sea salt, or more to taste**

1/2 **teaspoon freshly ground black pepper**

WORKING AHEAD
This recipe is best if the salsa has at least an hour or two for the flavors to meld, and it keeps nicely for up to 2 days.

1. Combine the pineapple, papaya, bell pepper, red onion, chiles, cilantro, and scallions in a bowl and cover with the orange and lime juice. Stir in the salt and pepper. Let stand for at least 1 hour (refrigerate if not serving within an hour).

2. Taste for seasoning and add more chiles and/or salt if needed before serving.

MAKES 4 CUPS

MAPLE LEMON GLAZE

ere is my Yankee version of sweet-and-sour sauce. It is terrific brushed on grilled shrimp and salmon, and even better on sea scallops, especially if they are skewered along with pieces of slab bacon. There is no need to use fancy Grade A maple syrup for this glaze. In fact, it's best to use Grade B pure maple syrup; it is less refined and has a richer flavor. Store this glaze at room temperature, not in the refrigerator.

For equipment, you will need a 1- to 2-quart saucepan.

1   **cup pure maple syrup, preferably Grade B**
1/4 **cup fresh lemon juice (2 lemons)**
Kosher or sea salt and freshly ground black pepper

1. Combine the maple syrup and lemon juice in a small saucepan and bring to a simmer over medium heat. (If the syrup boils rapidly, it will foam and cook over.) Simmer until the glaze has reduced to 3/4 cup, about 15 minutes.

2. Season the glaze with salt and pepper. Let cool to room temperature, then transfer to a covered container and store at room temperature; do not refrigerate. The glaze keeps well for up to 3 weeks.

MAKES 2/3 CUP, ENOUGH FOR 8 SKEWERS

COLD CUCUMBER SAUCE

This is one of my favorite sauces for grilled seafood, especially swordfish. It is also terrific with salmon, striped bass, halibut, tautog, and other white-fleshed fish suitable for grilling. Think of this recipe as a formula. The ratio of cucumber to the other ingredients is important, but from there you can adapt this sauce to match with different fish or even side dishes. For example, with a Latino or Caribbean dish like Black Beans and Rice (page 222), you could substitute fresh lime juice for the lemon juice and add chiles and cilantro. This recipe uses half yogurt and half sour cream, but you could use any combination of the two. Or, for salmon, you might want to use all sour cream, with dill. You could also make a low-calorie sauce using all low-fat yogurt. The first time you make the sauce, if you follow my guidelines but omit the jalapeño and use parsley and chives for the herbs, you will have a basic sauce. After that, you are on your own. The list of possible variations is extensive.

For equipment, you will need a stainless steel (or plastic) strainer.

1 1/2 pounds cucumbers (2 large), peeled, halved lengthwise, and seeded
Kosher or sea salt
1/4 cup minced red onion
1/2 cup whole-milk yogurt, drained of excess liquid
1/2 cup sour cream
2 to 3 tablespoons minced fresh herbs (dill, mint, cilantro, parsley, and/or chives)
2 teaspoons minced jalapeño chile (optional)
1 tablespoon fresh lemon juice, or more to taste
Freshly ground black pepper

1. Cut the cucumbers into 1/8-inch dice with a chef's knife, or pulse them in a food processor until chopped into 1/8-inch pieces (do not over-process). Place the cucumbers in a large stainless steel strainer set in the sink or over a bowl, sprinkle them with 1 teaspoon salt, and let them drain for 30 minutes.

2. Meanwhile, place the onion in a small bowl, cover with cold water, and let stand for 30 minutes.

3. Transfer the cucumbers to a large bowl, squeezing the last bit of excess moisture from them with your hands before you place them in the bowl. Drain the onion thoroughly and add to the cucumbers. Add the yogurt, sour cream, herbs, and jalapeño, if using. Mix gently, and add the lemon juice. Season with black pepper, taste, and add more lemon or salt as you wish. Refrigerate for at least 1 hour before serving. The sauce keeps refrigerated for 2 days.

MAKES 2 CUPS

CARIBBEAN HOT PEPPER OIL

I first tasted this flavored oil many years ago when I was working in the Caribbean, and I have kept a jar of it on my shelf ever since. I use the hot oil to enrich foods. It is a fabulous way to moisten and give a flavorful, spicy kick to grilled seafood such as red snapper, mahimahi, bluefish, sardines, shrimp, and lobster tails. The hot pepper oil can be transformed into another interesting condiment by adding a small dice of ripe papaya or avocado and a squeeze of fresh lime juice; see the variation below.

The fiery oil contained in the membranes of the habanero and other chile peppers, which is called capsaicin, is set free on your fingers when you mince chiles. Rubber gloves are highly recommended for this preparation.

3 cups canola oil
1   cup olive oil
4   habanero peppers, seeded and minced (2 tablespoons)
3   large shallots, minced (1/4 cup)
4   sprigs fresh thyme, leaves removed and chopped (2 teaspoons)
4   large sprigs fresh Italian parsley, leaves removed and chopped (1 tablespoon)
Grated zest of 1 large lemon
Grated zest of 1 large orange
1/2   small red bell pepper, minced (1/3 cup)
1   teaspoon kosher or sea salt

1. Combine all the ingredients in a bowl and mix well. Transfer to small jars with tight-fitting lids. Refrigerate for at least 1 week before using. The oil keeps 6 months refrigerated.

MAKES 4 CUPS

Variation: Avocado or Papaya Hot Oil

Halve and pit or seed 1 ripe avocado or papaya. Cut into 1/4- to 1/2-inch dice and add to 1/4 cup of the hot oil, along with the juice of 2 limes or 1 lemon. Let stand for an hour or more before serving, and spoon over grilled fish.

RED ONION VINAIGRETTE

This vinaigrette-salad hybrid does double duty as a flavorful sauce and a crunchy sweet-and-sour onion pickle. It complements grilled fish like halibut, striped bass, bluefish, mackerel, and swordfish.

For equipment, you will need a mandoline or a very sharp knife: the onions should be sliced into very thin rounds.

2   small red onions (5 to 6 ounces)
1/2   teaspoon kosher or sea salt
1/4   teaspoon freshly ground black pepper
1   tablespoon sugar
1/3   white wine vinegar or champagne vinegar
1/4   cup vegetable oil

1. Using a mandoline or a very sharp knife, slice the onions into the thinnest rounds possible. Transfer to a medium bowl, add the salt, pepper, sugar, and vinegar, and toss well. Let the onions sit and pickle for about 20 minutes, stirring occasionally, until they wilt and turn bright pink.

2. Stir in the oil, and transfer to a jar. Refrigerate until ready to use. The vinaigrette keeps well for 3 days.

MAKES 2 CUPS

BRAZILIAN RELISH

This refreshing and tasty relish is wonderful with all kinds of grilled seafood, including salmon, tuna, sardines, swordfish, bass, and other firm white-fleshed fish. There are dozens of versions, but most are similar to this one, which I learned years ago from Bella, one of my many Brazilian cooks. In her recipe, the bell pepper was raw, but I have an aversion to raw peppers—I like them better roasted, so my recipe is written accordingly. Feel free to try the raw pepper version if you like.

For equipment, you will need a coarse strainer.

1   pound ripe tomatoes
1   green bell pepper, roasted (see page 136), peeled, seeded, and cut into small dice (1/4 to 1/2 inch)
1   large cucumber (12 ounces), peeled, halved lengthwise, seeded, and cut into small dice (1/4 to 1/2 inch)
1/2 small onion, cut into small dice (1/4 to 1/2 inch; about 1/4 cup)
12   sprigs fresh cilantro, leaves removed and finely chopped (1/4 cup)
1 1/2 teaspoons minced garlic
1/2 teaspoon crushed red pepper flakes
3/4 cup red wine vinegar (5 to 6 percent acidity)
3/4 cup olive oil
1 1/2 teaspoons kosher or sea salt, or to taste
1/2 teaspoon freshly ground black pepper, or to taste

1. Core the tomatoes and halve them lengthwise. Using a small spoon, remove the pulp and seeds from each tomato half, and transfer the pulp to a coarse strainer set over a bowl. Using a ladle or a spoon, push the juices through the strainer into the bowl, leaving the seeds behind. Dice the flesh of the tomatoes and add it to the bowl.

2. Add the roasted pepper, cucumber, and onion, then add the cilantro, garlic, crushed red pepper, vinegar, oil, salt, and pepper. Cover and refrigerate until ready to serve. This relish keeps well for 3 days.

3. Taste the relish and add more salt and/or pepper if needed before serving.

MAKES 3 CUPS

FENNEL SLAW

My childhood friend Nick DiFidele grew up on a large family farm in South Jersey that specialized in fennel and tomatoes. I used to hang around the farm and play with Nick, and sometimes I assembled tomato boxes for a little extra spending money. At the farm, we would snack on tomatoes and fennel right out of the field (with only salt). I adored both vegetables before I ever had any idea of their profound importance in regard to cooking seafood.

This slaw goes well with many types of seafood, but it is especially good with grilled scallops, shrimp, striped bass, and tautog.

Sharpen your knife, because the thinner you cut the fennel, the better the slaw will be. (If you happen to have a meat slicer, it works perfectly; but don't use a food processor—it makes the fennel mushy and stringy.) I like to serve this at room temperature, spreading it on a platter and placing the grilled fish on top of the fennel. The fish warms the slaw and the juices mingle, creating a wonderful flavor combination. The slaw can also be served as a side dish or small salad.

2   small or 1 large head fennel (10 ounces)
1   small sweet onion (4 ounces), such as Vidalia, Texas Sweet, or Maui
1   teaspoon fennel seeds, chopped
3   tablespoons fresh lemon juice
1/4 cup green olive oil
1/2 teaspoon sugar
Kosher or sea salt
Freshly ground black pepper

1. Trim off the fennel stalks, reserving about 8 fronds. Finely chop the fronds (there should be about 2 tablespoons) and set aside. Halve the bulbs from top to bottom, and cut out and discard the cores. Use a paring knife to trim the leathery outer pieces down to the tender flesh. With a very sharp chef's knife, slice the fennel halves across the grain into very thin slices. Peel and halve the onion, then slice crosswise into very thin slices.

2. Toss the fennel, fennel fronds, onion, and fennel seeds together in a medium bowl. Add the lemon juice, oil, and sugar and toss to combine. Season to taste with salt and pepper. Cover and refrigerate until ready to serve. Bring to room temperature before serving.

MAKES 3 CUPS; SERVES 4 TO 6 AS A SIDE DISH

A FEW SPECIAL GRILLED SEAFOOD RECIPES

Although many of the recipes for accompaniments in this chapter can be used with almost any grilled seafood, some pairings are special. Grilled Oysters with Lemon Butter, Grilled Clams with Garlic Butter, and Grilled King Mackerel with Lime Marinade and Garlic Butter—recipes follow—are so perfect together that you simply must try these combinations as written. The Marinated and Grilled Calamari Accordion-Style and the Grilled Rock Lobster Tails can be served with different sauces (I give you those options in the recipes), but because the technique for both is complex, I wanted to share them with you in recipe form.

GRILLED OYSTERS WITH LEMON BUTTER

This is a simple version of what they call an oyster roast in the Carolina Low Country. You put some nice plump oysters over a hot fire, and when they pop open, you spoon over a little lemon butter and serve them immediately. A friend of mine, Tim Gilchrist, invented what he calls a GreatGrate, which holds the oysters upright and allows you to pick up the grate instead of the individual oysters (see the color photo for Grilled Clams). It's really a very special tool, made in various sizes that can hold from 6 to 30 oysters. The grate can also be used for clams; see the next recipe. GreatGrates can be purchased online at www.greatgrate.com, or call 877-768-5766.

You can use any medium to large plump oysters for this recipe, but I like to use wild oysters like bluepoints. Fancy half-shell oysters (such as Pemaquids or Malpeques) are expensive, and some of their nuances are lost in the cooking.

For equipment, you will need a grill brush and a pair of long tongs; the GreatGrate is optional but it makes the job much easier. You will also need a 1-quart saucepan.

FOR THE LEMON BUTTER SAUCE (MAKES ABOUT 1/2 CUP)

- 1/3 cup heavy cream
- 8 tablespoons (1 stick) cold unsalted butter, cut into small pieces
- 3 tablespoons fresh lemon juice
- 1 tablespoon chopped fresh chervil or Italian parsley

Kosher or sea salt and freshly ground white pepper

At least 2 cups rock salt
- 2 pounds oysters (about 24), well scrubbed

1. Prepare a medium fire following the directions on page 148.

2. To make the sauce: Pour the cream into a 1-quart saucepan and cook over low heat, whisking occasionally to prevent the cream from boiling over, until reduced by half, about 8 minutes. Increase the heat to medium and add the butter one piece at a time, whisking constantly until the sauce is shiny, emulsified, and thick enough to

coat the back of a spoon. Add the lemon juice and simmer briefly to blend the flavors. Remove the saucepan from the heat, add the chervil, and season to taste with salt and pepper. Set aside in a warm spot until ready to serve.

3. Line a serving platter or plates with a bed of rock salt. Set up the oysters on the GreatGrate with the cup side down (flat side up) or place them directly on the grill in the same fashion. Grill the oysters, without turning them, until they pop open, 8 to 10 minutes. Set the Great-Grate on a platter. Or, if you are not using the grate, immediately and carefully transfer the oysters with tongs to the platter or plates. Use the tongs to pry off the top shells. Spoon 1 teaspoon sauce over each oyster, and serve immediately.

SERVES 4 TO 6 AS AN APPETIZER

GRILLED CLAMS WITH GARLIC BUTTER

Once people taste these clams, they can't get enough. This dish has a flavor so exquisite that it belies this very simple preparation. We have served this appetizer at Summer Shack since the day we opened, and it is still one of our best sellers. Grilled clams are best made with small, special-count little necks (about 1 1/2 inches wide). You just put the clams directly over the hot fire—but you must take them off the grill as soon as the shells pop open, or they will burn, right through the shells. Place them on a bed of rock salt to hold them steady and spoon a few drops of sauce on each clam. Or, if you are using a GreatGrate (see Grilled Oysters, page 185), you can just set the grate on a platter—no rock salt needed.

For equipment, you will need a grill brush and a pair of long tongs; the GreatGrate is optional but it makes the job much easier. You will also need a 1-quart saucepan.

FOR THE GARLIC BUTTER SAUCE
(MAKES ABOUT 1/2 CUP)

  8 tablespoons (1 stick) cold unsalted butter, cut into small pieces
  4 large garlic cloves, minced (about 3 tablespoons)
1/4 cup dry white wine
1/4 cup heavy cream
  2 tablespoons minced fresh chives
Kosher or sea salt and freshly ground black pepper

At least 2 cups rock salt
1 1/2 pounds little neck clams (about 24), well scrubbed

1. Prepare a medium fire following the directions on page 148.

2. To make the sauce: Heat 3 tablespoons of the butter in a 1-quart saucepan over low heat until it is foamy. Add the garlic and sauté, stirring, until it is fragrant but has not colored, about 30 seconds. Add the white wine and heavy cream, increase the heat to medium-high, and simmer to reduce by half, about 8 minutes. Add the remaining 5 tablespoons butter one piece at a time,

whisking constantly until the sauce is shiny, emulsified, and thick enough to coat the back of a spoon. Remove the saucepan from the heat, add the chives, and season with salt and pepper. Set aside in a warm spot until ready to serve.

3. Line a serving platter or plates with a bed of rock salt. Set up the clams on the GreatGrate or place them directly on the grill. Grill the clams,

without turning them, until they pop open, 8 to 10 minutes. Set the GreatGrate on a platter. Or, if you are not using the grate, immediately, and carefully, transfer the clams with tongs to the platter or plates. Use the tongs to pry off the top shells. Spoon 1 teaspoon sauce over each clam and serve immediately.

SERVES 4 TO 6 AS AN APPETIZER

MARINATED AND GRILLED CALAMARI ACCORDION-STYLE

This is a basic recipe for grilled calamari. I call my method of cutting the squid for grilling accordion-style because of the way the squid looks after it is cooked. After cutting the squid, I marinate it in my All-Purpose Vinaigrette, which both adds flavor and tenderizes the squid. When it has marinated for at least six hours, I pull it out of the marinade, sprinkle it with salt, and put it right on the grill, where it cooks in minutes. As it grills over the hot coals, it puffs and bends, taking on the look of an accordion.

My favorite way to serve grilled squid is as a simple appetizer over slices of ripe summer tomatoes with a drizzle of good olive oil. It is also wonderful on a bed of greens, topped with Tomato Vinaigrette (page 342) or with fresh lemon juice and olive oil. Grilled squid is also very tasty served with pasta, beans, or creamy polenta and a spicy Fra Diavolo Sauce (page 350).

If you buy squid that isn't already cleaned, you will need to increase the weight to 2 pounds and follow the directions on page 265.

For equipment, you will need a wire grill brush and a pair of tongs.

1 1/2 pounds cleaned medium calamari (bodies and tentacles)
1 cup All-Purpose Vinaigrette (page 342)
Kosher or sea salt

1. To cut the squid: Place each squid body down on a cutting board and make vertical cuts every 1/3 inch, to about one-quarter of the way from the top of the body. This will create a series of rings that are attached at one end. Trim the tentacles and combine with the bodies in a bowl.

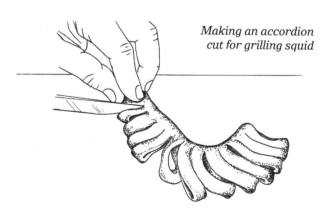

Making an accordion cut for grilling squid

2. Add the vinaigrette to the squid, turning to coat. Cover and refrigerate for at least 6 hours for the flavors to blend. You can let the squid marinate for up to 24 hours; after that, if not ready to grill, remove it from the marinade, cover, and refrigerate.

3. Build a hot grill fire following the directions on page 148. The trick to grilling squid is to cook it as quickly as possible over the hottest fire possible. That will give it a nice char and grill flavor while keeping it moist and tender.

4. Drain the squid, sprinkle with salt, and place directly over the hot flames. Cook for about 1 minute on each side, or until the squid bodies puff and take on an accordion shape. Serve hot.

SERVES 4 AS A MAIN COURSE OR 6 AS AN APPETIZER

GRILLED KING MACKEREL WITH LIME MARINADE AND GARLIC BUTTER

King mackerel are big fish that can weigh up to a hundred pounds—that's probably where they got their name. They range from North Carolina to Brazil; everyone in the Caribbean calls them kingfish. The average market kingfish is about 20 pounds. They are fatty and flavorful, like their little cousins, Atlantic mackerel (see page 155), and because of that, they can stand up to strong flavors. Common wisdom in Florida and the Bahamas is to marinate the fish in lime juice so it doesn't taste so strong. I like strong fish, so it was years before I tried this technique. I was skeptical, but the lime gave the fish a nice bright flavor. Topped with garlic butter, it is my favorite new (old) way to cook kingfish. You can also serve it with Wasabi Lime Vinaigrette (page 177), Caribbean Hot Pepper Oil (page 181), or Red Onion Vinaigrette (page 182).

Kingfish is firm and easy to grill. Just be sure to pat it dry after it comes out of the marinade and baste it with oil so it doesn't stick to the grill. The skin isn't good to eat, so remove it before cooking. If you are cutting your own fish, you can determine the thickness by cutting the fillets on a bias.

For equipment, you will need wire grill brush, a pair of long tongs, and a wide metal spatula.

Four 8- to 10-ounce skinless kingfish fillets, about 1 inch thick
Juice of 4 limes (about 1/2 cup)
About 1/4 cup vegetable oil
Kosher or sea salt and freshly ground black pepper
4   slices Garlic Herb Butter (page 352)
1   lime, cut into 4 wedges

WORKING AHEAD

I recommend that you make the garlic butter and keep it in your freezer as a staple item. Then, when you want to make a quick dinner of grilled fish, just pull it out and let it come to room temperature. Slice it about 1/4 inch thick and place it on top of the fish as soon as it comes off the grill.

1. Build a hot grill fire following the directions on page 148. Leave some space to move the kingfish fillets away from the high heat once they are seared. Scrape the rack clean with a wire brush, spray or moisten a rag with vegetable oil, and wipe the grill rack.

2. As soon as you start the fire, place the fillets in a baking dish and pour over the lime juice. Keep refrigerated, but turn the fish every 5 minutes so it marinates evenly.

3. After about 20 minutes, remove the fish from the lime juice (it will have absorbed most of it) and gently pat the fillets dry with a paper towel.

Brush the fillets on both sides with the oil and sprinkle them generously with salt and pepper.

4. Grill the fillets on the hottest part of the grill for 2 minutes, without moving them. Loosen gently with a spatula, turn, and grill 2 minutes more. Transfer the fillets to the cooler part of the grill and grill about 4 to 5 minutes more, turning once.

5. Transfer the fillets to a platter and top each piece with a slice of garlic butter, so it melts over the fish. Serve with the lime wedges.

SERVES 4 AS A MAIN COURSE

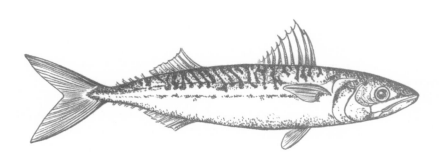

GRILLED ROCK LOBSTER TAILS WITH AJÍ VERDE

Living in New England, I don't get to eat rock lobster very often. In Massachusetts, it is illegal to market, purchase, or serve any lobster that isn't a true American lobster (*Homarus americanus*), the kind with the big claws. But rock lobster is available both fresh and frozen along most of the East Coast, and although different from true lobster (rock lobster are langostines, spiny lobsters, or *langoustes*, more closely related to shrimp than lobsters), it is very good. When I worked at Petite St. Vincent Resort in the Grenadines, rock lobsters were abundant. The local fishermen would bring them in live every morning and because they were (hard to believe) one of the least expensive local foods, we served them every day in all sorts of preparations. Each Friday night, we had a barbecue on the beach for our guests and everyone's favorite was the lobster tails grilled over a charcoal fire scented with nutmeg shells.

The tail of the rock lobster is the only part worth bothering with. There is very little meat in the body, and they don't have claws like American lobsters. The best way to grill the tails is to start by blanching them quickly in saltwater—that way, the meat will come out of the shell easily. Following this recipe is a variation for grilling American lobster tails in the same manner.

Rock lobster, like American lobster, is healthful, very high in protein and beneficial omega-3 fatty acids. It too is delicious with butter. You can serve these simply with Lemon Herb Butter (page 172), Garlic Herb Butter (page 352), or Caribbean Hot Pepper Oil (page 181). Because it is expensive to fill up on rock lobster, I like to serve it with hearty foods like Black Beans and Rice (page 222) or the very special sauce, from Mexico, made with avocado and hard-boiled egg and called *ají verde*.

For equipment, you will need a 5- to 6-quart pot, a wire grill brush, a basting brush, a pair of long tongs or a wide metal spatula, and a medium cleaver or heavy chef's knife.

Kosher or sea salt
  4 large uncooked rock lobster tails (5 to 6 ounces each)
About 1/4 cup olive oil
Freshly ground black pepper
Ají Verde (recipe follows)
  1 lime, cut into 4 wedges

WORKING AHEAD

The lobster tails can be blanched and split, ready for grilling, hours in advance; refrigerate until ready to cook. The sauce can also be made earlier in the day.

1. Fill a 5- or 6-quart pot with about 3 quarts of water and bring to a boil. Add about 1/4 cup salt, preferably sea salt, to make it taste like ocean water (or use ocean water). When the water is at a rolling boil, add the lobster tails and cook for about 3 minutes. Using tongs, remove the lobster tails from the water and let them cool to room temperature.

2. Using a cleaver or heavy knife, cut the tails lengthwise down the center. Remove the intestinal tract. Place the tails on a plate, cover with plastic wrap, and refrigerate until you are ready to grill them.

3. Prepare a medium grill fire following the directions on page 148—let the fire cook down so the lobster tails will cook evenly and not too fast. Clean the grill with a wire brush and wipe it with a cloth sprayed or moistened with vegetable oil.

4. Place the lobster tails on a large plate or in a shallow pan and brush them, on both the shell and meat side, with the oil. Sprinkle generously with salt and pepper.

5. Place the tails meat side down directly over the fire. Cook for 3 minutes, and turn them over. The meat should have grill marks and some brown spots from the grill. Brush the meat with oil and continue cooking for another 5 or 6 minutes, shell side down. If the shells become charred quickly, the fire is too hot and you should move the tails to indirect heat, or the periphery of the grill. Transfer the grilled tails to a platter or plates and spoon about 1/4 cup sauce over each tail. Serve with the lime wedges.

SERVES 4 AS A MAIN COURSE

Variation: Grilled American Lobster Tails

It was only recently, after the demand for rock lobster outstripped the supply, that it became viable to process lobsters from Maine and Canada as frozen tails. They are very good, but for now they remain a commercial item for the food service industry; I don't think you will find American lobster tails in a retail market—if you do, though, try them. You can handle the tails as if they were rock lobster, but because the shells are a little thinner, they may need to finish cooking away from the direct heat of the fire.

If you want to prepare tails from whole live lobsters, start with a minimum size of 1 1/2 pounds up to 2 1/2 pounds, depending on your budget. Steam the lobsters following the directions on page 71, but halfway through the steaming, quickly remove them from the pot and snap off the tails with a twisting motion. Quickly return the lobster bodies, with their claws still attached, to the pot, cover, and wait 2 minutes for the steam to recover; then finish the cooking as directed. (This cooked lobster meat can be used for another dish.) When the tails have cooled to room temperature, split them and remove the intestinal tract. Cover with plastic wrap and keep refrigerated until ready to grill. Proceed as for rock lobster tails, but keep in mind that you may need to adjust the timing, depending on the size of the tails.

AJÍ VERDE (YUCATÁN GREEN SAUCE)

This recipe comes from Brian Flagg, my right-hand man, who is currently running three of my restaurant kitchens. Brian has a passion for travel that coincides with his passion for food. He infuses our nightly blackboard specials with the dishes he has collected during his journeys. He bought this fabulous avocado dish back from the Yucatán. It is perfect with grilled lobster and can also be served with grilled shrimp, fish, chicken, or pork. Ají verde also makes a tasty snack/appetizer with tortilla chips, but if serving it this way, you will need to double the recipe, or it will be gone in five minutes.

1   ripe avocado
2   hard-boiled eggs, coarsely chopped
2   scallions, trimmed and thinly sliced
1   small plum tomato, cut into 1/3-inch dice
2   tablespoons fresh lemon juice
1   small jalapeño (or 1/4 habanero), seeded and minced
4   sprigs fresh cilantro, stems finely chopped, leaves coarsely chopped
1/2 clove garlic, minced
1   tablespoon olive oil
About 1/2 teaspoon kosher or sea salt
Freshly ground black pepper

WORKING AHEAD

This sauce tastes best the day it is made, but you can make it in the morning and serve later in the day.

1. Halve and pit the avocado, peel, and cut into 1/2-inch dice. Place the avocado in a mixing bowl.

2. Add the chopped eggs, scallions, tomato, lemon juice, jalapeño, cilantro, garlic, and olive oil and mix with a fork to create a creamy, chunky paste. Season with the salt and a little pepper. Cover and refrigerate until ready to use.

MAKES ABOUT 1 CUP

Grilled Sardines, page 154,
with Brazilian Relish, page 183

Grilled Sea Scallops,
page 152, with Maple Lemon
Glaze, page 179, over Fennel
Slaw, page 184

Grilled Clams with Garlic Butter,
page 186, on a GreatGrate

Grilled Rock
Lobster Tails
with Ají Verde,
page 191, and
Black Beans
and Rice,
page 222

Grilled Blue Cheese Long Burger, page 195, and Fried Peppers with Garlic and Olive Oil, page 219

Broiled Bluefish with Garlic Butter, page 230

Pan-Roasted Whole Flounder with Brown Butter, Lemon, and Capers, page 224, with broccoli rabe and steamed red bliss potatoes

Grilled Skirt
Steak, page 199,
with Grilled
Vegetables,
page 201

GRILLING POULTRY AND MEAT

Grilling poultry and meat is really not that different from grilling seafood. In fact, the best grilling technique for most seafood, which starts with a hot sear and then finishes grilling at a lower temperature, is one I learned from cooking thick steaks. One of the big differences between grilling meat and seafood concerns the desired smokiness. The object of grilling fish isn't to infuse it with smoke—it is to cook it so it is moist and juicy. But most grilled poultry and meat is greatly enhanced by the smoky flavor imparted by grilling. That is why with many dishes, I lower the lid during the final cooking to allow the poultry or meat to soak up some of the smoke. In order to be able to do this effectively, you must build the fire so it is large enough to cook the meat directly over the coals, but not so big that there is no room to move the poultry or meat away from direct heat.

The simple smoky flavors of grilled chicken, steaks, and chops lend themselves to a wide array of accompaniments, but they don't really need sauces. I don't like to mess with a good steak—salt, pepper, and proper cooking is all that is really needed, although a little Garlic Herb Butter (page 352) doesn't hurt. Grilled pork chops can be more versatile; see page 200.

GRILLED MARINATED CHICKEN

ere is a simple and delicious way to grill chicken. If you have my All-Purpose Vinaigrette made up, then all you need to do is cut up the chicken and pour the marinade over it. Turn it occasionally, so the marinade is absorbed evenly. I won't tell you how much to spend on chicken, but if you can buy kosher chicken, such as Empire, they are usually excellent quality at a fair price. Free-range chickens can be expensive, but they do have a wonderful flavor. My recipe calls for a chicken cut into ten pieces, the same way I cut chicken for frying, because it cooks very evenly that way. If you don't want to butcher a whole chicken yourself, you can replace it with 3 pounds of chicken parts.

For equipment, you will need a wire grill brush and a pair of long tongs.

One 2 1/2- to 3-pound chicken, cut into 10 pieces (see page 274)

1   cup All-Purpose Vinaigrette (page 342)

4   cloves garlic, finely chopped

Kosher or sea salt and freshly ground black pepper

WORKING AHEAD

The flavor of the marinade will continue to penetrate the chicken for up to 24 hours, so don't be afraid to make this way ahead. Do try to let the chicken marinate for at least 4 hours, but if you don't have time, you can skip the marinade and instead season the chicken well with Seasoned Salt for Chicken (page 273).

1. Place the chicken in a 1-gallon zip-lock bag or in a deep bowl or baking dish. Add the vinaigrette and chopped garlic. If you are using a zip-lock bag, seal the bag, squeezing out most of the air, and move the chicken around in the marinade to coat. If you are using a bowl or baking dish, coat the chicken well with the marinade, using tongs to turn the pieces; cover with plastic wrap. Refrigerate for up to 24 hours.

2. Prepare a medium grill fire following the directions on page 148—let the fire cook down so the chicken cooks evenly and not too fast. Clean the grill with a wire brush and wipe with a cloth sprayed or moistened with vegetable oil.

3. Place the marinated chicken pieces on a large plate and let them drain for a few minutes. Sprinkle generously with salt and pepper.

4. Place the chicken skin side down over a medium-hot part of the fire and grill for 2 1/2 minutes, without moving the pieces. Loosen gently with tongs, turn, and grill 2 1/2 minutes more. Transfer the chicken to the cooler part of the grill and cover the grill with the lid, leaving the vents open so the fire does not die down too much. Cook for an additional 15 to 20 minutes, turning and moving the pieces around twice so they cook evenly.

5. Transfer the chicken to a platter and serve.

SERVES 4 AS A MAIN COURSE

GRILLED LONG BURGERS

The most American of American foods, the hamburger (along with the hot dog) is a staple of summer cooking: quick, simple, delicious, and satisfying. Hamburgers or cheeseburgers can be cooked indoors, but to cook them properly—at a fairly high heat—is pretty messy. I like the smoky flavor of grilled burgers, as well as the fact that the job is clean and easy.

Almost thirty years ago, I worked at an Italian restaurant called Marenzi in San Francisco. The owner, Luigi, would gladly oblige the occasional request for a hamburger or cheeseburger, but since he didn't have hamburger buns on hand, he would serve the burger on a section of baguette. To do this, he had to shape the burger into a long tube. I grew very fond of Luigi's burgers, preferring crisp French bread to soft white buns, and I have made them for myself for many years. When I opened Summer Shack in 2000, I decided to resurrect Luigi's burger as the "long burger." Some people didn't like the chewy baguette for their burger, so eventually we started baking special long burger buns. We kept the shape, but not the French bread—which I still prefer.

My favorite hamburger meat is ground chuck, which comes from the shoulder. The shoulder is tough unless made into stew or ground for burgers or meat loaf, but, like other tough cuts of beef, it can be one of the most flavorful. And, because it is fatty, it has even more flavor, making excellent meat for burgers. When it comes to the actual grilling, there are a couple of things to remember: Don't press down on the burgers with a metal spatula—a burger will get plumper as it cooks, and pressing down on it just squeezes out the juices; instead, make the patties about 25 percent bigger than you want the cooked burgers to be. Since burgers cook quickly, I build a medium fire and cook them directly over the coals. And don't keep flipping the burgers back and forth: a burger needs just one flip halfway through grilling. Four to 5 minutes per side will cook a 6-ounce burger to medium-rare.

For equipment, you will need a wire grill brush, a basting brush, and a wide metal spatula.

1 1/2 pounds ground chuck

1 or 2 ripe tomatoes, sliced

1   medium red onion, sliced 1/4 inch thick

4   or more pieces of iceberg lettuce

1   Kosher dill pickle, thinly sliced

Ketchup (Heinz)

Mustard (your choice)

2   tablespoons vegetable oil

Kosher or sea salt and freshly ground black
    pepper

4   ounces cheddar, American, or Swiss
    cheese, sliced, or blue cheese, crumbled
    (optional)

Four 6-inch-long pieces of baguette, split in
    half

1. Divide the meat into 4 portions and shape each one into a 7-inch-long cylinder or tube. Press it down so it is about 3/4 inch thick. Keep refrigerated until ready to grill.

2. Prepare a medium grill fire following the directions on page 148. Clean the grill with a wire brush and wipe with a cloth sprayed or moistened with vegetable oil.

3. Arrange the tomatoes, onion, lettuce, and pickle on a platter. Place on the table with the condiments—ketchup, mustard, and any other you might enjoy.

4. Place the long burgers on a large plate or in a pan and brush one side of each burger lightly with the oil. Sprinkle them generously on both sides with salt and pepper.

5. Place the burgers oiled side down directly over the coals. For medium-rare, grill for 4 to 5 minutes, without moving them, then loosen gently with a spatula, turn, and grill on the second side for 4 to 5 minutes more. For medium burgers, increase the time on each side by 1 to 2 minutes. For cheeseburgers, about a minute before the burgers are done, lay a slice or two of cheese or press 1 1/2 tablespoons crumbled blue cheese over each burger, cover the grill, and cook for 1 minute (for blue cheese, 2 minutes). Transfer the burgers to a platter.

6. Quickly grill the baguettes, mostly on the inside and just a little on the crust side. Place the burgers on the bottom halves of the bread, lean the top halves against the burgers, and serve immediately.

SERVES 4

GRILLED SAUSAGES

Sausages must be handled very carefully and cooked very slowly on the grill to prevent the casings from splitting open and losing some of their fatty juices. Searing on high heat will usually split the casings and cause the sausages to become dry. So, you need to have plenty of room on the grill away from the coals to cook the sausages slowly. This usually works out nicely, because often sausage is served as part of a mixed grill. You can cook the sausages off to the side while you are cooking steaks or burgers directly over the coals. Although there are hundreds of types of sausage, in terms of grilling them, there are really only two: fresh raw sausage, like Italian sausage, and fully cooked sausage, like Polish kielbasa or Portuguese linguiça.

For all types of sausage, start by preparing a medium fire following the directions on page 148. Let the fire cook down to glowing embers. Clean the grill with a wire brush and wipe with a cloth sprayed or moistened with vegetable oil. It is important that the grill be well oiled so the sausages don't stick and tear.

For equipment, you will need a wire grill brush and a pair of long tongs.

To grill fresh Italian or other raw sausages, you must start them very slowly, off to the side, where they will cook steadily, and turn them every couple of minutes to ensure even cooking.

Most raw sausages will take a good 15 minutes to cook through. When they are fully cooked, they will feel very firm to the touch. You can always cut into one to check for doneness if you are not sure. Just before you take the sausages off the grill, place them directly over the coals and brown them to your liking.

To grill fully cooked sausages like kielbasa, linguiça, or frankfurters, the idea is just to heat them through. There is (obviously) no need to worry about cooking them through. Most already cooked sausages will take less than 10 minutes to heat through. Cook them over indirect heat, off to the side, and then, just before you take the sausages off the grill, place them directly over the coals and brown them to your liking.

I usually serve sausages as one of several grilled items when I am having a cookout for lots of people. If you are making a meal of grilled sausages, you might want to use the center of the grill to cook some potatoes, peppers, and onions—then you will have a pretty complete meal all cooked on the grill. Because most sausages are fatty (that's what makes them so good), I recommend that you serve something acidic to balance the experience, like pickles, tangy slaw, sauerkraut, and/or various relishes. Mustard is also important.

GRILLED STEAKS AND CHOPS

I don't eat red meat very often, but there are times when I crave it in a way that is beyond preference; it's a primitive urge. Thick slices of grilled beef—charred on the outside, juicy and pink in the center—are something I find so satisfying that I think about the meat before and after eating.

One of the great American clichés is that grilling steak, chops, and burgers is "man's work." This stereotype, like many others, draws from reality: Grilling is the only cooking that some men have ever done. My dad didn't ever cook in the kitchen, but he was perfectly comfortable at the outdoor grill. Fortunately things are changing. I have been teaching cooking classes for more than twenty years, and they have gone from the odd guy here and there to one out of three. And I know many women who don't cook at all. That said, I think that the approach to cooking meat outdoors needs to be macho, whether you are male or female.

To cook a perfect steak, the fire needs to be powerful—very hot. It is the initial sear over intensely hot coals that has the greatest effect on the final outcome. You must be fearless, not shying away from the heat and occasional flare-ups, and you must remain focused at all times, ignoring most of the other things going on around you. Be sure you lightly oil each steak and then season very generously with coarse salt and pepper.

For equipment, you will need a wire grill brush, a basting brush, and a pair of long tongs. Although it is not essential, I recommend that you have a squirt bottle filled with water for controlling flare-ups.

Porterhouse and T-Bone Steaks

When I am entertaining and I really want to impress, I cook what I call my "Yabba Dabba Doo" steak, in honor of Fred Flintstone. I call the butcher well in advance and ask for a couple of porterhouse steaks cut 3 to 3 1/2 inches thick. By the way, the only difference between the porterhouse and the T-bone is the part of the loin it is cut from: the porterhouse has less tenderloin (more sirloin) attached; the T-bone has a more substantial piece of tenderloin. Both are terrific, but I prefer the porterhouse because I like the sirloin best. To cook these, you will need to build a very hot fire (if using a chimney starter, add extra coals as described on page 148). These steaks are so thick that you have to sear the sides as well as the surface, and it will take a good 10 minutes to char them all around. Then move them over to the side, away from direct heat, and cover the grill. Let them cook for about 10 minutes, then flip and cook for 10 more. They will pick up a wonderful smoky flavor. Let them rest for at least 10 minutes before slicing. To grill thinner—1-inch-thick—T-bone or porterhouse steaks, sear them over high heat, directly over the coals, for about 5 or 6 minutes on each side, and they will be ready.

Sirloin Steaks

Have your butcher cut these expensive steaks, also called New York or strip steaks, about 1 inch thick, 10 to 12 ounces each, with about 1/3 inch of fat left on. Cook them directly over hot coals, giving them a very hard sear, for about 5 minutes per side for medium-rare. When cooked perfectly, this is a hard steak to beat.

Rib-Eye Steaks

This is probably the most flavorful of all steaks, because of its high fat content. For a big wow, ask your butcher to cut what the French call a *Côte de boeuf*, a double-thick bone-in rib steak, about 2 to 3 inches thick. Cook it the same way as described for a thick porterhouse, above. Let it rest and slice it like a roast. The other option is the boneless individual rib-eye steak, also known as a Delmonico. Cook these as you would sirloin, directly over the coals. I like rib-eye steaks cooked medium-rare to medium, not rare. The extra cooking develops the flavor of the fat. Allow about 6 to 8 minutes per side for medium-rare to medium.

Tenderloin/Filet Mignon

The lean, soft little used muscle inside a loin of beef is called the tenderloin, a very descriptive name. Unfortunately, being tender is its most notable quality. It doesn't have anywhere near the flavor of a sirloin or rib-eye steak. That being said, it is very popular (and expensive). I think it is best cooked rare to medium-rare. Because the tenderloin itself is long and round, it has to be cut into thick steaks that will need to be cooked on the sides as well as the surface. Depending on thickness, however, you should be able to sear these steaks start to finish over hot coals. They will have a better flavor if you really char them.

Flank Steak and Skirt Steak

Although they are not as expensive as sirloin, rib-eye, or tenderloin, flank steak and skirt steak are no longer inexpensive as they once were. These are lean steaks with very rich flavor. They should be cooked to rare or medium-rare at most; any more, and they become very tough. The trick to cooking these steaks properly is to give them a very intense sear directly over hot coals. Cook flank steak about 6 minutes per side, a bit longer if it is more than 2 pounds. Skirt steaks will take only 4 or 5 minutes per side. Once the steaks are cooked, let them rest for at least 5 minutes, then slice them thinly on a bias across the grain.

Both these steaks will benefit from being marinated. The All-Purpose Vinaigrette (page 342) is terrific for this purpose. Use about 1 cup for 2 pounds of meat and let the steak marinate for up to 24 hours, giving the meat a turn once in a while so it marinates evenly. You could also use the Soy-Ginger Sauce (page 348) as a marinade; however, in that case, don't let the meat marinate for more than 1 hour.

Steak Tips

Steak tips can be tricky to grill, depending on the cut of meat used for the tips. Sirloin tips are best. I recommend that you purchase them from a reputable butcher or market that is known for high-quality meat, or you may end up spending a disproportionate amount of time chewing the meat. Ask for tips that are about 2 ounces each. I recommend that you marinate the tips in All-Purpose Vinaigrette (page 342) for up to 24 hours. It will help to tenderize them as well as add great flavor. Put 3 or 4 pieces on each skewer (soaked if wooden). Sear them directly over hot coals, turning every 2 minutes so they cook evenly, for a total of about 8 minutes for medium-rare. Cooked much longer, they will be very tough.

Pork Chops

I love pork chops on the grill, especially when they are thick and juicy. Ask for chops that are about 1 inch thick. Season them with salt and pepper or your favorite spice rub. Sear them directly over hot coals for 2 minutes on each side, then move them away from the direct heat to finish cooking. I like to cover the grill and let them become nice and smoky as they cook (turn them once) for another 8 to 10 minutes. When you move them away from the direct heat, you might glaze them with Maple Lemon Glaze (page 179) or Roasted Garlic and Mustard Glaze (page 175).

Lamb Chops

Grilled lamb chops are a very special treat that deserve a little extra attention. Early in the day, chop a little rosemary and garlic and mix it with black pepper. Rub it all over the chops. If the bones are "frenched" (no meat attached) cover them with foil, or they will burn and snap off. Cover the chops with plastic wrap and keep refrigerated until you are ready to cook them. Lightly oil and salt them before you grill them. Sear the chops directly over hot coals for 2 minutes on each side, then move them away from the direct heat and grill for another 4 or 5 minutes on each side for medium-rare to medium. Lamb chops are fatty, so they tend to cause flare-ups; keep a spray bottle of water nearby.

GRILLED VEGETABLES

Grilling vegetables is more of a convenience than an important technique—I would rarely start up a wood fire just to grill vegetables. However, if you already have a hot grill going, why not use it to cook some vegetables? That will save you from cooking indoors and from cleaning an extra pan. Best of all, some vegetables taste really good cooked on the grill.

No recipe is really needed for grilling vegetables—it is a very simple process. To a certain extent, it is something that you will need to teach yourself, because the technique will need to be adapted to your grill. Ideally, you want to grill most vegetables directly over medium or low coals, so if you have a small grill, you might want to cook your main dish first and then quickly grill the vegetables right afterward. If you have a big grill and are cooking the main course on a hot fire, you may be able to cook the vegetables off to the side. Another option is to spread out the coals after you finishing searing the main dish. That will create a medium fire, and you can grill the vegetables while the main dish finishes cooking. Remember, this is about convenience, so make it work in the way that best fits your circumstances.

Grilled Corn

Sweet summer corn charred on the grill is a real treat: I love the complex flavors of the sweet kernels mingled with bits of toasted and charred corn. To prep sweet corn for the grill, pull back the husks, leaving them attached, and remove the silk. Pull the husks back up over the corn to keep the corn from burning and drying out. Soak the corn in salted water for 5 to 10 min-

utes (at the beach, I use seawater) so the husks won't dry out too quickly on the grill.

Try to find a spot on the grill with low to medium coals—where the corn will take about 15 minutes to grill. It is okay if the husks eventually burn and even if the corn gets some brown color, but if it seems that the kernels are drying out, dunk the corn into the bucket of saltwater for 10 seconds and then put it back on the grill. Watch for the color of the kernels to change, the way steamed or boiled corn does. Remove the husks, brush with butter, and serve immediately.

Grilled Mushrooms

The best mushrooms for grilling are large flat ones such as portobellos or shiitake. Large button mushrooms can also be grilled. Expensive and rarer mushrooms like cèpes or chanterelles are best sautéed so you can appreciate their special flavor. To grill mushrooms, cut the stems off and brush the mushrooms with olive or vegetable oil. Season them with salt and pepper and cook for a couple of minutes on each side, directly over the coals, until they are tender and moist. Instead of using oil, you can brush the mushrooms with All-Purpose Vinaigrette (page 342) before grilling them; they taste wonderful this way.

Grilled Potatoes

Red or white new potatoes or small Yukon Gold potatoes are my favorites for grilling, but any low- to medium-starch potato, like a Maine

(Kennebec) or PEI is fine. Earlier in the day, start the potatoes (as many as you need) in a pot of cold water. Throw in a big handful of salt and bring them up to a boil. Lower the heat and simmer the potatoes until they are just tender—it is best to undercook them slightly, but not too much. Drain them and run them under cold water to stop the cooking. Keep refrigerated.

When the potatoes are completely chilled, trim off the ends and slice the potatoes into 1/2-inch-thick pieces. Brush the potato slices with olive or vegetable oil and season with salt and pepper. Grill over medium coals for about 4 or 5 minutes on each side, until browned and crisp.

Grilled Onions

Grilled onions are very good on burgers and other sandwiches; they are also nice as a side dish for steak. Cut the onions crosswise into rings that are about 1/2 inch thick, leaving the skin on. Brush the slices with oil and season with salt and pepper. Grill the slices for about 5 minutes on each side, using a spatula to turn them. Try to keep them intact so the slices only char on the edges. When they are soft and well charred, use tongs to remove the skin and outer layer or two of each slice, then break them up so that they are mostly individual rings. Spread them on the grill to let them briefly absorb a little smoke, and remove them from the grill before they are too charred.

Grilled Bell Peppers

Start by cutting the peppers into quarters and trimming off the curly top and bottom ends so they will lie flat on the grill. Oil and season the peppers, then place them skin side down on the grill over low to medium coals; move them around as necessary to find a place where they won't burn quickly. Expect a little black on the peppers, but not too much. The skin on peppers cooks more slowly than the flesh, so once you turn them, they will only take a couple more minutes to finish.

Grilled Zucchini or Summer Squash

Cut squash about 1/2 inch thick on a bias, to make fairly long slices. Brush the slices with olive or vegetable oil and season them, then place directly over the coals. They will cook very fast, about 2 minutes on each side. When you see the slices bubbling in the center, they are done.

Grilled Eggplant

Eggplant is a vegetable that most people love but shy away from cooking. Grilling is the simplest way to cook it. Cut small to medium regular eggplants (large ones aren't as good on the grill) straight across into 1/2-inch-thick rounds. Brush with olive or vegetable oil and season right before they go on the grill. (If you do this early, the eggplant will absorb the oil.) Cook them directly over medium coals for 2 or 3 minutes on each side, until they are soft and bubbling in the center. Japanese eggplant can also be grilled. Cut them and cook them as you would zucchini or summer squash.

Grilled Cherry or Grape Tomatoes

Small tomatoes taste really good cooked on the grill. The trick is to put them on wooden skewers that have been soaked in water—that way you only have to turn a few skewers instead of a lot of little tomatoes. Brush the skewered tomatoes with oil and place them over low to medium coals. Turn them once or twice, cooking them until they are soft and hot. Be careful—if you cook them too long, they will burst and deflate. Grilled cherry tomatoes are an excellent garnish for many types of grilled fish.

INSIDE THIS CHAPTER

Pan-Seared Tuna with
Japanese Flavors   207

Sautéed Soft-Shell Crabs
with Garlic and Parsley   208

Box: Soft-Shell Crabs   209

Box: How to Clean Soft-Shell
Crabs   210

Mostly Crab Crab Cakes
with English Mustard
Sauce   211

   English Mustard Sauce   212

Salt Cod Cakes   213

Perfect Panfried Breaded
Fish   215

   Almond and Parmesan
   Bread Crumbs   216

Portuguese-Style Panfried
Hake   217

Fried Peppers with Garlic
and Olive Oil   219

Home Fries   221

Black Beans and Rice   222

Pan-Roasted Whole Flounder
or Fluke with Brown Butter,
Lemon, and Capers   224

Pan-Roasted Lobster with
Tomatoes, Butter, and
Herbs   226

Broiled Butterfish with
Mirin Glaze   228

Broiled Bluefish with
Garlic Butter   230

Scallop and Bacon Hors
d'Oeuvres   231

Baked Oysters "Casino"   232

Boston Baked Scrod   234

   Buttery Crumbs   235

Plank-Roasted Salmon
(or Bluefish)   236

   Herb Rub for Planked
   Fish   237

Slow-Roasted Whole Fish
with Onion and Fennel
Stuffing   238

Caribbean "Jammed"
Crabs   240

Baked Stuffed Rock
Lobster Tails   242

Baked Plum Tomatoes
Gratinée   244

INDOOR COOKING

FLASH IN THE PAN

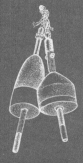

You can try, but you can't stay outside all summer. In this chapter, I invite you back into your home kitchen and show you some simple, and a few not so simple, dishes that can be made on top of your stove, under your broiler, or in your oven. Many of these dishes are served often in my restaurants, but they are not restaurant dishes—they are uniquely home-style dishes with a wide variety of textures and flavors. These are recipes that I hope you will come back to time and time again.

Quite a few of these recipes call for a well-seasoned heavy skillet. This cast-iron pan, sometimes called a Griswold, available at almost any hardware store or housewares department, is indispensable for pan-roasting, searing, and several other techniques. Always lightly oil the pan before you put it away to prevent rust. Not all your pans need to be as sturdy as this one, but in general, the heavier the pan, the better it will conduct heat and the more evenly your food will cook. When broiling, a heavy stainless steel baking sheet will perform far better than thinner versions, and it won't buckle. A "strapped" roasting pan (reinforced with a steel band) will not buckle either, and so is useful for roasts and some baked dishes. These pieces of equipment will become the workhorses of your kitchen, and it's worth spending a few extra dollars on them.

In quite a few recipes, you are asked to turn items in a pan. Whether it's a cod cake, a piece of fish, or a soft-shell crab, remember this simple and important technique: When you flip or turn an object in a pan, hold the spatula directly in front of you and turn the item so it falls over backward. That way, when it lands, any splattering grease will splash toward the back, away from you and your hands. No unnecessary burns.

When a recipe calls for olive oil for cooking, I am referring to good-quality refined olive oil that has a golden, not green, color. The good stuff, extra virgin or cold-pressed olive oil, is best used as a condiment for flavoring foods. I specify when you need this type of oil. Don't use olive oil or corn oil in recipes that call for vegetable oil. When I call for vegetable oil, I am looking for a neutral flavor. Olive oil imparts its own unique flavor to the foods cooked in it, desirable for some dishes but not for all. Corn oil also has its own flavor and is best used for corn fritters, hush puppies, and other dishes made with cornmeal.

In a few recipes, I call for "peanut oil, canola oil, or other vegetable oil." Peanut oil is superior because it has a high burning point and a very clean flavor (virtually no flavor) that allows the flavor of the food cooked in it to come through. However, many people have peanut allergies, so you should let your guests know when you are using it. Grapeseed oil is actually the best cooking or salad oil you can buy, but it is very expensive and not widely available. Canola oil is always a good choice; it is moderately priced, available in any market, and clean tasting.

I don't use clarified butter (clear, pure butterfat, with the milk solids removed) at home. Making it is an extra step that I find unnecessary. Instead, for many recipes, I use a combination of vegetable oil and butter. The oil raises the burning point and the butter gives great flavor.

As with most of my recipes, I have taken special care to point out what you can make ahead. The recipes here that don't have Working Ahead comments can be cooked from start to finish in less than an hour, and less than 30 minutes in many cases. So break out the cast-iron skillet, crank up your oven, and fill your kitchen with the aromas of great home-cooked seafood.

PAN-SEARED TUNA WITH JAPANESE FLAVORS

All along the Atlantic Coast, sports fishermen chase after the migratory tuna, especially the *bluefin tuna*, whose market value can help offset this expensive hobby. Commercial fisherman also target the highly prized *bluefin*, along with *yellowfin* and *big-eye tuna*. All three of these red-meat tunas are superb, especially when the prime cuts are served raw or rare. The easiest way to control the cooking of perfect rare tuna is to sear it in a heavy pan, because you can see the doneness as it cooks.

Pan-seared tuna can be paired with Mediterranean flavors, such as tomatoes, capers, olives, citrus, and herbs, or with Asian flavors, as in this recipe. Another option is to season the tuna with my Spiced Seafood Salt (page 168) and serve it with lemon or lime wedges. For this dish, I recommend that you set out small bowls of Soy-Ginger Sauce and Wasabi Lime Vinaigrette for your guests to serve themselves. Of course you can serve either one of the sauces individually—both are terrific, but the combination is even better. You'll need a total of at least 1 cup of sauce (or sauces). Keep the side dishes simple. Plain rice and a green salad are perfect. Or, if your fish market sells Japanese seaweed salad (wakame), it is a wonderful accompaniment.

For equipment, you will need a well-seasoned heavy 12-inch skillet and a pair of tongs.

Four 8-ounce tuna steaks, 1 1/2 to 2 inches thick
1/4 cup vegetable oil
Kosher or sea salt and freshly ground black pepper
4 scallions, trimmed and sliced very thin on a bias
1/2 cup Soy-Ginger Sauce (page 348)
1/2 cup Wasabi Lime Vinaigrette (page 177)

WORKING AHEAD
Prepare the sauces well in advance; both keep for days.

1. Place a well-seasoned heavy 12-inch skillet over high heat and heat it for 5 minutes.

2. Meanwhile, place the tuna steaks in a shallow dish and pour the oil over them. Turn to coat them evenly with the oil, and season them generously with salt and pepper.

3. With tongs, lift the tuna steaks one by one from the oil, letting excess oil drip back into the dish, and lower them into the hot pan. Do not reduce the heat. Sear on one side until nicely browned with slightly blackened edges, about 1 1/2 minutes. If you look at the side of the fish, you can tell the doneness: the color will change

from brilliant red to a beige-brown color. Once it has cooked up to about 1/3-inch from the bottom, turn the fish. (If you would prefer the fish to be medium-rare, let it cook longer on each side.) Pour any remaining oil in the seasoning dish into the skillet as you turn the fish, and sear the second side until well browned, about 1 1/2 minutes more. Transfer the tuna to a platter and garnish with the sliced scallions. Serve immediately, with the sauces on the side.

SERVES 4 AS A MAIN COURSE

SAUTÉED SOFT-SHELL CRABS WITH GARLIC AND PARSLEY

There are many ways to cook soft-shell crabs and there are dozens of different flavors that can be paired with them. My favorite is very simple: I sauté the crabs until crisp and make a foaming brown butter–garlic sauce to spoon over them. The flavors go beautifully together and the garlic doesn't overpower the flavor of the crab. To cook all the crabs at once, you will need two 10- or 12-inch sauté pans. Since the cooked crabs can get soggy quickly, it is important to serve them as soon as they are done.

Keep the side dishes simple. I recommend Baked Plum Tomatoes Gratinée (page 244) and plain rice. Spoon the rice onto the plates to soak up some of the crabs' juices—they make the rice taste great.

For equipment, you will need sharp kitchen shears or a sharp chef's knife for cleaning the crabs, two heavy 10- or 12-inch sauté pans, and a pair of long tongs or a wide metal spatula.

8 **live medium soft-shell crabs (hotels or primes—see page 209)**
1 1/2 **cups whole milk**
1 1/2 **cups all-purpose flour**
Kosher or sea salt and freshly ground black pepper
6 **tablespoons peanut, canola, or other vegetable oil**
6 **tablespoons unsalted butter**
6 **garlic cloves, minced (2 tablespoons)**
Juice of 1/2 lemon
6 **sprigs fresh Italian parsley, leaves removed and chopped**

1. Clean the crabs as described on page 210.

2. Set two heavy 10- or 12-inch sauté pans over medium-high heat and heat for 5 minutes.

3. Meanwhile, pour the milk into a medium shallow bowl. Put the flour in a shallow bowl or pie plate, add about 1 tablespoon salt and 1/2 teaspoon pepper, and mix well. Spread out the flour.

4. Dip the crabs one by one into the milk, making sure to submerge each one completely, and then into the seasoned flour, making sure each is

evenly coated; set on a plate. Pour 3 tablespoons of the oil into each hot pan. Shake the excess flour off each crab and carefully lower them shell side down into the hot oil—stand back: the crabs will splatter and pop. Do not move or flip the crabs for about 4 to 5 minutes, at which point they will be cooked two-thirds of the way on the shell side. (Shake the pan gently after a couple of minutes to make sure the crabs are not sticking. If they are, loosen them with tongs or a spatula.) After 4 or 5 minutes, carefully flip the crabs (the shell side should be deeply browned), and fry on the second side for 3 minutes.

5. Transfer the crabs to dinner plates. Pour off the oil from both pans, and return one pan to the heat. Add the butter and let it bubble. As soon as it begins to brown, add the garlic. Let the garlic cook until it begins to brown and become fragrant. Squeeze the lemon juice into the pan and add the chopped parsley. Season with salt and pepper.

6. Spoon a little of the foaming garlic brown butter over each crab and serve immediately.

SERVES 4 AS A MAIN COURSE

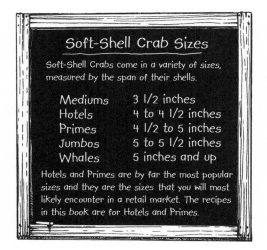

Soft-Shell Crab Sizes

Soft-Shell Crabs come in a variety of sizes, measured by the span of their shells.

Mediums	3 1/2 inches
Hotels	4 to 4 1/2 inches
Primes	4 1/2 to 5 inches
Jumbos	5 to 5 1/2 inches
Whales	5 inches and up

Hotels and Primes are by far the most popular sizes and they are the sizes that you will most likely encounter in a retail market. The recipes in this book are for Hotels and Primes.

Soft-Shell Crabs

Soft-shell crabs are blue crabs that have shed their shells and are, for the most part, completely edible. One of America's truly great delicacies, they are universally popular, and in May, when they come into season, soft-shell crabs appear on menus all across the United States. Even in New England, where lobsters are king, soft-shell crabs often outsell lobsters in my restaurants, especially at the beginning of the season. A few summers ago, I was visiting friends on Tilghman's Island, in Maryland, the heart of crab country. The first night was so hot that I couldn't sleep, so I went for a walk. I stumbled on a small soft-shell crab facility (I think it was called Harrison's) and met a gentleman who was tending the tanks. Since it is essential that the crabs are removed as soon as they shed, the business of harvesting soft-shell crabs is a twenty-four-hour-a-day operation. He had a lonely job and was happy to explain how they placed the hard-shell crabs in the tanks and then removed them individually as they shed.

How to Clean Soft-Shell Crabs

1. Be sure the crabs are alive and kicking. Rinse them under cold water.

2. With a pair of scissors, cut off the face of each crab about 1/3 inch behind the eyes. This will kill the crab. Squeeze behind the cut to push out the little balloon-like innards.

3. Turn each crab over and remove the apron (tail flap).

4. Lift the pointed ends of the shell and remove the gills by gently pulling them away from the body or by cutting them with a paring knife. As you do this, be careful not to knock off the legs.

Cutting off the face of a soft-shell crab

Removing the apron of a soft-shell crab

Cutting away the gills of a soft-shell crab

MOSTLY CRAB CRAB CAKES WITH ENGLISH MUSTARD SAUCE

To make great crab cakes, you need great crabmeat, and lots of it. The more crab in your crab cakes, the better they will be. The original American crab cake is from the Chesapeake region, where it is made with blue crab. Although there are many delicious varieties of crab, I still like cakes made with blue crabmeat the best. You can use any high-quality crabmeat in this recipe, but if you can afford blue crab, by all means try it. Blue crabmeat is sold as backfin lump or jumbo lump backfin, the latter being the best and most expensive. If you ever find yourself in Baltimore, stop by Faidley's at Lexington Market and try their crab cake—it is one of the best I have ever had. Peekytoe Maine crabmeat (from rock crabs) also makes a delicious crab cake.

Crab cakes are a bit expensive to serve for a main course; I prefer them as appetizer. Coleslaw is a traditional accompaniment and is really all that is needed, but a small green salad is also a nice accompaniment. If these cakes are made far in advance, they require less bread crumbs to hold their shape. The 1/4 cup of bread crumbs listed below is enough if you make the cakes 8 hours or more in advance. If you plan to cook them within 2 to 4 hours of making them, add another 2 tablespoons of crumbs. The recipe can be easily doubled.

For equipment, you will need a heavy 10-inch skillet and a wide metal spatula.

1   **pound lump blue crabmeat**
1/3   **cup Hellmann's mayonnaise**
1   **tablespoon Dijon mustard**
2   **teaspoons Old Bay seasoning**
1   **tablespoon fresh lemon juice**
1/4   **cup fine dry bread crumbs, or as needed (see headnote)**
1   **large egg, beaten**
1/2   **teaspoon freshly ground black pepper**
2   **scallions, trimmed and minced**
Kosher or sea salt
1   **cup all-purpose flour**
1/4   **cup peanut, canola, or other vegetable oil**
Lemon wedges and fresh parsley sprigs for garnish
English Mustard Sauce (recipe follows)

WORKING AHEAD

The cakes should be formed at least 2 hours before frying. It is actually best to make them 8 hours in advance, or even the day before.

1. Pick over the crabmeat and discard any bits of shells or cartilage, taking care to leave the crab pieces as large as possible.

2. Combine the mayonnaise, mustard, Old Bay seasoning, lemon juice, bread crumbs, egg, pepper, and scallions in a medium bowl and mix well. Add the crabmeat and fold gently with a rubber spatula to combine. The mixture will be loose and wet. Season it with salt if needed— that will depend on the crabmeat. Divide the mixture in half and then divide each half into 2 or 3 portions, to make 4 or 6 crab cakes. Shape

them into perfect round disks, about 1 inch thick. Place on a plate or in a baking pan and cover tightly with plastic wrap. Refrigerate for at least 2 hours, or, preferably, 8 hours or overnight.

3. To fry the cakes, set a heavy 10-inch skillet over medium heat and heat for 5 minutes.

4. While the skillet is heating, remove the cakes from the refrigerator. Spread the flour in a shallow bowl or pie plate and gently coat the crab cakes with flour, brushing off the excess. Add the oil to the skillet and lower the crab cakes into the skillet, so they are not touching. Cook, without turning, until golden brown on the first side, 3 to 4 minutes. Turn the cakes and cook on the other side until golden brown, about 3 minutes. (Because the thickness will be the same, the timing is the same for 4 or 6 cakes.)

5. Drain the crab cakes briefly on paper towels and serve immediately, garnished with the lemon wedges and parsley sprigs, and with the mustard sauce on the side.

MAKES 4 LARGE CRAB CAKES OR 6 SMALLER CRAB CAKES

ENGLISH MUSTARD SAUCE

Crab cakes are good with Tartar Sauce (page 344), Summer Shack Rémoulade (page 345), Creamy Mustard Sauce (page 127), or just plain with lemon wedges. However, if you really want to serve them with something special, make this mustard sauce. It is creamy, spicy, and tangy, with a hint of sweet and sour. Serve it on the side and let your guests decide how much to dollop on.

For equipment, you will need a small saucepan, a whisk, and a small sieve.

2   **teaspoons all-purpose flour**
1   **tablespoon Colman's dry mustard**
1   **teaspoon sugar**
3/4 **cup milk**
1   **tablespoon apple cider vinegar, or to taste**
Kosher or sea salt
Pinch of cayenne pepper
1   **tablespoon unsalted butter**

1. Combine the flour, dry mustard, and sugar in a small heavy saucepan, off the heat, and whisk together. Add 2 tablespoons of the milk and the vinegar and whisk until no lumps remain. Place the pan over medium heat and slowly add the remaining milk, whisking to incorporate. Bring to a simmer over medium-low heat, whisking frequently, about 5 minutes. Simmer 5 additional minutes to cook out the starchiness of the flour.

2. Season the sauce with salt and the cayenne pepper. Taste for seasoning—you may want to add a little more vinegar. Remove from the heat, whisk in the butter, and pour through a sieve into a warm sauceboat.

MAKES 2/3 CUP

SALT COD CAKES

People never seem to tire of this old-fashioned dish made with dried salt cod and potatoes. The unique, pungent flavor of salt cod may be an acquired taste, but once you get it, you can't get enough. Today preparing salt cod is not a necessity, as it was in the days before refrigeration, yet it is still produced in large quantities, because people love it.

In New England, cod cakes are usually served with baked beans and Tartar Sauce, resulting in an array of aromas and flavors that stirs the soul. It is true American comfort food. It is also customary to have cod cakes for breakfast. Panfry some smoky bacon, then panfry the cod cakes in the bacon fat and serve the cod cakes with the strips of bacon. You can serve an egg with the cakes if you like and, if you are really hard-core, "refried" baked beans (reheated left-over beans).

Boneless salt cod is usually packed in 1-pound boxes. This recipe uses half a pound, so you can freeze half to make these again, or double the recipe.

For equipment, you will need a 2-quart saucepan, a potato ricer or food mill, an 8-inch skillet, a 10- to 12-inch skillet, a well-seasoned cast-iron 12-inch skillet or 12-inch nonstick skillet, a slotted spoon, and a wide metal spatula.

8   ounces boneless salt cod
2   medium Yukon Gold, PEI, or other all-purpose potatoes (12 ounces), peeled and cut into quarters
4   tablespoons unsalted butter
1/2 small onion, minced (1/4 cup)
1   teaspoon Colman's dry mustard
1   large egg, lightly beaten
4   drops Tabasco sauce
1/4 cup panko crumbs (Japanese bread crumbs)
1/4 teaspoon freshly ground black pepper
1   cup all-purpose flour
2   tablespoons peanut, canola, or other vegetable oil
1/2 cup Tartar Sauce (page 344)
Lemon wedges

WORKING AHEAD

The salt cod should be soaked for a minimum of 6 hours, or as long as overnight, before you start making the recipe. The cakes can be formed in the morning, then covered and refrigerated until ready to fry. They can also be made the night before and cooked in the morning for breakfast.

1. Place the salt cod in a large bowl in the sink and run cold water into the bowl for 5 minutes. Fill the bowl with fresh cold water, cover, and refrigerate for at least 6 hours, changing the water once during the soaking. You can soak the fish overnight if you wish.

2. Place the potatoes in a 2-quart saucepan and cover with water (unsalted). Bring to a boil and simmer until they are very tender,

about 15 minutes. Drain well and pass through a food mill or potato ricer into a bowl. Cover the mashed potatoes and set aside (do not refrigerate).

3. Heat 2 tablespoons of the butter in an 8-inch skillet over medium heat until bubbling. Add the onion and sauté until golden brown, about 5 minutes. Remove from the heat and stir in the dry mustard.

4. Drain the salt cod, place it in a large skillet, and cover it with cold water. Cover the pan and bring the water to a simmer over low heat. Use a slotted spoon to break up the pieces of fish, starting with the thinner pieces: when they are cooked through, they will be pure white and will flake easily. Remove the pieces as they cook, and drain well.

5. Place the cod on a cutting board and chop until very finely shredded. Transfer to a mixing bowl and add the potatoes, onion-butter mixture, egg, Tabasco sauce, bread crumbs, and pepper. Stir lightly with a fork until well combined. The mixture will be thick and easy to handle. Taste for seasoning; it should not need salt unless the cod was soaked for too long. Divide the mixture into 8 portions. Shape into cakes about 3/4 inch thick and place on a plate. If not ready to cook the cakes, cover and refrigerate.

6. To fry the cakes, spread the flour in a shallow bowl or pie pan and dredge the cakes in the flour, knocking off the excess; place on a plate. Heat the oil and the remaining (2 tablespoons) butter in a 12-inch well-seasoned cast-iron or nonstick skillet over medium heat until bubbling. Add the cakes and cook, without turning, until golden brown on the first side, about 3 minutes. Turn the cakes and cook on the other side until golden brown, about 3 minutes. Serve with the tartar sauce and lemon wedges.

MAKES 8 CAKES

PERFECT PANFRIED BREADED FISH

The age-old method of breading fish *à l'anglaise*, also called standard breading, is one of the perfect ways to prepare a piece of fish. Creating an airtight seal around a fillet with the breading means that, in essence, the fish steams in its own juices, bringing out the natural flavors. It's simple: dredge the seasoned fillets in flour, dip in an egg wash, and dredge in bread crumbs. The same breading can be used for chicken, pork, and shrimp, as well as most fish fillets, which can then be deep-fried or panfried. I prefer panfrying breaded fish fillets because it means I can use some butter in the cooking. When properly executed, this technique will bring out the true flavor of the fish, with only the mild, buttery crunch of the breading to complement it.

Because you add fat when you panfry the fish, lean fish are especially suited to this preparation. The fillets you use can be naturally thin, such as flounder or fluke, baby cod or haddock, silver hake, or small snapper, or you can make thin portions from larger fillets by cutting them on the bias so they are no thicker than 3/4 inch. Large cod or haddock, halibut, striped bass, and grouper are all lovely when breaded and panfried.

No sauce or relish is needed for this dish, but I like to serve a lightly dressed green salad and maybe a couple of slices of ripe tomato on the same plate. The fresh flavors mingle delightfully. Serve lemon wedges on the side. Because of the pure flavor of fish cooked this way, the choice of side dishes is almost limitless.

For equipment, you will need 3 shallow bowls or pie plates, a wire rack, a baking sheet, a well-seasoned 12-inch cast-iron skillet, and a slotted spatula.

2   **large eggs**
1/4 **cup whole milk**
2   **cups all-purpose flour**
2   **cups panko crumbs (Japanese bread crumbs) or fresh white bread crumbs**
Four 8-ounce skinless fish fillets, no thicker than 3/4 inch (see headnote for suggestions)
Kosher or sea salt and freshly ground black pepper (or Spiced Seafood Salt, page 168)
3   **tablespoons vegetable oil, or as needed**
3   **tablespoons unsalted butter, or as needed**
Lemon wedges and fresh parsley sprigs for garnish

1. Crack the eggs into a large shallow bowl, add the milk, and beat well. Spread the flour and the crumbs in two separate bowls or pie plates. Set a wire rack over a baking sheet.

2. Season the fish fillets on both sides with salt and pepper (or spiced salt). Dredge one fillet in the flour, then lift it out, knocking off the excess, and place it in the egg wash, making sure that the entire fillet is coated. Remove the fillet from the egg wash, letting the excess drip off, and place in the crumbs. Gently press the crumbs onto the fish on both sides, coating it completely. Transfer the breaded fillet to the cooling rack, and repeat the process with the remaining fillets.

3. Place a well-seasoned 12-inch cast-iron skillet over medium-high heat and heat for 5 minutes. Add the oil and butter to the skillet. Sprinkle a few crumbs into the pan to test the temperature—they should sizzle when they hit

the fat. Lower the fish fillets into the hot fat, which should come halfway up the sides of the fish. As soon as the crumbs begin to darken, turn the heat down a bit. The key is even cooking, so that when you turn the fillets, they are a perfect golden brown. This will take about 3 to 4 minutes per side; the thicker the fish, the more slowly you should cook it—turn the heat down a bit more if necessary. Turn the fillets and cook for another 3 to 4 minutes, until golden brown. Add a little more oil and butter to the pan if it appears dry.

4. Using a slotted spatula, transfer the fish to individual plates or a platter. Serve garnished with lemon wedges and sprigs of parsley.

SERVES 4 AS A MAIN COURSE

ALMOND AND PARMESAN BREAD CRUMBS

Although this might sound Italian, it isn't. Italians rarely combine cheese and seafood. This recipe is mine and I make no apologies for the combination—it's absolutely scrumptious. The flavors of the almonds and Parmesan cheese are subtle and don't overpower the fish. True Italian Parmesan cheese has an earthy flavor that is both sweet and pungent. It is much more complex than the many similar styles of cheese that are available. Please don't compromise—only the imported stuff will do.

Substitute this mixture for the bread crumbs in the recipe above and use olive oil or a combination of olive oil and butter for panfrying. Serve the crisp almond-Parmesan fried fish with lemon wedges and sliced tomatoes, or, for a real treat, make my Portuguese Salad (page 135) and serve it alongside.

1/2 **cup coarsely chopped sliced almonds**
  2 **ounces Parmigiano-Reggiano, grated (1/2 cup)**
1/2 **cup panko crumbs (Japanese bread crumbs)**
  2 **tablespoons minced fresh Italian parsley**
1/2 **teaspoon kosher or sea salt**
1/4 **teaspoon freshly ground black pepper**

1. Combine all the ingredients in a medium bowl and stir well. Store in an airtight glass jar in the refrigerator. The crumbs will keep for up to 3 weeks.

MAKES 1 1/2 CUPS

PORTUGUESE-STYLE PANFRIED HAKE

Silver hake, called whiting in some regions, is a true member of the cod family, of which only cod, haddock, pollock, and hake are legitimate members. Lean and flaky, this flavorful fish is very popular among the Portuguese community, who are brilliant seafood cooks. You could substitute small cod or haddock in this recipe, but if you can purchase hake, I highly recommend that you do.

The hake is coated in cornmeal and panfried in olive oil. You make a quick sauce with onions, peppers, tomatoes, and olives in a separate pan, and then spoon the sauce around the fish when it is cooked. Although the dish is somewhat similar to a seafood stew, it is less intense, with lighter flavors, and, because the fish is cooked separately, it keeps its natural flavor. The combination is magic. Serve with Home Fries (page 221) or plain rice.

For equipment, you will need a 3-quart saucepan, an 8- to 10-inch skillet, a 12- or 14-inch well-seasoned cast-iron skillet, and a slotted spatula.

FOR THE SAUCE

- **2** medium ripe tomatoes (12 ounces)
- **3** tablespoons olive oil, preferably Portuguese
- **2** dried bay leaves
- **3** whole allspice berries, cracked and finely chopped
- **3 to 4 cloves garlic, minced**
- **1** medium green bell pepper (6 ounces), cored, seeded, and thinly sliced
- **1** medium onion (6 ounces), thinly sliced
- **1/4 cup dry white wine**
- **1/2 cup small black Portuguese or Niçoise olives, pitted and rinsed**
- **Kosher or sea salt and freshly ground black pepper**

1/4 cup olive oil, preferably Portuguese
Four 6- to 8-ounce skinless hake fillets
Kosher or sea salt and freshly ground black pepper
- **2** cups cornmeal

WORKING AHEAD

The sauce for this dish needs to be very fresh and light and therefore cannot be made ahead. However, you can prepare the tomatoes well in advance, and you can cut the vegetables and pit the olives for the sauce up to 4 hours ahead.

1. Fill a medium saucepan with water and bring it to a boil over high heat. Fill a medium bowl with ice and water. Score an X in the base of each tomato with a small paring knife. Blanch the tomatoes in the boiling water just until the skin splits, about 30 seconds. Plunge them into the ice water to stop the cooking,

then drain and peel them. Cut the tomatoes lengthwise in half. With a small spoon, remove the seeds and pulp. Cut the tomatoes into 1/3-inch-wide strips (julienne); there will be about 1 1/2 cups. Set aside.

2. Start the sauce about 15 minutes before you want to serve the fish; start heating a 12-inch well-seasoned skillet for the fish over medium heat when you begin the sauce. Place an 8- to 10-inch skillet over medium-high heat and add the 3 tablespoons olive oil and the bay leaves. Cook the bay leaves until they are lightly browned, 2 to 3 minutes. Add the allspice and garlic and cook for 30 seconds, stirring constantly. Add the bell pepper and onion and sauté, stirring frequently, until the vegetables are golden, about 5 minutes. Add the tomatoes, white wine, and olives and simmer until the sauce is fragrant and has thickened slightly, about 5 minutes. Season with salt and pepper and remove from the heat.

3. Meanwhile, just before you add the tomatoes to the sauce, add the 1/4 cup olive oil to the hot large skillet. Quickly season the fillets on both sides with salt and pepper. Spread the cornmeal in a shallow bowl and, one at a time, dredge the fillets in the cornmeal, pressing to make the cornmeal adhere and then gently shaking off the excess. Work quickly, and put each fillet into the hot oil as you prepare it. As soon as the cornmeal begins to darken, turn the heat down a bit. The key is even cooking, so that when you turn the fillets, they are a perfect golden brown. This will take about 3 to 4 minutes per side; the thicker the fish, the more slowly you should cook it—turn the heat down a bit more if necessary. Turn the fillets and cook for another 3 to 4 minutes, until crisp and golden brown.

4. Using a slotted spatula, transfer the fish to individual plates or a platter. Spoon a small amount of the chunky sauce over each fillet and spoon the rest around the fish. Serve immediately.

SERVES 4 AS A MAIN COURSE

FRIED PEPPERS WITH GARLIC AND OLIVE OIL

*L*ong, thin pastel-green frying peppers, also called Italian peppers or cubanelle peppers, panfried in olive oil with lots of garlic, are one of my favorite summer foods. There is more than one variety of frying pepper, but they are not distinguishable at the market. Some are mild, some are mildly spicy. Colors range from pale yellow to green, or, once in a while, a darker shade of green. However, they all cook the same and their taste is similar. The skin is very thin, so unlike bell peppers, there is no need to roast and peel them. I like to make big batches of these, because they will keep for over a week refrigerated; feel free to double or triple this recipe. The peppers should be served at room temperature. They make a great side dish for grilled fish, steak, or lamb. They are also wonderful as part of an antipasto, in a salad, or as a condiment for sandwiches.

For equipment, you will need a 12-inch cast-iron skillet, a slotted spoon, and a pair of tongs.

8 **frying peppers, about 8 inches long**
1/4 **cup olive oil, or as needed**
8 **cloves garlic, thinly sliced**
Kosher or sea salt and freshly ground black pepper
Approximately 2 tablespoons extra virgin olive oil (the good green stuff)

1. Trim the tops and bottoms from the peppers and halve them lengthwise. Remove the seeds.

2. Heat the olive oil in a 12-inch cast-iron skillet over medium-low heat. Add the garlic and toast it, stirring frequently, until fragrant and golden brown, about 3 to 4 minutes. With a slotted spoon, transfer the garlic to a small plate and set aside (leave the oil in the pan).

3. Arrange a layer of peppers skin side down in the skillet, flattening them slightly with tongs to expose as much of their surface to the heat as possible, then add the remaining peppers skin side down over the first layer. Cover the pan and lightly brown the bottom layer of peppers over medium heat, without turning them or lifting the lid, about 5 minutes. Uncover the skillet and rearrange the peppers with the tongs so that the peppers that were on top are now on the bottom. Cover the skillet and cook the peppers for another 5 minutes. Move the peppers around again so they cook and brown evenly, cover, and cook for another 5 minutes. At this point the peppers should be starting to become tender. Turn the heat up to medium and leave the peppers uncovered. Set a large shallow bowl or

soup plate next to the stove. As the peppers become soft and nicely colored, remove them and place in the bowl. Once you have a layer of peppers in the bowl, season with salt and pepper and sprinkle with some of the toasted garlic chips. Continue layering and seasoning the peppers as they brown until they are all cooked; scatter any remaining toasted garlic over them. Pour the olive oil that remains in the pan over the peppers, cover them very loosely with plastic wrap, and let them cool to room temperature.

4. When the peppers are completely cool, move them around to be sure the garlic is evenly dis-tributed. Taste a pepper and adjust the salt and pepper if necessary to your liking. The peppers will be immersed in their own juices and the olive oil they were cooked in; if necessary, add a little more olive oil so the liquid just barely covers the peppers. Drizzle the good green extra virgin oil over the peppers. Refrigerate the peppers, uncovered, until cold. Once they have chilled, cover tightly with plastic wrap. They will keep for up to 10 days refrigerated. Take out of the refrigerator at least 1 hour before serving.

SERVES 4 TO 6 AS A SIDE DISH

HOME FRIES

Whether you eat them with eggs, fish, or meat, or by themselves, there's nothing like crisp home-fried potatoes. One of the greatest of all comfort foods, home fries, laden with bits of caramelized onion, are easy to make and a great way to use up leftover potatoes. This recipe calls for Yukon Gold potatoes, which make terrific home fries, but you can use any all-purpose (medium-starch) or boiling potato (low-starch), such as Red Bliss new potatoes. The only potatoes that don't make great home fries are baking potatoes—they are too mealy. If using leftover potatoes, ideally they are cooked through, soft on the outside, yet still firm in the center. When you cook potatoes especially for home fries, it is easy to achieve this perfect texture.

For equipment, you will need a 4- to 6-quart pot, a 12-inch cast-iron skillet, and a spatula.

2 **pounds Yukon Gold potatoes (4 large potatoes)**
Kosher or sea salt
2 **tablespoons unsalted butter**
1 **medium onion (4 ounces), cut into 1/4-inch slices**
Freshly ground black pepper
1/4 cup vegetable oil

WORKING AHEAD

If you want home fries for breakfast, you must cook them the day before. Follow Steps 1 and 2, and you are ready for the morning. If you have leftover potatoes, start with Step 3.

1. Scrub the potatoes and cut them lengthwise in half. (If you are using smaller potatoes, leave them whole.) Place them in a large pot and add enough cold water to cover them by 2 inches. Add 2 teaspoons salt, cover, and bring to a boil over high heat. Simmer for 10 minutes, and check for doneness—they should be very firm in the center.

2. When they are ready, drain the potatoes and rinse under cold running water to stop the cooking. Refrigerate until they are completely chilled.

3. Melt the butter in a 12-inch cast-iron skillet and add the onion. Sprinkle with salt and pepper and sauté until tender and golden brown, about 5 minutes.

4. Meanwhile, peel the skin off the potatoes and slice crosswise into 1/2-inch-thick slices.

5. When the onions are cooked, transfer them to a bowl, along with the butter, and wipe out the skillet with paper towels. Place the skillet over medium-high heat and heat for 5 minutes.

6. Add the oil to the hot pan. When it is smoking hot, add the potatoes, season them with salt and pepper, and fry, turning them as they brown, for 5 minutes. Turn the heat down to medium and continue to cook until the potatoes are crisp and browned on both sides, about 10 to 12 minutes.

7. Add the onions with the butter, and cook for a few minutes more until the onions darken along with the potatoes. Check the seasoning and serve immediately.

SERVES 4 TO 6 AS A SIDE DISH

BLACK BEANS AND RICE

This is a very special Caribbean rice dish with different versions from island to island. It has a wonderful bean flavor throughout, because the rice is cooked in the dark liquid left from cooking the beans. Serve this with grilled or jerked (see page 170) fish or chicken, panfried or fried fish, or roast chicken or pork.

The recipe makes a good amount, but leftovers will keep in the refrigerator for 3 days and can be easily reheated in a microwave or warm oven.

For equipment, you will need a 3-quart saucepan, a 10-inch skillet, and a slotted spoon.

1 **cup black beans, soaked in cold water to cover generously for at least 6 hours, or overnight**
1 **tablespoon vegetable oil**
6 **ounces meaty salt pork, rind removed and cut into 1/4-inch dice (1 cup)**
2 **cloves garlic, thinly sliced**
1 **large Spanish onion (about 14 ounces), sliced 1/4 inch thick**
1 **large green bell pepper (8 ounces), cored, seeded, and cut into 1/2-inch dice**
Freshly ground black pepper
2 **teaspoons chopped fresh thyme or 1 teaspoon dried thyme**
1/2 **teaspoon ground cumin**
1 **tablespoon tomato paste**
2 **cups jasmine rice, rinsed and drained**
Kosher or sea salt

1. Drain the beans and pick them over for shriveled or broken beans or small stones. Bring 6 cups of water to a boil in a medium saucepan over medium-high heat. Stir in the beans, lower the heat, and simmer, partially covered, until the beans are tender, 45 minutes to 1 hour. Remove from heat and cool slightly.

2. While the beans are cooking, place the oil and diced salt pork in a 10-inch skillet and cook the pork over medium heat, stirring frequently, until most of the fat has been rendered and the meat is crisp and golden, about 15 minutes. Using a slotted spoon, transfer the salt pork to a small bowl and reserve. Add the garlic, onion, green pepper, and 1/2 teaspoon pepper, to the skillet and sauté over medium-low heat until the onion is tender and golden, 7 to 10 minutes. Stir in the thyme, cumin, and tomato paste, cover, and set aside.

3. When the beans are cooked, drain in a colander set over a bowl, and transfer them to a bowl or baking dish. Cover to keep warm. You should have 4 cups of cooking liquid—if you are short, add enough water to equal 4 cups. Set aside.

4. Pour the bean cooking liquid back into the same pot and bring to a simmer over medium-high heat. Stir in the rice, cover, and reduce the heat to very low. Cook, without stirring, until the rice is tender and has absorbed the liquid but is not dry, about 20 minutes. Remove from the heat and let stand, covered, 5 minutes.

5. Combine the cooked rice, beans, onion and pepper mixture, and pork cracklings in a large bowl and stir lightly to combine. Add salt and pepper to your liking. Transfer to a serving dish and serve without delay.

MAKES ABOUT 2 QUARTS; SERVES 10 TO 12 AS A SIDE DISH

PAN-ROASTED WHOLE FLOUNDER OR FLUKE WITH BROWN BUTTER, LEMON, AND CAPERS

If you or a friend catch a few nice medium-sized flounder or fluke, you owe it to yourself to cook some on the bone—it is by far the best way to experience the full flavor and juiciness of the fish. This is a special dish, beautiful to behold and perfect for a quiet dinner for two (see the color photo). The only problem is that you can only cook one fish in each pan. You could cook one fish and serve it as a first course for two people. Or, if you have two suitable pans, you can cook two fish at the same time and make a starter for 4 or a main dish for 2. If you decide on the latter, serve it with boiled new potatoes and a green vegetable or salad.

The hardest part of this recipe is skinning the whole flounder, so if you didn't catch your own, ask your fish market to do it for you.

For equipment, you will need a 12-inch well-seasoned cast-iron skillet, an 8-inch skillet, and a long metal spatula.

One 1- to 1 1/2-pound whole fluke or flounder, preferably skinned by the fish market (see headnote)
3/4 cup all-purpose flour
Kosher or sea salt and freshly ground black pepper
1/4 cup vegetable oil
4 tablespoons unsalted butter
1 tablespoon fresh lemon juice
1 tablespoon capers, rinsed
1 tablespoon chopped fresh Italian parsley

1. If necessary, skin the fish: Start by cutting off the head. Then make a little V-cut at the tail in order to loosen the skin enough to get a firm grip on it. Peel the skin back far enough to get your thumb under the loose skin. To prevent slipping, hold a towel in your hand as you grip the skin. In one strong, swift motion, pull the skin away from the tail—it should come off in one piece. Flip the fish over and remove the skin from the other side. Then trim the small bones away from the sides of the fish, and remove the roe sac (if any) and any viscera from the cavity. If necessary, cut off the tail of the fish so that it will fit into your pan. Rinse and dry the fish. Keep refrigerated until you are ready to cook.

2. Adjust a rack to the lower third of the oven and preheat the oven to 400°F.

3. Place a 12-inch well-seasoned skillet over high heat and heat for 5 minutes. Meanwhile, spread the flour in a large shallow bowl or a baking dish. Sprinkle the fish generously with salt and pepper and dredge it in the flour, turning it well to coat; shake gently to remove the excess.

4. Add the oil to the hot skillet. Lower the fish into the skillet and reduce the heat to medium-high (at this point, you should start cooking the butter; see step 5). Brown the fish on one side without turning, about 4 minutes. Turn the fish and immediately place the skillet in the oven. Roast until the fish is pure white and firm to the touch, about 8 minutes. Transfer the fish to a platter and keep warm.

5. Meanwhile, as soon as the fish goes into the pan, place the butter in an 8-inch skillet and melt it over medium-low heat. Reduce the heat to low and cook the butter gently until it browns—keep an eye on it, but let it cook undisturbed until it is nutty brown. This will take about 8 minutes (about the same time it takes to cook the fish). When the butter is nutty brown, remove the skillet from the heat and immediately add the lemon juice, capers, parsley, and a pinch of salt. Pour the still-foaming butter into a sauceboat or serving bowl and spoon just a bit over the fish.

6. Present the fish at the table and allow a minute for your guest to admire it. To fillet the fish, hold an ordinary tablespoon upside down at the center of the fish, near the head, and loosen the top fillet, pushing out from the center of the fish. The bones on a flounder are very strong and won't pull away with the meat. You should have no problem removing the two fillets on the top side. Transfer them to a dinner plate. Flip the fish over and repeat with the two remaining fillets. Spoon the brown butter over the fish and enjoy this special treat, noticing how much more flavorful fish is when cooked on the bone.

SERVES 2 AS A FISH COURSE OR 1 AS A MAIN COURSE

PAN-ROASTED LOBSTER WITH TOMATOES, BUTTER, AND HERBS

Pan-roasted lobster is a dish I created more than twenty years ago, and it became famous because of its close association with my late friend Julia Child, through her cooking shows, her biography, and her dozens of visits to Jasper's and then Summer Shack, where she almost always ordered it. I was inspired by watching Chinese cooks chop up lobsters and then stir-fry them in a wok. I modified the technique and infused classic French flavors: wine, shallots, chervil, chives, and butter. At Summer Shack, we still serve the dish exactly the same way as I did the day I first put it on the menu at Jasper's in 1984, but during August and September, I also offer this version, which features ripe tomatoes and fresh herbs. You have a choice of using mint or sweet basil in the sauce—both are terrific, and each adds its own special nuance, but don't try to use them together.

For equipment, you will need a 3-quart saucepan, a coarse strainer, a Chinese cleaver or large chef's knife, a heavy ovenproof 14-inch skillet, a pair of tongs (if you don't have a 14-inch skillet, use two 9- or 10-inch pans).

2 ripe medium tomatoes (12 ounces)
2 live hard-shell lobster, 1 1/2 to 1 3/4 pounds each
Kosher or sea salt and freshly ground black pepper
2 tablespoons olive oil, or as needed
2 medium shallots, finely chopped
1/4 cup dry white wine
4 tablespoons unsalted butter, cut into hazelnut-sized pieces and chilled
2 tablespoons chopped fresh mint or basil

WORKING AHEAD

You can prepare the tomatoes, dice the shallots, and chop the herbs, hours ahead, but you must cut up the lobster only minutes before you cook it.

1. Fill a medium saucepan with water and bring it to boil over high heat. Fill a medium bowl with ice and water. Score an X in the base of each tomato with a small paring knife. Blanch the tomatoes in the boiling water just until the skin splits, about 30 seconds. Plunge them into the ice water to stop the cooking, then drain and peel them. Quarter the tomatoes lengthwise. With a small spoon, remove the seeds and pulp and transfer the pulp to a coarse strainer set over a glass measuring cup. Press on the pulp with a ladle or spoon to extract the juices—there should be about 1/4 cup juice. Cut the tomatoes into 1/2-inch dice and combine with the juice in a bowl. Set aside.

2. Adjust an oven rack to the middle position and preheat the oven to 500°F.

3. Using a Chinese cleaver or large chef's knife, chop off the front of each lobster's head about 1 inch back from the tip (rostrum); this will kill the lobster instantly and will also remove the inedible head sac. Split each lobster lengthwise in half. Separate the knuckle and leg sections by twisting or by cutting them away with a knife. Chop the lobster halves in half where the carcass and tail meet. If either lobster contains roe, remove it, along with the green tomalley; discard half of the tomalley and transfer the remainder, and any roe, to a small bowl. Break into small pieces with a fork, cover the bowl with plastic wrap, and reserve.

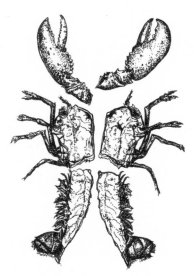

Lobster cut into 6 pieces for pan-roasting

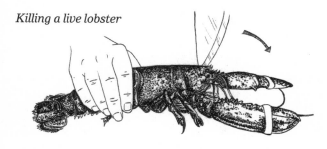

Killing a live lobster

4. Place a heavy ovenproof 14-inch skillet over high heat and heat for 5 minutes (or use 2 pans). Meanwhile, season the lobster pieces very lightly with salt and pepper.

5. Add the oil to the hot skillet. Put the lobster claws in first and, using tongs to move them around, cook them in the oil for about 1 minute. Add the remaining pieces shell side down and use the tongs to roll and press the shells into the hot fat to sear them evenly. If the pan gets dry, add a little more oil. Sear until the shells are bright red, about 2 minutes. Add the shallots, spreading them out in the bottom of the pan. Turn the lobster pieces so the shell sides are facing up. Add the tomalley (and roe) to the skillet and place it in the oven. Roast until the shells are lightly browned or a bit charred, about 4 to 5 minutes.

6. Remove the skillet from the oven and set it over high heat. Using an oven mitt to protect your hand and forearm, add the wine and the tomatoes, with their juices and simmer over high heat until the juices thicken slightly, about 2 minutes. Stir with a wooden spoon to loosen any particles stuck to the bottom of the pan, remove the pan from the heat, and, using tongs, quickly transfer the lobster to a platter, arranging the pieces shell side down.

7. Add the butter and mint to the sauce and stir until the butter has emulsified and the sauce has a creamy consistency, then season with salt and pepper to taste. Spoon the sauce over the roast lobster pieces and serve immediately.

SERVES 4 AS AN APPETIZER OR 2 AS A MAIN COURSE

BROILED BUTTERFISH WITH MIRIN GLAZE

Butterfish are small round fish that are tasty and luscious, with a melt-in-your-mouth texture because of their high fat content. (Remember, fatty fish are high in beneficial omega-3 acids, which can reduce cholesterol and the incidence of heart attacks.) A whole fish only weighs between 4 and 6 ounces; they can be cooked whole or filleted. Although butterfish are abundant on the East Coast, they are rarely offered as a retail item because so few people know what to do with them—the majority of the catch is shipped to Japan. But you can ask your fish market to get butterfish, which shouldn't be much trouble. Or, if you have an Asian market nearby, they just might have them. Once you try these fish, you will want to eat them often.

It may seem odd to fillet such a small fish, but because butterfish is so soft and tender, it is easier to eat if it has been filleted. The bone structure of a butterfish is similar to that of other round fish, just much smaller, but it is actually quite easy to fillet these little fish, using a sharp paring knife (follow the directions for filleting round fish on page 42). The skin is very thin and should be left attached; it will practically disappear during broiling. And you don't have to fuss over any small bones that might have been missed, because they will melt in your mouth with the fish. The best way to handle these small fillets is to bend each one, like a wave, and put a wooden skewer through the two crests—this will help to hold the fish together as it cooks.

Butterfish cooks very quickly (only about 2 minutes under the broiler), during which time I like to brush the fillets with a glaze made from mirin (a sweet sherry-like Japanese wine used for cooking) mixed with a little soy sauce. The salty, sweet, and exotic flavors of this combination make for a wonderful appetizer, one that will excite your taste buds. The small size and the richness of the butterfish also sets it apart as a very special appetizer. For an interesting variation, substitute the Maple Lemon Glaze (page 179) for the mirin glaze.

For equipment, you will need a baking sheet, preferably nonstick, bamboo skewers (soaked in water for at least 1 hour), a small saucepan, a whisk, a small skillet, a pastry brush, and a thin spatula.

8	small or 4 large butterfish (about 2 pounds), filleted (have the fish market do this, or see page 42)
3	tablespoons peanut or other vegetable oil
1/2	cup mirin
1/4	cup light soy sauce
	A pinky-tip-sized piece of fresh ginger
1/4	teaspoon freshly ground white or black pepper
1	teaspoon cornstarch, mixed with 2 teaspoons water
1	tablespoon sesame seeds
4	ounces tat tsoi, watercress, or baby spinach
	Kosher or sea salt
2	scallions, trimmed and thinly sliced on a bias

All the preparation of this dish up to the point where the fish is broiled can be done earlier in the day. Keep the glaze at room temperature.

1. Brush the fillets on both sides with 2 tablespoons of the oil. Thread the butterfish onto skewers (see the headnote above): If you are using small butterfish, put 2 fillets on each skewer and serve 2 skewers per person. If you are using larger fish, put 2 fillets on each skewer but serve only 1 skewer per person. Place the skewers on a baking sheet, preferably nonstick, and refrigerate.

2. To make the glaze: Combine the mirin and soy sauce in a small saucepan over low heat. Use the flat side of your knife to smash the fresh ginger, and add that to the pan along with the pepper. Heat slowly to a simmer, then stir in the cornstarch mixture (slurry) and simmer, stirring, for another minute. Whisk in the remaining 1 tablespoon oil and remove from the heat. Let the glaze cool to room temperature, and remove the ginger.

3. Toast the sesame seeds in a small skillet over low heat for about 2 minutes, until they begin to darken. Remove from the heat.

4. Set an oven rack about 8 inches from the heat source and preheat the broiler to 550°F, or as high as it will go.

5. To cook, place the baking sheet of skewers under the broiler for about 30 seconds. Remove the pan and gently brush the top of the fish with the mirin glaze. Place the butterfish back under the broiler and broil for another minute for small fillets or up to a minute longer for larger ones. Remove from the heat.

6. Lightly season the tat tsoi with salt and arrange in the centers of four small plates. Using a spatula, gently place the fish skewers over the greens—be careful with the fish, as it is very delicate. Lightly glaze the skewers again, letting a bit of the glaze drip onto the greens. Sprinkle with the sliced scallions and toasted sesame seeds and serve immediately.

SERVES 4 AS AN APPETIZER

BROILED BLUEFISH WITH GARLIC BUTTER

This is one of the very best bluefish preparations I know. Small bluefish are terrific on the grill, but larger fish (over 8 pounds) can be too fatty and flaky to grill—baking or broiling is best. For large bluefish, I cut skin-on portions from fillets and score the top of the bluefish with a sharp knife to allow it to cook more evenly. As the bluefish broils, it creates contrasts in color that make the fish look very special. (Don't use this technique on other fish, though, except maybe a fatty salmon, because scoring a leaner fish would tend to dry it out.) Then I melt garlic herb butter over the fish, so it seeps into the cracks and adds great flavor. Bluefish and garlic were meant for each other.

For equipment, you will need a basting brush, a heavy rimmed baking sheet or shallow roasting pan, and a large metal spatula.

Four 8-ounce skin-on bluefish fillets
1   tablespoon olive oil
Kosher or sea salt and freshly ground black pepper
8   thin slices Garlic Herb Butter (page 352), cool
Lemon wedges and fresh parsley sprigs for garnish

1. Adjust the broiler rack to about 6 inches from the heat source and preheat the broiler. For easy cleanup, line a heavy rimmed baking sheet or roasting pan with aluminum foil.

2. Using a sharp knife, score diagonal incisions in each direction to create a crosshatch pattern in the skin of each fillet (see the color photo): Make them about 1/2 inch deep in the thickest part of the fillet and 3/4 inch apart. Pour the olive oil onto the baking sheet and place the fillets on the pan. Season them with salt and pepper as you turn to coat them in the oil. Leave them skin side down on the pan.

3. Place the baking sheet under the broiler and broil the fillets for 6 minutes. Remove from the broiler and place 2 medallions of butter on top of each fillet. Return to the broiler and cook for 2 to 3 minutes more, until the fish is firm and the tops of the fillets are well colored and a little crisp. If you're uncertain whether the fish is done, use a paring knife to peek into the center of the thickest part of one fillet. Transfer to plates, using a spatula, and garnish with lemon wedges and parley sprigs. Spoon the butter and juices in the broiling pan over the fish, and serve immediately.

SERVES 4 AS A MAIN COURSE

SCALLOP AND BACON HORS D'OEUVRES

ere is a timeless combination that is always a crowd pleaser at cocktail parties. This is a great way to serve scallops without splurging on them for a main course. My version of this classic uses a pinch of fresh thyme, which tastes lovely with the sweet scallops and smoky bacon. I roll the scallops and bacon in crumbs before I bake them. As they bake, the fat from the bacon soaks into the crumbs, giving them a nice crunch and extra bacon flavor.

For equipment, you will need 20 wooden toothpicks, a baking sheet, and a pastry brush.

1   **pound medium sea scallops (16–20 per pound)**
Kosher or sea salt and freshly ground black pepper
4   **sprigs fresh thyme, leaves removed and chopped (1 tablespoon)**
10 **slices thin-sliced bacon (about 8 ounces), cut crosswise in half**
1   **cup panko crumbs (Japanese bread crumbs) or fine fresh bread crumbs**
About 3 tablespoons olive oil

WORKING AHEAD
The scallops can be seasoned and wrapped in the bacon hours before cooking. They should be rolled in crumbs at the last minute.

1. Prepare the scallops by picking over them for pieces of shell and removing the straps (the muscle attached at the side). Place them in a bowl and season them with salt, pepper, and the thyme. Wrap a half slice of bacon snugly around each scallop so it overlaps slightly and secure with a toothpick, inserting it through the bacon overlap at the center of the scallop and out the other side. The scallops can be cooked now or refrigerated until ready to cook.

2. Adjust a rack to the middle of the oven and preheat the oven to 450°F. Line a baking sheet with parchment paper or aluminum foil, and set aside.

3. Put the bread crumbs in a food processor and pulverize them until very fine. Place in a shallow bowl.

4. Brush each scallop lightly with olive oil and roll in the crumbs, pressing it gently into the crumbs so they adhere, and place on the baking sheet. Put the pan in the hot oven and bake for 5 to 6 minutes, until the bacon is crisp and the crumbs turn golden brown. Place on a platter and serve.

MAKES 16 TO 20 HORS D'OEUVRES

BAKED OYSTERS "CASINO"

Owning a restaurant in a casino (Summer Shack at Mohegan Sun), it is always tempting to come up with new versions of the classic clams casino. My baked oysters are made with garlic, peppers, and bacon—all typical ingredients—but I use only a small amount of garlic, so the oysters aren't overpowered. And instead of bell pepper, I prefer the richer, spicier flavor of roasted poblano chile, which together with the cinnamon and corn bread give this version nuances of the American Southwest. The bacon cooked on top is traditional. It adds smokiness and rounds out the flavors of the oysters.

There is no need to purchase fancy cultivated oysters on the half-shell for baking (although it won't hurt). Better to save a little money and buy bluepoints, Falmouths, Watch Hill, or other wild oysters—they are usually a little larger than cultivated oysters, which is good for baking. The topping in this recipe will make enough for 16 large oysters or 20 slightly smaller ones; serve 4 or 5 oysters each as an appetizer.

For equipment, you will need an oyster knife, a small skillet, and a baking sheet. You will also need plenty of rock salt to steady the oysters as they bake and to use in the presentation.

16   **large or 20 medium to large oysters, scrubbed**
4   **tablespoons unsalted butter**
2   **cloves garlic, minced (1 teaspoon)**
1   **large shallot, finely diced (2 tablespoons)**
1/4   **teaspoon ground cinnamon**
1/2   **cup finely diced roasted (see page 136) poblano or Anaheim pepper**
Freshly ground black pepper
1/2   **cup coarsely ground dried corn bread (i.e., coarse crumbs)**
4   **slices thin-sliced bacon**
At least 2 cups rock salt
4   **lime wedges**
4   **big sprigs of fresh Italian parsley or watercress**

WORKING AHEAD
The oysters can be assembled a couple hours in advance and kept refrigerated. Pull them out 10 minutes before you want to cook them.

1. Carefully shuck each oyster (see page 50), cutting the abductor muscle, so the oyster is not attached to the shell, leaving the oysters on the half-shell. Pour the oyster juices into a cup and reserve. As you shuck the oysters, place them on a baking sheet lined with rock salt, to keep them level.

2. Melt the butter in a small skillet over medium heat. Add the garlic and shallot and sauté for 5 minutes, or until soft. Stir in the cinnamon and then the oyster juices, roasted poblanos, and black pepper to taste. Bring to a boil, and remove from the heat. While the mixture is still warm, fold in the corn bread crumbs.

3. When the mixture has cooled a bit, use a teaspoon to distribute it evenly among the oysters. Cut the bacon strips into 4 or 5 pieces each, depending on whether you have 16 or 20 oysters, and put a piece of bacon on top of each oyster. Refrigerate the oysters until you are ready to bake them.

4. Place a rack in the upper third of the oven and preheat the oven to 450°F. Line four serving plates with rock salt.

5. Place the sheet of oysters in the oven and bake for 8 to 10 minutes, until the bacon is crisp and the oysters are bubbling. Place 4 or 5 oysters on each plate, garnish each with a lime wedge and sprig of parsley, and serve immediately.

SERVES 4 AS AN APPETIZER

BOSTON BAKED SCROD

Scrod is one of the most famous seafood dishes in New England, and yet if you ask five people what it is, you will get at least three different answers. The term *scrod*, sometimes spelled *schrod*, is used in the fish business to market the smallest cod, 3 to 5 pounds, which is also called baby cod. But if you cook baby cod in any way other than baked or broiled with bread crumbs, then it isn't scrod. And some people contend that scrod simply means "fish of the day." Amid all the confusion, there is plenty of room to personalize this dish. My version uses baby cod or small haddock, topped with slices of ripe tomato and a buttery cracker crumb topping. The tomato certainly isn't traditional, but I like the way it brightens the flavor of the mild fish. When tomatoes are out of season, omit them.

This is a mild-flavored dish that goes well with many sides. If you want to continue the Boston theme, serve it with Summer Shack Coleslaw (page 140) and Succotash Salad (page 138). If you want to keep it easy, a green salad and/or fresh green vegetables along with boiled new potatoes will round out the meal nicely.

For equipment, you will need a basting brush, a baking sheet, and a large metal spatula.

WORKING AHEAD

The buttery crumbs can be made well in advance and kept refrigerated or frozen. Pull them out an hour before you start the recipe and let them come to room temperature.

4   skin-on baby cod or small haddock fillets, about 8 ounces each
About 3 tablespoons vegetable oil
Kosher or sea salt and freshly ground black pepper
2   ripe medium tomatoes, thinly sliced
1   cup Buttery Crumbs (recipe follows)

1. Adjust an oven rack to the middle position and preheat the oven to 375°F. Brush a baking sheet with oil.

2. Place the fillets skin side down on the sheet pan. Brush the tops lightly with the oil and sprinkle them with salt and pepper. Layer the tomato slices over the fillets, overlapping them slightly. Sprinkle each piece of fish with 1/4 cup of the crumbs and pack the crumbs lightly with cupped hands to cover the fish.

3. Place the fish in the oven and bake until the fish feels very firm and the crumbs have turned golden brown, about 12 minutes. If you're uncertain about whether the fish is cooked through, use a paring knife to peek into the center of one fillet—it should be pure white all the way through.

4. Use a large spatula to carefully transfer the baked scrod to dinner plates. The fish is very flaky and will break easily. Serve immediately.

SERVES 4 AS A MAIN COURSE

BUTTERY CRUMBS

If you don't have a food processor, you can make the cracker crumbs by putting the crackers in a 2-quart zip-lock bag, sealing the bag, and crushing them with a rolling pin. These crumbs can be used for other baked dishes as well, such as Baked Plum Tomatoes Gratinée (page 244).

One 6-ounce box oyster crackers
8 sprigs fresh Italian parsley, leaves removed and coarsely chopped (3 tablespoons)
4 sprigs fresh thyme, leaves removed and chopped (1 tablespoon)
1/2 teaspoon kosher or sea salt
1/4 teaspoon freshly ground black pepper
8 tablespoons (1 stick) unsalted butter, melted and cooled

1. Place the oyster crackers in a food processor and pulse until they are fairly fine, with pieces no larger than 1/4 inch. Transfer the crumbs to a large bowl. Add the chopped parsley, thyme, salt, and pepper and stir to combine. Drizzle in the melted butter and mix well with a rubber spatula so all the crumbs are coated with butter.

2. Transfer the crumb mixture to a tightly sealed glass jar container and refrigerate or freeze until ready to use. The crumbs can be refrigerated for up to 2 weeks or frozen for up to 1 month.

MAKES ABOUT 2 CUPS, ENOUGH FOR 8 PORTIONS OF SCROD

PLANK-ROASTED SALMON (OR BLUEFISH)

Plank-roasted salmon is an impressive, sensual dish that has enormous visual appeal and delivers a most exotic aroma of cedar, herbs, and fish. It is actually quite easy to prepare, as long as you are willing to take a trip to Home Depot or a lumber supply company. Native Americans baked fish on cedar planks in hot boxes, which were placed next to an open fire to capture the heat—much more exotic than a baking sheet and an oven, but basically the same thing. At our Summer Shack at Mohegan Sun in Connecticut, a Native-American–owned resort and casino, we often serve dishes inspired by the heritage of the Mohegan tribe. Most often we serve salmon planked, but I love freshly caught bluefish on a plank as well. Watercress, one of the wild greens that is common to the Native American diet, is an appropriate garnish. The filé powder in the herb rub is made from sassafras, another favorite of the original Americans.

I usually buy planks at Home Depot, where they have always been happy to cut them to the size I request. Cedar is not usually pressure-treated (which uses toxic substances), but you should always ask—you must make this dish only with pure untreated cedar planks.

For equipment, you will need a plank of untreated cedar, 8 to 10 inches wide by 12 to 14 inches long and about 3/4 inch thick (you can reuse the plank three or four times, until it no longer exudes the beautiful cedar fragrance); you will also want to have a heatproof platter or wooden mat, or a large trivet, to place the hot plank on when you serve it.

1/4 **cup vegetable oil**
1 1/2 to 2 **pounds skinless salmon or bluefish fillet in one piece from a 5- to 6-pound fish**
Kosher or sea salt and freshly ground black pepper
Herb Rub for Planked Fish (recipe follows)
1 **bunch watercress, trimmed**
Lemon wedges

WORKING AHEAD
You can sand and oil the plank as much as a day ahead. You can also make the herb rub up to 1 day in advance.

1. With fine sandpaper, lightly sand the cedar plank. Wipe it well with a dry towel and then rub it on both sides with 3 tablespoons of the vegetable oil.

2. Adjust an oven rack to the middle position and preheat the oven to 400°F.

3. Rub the top of the cedar plank with the remaining 1 tablespoon vegetable oil. Season the bottom (the skinned side) of the fish with salt and pepper and lay it in the center of the plank. Rub the surface of the fish with the herb rub.

4. Place the plank in the oven, directly on the oven rack. Bake until the fish is very firm to the touch and cooked through to the center: 20 to 25 minutes for salmon, 25 to 30 minutes for bluefish. (If the fillet is thicker than 1 inch, it will take a little longer.)

5. Remove the plank from the oven and place it on a platter or trivet. Garnish with the watercress and lemon wedges and serve family-style. When you dish it up, place the watercress on the plate first and then put the hot fish on the cress to wilt it.

SERVES 4 AS A MAIN COURSE

HERB RUB FOR PLANKED FISH

It is best to make this at least a few hours in advance to allow the flavors to expand and combine.

1   teaspoon filé powder
1   teaspoon chili powder
One large sprig of fresh tarragon, leaves removed and coarsely chopped (1 teaspoon)
4 to 6 sprigs fresh thyme, leaves removed and coarsely chopped (2 teaspoons)
6   large sprigs fresh Italian parsley, leaves removed and coarsely chopped (3 tablespoons)
3   scallions, trimmed and coarsely chopped
2   tablespoons vegetable oil
1   teaspoon kosher or sea salt, or to taste
1/4   teaspoon freshly ground black pepper, or to taste

1. Combine the filé powder, chili powder, tarragon, thyme, parsley, and scallions in a food processor and pulse to mix about ten 2-second pulses.

2. With the machine running, add the oil, and process until the mixture forms a wet paste. Add the salt and pepper and pulse again. Taste and season a little more if you like. Transfer the rub to a small bowl or plastic container, cover, and refrigerate until ready to use. The rub keeps for up to 2 weeks.

MAKES 2/3 CUP

SLOW-ROASTED WHOLE FISH WITH ONION AND FENNEL STUFFING

When I catch a striped bass, as I often do in July and August, this is my favorite way to cook it for friends and family. I have also made this dish with cod, salmon, bluefish, and smaller fish such as black sea bass and red snapper, with tasty results. The presentation of a whole fish, like a whole turkey, creates a primal sense of joy. The dish is easily put together and you have about 1 1/2 hours after the fish goes into the oven to prepare the rest of the meal. Since I usually serve this with simple accompaniments like fresh green vegetables, salad, rice, or Home Fries (my favorite—page 221), there is plenty of time for relaxing with a glass of wine before dinner.

I almost always add a little chouriço, linguiça, or other spicy sausage to my stuffing. Any of these adds a pleasant kick and a new dimension to the flavor, but they are not essential, because it is the moisture from the onions that makes the fish so juicy and tender. If you omit the sausage, use a couple of tablespoons of butter instead, as described below.

The proportions of ingredients and the timing given in this recipe are for a 6- to 8-pound fish. You can cook a fish as big as 12 pounds—larger than that and it probably won't fit in your oven. A 6-pound fish will take about 1 hour and 15 minutes to cook, an 8-pound fish about 1 hour and 30 minutes. For larger fish estimate 12 to 15 minutes per pound. For smaller fish like snapper or haddock, in the 4- to 5-pound range, reduce the cooking time to about 1 hour.

For equipment, you will need a 10-inch skillet, a large roasting pan, and two large spatulas.

1 6- to 8-pound striped bass or other whole fish (see headnote), cleaned and scaled
6 tablespoons olive oil or vegetable oil, plus a little for drizzling
3 medium cloves garlic, minced
2 small onions (8 ounces), thinly sliced
1 fennel bulb (8 to 10 ounces), branches and tough outer sections removed, fronds reserved for garnish
1 tablespoon minced thyme (leaves from 4 to 6 sprigs)
6 ounces Portuguese chouriço, linguiça, or other spicy dry sausage, casings removed and cut into 1/3-inch dice (optional)
2 tablespoons butter if not using sausage
2 tablespoons minced chives or scallions
1/2 bunch Italian parsley, leaves removed and chopped (1/2 cup)
2 ounces hard dry crackers, such as common crackers, oyster crackers, or pilot crackers, coarsely crumbled or chopped (about 3/4 cup)
Kosher or fine sea salt and freshly ground black pepper
1 lemon, cut into wedges

WORKING AHEAD
You can make the stuffing the morning of the day you plan to serve the fish. Cover and refrigerate. Pull the stuffing out of the refrigerator about an hour before you stuff the fish and let it come to room temperature.

1. Run the back of a knife over the fish to make sure all the scales have been removed. Using kitchen scissors or a sharp knife, cut off all the fins. Rinse the fish inside and out to remove any blood. Dry it on paper towels, wrap it in plastic, and refrigerate until ready to cook.

2. Heat 3 tablespoons of the oil in a 10-inch skillet over medium heat. Add the garlic, onions, fennel, and thyme and sauté, stirring frequently, until the vegetables are tender and beginning to brown, about 10 minutes. Add the diced sausage, if using, and sauté until the sausage is fragrant, about 1 minute more. Or, if you are not using sausage, add the butter and stir to melt. (The butter is comparable to the amount of fat the sausage would add and is essential to the recipe.) Remove the skillet from the heat and cool slightly.

3. Add the chives, parsley, and cracker crumbs. Season to taste with salt and pepper and mix to combine. The stuffing will be fairly loose. Set aside.

4. Adjust an oven rack to the lower position and preheat the oven to 325°F. Rub the bottom of a large roasting pan with 1 tablespoon of the olive oil.

5. Remove the fish from the refrigerator and rub the outside with the remaining 2 table-spoons olive oil. Season it generously with salt and pepper. Spoon the stuffing into the fish's cavity and place the fish in the roasting pan. Drizzle it with a little more olive oil.

6. Cover the roasting pan loosely with alu-minum foil, place in the oven, and roast for 45 minutes. Remove the foil and baste the fish with its pan drippings. Continue to roast uncovered for 15 minutes, then baste again with pan drip-pings. Roast 15 minutes more, then remove from the oven and turn up the heat to 450°F.

7. To check for doneness, slip a knife into the thickest flesh of the fish to see if it is opaque. If the fish isn't done, return the roasting pan to the oven, turn down the temperature to 375°F, and roast for an additional 10 to 15 minutes. Once it is done, return the fish to the 450°F oven for 5 minutes to crisp the skin. Remove the fish from the oven and let it rest for 5 min-utes. Turn off the oven and place a platter in it to warm.

8. Transfer the fish to the warm platter with two spatulas. Garnish the platter with lemon wedges and the reserved fennel fronds, and present the fish whole. To serve, slide a large serving spoon between the backbone and the top fillet to loosen the fillet. Serve each portion with a spoonful of the stuffing and a piece of the crisp skin. After the top fillet has been served, pull the frame of bones away to expose the bot-tom fillet. Warn your guests to be on the lookout for pin bones—it is impossible to serve a whole fish without getting a few.

SERVES 6 TO 8, DEPENDING ON THE SIZE OF THE FISH; FIGURE ON 1 PORTION PER POUND OF WHOLE FISH

CARIBBEAN "JAMMED" CRABS

In parts of the Caribbean, stuffed, or deviled, crab backs are called "jammed" crabs. Don't take the name literally—the stuffing should be put into the crab backs loosely so they are not heavy when baked. This dish offers the lovely aroma of Caribbean spices, such as nutmeg and clove, as well as the scent of fresh thyme and toasted coconut. You have the option of making it spicy with one chile or very spicy with two chiles, the latter being most authentic. Serve this with Black Beans and Rice (page 222) and some wedges of watermelon to cool down the spice. You might like to start the dinner off with a glass of Petite St. Vincent Rum Punch (page 339) or Jamaican beer.

To make this dish, you will need 8 crab backs (shells) from large blue crabs, large rock crabs, or medium Jonah crabs. Call your seafood market ahead, as they might need to special-order the crab backs for you. You can use lump or jumbo lump crabmeat from blue crabs, leg and body meat from rock crabs, or, as long it is a good-quality mix (at least 50 percent leg and claw meat), Jonah or snow crabmeat. Snow crab meat will have to be cut into 3/4-inch chunks.

For equipment, you will need 8 empty crab shells (backs), a 10-inch skillet, an 8-inch skillet, and a 12 by 18-inch baking sheet.

6 tablespoons unsalted butter
1/2 large onion (3 ounces), cut into 1/4-inch dice (1 cup)
1 small red bell pepper, cut into 1/4-inch dice (3/4 cup)
1 or 2 Jamaican bird chiles or Thai chiles, seeds removed and finely minced
1 1/2 teaspoons minced fresh thyme
2 teaspoons Caribbean Spiced Salt (page 169)
1/2 teaspoon freshly ground black pepper
1 pound crabmeat (see headnote), picked over for shell or cartilage, legs cut into 3/4-inch chunks (if using snow crab)
1 tablespoon dark rum
2 large eggs, beaten
1/4 cup unsweetened coconut milk or heavy cream
Juice of 1 large lime
1/2 cup unsweetened flaked coconut
1/3 cup minced fresh chives
1 1/2 cups panko crumbs (Japanese bread crumbs)

WORKING AHEAD

The dish can be prepared up through Step 4 in the morning and refrigerated. Remove the crab backs from the refrigerator 30 minutes before baking.

1. Heat 3 tablespoons of the butter in a 10-inch skillet over medium heat until bubbling. Add the onion, bell pepper, chile peppers, and thyme and sauté until the vegetables are tender, about 4 minutes. Remove from the heat and stir in the seasoned salt and pepper. Let the mixture cool.

2. Adjust an oven rack to the middle position and preheat the oven to 375°F.

3. Place the crabmeat in a large bowl. Add the cooled vegetables, the rum, eggs, coconut milk, lime juice, 1/4 cup of the coconut, the chives, and 1 cup of the bread crumbs and mix gently.

4. Divide the filling equally among the 8 crab backs; do not compress it. Arrange them on a large baking sheet.

5. Heat the remaining 3 tablespoons butter in a small skillet over medium heat until bubbling. Add the remaining 1/2 cup bread crumbs and stir to coat them with butter.

6. Spread the bread crumbs evenly over the crab backs, then sprinkle the remaining 1/4 cup coconut over them. Bake until the filling is heated through and the bread crumbs are deep golden brown, about 20 minutes.

SERVES 4 AS A MAIN COURSE

BAKED STUFFED ROCK LOBSTER TAILS

althought I've written a book about American lobster, I'm really not a snob about rock lobsters. The two species are not very closely related, so if you forgo comparisons and enjoy rock lobsters for what they are—tasty, firm fleshed, white, and sweet, with a flavor similar to shrimp—you are in for a treat. Because it is illegal to buy or sell rock lobster in Massachusetts, where I have lived for almost thirty years, my experience with rock lobster is somewhat limited. But I have cooked enough rock lobsters in Florida and the Caribbean to know that you need to cook them gently, whether they are steamed, broiled, grilled, or baked.

In this recipe, I stuff the lobster tails with buttery onions, celery, and aromatics, bound with a minimal amount of crumbs. I don't stuff them in order to stretch them and get a bang for my buck—I stuff them to add moisture, which protects the tails from drying out and toughening. But I make a tasty stuffing chock-full of extra lobster meat. I don't normally use sweet onions for cooking, but in this recipe, it is the moisture, not the pungent flavor, I want from the onion. If you can't find sweet onions from Vidalia (Georgia), Florida, Texas, or Hawaii, buy the freshest, mildest onion you can find.

For equipment, you will need a 2-quart saucepan, an 8-inch skillet, a roasting pan, a pastry brush, and a large metal spatula.

5   **rock lobster tails, 5 to 6 ounces each, preferably fresh**
8   **tablespoons (1 stick) butter**
1   **small clove garlic, finely minced (1 teaspoon)**
A pinky-tip-size piece of fresh ginger, peeled and finely minced (1 teaspoon)
1/2   **small sweet onion (2 ounces), cut into 1/4-inch dice**
1   **small stalk celery (1 1/2 ounces), cut into 1/4-inch dice**
1/4   **teaspoon freshly grated nutmeg**
1/2   **cup panko crumbs (Japanese bread crumbs)**
4   **sprigs fresh Italian parsley, leaves removed and coarsely chopped (2 tablespoons)**
Kosher or sea salt and freshly ground black pepper

WORKING AHEAD

The lobster tails can be stuffed as much as 4 hours in advance and kept refrigerated. Remove them from the refrigerator 20 minutes before you bake them.

1. Fill a small saucepan with lightly salted water and bring to a boil. Add 1 lobster tail (in the shell), reduce the heat, and simmer for 5 minutes. Remove the pan from the stove and let the lobster tail steep in the hot water for another 5 minutes.

2. Drain the lobster tail, cut lengthwise in half, and remove the meat. Clean the meat of any intestinal tract, and cut the lobster into 1/3-inch dice. Place in a small mixing bowl.

3. Melt 4 tablespoons of the butter in an 8-inch skillet over medium heat. Add the garlic, ginger, onion, and celery and sauté until the vegetables are beginning to soften, about 4 minutes. Remove from the heat and stir in the nutmeg. Let the mixture cool a bit.

4. Add the onion mixture, with the butter it was cooked in, to the diced lobster meat, then add the panko crumbs and chopped parsley. Season with salt and pepper. Toss only enough to distribute all the ingredients evenly.

5. Set an oven rack in the middle position and preheat the oven to 350°F. Bring a small pan of water to a boil.

6. Meanwhile, place the remaining 4 lobster tails shell side down on a cutting board. With a sharp knife, split each tail lengthwise, without cutting completely through the bottom shell; try to crack the shell a little as you press down. Now take each lobster tail in both hands and pry it open. Remove the intestinal tract. Season the meat, still inside the tail shells, very lightly with salt and pepper. Place the lobster in a roasting pan.

7. Divide the stuffing evenly among the cavities of the 4 tails. Do not pack the filling down—just press lightly so it stays in place. Melt the remaining 4 tablespoons butter and, using a pastry brush, glaze the top of the stuffing and any exposed lobster with butter.

8. To bake the lobsters, place the baking pan on the oven rack and carefully pour the boiling water into the pan so it comes up about 1/2 an inch; don't let the water splash onto the lobsters. (The hot water helps to prevent the lobster meat from sticking to the shells.) Bake for about 20 minutes. To check for doneness, peek under the stuffing at the thickest end of a tail—the meat should be pure white. Serve immediately.

SERVES 4

Rock lobster tail split for stuffing

BAKED PLUM TOMATOES GRATINÉE

Baked plum tomatoes are a terrific vegetable to serve with simple grilled foods, because they do double duty as a side dish and as a stand-in for a sauce. Whether you are serving plain grilled swordfish or a sirloin steak, I think you will find this summer dish delicious and useful. Use only ripe tomatoes. You can substitute other small tomatoes for the plum tomatoes, but they should be meaty and firm even when ripe—soft slicing tomatoes won't hold up for this recipe.

For equipment, you will need a 12 by 15-inch baking sheet, a wire rack that fits over it (you can omit the rack, but it helps to dry the tomato and intensify the flavor), and a shallow 1-quart baking dish.

2 1/2 pounds ripe plum tomatoes, halved lengthwise
1/2 cup Buttery Crumbs (page 235)
2 garlic cloves, finely minced
2 tablespoons very thinly sliced (chiffonade) fresh basil
2 tablespoons olive oil
1/2 teaspoon kosher or sea salt, or to taste
1/4 teaspoon freshly ground black pepper, or to taste

WORKING AHEAD

You can roast and season the tomatoes in the morning, then top them with the crumbs and bake just before dinner. The crumbs can be prepared a few days in advance or even up to a month ahead and then kept frozen.

1. Adjust an oven rack to the middle position and preheat the oven to 500°F.

2. Set a wire rack on a small baking sheet and lay the tomato halves cut side down on the rack (the fit will probably be snug). Roast until the skins curl back and have black splotches, about 10 minutes. Remove the tomatoes from the oven and cool slightly. Reduce the oven temperature to 400°F.

3. Meanwhile, toss the crumbs with the garlic; set aside.

4. While the tomatoes are still on the rack, pull the skins off, then lift each half from the rack and remove the seeds by running your index finger up both sides of the center section. Place the tomato halves in a medium bowl, add the

basil and olive oil, and season with the salt and pepper. Stir to combine.

5. Turn the tomatoes into a shallow 1-quart baking dish and sprinkle evenly with the bread crumbs. Bake until the crumbs are brown and the filling is bubbly, about 20 minutes.

SERVES 4 AS A SIDE DISH

INSIDE THIS CHAPTER

The Basics of Deep Frying
(Fry Cook 101)   249

Crispy Fried Seafood
(Master Recipe)   250

Dry Mixes for Deep-
Frying   252

New England–Style
Fry Mix   252

Southern-Style Fry Mix   253

Fried Ipswich Whole
Belly Clams   254

Fried Oysters   255

Fried Scallops   256

Shack-Style Fried Fish
Fillets   257

Fried Smelts   258

Fried Grouper Fingers   259

Crispy Fried Soft-Shell
Crabs   260

Fried Shrimp   261

Special Deep-Fried
Recipes   262

Spicy and Greasy Rhode
Island Calamari   262

Box: How to Clean Whole
Squid   265

Beer-Battered Fish and
Chips   266

Boardwalk French Fries   268

Clam Cakes (Fritters)   270

Jasper's Fried Chicken   272

Seasoned Salt for
Chicken   273

Box: How to Cut a
Chicken into Ten Pieces   274

Summer Shack Corn
Dogs   276

Great Sandwiches   278

Classic Maine Lobster
Roll   278

Clam Roll   279

Jersey Shore Tuna Sub   281

Tuna Salad   282

Sausage Sandwich,
Loaded   283

Hot Dogs   285

Jersey Shore Italian
Hot Dogs   286

Italian Pepper and Potato
Stew   287

Quick Onion Chili   287

-8-

CRISPY FRIED FOODS AND OTHER FUN STUFF

BOARDWALK AND SHACK FAVORITES

$\mathcal{I}$ have always lusted for food sold from carts and stands on boardwalks, at county fairs, at city festivals, outside ballparks, at New England clam shacks, at beachside cafés in Florida, and at jerk shacks in the Caribbean. I am fearless when it comes to eating street foods, and I am almost always impressed with the way the folks who sell those foods can make things taste so great with so little space and equipment. I grew up at the Jersey Shore, where my siblings, friends, and I could visit boardwalks on a regular basis. Of course we all loved to eat fried food—what kid, or adult, for that matter, doesn't?

This chapter is about my favorite shack-style fried foods and shore-style sandwiches. Most of these dishes are served at Summer Shack quite often, if not every day. When people leave New England, the thing they seem to miss the most (other than their families) is real fried clams. Crisp, deep-fried belly clams are a favorite with many New Englanders, maybe even more so than lobster. Although most people don't often cook fried clams (see page 254), fish and chips (page 266), or Rhode Island–style calamari (page 262) at home, it isn't as intimidating as it might seem—it is actually very simple. I was surprised one recent Thanksgiving by how many people told me that they had successfully deep-fried their turkeys. That's heavy-duty frying. Frying seafood or chicken is much more manageable—try it, and see for yourself.

This book, like the Summer Shack menu, is full of healthy dishes, but they aren't on the top of my agenda for this chapter. Fried foods, by definition, cannot be viewed as light or healthful—but the truth is that they certainly don't have to be greasy. It is all in the technique. And while I don't expect that you will heat up a deep fryer as often as you fire up your grill, I will explain how to make deep-frying a very special treat.

The fried foods and sandwiches that follow prove that culinary greatness comes in many forms and is often disguised by its lack of pretense. These dishes may appear humble and simple, but as you bite into the thin crispy crust of a great fried clam, oyster, scallop, or shrimp and the flavor explodes on your palate, the experience is amazing. So take off your watch and roll up you sleeves—it might get a little messy, but I promise it will be fun, and the results crisp and delicious.

THE BASICS OF DEEP-FRYING (FRY COOK 101)

When deep-fried foods are cooked perfectly, they are a thing of beauty. The foods are crisp, not greasy, and their flavor is intensified, because what deep-frying really does is to allow the breading to create a total seal around the food so it steams in its own juices. Deep-frying enhances the natural flavor of ingredients as no other cooking technique does.

The fried seafood in this chapter is cooked "shack-style," which I define as using a simple breading that consists of dipping the food in buttermilk and then dredging it in a dry mix. This should be done at the last minute, right before the food is fried. The goal is to make the fried food crispy and light. A "standard breading" (flour, then egg wash, then crumbs), also called *à l'anglaise* is a more traditional restaurant-style type of breading and makes a heavier coating than shack-style; I prefer to use that type for panfrying (see page 215).

Here are some important rules for successful deep-fat-frying.

1. **Always use clean high-quality oil.** Use oil that has a high tolerance for heat and won't break down or start smoking at high temperatures. If you don't have a peanut allergy, refined peanut oil is a great choice. It has a very clean flavor and a high burning point, which means that it can be heated to high temperatures without breaking down. High-quality canola oil is also good for deep-frying and is readily available. Corn oil is perfect for frying dishes like hush puppies and corn fritters, where corn or cornmeal is the predominant flavor. Grapeseed oil is excellent but very expensive.

2. **You can reuse the oil for frying at least one or two times.** That is, as long as you strain it through a coffee filter or cheesecloth after each use. When the oil darkens to brown or starts to smoke at around 325°F or so, discard it.

3. **Carefully bread the foods to be fried at the last minute.** Whether you are using the shack-style combination of buttermilk and fry mix for breading or the standard breading described above, it is extremely important that the foods be breaded as close to the time you are going to cook them as possible—no more than 5 minutes ahead. If the food is breaded too far ahead, the breading will become wet and adhere to it, which could result in breaking the seal created by the breading—and, in turn, allowing the hot oil to get inside the breading. It is also important that when you bread the foods, you make sure that every part of the item is coated, so the oil will touch breading only, never the food.

4. **Do not overcrowd the fryer.** Whether you are using an electric fryer or a heavy pot, if you put too much food in at once, bad things will happen. The foods touch and either stick together and/or break the seal the breading has created around the food. Even worse, the temperature drops to a point that is too low to seal the breading, and instead the breading absorbs the oil.

5. **Always handle fried foods gently.** When you are dredging foods in fry mix or bread crumbs, don't shake them hard. And don't move the food around when you first drop it in the oil—give it 15 to 20 seconds before you stir the pot (so to speak) to prevent the food from sticking

together, and then stir it occasionally so that it cooks evenly.

6. **Drain the food before you serve it.** When you lift the food out of the hot fat, using a Chinese wire-mesh skimmer (my favorite) or a slotted spoon, let it drain over the pot, then place on a pan or tray lined with paper towels and let the paper absorb the excess oil. Gently transfer the fried food to a plate or platter and serve hot.

CRISPY FRIED SEAFOOD (MASTER RECIPE)

For equipment, you will need a 4- to 5-quart Dutch oven and a deep-frying thermometer or an electric deep fryer, a Chinese wire-mesh skimmer or a pasta basket, a pair of tongs, and a baking sheet.

For the average dinner for 4, where you will fry about 1 1/2 pounds of seafood, you will need:

> About 6 cups peanut, canola, or other vegetable oil for deep-frying
> 1 cup buttermilk
> 2 cups New England or Southern-Style Fry Mix (page 252 or 253), depending on the type of seafood

1. In many cases, you will be frying in batches to avoid the problems that can happen if you overcrowd your fryer. In anticipation of this, line a baking sheet with paper towels and preheat the oven to 250°F.

2. Heat 3 inches of oil to the desired temperature (see chart on page 253) in a 4- to 5-quart Dutch oven over medium heat or in a deep fryer.

3. While the oil is heating, pour the buttermilk into a large bowl, and put the fry mix in another. Drop the seafood into the buttermilk and stir gently. Using a Chinese wire-mesh skimmer or a pasta basket, carefully lift up a small batch (in this case, about half of the seafood you are frying), allowing the excess buttermilk to drip back into bowl, then drop the seafood into the fry mix and gently toss it to coat evenly with the mix. Quickly dry off the skimmer.

4. When the oil is hot, lift the food out of the fry mix with the skimmer, gently shake off the excess, and drop it carefully into the oil. Try to spread the food out in the pot so there is less chance of the pieces sticking to each other. The first few moments are crucial: let the seafood cook for 15 to 20 seconds without moving the seafood (or the fryer basket)—if you do, some of the breading could fall off, making the dish greasy. Then stir the seafood so that it cooks evenly. This also helps to loosen any pieces that might have stuck together. If anything sticks to the bottom of the pot, loosen it with tongs. Stay right there at the fryer, moving the seafood occasionally so it cooks evenly, following the timing given in the chart on page 253.

5. Transfer the first batch of seafood from the hot oil to the paper towel–lined baking sheet to drain. You can keep the seafood warm in the oven while you fry the second batch, but with clams or oysters, you should consider serving them as soon as they have drained. Because they are whole creatures with wet innards, they tend to lose their crunch faster than shrimp, scallops, and other seafood. Set the food on a plate or platter and send it to the table with lemon wedges and parsley sprigs. A nice casual, and very appropriate, touch when serving fried foods is to serve it on deli paper or butcher's paper. At Summer Shack, we serve most of our fried foods on colorful deli paper printed with our logo—the paper isn't really intended to soak up excess oil, it's more to show off how greasy it isn't (see the color photo).

DRY MIXES FOR DEEP-FRYING

efore you get started with the many fried seafood dishes in this chapter, you will need a dry fry mix to coat the food. There is no need to make the mix the day you are frying—they both keep very well, almost indefinitely, when sealed in an airtight jar and refrigerated. I recommend you have at least one of these mixes on hand.

There are basically two types of East Coast (American-style) dry flour mixes for frying seafood. The first is the authentic New England–style mix, made with fine corn flour and all-purpose flour. It is fantastic for deep-frying small items, such as belly clams, shrimp, scallops, and smelts, but it can also be used for

pan-frying or deep-frying large pieces of fish. Because corn flour is not always readily available, I give you the option of substituting masa harina (very fine cornmeal) for the corn flour. Masa harina can be found in any Latin grocery store and in many regular grocery stores.

The second style of fry mix is from the Mid-Atlantic and the South, and it uses yellow cornmeal instead of corn flour. It is an all-purpose fry mix that is fine for frying shrimp and scallops, but I think it is especially good for fish fillets and larger pieces of seafood.

I recommend the type of mix that I prefer with each recipe, but for all intents and purposes, they can be used interchangeably.

NEW ENGLAND–STYLE FRY MIX

2   cups corn flour (or masa harina)
2   cups all-purpose flour
2   teaspoons fine sea salt or table salt
1   teaspoon freshly ground black pepper
1/2 teaspoon cayenne pepper

1. Combine the flours, salt, and both peppers in a large mixing bowl and mix well.

2. Store in an airtight glass container in the refrigerator for several weeks or more.

MAKES 4 CUPS

SOUTHERN-STYLE FRY MIX

2 1/2 cups all-purpose flour

1 1/2 cups yellow cornmeal

1 tablespoon finely grated lemon zest

1 teaspoon dried thyme

2 teaspoons freshly ground black pepper

1/2 teaspoon cayenne pepper

1/2 teaspoon kosher or sea salt

1. Combine the flour, cornmeal, lemon zest, thyme, black pepper, cayenne pepper, and salt in a large bowl and mix well.

2. Store in an airtight glass container in the refrigerator for up to several weeks.

MAKES 4 CUPS

Crispy Fried Seafood Cooking Times

NE = New England–Style Fry Mix   SO = Southern-Style Fry Mix

Species	Dry Mix	Temperature	Minutes
Belly Clams	NE	375	1 to 1 1/2
Oysters	SO	360	1 to 1 1/4
Scallops, medium	NE	360	2
Scallops, small	NE	375	1 1/2
Cape Scallops	NE	375	1
Fish Fillets	SO	350	4 to 5
Smelts	NE	375	2 to 3
Grouper (fingers)	SO	360	3
Soft-Shell Crabs	NE	360	3 1/2 to 4
Shrimp, 21 - 25	NE	360	3
Shrimp, 26 - 30	NE	360	2 1/2
Florida Rock Shrimp	NE	375	1 1/2
Popcorn Shrimp	NE	375	1
Squid	see page 262	360	1 1/2

FRIED IPSWICH WHOLE BELLY CLAMS

When people who are not from New England come to visit, they are looking for two things: lobster and fried clams. The town of Ipswich has become synonymous with fabulous fried clams, but the truth is that fried clams were invented at Woodman's, a shack in Essex, the next town over. Woodman's is a mecca for fried clam lovers, and it still lives up to its reputation. Back in Ipswich, the best place for fried clams is the ClamBox. During the summer, expect to stand in line at either of these clam shacks.

In the Ipswich-Essex region of Massachusetts, called Cape Ann (the "Little Cape," north of Cape Cod), there is an abundance of high-quality soft-shell clams, which are called steamers by most people. Whole belly clams, or fryer clams, are soft-shell clams that have been shucked, with the top of the siphon removed. To be honest, the soft-shell clams from Maine are just as good as those from Ipswich, but the big clam distributors are in Ipswich, so whether they are selling local clams or clams from Maine, they always seem to be called Ipswich clams—and they are all incredibly delicious. Clam strips, popularized by the Howard Johnson chain of restaurants, are strips of muscle from sea clams. They are tasteless in comparison to true belly clams. Belly clams used to be inexpensive, but in the last ten years they have become very pricey, selling for up to $15 a pint in the summer. The high prices have made clam strips more popular, but don't be misled—one has little to do with the other.

Specifics

Ask for medium-sized frying clams; small ones overcook easily and large ones can be tough. A pound of medium-sized clams equals about 60 clams. For appetizers, serve about 4 ounces per person; for a main course, serve 6 to 8 ounces per person. To re-create the classic shack-style fried clams, dip them in buttermilk and then dredge them in New England–Style Fry Mix (page 252). Deep-fry them in oil heated to 375°F, in batches if necessary. Stir after 15 seconds to prevent them from sticking together, then cook until lightly colored but crisp, 1 to 1 1/2 minutes. Because clams are very wet, they sizzle more loudly than most foods when fried. Listen closely, and when the sizzling becomes muted, pull the clams from the hot oil. Refer to the master recipe for fried seafood (page 250) for a more detailed explanation.

Serving Suggestions

Because fried clams get soggy faster than most fried foods, it is very important to serve them quickly. I recommend that you have bowls of Summer Shack Coleslaw (page 140) and Tartar Sauce (page 344) set out on the table. In addition to these two mandatory items, serve some other favorite salads and side dishes. Fry the clams in batches and send them to the table as they come out of the fryer. They cook very quickly, so it will be only a few minutes before the cook joins the table.

FRIED OYSTERS

ooked oysters can be a very tasty treat, especially deep-fried with a cornmeal crust. From the Mid-Atlantic down through the South, they are even more popular then fried clams. Most oysters that are sold shucked are wild. Some come from Cape Cod and other New England waters, but the bulk of them come from the Chesapeake and the Gulf of Mexico. These shucked oysters are milder than cultivated half-shell oysters, and less briny too. These plump sweet oysters are delicious served as an appetizer with Summer Shack Rémoulade (page 345) or in a sandwich as a po'boy (see below).

Specifics

Because shucked oysters come from wild stock, their size can vary widely. They are graded by size, but even then there is still some variation. At Summer Shack, we buy "standard" (medium) shucked oysters—about 35 per pound. For an appetizer, serve about 4 ounces per person; for a main course, serve 6 to 8 ounces per person. Dip the oysters in buttermilk and then dredge in Southern-Style Fry Mix (page 253). Deep-fry the oysters in oil heated to 360°F, in batches if necessary. Stir after 15 seconds to prevent them from sticking together, then cook until lightly colored but crisp, 1 to 1 1/4 minutes. Because oysters are very wet, they sizzle more loudly than most foods when fried. Listen closely, and when the sizzling becomes muted, pull them from the fryer. Refer to the master recipe for fried seafood (page 250) for a more detailed explanation.

Serving Suggestions

Unlike shrimp, fritters, or fish fillets, oysters and clams are whole creatures with wet innards. If they are not served right away, they can get soggy. I recommend that you have bowls of Summer Shack Coleslaw (page 140) and Summer Shack Rémoulade (page 345) set out on the table. In addition to these two mandatory items, serve some other favorite salads and side dishes. Fry the oysters in batches and send them to the table as they come out of the fryer. They cook very quickly, so it will be only a few minutes before the cook joins the table.

To make a Fried Oyster Po'Boy, cut a loaf of French bread into 6- to 8-inch sections, then split them open (not all the way through). Spread the bread with rémoulade sauce and add lettuce leaves, sliced tomatoes, and a few slices of pickles. Fill them with fried oysters and serve immediately.

FRIED SCALLOPS

Scallops are very versatile. They can be served raw, sautéed, stir-fried, grilled, broiled, or baked, and they can be paired with classic American flavors such as bacon and bitter greens, Provençal flavors like garlic and tomatoes, or Asian flavors like ginger and scallions. The greatest flavor of all, however, is the scallop itself and no other cooking technique delivers that pure flavor the way deep-frying does, which seals in all the juices and flavor. So the next time you see beautiful fresh medium or small scallops at the market, consider deep-frying them.

Specifics

Medium-sized bay or sea scallops (20–30 per pound) or even smaller sizes (30–40 per pound) are best suited for deep-frying. Large scallops are better for grilling or sautéing. The tiny but famous Cape scallops from Nantucket and Cape Cod, considered by many to be the sweetest scallops in the world, are also wonderful deep-fried. For an appetizer, serve about 4 ounces per person; for a main course, serve about 6 ounces per person. Dip the scallops in buttermilk and then dredge them in New England–Style Fry Mix (page 252). (The New England–Style mix is my preference for scallops, but the Southern-Style Fry Mix (page 253) also works very well.) Deep-

fry medium (20–30 per pound) scallops in oil heated to 360°F. Deep-fry small (30–40 per pound) scallops or small Cape scallops at 375°F. Stir after 15 seconds to prevent them from sticking together, then cook until the batter is golden brown and crisp. Medium scallops will take about 2 minutes, small scallops will take about 1 1/4 to 1 1/2 minutes, and Cape scallops will take only 1 minute. Refer to the master recipe for fried seafood (page 250) for a more detailed explanation.

Serving Suggestions

Fried scallops are terrific with Tartar Sauce (page 344) or Summer Shack Rémoulade (page 345), and they go well with a variety of salads, including Summer Shack Coleslaw (page 140). Home Fries (page 221) or plain rice would be a good side dish. I have already mentioned the great versatility of scallops—don't hesitate to venture beyond my traditional suggestions if the mood strikes you. For example, you could serve a curry mayonnaise with fried scallops, along with chutney and basmati or brown rice. Or you could serve a small salad topped with crispy fried scallops. You really have a lot of options here, but in the end it's the crispy fried scallops that will steal the show, no matter what the accompaniments.

Spicy and Greasy Rhode Island Calamari, page 262

Beer-Battered Fish
and Chips, page 266

Classic Maine Lobster Roll,
page 278

Dinner at the Summer Shack

Jersey Shore Italian Hot Dog,
page 286, topped with Italian
Pepper and Potato Stew,
page 287

FOOD IS LOVE

Some of the Summer Shack cooks
(left to right): "Del" Delcilandio,
Marcelo Santos, Nick Wilson,
Carlos Venancio, Leia Santos,
Jasper White, Brian Flagg, and
Steve Nevulis

Blueberry Pie, page 3

SHACK-STYLE FRIED FISH FILLETS

There are several ways to fry fish fillets. They can be breaded using the standard breading procedure (see page 215) and either deep-fried or panfried. They can be deep-fried in a batter as for Beer-Battered Fish and Chips (page 266), and they can be dipped in buttermilk and dredged in a dry mix—shack-style. By rights, any fish can be deep-fried, but I like the technique best with lean fish such as flounder, fluke, halibut, haddock, cod, hake, and tautog. Striped bass and snapper, although not as lean, are also tasty when deep-fried. It is best to fry fish that are no thicker than 3/4 inch. Many fish, such as flounder or fluke, baby cod or haddock, hake, and small snapper, are naturally thin, and you can make thin portions from large fillets simply by cutting them on a wide bias. Large cod, large haddock, halibut, large snapper, and striped bass are all terrific when cut on a bias and deep-fried shack-style.

Specifics

It is nice to serve one large piece (about 6 to 8 ounces) to each guest, but sometimes you will need to cut the fish into smaller pieces and serve two per person. Season the fish lightly with salt and pepper or Spiced Seafood Salt (page 168) before you dip the fillets in buttermilk. I prefer to dredge the fillets in Southern-Style Fry Mix (page 253), but you can use the New England–Style Fry Mix (page 252) with very tasty results. Heat the oil to 350°F. Gently lower the fish into the oil. Stirring only occasionally, cook for about 4 to 5 minutes, until golden brown. Refer to the master recipe for fried seafood (page 250) for a more detailed explanation.

Serving Suggestions

Like most fried seafood, fish fillets are always good served with Summer Shack Coleslaw (page 140) and Tartar Sauce (page 344) or Summer Shack Rémoulade (page 345) and garnished with lemon wedges and sprigs of fresh parsley. Since you probably don't fry fish very often, you may not feel the need to stray from the traditional. However, because the technique of deep-frying fish fillets leaves the fish with its most natural flavor, it could be considered a blank canvas. Sliced ripe tomatoes or a tomato salad like Portuguese Salad (page 135) could be used to stand in the acidity that coleslaw offers. A tossed green salad could also do the job. Plain rice, brown rice, Home Fries (page 221), New Potato Salad Vinaigrette (page 142), or just plain boiled new potatoes could replace the French fries that most restaurants serve with fried fish. Succotash Salad (page 138) is also a good accompaniment to fried fish.

FRIED SMELTS

nyone who likes seafood but says they don't like smelts has probably never actually tried them. They are sweet and moist, with a pleasing mild flavor. I think some people are put off eating any whole bone-in fish, even little ones, while others confuse smelts with sardines, which are very full flavored. There is little to discuss when it comes to cooking smelts—deep-frying is, hands down, the method that is most complementary to these wonderful tiny fish. The season for fresh New England and Canadian smelts is from October into early winter. Frozen are available year-round, but at Summer Shack we feature fresh smelts every day while they are in season, and when it's over, we just wait until the next year.

Specifics

Smelts are usually sold head off and gutted; they do not need to be scaled. They generally weigh about 1 ounce each, but they can be larger at times, up to 2 ounces. I prefer the smaller ones, but the large ones can be quite good. I like to eat fried smelts as an appetizer; as a main course, they can cross over into the "too much of a good thing" category. Purchase 4 or 5 fish for each person. For a light coating, dip the smelts in buttermilk and then dredge in New England Style–Fry Mix (page 252). If cook-

ing smaller smelts (about 1 ounce) heat the oil to 375°F. Carefully drop in the fish and cook for 2 minutes, or until they are very crisp and golden brown. I prefer my smelts cooked very crisp—they really don't dry out and I think this makes the bones and tail more edible. If cooking larger smelts, heat the oil to 360°F, and cook them for about 3 to 4 minutes, until they are very crisp and golden brown.

I have also had great success frying smelts with the standard breading (flour, egg wash, and crumbs—see page 215), using panko (Japanese bread crumbs) that I pulse in the food processor to make them finer. The crust is very crunchy, although a little heavier than shack-style. Refer to the master recipe for fried seafood (page 250) for a more detailed explanation of either method.

Serving Suggestions

The timeless combination of crisp fried smelts with Tartar Sauce (page 344) is tough to improve upon—keep it simple, and serve the smelts with lemon wedges, parsley sprigs, and the tartar sauce. Coleslaw (page 140) is always a nice accompaniment, and at Summer Shack we often pair fried smelts with a slaw made from crisp celery root (which is in season the same time as smelt).

FRIED GROUPER FINGERS

Grouper is one of the very best fish from Florida and the tropics. It has beautiful white, flaky flesh and a lovely sweet, somewhat mild flavor. There are many species of grouper on the market, but black grouper, red grouper, and strawberry grouper are the most common. I have yet to taste a type of grouper that I don't like, but my favorite is black grouper. Grouper is versatile and can be pan-roasted or grilled as well as deep-fried.

Specifics

Because grouper are big fish with thick fillets, it is common to cut them into "fingers," anywhere from 3 to 4 inches long and 3/4 to 1 inch thick. This cut allows the grouper to cook evenly without overcooking the outside of the fillet before the center is done. The fingers should weigh about 1 1/2 ounces each; 4 or 5 pieces per person are ample for a main course (1 1/2 to 2 pounds of fillets for 4 people). Season the fish lightly with salt and pepper or Caribbean Spiced Salt (page 169) before you dip it in buttermilk. I prefer to dredge the fingers in Southern-Style Fry Mix (page 253), but you can use the New England–Style Fry Mix (page 252) with tasty results. Heat the oil to 360°F. Gently lower the fingers into the oil, in batches if necessary. Cook, stirring only occasionally, for about 3 minutes, until golden brown. Refer to the master recipe for fried seafood (page 250) for a more detailed explanation.

Serving Suggestions

In keeping with grouper's tropical roots, I like to serve it with Curry Mayonnaise (page 133). Curry is a popular seasoning throughout the Caribbean because so many people from India settled there, and the flavors go very well together. You could also serve fried grouper with my Green Goddess Dressing (page 346). The traditional Rémoulade (page 345) or Tartar Sauce (page 344) is always good with fried fish. For a very special accompaniment, serve the grouper with Black Beans and Rice (page 222) and a green salad or green vegetable.

CRISPY FRIED SOFT-SHELL CRABS

Soft-shell crabs are truly a special treat, to be eaten in late spring and summer. Although they are available well into autumn, they tend to have thicker, tougher shells after August; crabbers have dubbed these "leatherbacks." Soft-shell crabs need to be cooked until crisp, to create a delicious contrast between the crunchy exterior and the luscious, soft interior. This limits cooking techniques to deep-frying and sautéing (see page 208).

Specifics

Whether soft-shell crabs are deep-fried or sautéed, the method of cleaning them is the same; see page 210. I recommend that you purchase "prime" (medium-sized) crabs. "Primes" are the most common size for retail; I don't recommend the smaller sizes for deep-frying. Serve 2 per person. After you dip the crabs in buttermilk, dredge them in New England–Style Fry Mix (page 252); be careful to coat all the nooks and crannies nicely, so every bit of the crab will be crunchy. Heat the oil to 360°F. Add the crabs, in batches if necessary, and cook for 3 1/2 to 4 minutes, until the crabs are very crisp and golden brown. You can also fry jumbo soft-shell crabs if you reduce the frying temperature to 350°F and cook them 1 1/2 to 2 minutes longer. (For more information on sizes, see page 209). Refer to the master recipe for fried seafood (page 250) for a more detailed explanation.

Serving Suggestions

Deep-fried soft-shell crabs can be served plain with Summer Shack Rémoulade (page 345) or Creamy Mustard Sauce (page 127) and Summer Shack Coleslaw (page 140), but one of my favorite ways to eat them (and very popular at the restaurant) is to add them to a BLT. To make a soft-shell-crab BLT, simply prepare the sandwich as you normally do and stick a deep-fried crab in the center. I also enjoy fried soft-shell crabs on a simple green salad or with my Succotash Salad (page 138).

FRIED SHRIMP

Shrimp are America's favorite seafood and fried shrimp are probably the most popular preparation of all. People can never seem to get enough of them. Unfortunately, there is a lot of bad fried shrimp out there—a good reason to make them at home, especially if you can buy them fresh. You can use any type or size of shrimp for frying—the better the quality, of course, the better the fried shrimp—but I don't think deep-frying is a good way to use large (16–20 per pound) or jumbo shrimp (U–16 and U–10). It is not that they don't taste great, it's just that they don't taste better deep-fried than smaller sizes, which are significantly less expensive.

In fact, my favorite version of fried shrimp, which we serve often at Summer Shack, uses fresh Florida rock shrimp, which are quite small (about 60 per pound). They are sweet shrimp that have a dense texture, like European langostinos. They are readily available, moderately priced, and perfect for deep-frying. In some places, these are sold as "popcorn shrimp," but where I come from, the red *aborealis* shrimp (Maine shrimp), which are even smaller than rock shrimp (about 80 to a pound), are called popcorn shrimp (see page 131).

Specifics

Purchase 3 to 4 ounces of shrimp per person for an appetizer or about 6 ounces per person for a main course. Peel and devein the shrimp (see page 120); for medium-size shrimp (21–25 or 26–30 per pound), I like to leave the tail fins attached. Rock shrimp and Maine shrimp are usually sold already peeled, but if you have to peel these, remove all the shell, including the tail fins. Dip the shrimp in buttermilk and then dredge them in New England–Style Fry Mix (page 252). For medium-sized shrimp, heat the oil to 360°F. Cook until crisp and golden, about 3 minutes for 21–25 count shrimp, a little less, about 2 1/2 minutes, for 26–30 count shrimp. Florida rock shrimp should be cooked in 375°F oil for only 1 1/2 minutes, Maine shrimp for only 1 minute. In any case, stir after 15 seconds to prevent the shrimp from sticking together. Refer to the master recipe for fried seafood (page 250) for a more detailed explanation.

Serving Suggestions

You can, of course, serve fried shrimp in the traditional way, with Coleslaw (page 140) and Tartar Sauce (page 344) or Rémoulade (page 345), with lemon wedges and parsley sprigs as garnish. If you want to try something different, set them atop a beautiful garden salad or a romaine salad. These crisp morsels serve as the protein and the crunch, replacing the croutons. Deep-fried tiny Maine shrimp (popcorn shrimp) are more appropriate at very casual gatherings, served as a snack or hors d'oeuvre rather than as part of a meal. So have fun: pop open some beers and fry up some shrimp—it beats the hell out of chips and dip.

SPECIAL DEEP-FRIED RECIPES

alth</a>ough deep-frying is essentially a very systematic way to cook, not all of my dishes fit neatly into the master recipe formula. The few recipes that follow need more detailed explanation, so I am offering these dishes to you in my regular recipe format.

SPICY AND GREASY RHODE ISLAND CALAMARI

If you think tossing crispy fried squid in a mixture of garlic butter and slices of hot cherry peppers is strange, welcome to Rhode Island! It's unusual but addictively delicious. In recent years, Rhode Island–style squid has gained popularity as a regional favorite all over New England. When I first started serving this dish at Summer Shack, we would hear complaints once in a while that it was "spicy" or "greasy"—which it was. So I changed the menu and called it just that, "Spicy and Greasy Rhode Island Calamari," and I've never had a complaint since. You could omit the garlic, butter, and hot peppers, and serve a simple and less "greasy" crisp fried calamari with a side of Red Sauce (page 349).

Point Judith, Rhode Island, has the largest squid-fishing fleet on the East Coast; it is the hub of the squid business in the United States. The fleet follows the huge schools of squid all over the Atlantic, bringing them home to Point Judith for processing. The longest and best season is summer, but we see fresh squid periodically in the spring and fall too.

When fresh squid is available, it is often reasonably priced, even when already cleaned. Frozen squid is available throughout the year, and its quality varies according to the packer and its place of origin. The most dependable brands are packed in Point Judith; you probably won't ever see the brand in a retail market, but you can ask your retailer. A lot of squid is imported from China, some of it good, some of it tasteless and rubbery. If you have a good fish market, it will most likely sell you domestic squid. If you run across fresh domestic squid, I highly recommend you buy it. Look for medium-sized squid (about 8 to a pound) for frying. Smaller squid are good for stuffing, larger ones for grilling (see page 187).

If the squid you find isn't already cleaned, increase the amount to about 1 1/4 pounds; see page 265 for how to clean squid.

For equipment, you will need a baking sheet, a 4-quart Dutch oven and a deep-frying thermometer or an electric deep fryer, a Chinese wire-mesh skimmer, a 10- to 12-inch sauté pan, and a pair of tongs.

1 **pound cleaned medium squid (4- to 5-inch), with tentacles (see headnote)**

FOR THE FRY MIX

3/4 **cup cornstarch**

3/4 **cup all-purpose flour**

1/2 **cup yellow cornmeal**

2 **teaspoons table salt**

1/2 **teaspoon freshly ground black pepper**

1/2 **teaspoon cayenne pepper**

About 6 cups peanut, canola, or other vegetable oil for deep-frying

2 **cups buttermilk**

4 **tablespoons unsalted butter**

4 **large cloves garlic, finely chopped**

1 **cup sliced hot cherry peppers in vinegar, drained**

2 **tablespoons chopped fresh Italian parsley**

WORKING AHEAD

The squid can be cleaned if necessary and cut in the morning, covered, and refrigerated. The fry mix can also be made early in the day.

1. Cut the squid bodies into 1/2-inch rings and put in a colander set over a bowl; add the whole tentacles. Cover and refrigerate until ready to use (up to 6 hours).

Cutting rings for deep-frying squid

2. To make the fry mix: Combine the cornstarch, flour, cornmeal, salt, and both peppers in a large bowl and whisk well. Refrigerate if not using within an hour or two, to prevent humidity from changing the mixture.

3. Line a baking sheet with paper towels. Heat 3 inches of oil to 360°F in a 4-quart Dutch oven over medium heat or in a deep fryer.

4. While the oil is heating, pour the buttermilk into a large bowl and drop the squid into it. Stir with a Chinese wire-mesh skimmer to coat, then lift about half the squid from the buttermilk, allowing the excess buttermilk to drip back into bowl, and drop them into the dry mix. Rinse and dry the wire skimmer. Toss the squid to coat evenly with the mix, then lift them out with the skimmer, gently shake off excess fry mix, and transfer to a plate. Bread the other half of the squid. Rinse and dry the skimmer.

5. Heat a 10- to 12-inch sauté pan over medium heat and add the butter. Once it melts, add the garlic and sauté until golden. Add the drained cherry peppers and toss to combine. Turn the heat down to low to keep warm when you fry the squid.

6. When the oil is hot, carefully drop half of the squid into the oil. If any of the squid sticks to the bottom of the pot, loosen the pieces with tongs. Turn the squid occasionally so they cook evenly: it will only take about 1 1/2 minutes until they are crisp and golden. Transfer the squid from the hot oil to the lined baking sheet. Fry the other half of the squid and drain them.

7. Add all of the fried squid to the hot pan with the garlic and sliced peppers, sprinkle with the chopped parsley, and quickly and gently toss (only twice) the squid. Divide among four small plates and serve immediately.

SERVES 4 AS AN APPETIZER

How to Clean Whole Squid

When I first started cooking more than thirty years ago, if you wanted to make a dish with squid, you had to clean it yourself. Back then, squid was served only in Asian, Portuguese, and Italian restaurants or at home. Calamari didn't become mainstream until fish markets began selling it already cleaned. (It also became more popular when they started marketing it as calamari instead of squid.) Nowadays you would be hard-pressed to find squid that hasn't been already cleaned. I think that's great. If, however, you find yourself faced with this somewhat messy job, don't be intimidated. It really is simple.

1. Pull the head and tentacles away from each body. You can save the black ink that is in the body, if you like. (I don't bother, because I don't make homemade pasta and I don't particularly like squid risotto.) If you squeeze behind the tentacles, you will find a small ball—cut that off and discard it, along with anything attached to it. Trim off the two long tentacles. If the squid is large, split the tentacles into 2 or 3 pieces each. Place in a colander.

2. Reach inside the tube (body) to find the long, thin, plastic-like vertebra and pull it out in one piece. Use your finger to push/pull out all the creamy stuff inside the body and discard it.

3. Use your fingernail to get under the purple skin at the head side of the tube. Loosen that skin, and when you have enough to grab onto, peel it away from the tube. It may tear—just keep peeling until the job is done. Add the tubes to the colander and rinse and clean all the tubes and tentacles. Drain well and refrigerate until ready to use.

1. Removing the head and tentacles from the body of a squid

2. Removing the vertebra of the squid

3. Peeling the skin from the squid

BEER-BATTERED FISH AND CHIPS

Fish and chips may have originated in England, but the dish has definitely taken root in the United States, especially here on the East Coast. In my restaurants, I serve hundreds of orders a day. People just love the crispy fried beer batter and the perfectly moist fish inside. It's easy to make fish and chips in a restaurant, using a large commercial fryolator (deep fryer), but making the dish at home is a substantial undertaking. It is not that fish and chips is hard to make, it's just that you need to cook the fish and the fries in separate pots in order to get all the food out at the same time, both hot and crisp. In fact, after testing this recipe at home, I have decided that making fish and chips in a home kitchen is crazy. But I also know there are a lot of crazy cooks out there, possibly a few who may want to quadruple this recipe, or more, and set up two big pots on portable propane burners (see page 31) for an outdoor fish fry.

This recipe is for the fish; the recipe for the chips, Boardwalk French Fries, follows—but you may want just to make the fish and serve it with coleslaw or a green salad.

The varieties of fish that make good fish and chips are many. Since the fish fillets should be fairly thin, you will need to cut thicker fish (more than 3/4 inch thick), such as cod or striped bass, on a thin bias. Flounder and other thin fish fillets (3/4 inch or less) can be cut straight down. It is nice to have one big 6- to 8-ounce piece per portion, but if that doesn't work out, it's fine to serve two smaller pieces.

For equipment, you will need a 4- or 5-quart Dutch oven and a deep-frying thermometer or an electric deep fryer, a whisk, a baking sheet, and a pair of tongs.

FOR THE BATTER

1   **cup all-purpose flour**
1   **cup cornstarch**
One 12-ounce can beer or ale
1   **large egg**
1   **teaspoon kosher or sea salt**

About 6 cups peanut, canola, or other vegetable oil for deep-frying
1 1/2 pounds (or a little more) skinless fish fillets (large flounder and fluke, haddock, hake, cod, pollock, ocean perch, or tautog), cut into 4 thin (less than 3/4 inch) slices
About 3 tablespoons Spiced Seafood Salt (page 168), or salt and freshly ground black pepper to taste

ACCOMPANIMENTS

Boardwalk French Fries (recipe follows)
Summer Shack Coleslaw (page 140)
Tartar Sauce (page 344)
Lemon wedges
Malt vinegar

WORKING AHEAD

The batter can be made several hours in advance and refrigerated until ready to use.

1. To make the batter: Combine the flour, cornstarch, beer, egg, and salt in a large mixing bowl and whisk well. The batter will be very light—slightly thinner than a regular pancake batter. Cover and refrigerate for at least 20 minutes, or up to 3 hours.

2. Line a baking sheet with paper towels. Heat 3 inches of oil to 375°F in a 4- to 5-quart Dutch oven over medium heat or in a deep fryer.

3. While the oil is heating, dry the fish fillets between several thicknesses of paper towels. Season with the spiced salt (or salt and pepper). Drop the fillets into the batter and toss with tongs to coat evenly.

4. When the oil is hot, lift the fillets one by one from the batter with the tongs, letting excess batter drip back into the bowl, and lower them into the oil, holding each fillet suspended in the oil for a few seconds to set the batter and prevent it from sticking to the bottom of the pot. The temperature of the oil will drop when the fish is added, but you overheated the oil, to 375°F, to compensate for this. Don't let the oil come back over 350°F once it recovers. Fry the fillets until deep golden brown, about 5 minutes. Transfer them to the paper towel–lined baking sheet with tongs. Serve the fish hot with the French fries, coleslaw, tartar sauce, lemon wedges, and malt vinegar.

SERVES 4 AS A MAIN COURSE

BOARDWALK FRENCH FRIES

As a kid, I loved hanging out at the different boardwalks at the Jersey Shore. One of my favorite treats was the oversized French fries sold there, greasy, crispy, and delicious. These are easy to make at home with great success. The only trouble you might run into is when the potatoes are old, during spring and early summer. Over time, the natural starches in potatoes convert to sugar, which will yield soggy fries. The key to successful crispy fries is a high starch content in the potatoes; I recommend that you use russets or Idaho baking potatoes. You can use a medium-starch potato, such as Yukon Gold or Penobscot, but although they will taste great, they won't be nearly as crisp as a baking potato. And don't put the cut potatoes in a bowl of water before frying them—the water will wash the starch off and the potatoes won't be as crisp as they should be.

It is important to start by cutting the potatoes lengthwise into even planks, about 3/8 to 1/2 inch thick. The evenness of the planks is more important than the length or width of the fries; it will ensure even cooking. After the planks are cut, you simply cut them lengthwise into wide fries. Frying the potatoes twice is the key to good crispy fries.

For equipment, you will need a 4- to 5-quart Dutch oven and a deep frying thermometer or an electric deep fryer, 2 baking sheets, a Chinese wire-mesh skimmer, and a pair of tongs.

2　pounds Idaho or russet potatoes of uniform size and shape (about 6 to 8 ounces each), washed
About 7 cups peanut, canola, or other vegetable oil for deep-frying
Kosher or sea salt
Ketchup or cider or malt vinegar
Cracked black pepper (optional)

WORKING AHEAD
Although you must cut the French fries right before you cook them the first time, the first frying can be done up to 3 hours before you cook the potatoes the final time to serve.

1. Line a baking sheet with paper towels. Heat 3 inches of oil to 325°F in a 4- to 5-quart Dutch oven over medium heat or in a deep fryer.

2. While the oil heats, slice the potatoes lengthwise into 1/2-inch-thick planks. Stack the planks 2 or 3 high and cut them into 1/2-inch-wide fries.

3. Drop all the potatoes into the oil and swirl them with tongs. Fry until the middle of a fry is hot when tested and doesn't snap when broken in half, about 3 minutes. The fries should not pick up much color at all—do not let them brown. Using a wire-mesh skimmer, lift up the fries and drain over the pot, then transfer them to the lined baking sheet and allow them to cool completely at room temperature, at least 20 minutes (or up to 3 hours). Let the oil cool as well.

4. When ready for the second frying, line a second baking sheet with paper towels. If you want to keep the first batch of French fries warm until they are all cooked, preheat the oven to

200°F. Add additional oil as needed to come 3 inches up the sides of the Dutch oven or deep fryer and heat to 375°F.

5. Drop half the potatoes into the hot oil and swirl them with tongs. Fry until deep brown, a full 5 minutes or so. Transfer the fries to the lined baking sheet and sprinkle with salt. You can serve them immediately or keep them warm in the preheated oven. Fry the remaining potatoes, making sure to let the oil come back to 375°F before adding the second batch. Drain on the lined baking sheet, sprinkle with salt, and serve hot with ketchup or cider vinegar. I also like black pepper cracked over my fries.

SERVES 4 AS A SIDE DISH

CLAM CAKES (FRITTERS)

Clam cakes, as they are called in most of New England, are fritters made with chopped clams and clam broth. They are sold in clam shacks and seafood restaurants all up and down the coast, where, all too often, the clams in the clam cakes are hard to find. My standard joke when eating these commercial clam cakes is, "Find the clam—win a free trip to Bermuda." Even without many clams, when the fritters are made with a strong clam broth, they are pretty good. My recipe is chock-full of clams—no free trips offered.

Clam chowder (see pages 97–100) and clam cakes are a classic combination. Together they make a wonderful casual meal. Since chowder should be made ahead, all you need to do is reheat it slowly. That gives you plenty of time to focus on cooking the fritters. Clam cakes also make a very nice starter or pass-around item at a party.

For equipment, you will need a 4-quart pot with a lid, a fine strainer, a 1-quart saucepan, a 4- to 5-quart Dutch oven and a deep-frying thermometer or an electric deep fryer, a whisk, a baking sheet, a pair of tongs, and a Chinese wire-mesh skimmer.

4 pounds small quahogs or large cherry-stones, well scrubbed
1 cup johnnycake meal or yellow cornmeal
3 scallions, trimmed and minced
1 cup whole milk
4 tablespoons unsalted butter or 1/4 cup bacon fat
4 large eggs, lightly beaten
2 cups all-purpose flour
2 teaspoons baking powder
1/2 teaspoon kosher or sea salt
1 teaspoon freshly ground black pepper
About 6 cups peanut, canola, or other vegetable oil for deep-frying

WORKING AHEAD

The clams can be steamed and chopped in the morning, then refrigerated until ready to use. The fritter batter should be made at least 1 hour, or up to 8 hours, in advance.

1. Add 1/2 cup water to a 4-quart pot, cover, and bring to a boil over medium-high heat. As soon as the water boils, add the clams and cover. After 5 minutes, uncover and stir the clams. Cover and steam until most of the clams have opened, about 5 minutes more for cherrystones, as much as 10 minutes more for quahogs. Remove from the heat and let cool.

2. Pull the clams from their shells and finely chop them. Strain and reserve 1 cup of the clam broth.

3. Place the johnnycake meal and scallions in a large mixing bowl. Combine the milk, the reserved clam juice, and the butter in a small

saucepan and bring to a simmer over medium heat. Pour the hot milk mixture over the corn meal and stir to combine. Let rest for 5 to 10 minutes.

4. Add the eggs, then whisk in the flour, baking powder, salt, and pepper. Fold in the clams. The batter should be fairly thick. Cover and refrigerate for 1 hour.

5. Preheat the oven to 200°F, and line a baking sheet with paper towels. Heat 3 inches of oil to 360°F in a 4- to 5-quart Dutch oven over medium heat or in a deep fryer.

6. Using two regular tablespoons (one to scoop and one to shove), one at a time, drop 6 fritters, about 1 1/2 inches across, into the hot oil. Loosen the fritters from the bottom of the pot with tongs and fry, turning them frequently so they cook evenly, until a deep golden brown, 3 to 4 minutes. Transfer them to the lined baking sheet with a Chinese wire-mesh skimmer, and then into the oven. Fry the remaining fritters, making sure to let the oil come back to 360°F between batches. Serve the fritters hot.

Note: If you are making these as a pass-around hors d'oeuvre, make them smaller (about 1 inch across) and shorten the frying time by about 1 minute.

MAKES TWENTY-FOUR 1 1/2-INCH OR THIRTY-SIX 1-INCH FRITTERS

JASPER'S FRIED CHICKEN

Although fried chicken is most commonly associated with the South, it is a dish that has been popular all along the East Coast for almost two centuries. I have yet to see an old cookbook from New England or the Mid-Atlantic states that doesn't have a recipe for fried chicken. I used to marinate my chicken with lemon, garlic, and herbs before frying it, but I have found that by using lemon pepper and granulated garlic in a seasoned salt mixture (recipe follows), I get a very similar flavor with a lot less work. Despite my reputation as a seafood chef, my fried chicken is quite well known and very popular at my restaurants. Last summer, the *Boston Globe* picked Summer Shack as one of the three best places to eat fried chicken; I'm proud to say the other two places were soul food restaurants.

I love cold fried chicken for lunch, especially on a picnic. It is easy to double this recipe and have it hot for lunch or dinner the first day and cold the next day.

For equipment, you will need a large wire rack and a rimmed baking sheet, a heavy 12-inch cast-iron skillet or a 4- to 5-quart Dutch oven and a lid, a deep-frying thermometer, an instant-read thermometer, and a pair of tongs.

2   cups buttermilk
New England–Style Fry Mix (page 252)
One 2 1/2- to 3-pound chicken cut into 10
**   pieces (see page 274)**
Seasoned Salt for Fried Chicken (recipe follows)
4   cups peanut, corn, canola, or other
**   vegetable oil for frying**

WORKING AHEAD

The seasoned salt and fry mix can be made days in advance. Store the fry mix covered tightly in the refrigerator. With those two items ready, this dish will take less than half an hour to prepare.

1. Set a large wire rack over a baking sheet. Pour the buttermilk into a large shallow bowl and the fry mix into another. Sprinkle the chicken pieces generously with the seasoned salt.

2. Pour the oil into a heavy 12-inch cast-iron skillet or a 4- to 5-quart Dutch oven (the oil should be 1 inch deep) and heat to 325°F over medium heat.

3. Meanwhile, one by one, dip the chicken pieces into the buttermilk, turning them with tongs to coat and letting the excess buttermilk drip back into container, then drop into the fry mix and use your hand to turn the pieces and gently press them into the fry mix, making sure each one is completely coated. Gently shake off the excess and place the chicken on the wire rack.

4. Place the chicken pieces skin side down into the hot oil, cover, and fry for 8 minutes, lifting the pieces once halfway through to make sure they are browning evenly and not too quickly. (The oil should register about 300°F.) Turn the chicken pieces with tongs and continue to fry, uncovered, until a deep golden brown, about 8 to 10 minutes longer. Remove a thick piece of thigh or breast meat and check the internal temperature; it should read 145°F. Remove the chicken from the oil with tongs and transfer to the wire rack to drain.

5. Let the chicken sit for at least 5 minutes; it will finish cooking during this time. After the chicken has rested, the internal temperature should be 160°F. Serve hot or chilled.

SERVES 4 AS A MAIN COURSE

SEASONED SALT FOR CHICKEN

I created this seasoned salt for a very specific purpose, to season fried chicken. But it is also very good on roasted or grilled chicken. Make a batch and keep it tightly sealed in the refrigerator or freezer. It will come in handy all summer. The recipe can be doubled easily.

1/4 cup fine sea salt or table salt
1/4 cup lemon pepper
1 tablespoon granulated garlic
1 1/2 teaspoons Old Bay seasoning
3/4 teaspoon crushed red pepper flakes
3/4 teaspoon dried oregano
1 tablespoon all-purpose flour

1. Combine the ingredients in a small bowl and mix well. Place the mixture in a tightly sealed container and refrigerate or freeze until ready to use.

MAKES 2/3 CUP, MORE THAN ENOUGH TO SEASON ONE CHICKEN FOR FRYING

How to Cut a Chicken into Ten Pieces

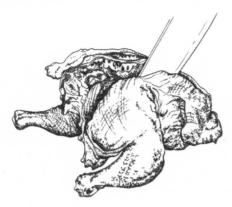

1. Splitting a chicken by cutting down the backbone

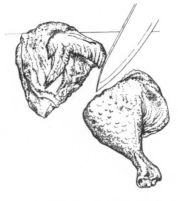

3. Separating the breast and wing from the thigh and leg

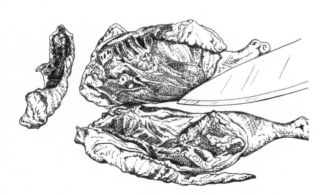

2. Split chicken with the backbone removed

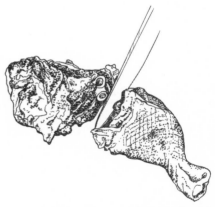

4. Separating the drumstick from the thigh

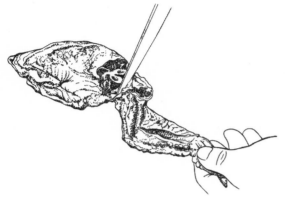

5. Separating the wing from the breast

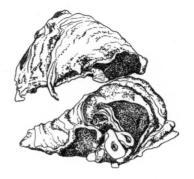

6. Chicken breast split into 2 pieces

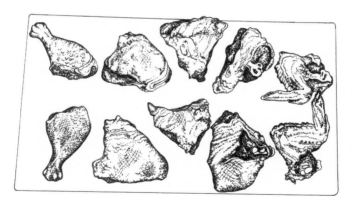

7. Chicken cut into 10 pieces, ready for frying or grilling

SUMMER SHACK CORN DOGS

all up and down the East Coast, corn dogs are sold at vendor stands, boardwalks, and county fairs. Wrapped in a crisp, slightly sweet cornmeal batter, similar to fritter or hush puppy batter, they are one of America's greatest ways to cook our beloved hot dogs. When I opened Summer Shack, I knew that I wanted to serve corn dogs. For me they were a metaphor for my new life, away from all the trappings of fine dining. To that extent, they have become a metaphor for my restaurant as well. Any place that serves corn dogs is family friendly, because, more than anyone, kids love them. To make a great corn dog, you need to start with a great hot dog—all beef, natural casings, kosher or kosher-style (see page 285); the rest is pretty easy.

For equipment, you will need 10 heavy 8-inch wooden skewers, a 12-inch or larger deep skillet and a deep-frying thermometer, a baking sheet, a pair of tongs, and a Chinese wire-mesh skimmer. (Because the entire dog-on-stick is about 10 inches long, a Dutch oven or electric deep fryer won't work for this recipe.)

FOR THE BATTER

1/2	cup all-purpose flour
1/2	cup yellow cornmeal
1	heaping teaspoon baking powder
2	teaspoons sugar
1/2	teaspoon salt
1/2	teaspoon freshly ground black pepper
1	tablespoon finely minced scallion or onion
1	large egg, beaten
1/2	cup whole milk

10	beef hot dogs (1 1/2 to 2 ounces; 5 to 6 inches long)

About 4 cups corn oil, canola oil, or other vegetable oil for deep-frying
Mustard (your favorite) and dill pickle spears

WORKING AHEAD

The hot dogs can be skewered in the morning and kept covered and refrigerated until ready to use. The batter can be made in the morning and refrigerated, covered, until right before you fry the dogs.

1. To make the batter: Combine the flour, cornmeal, baking powder, sugar, salt, and pepper in a large mixing bowl (a deep narrow bowl if you have one) and whisk well.

2. Combine the scallion, egg, and milk in a small bowl and whisk well. Gently fold the wet ingredients into the dry ingredients. Do not overmix. Cover the batter and allow it to rest at room temperature for 20 minutes.

3. Preheat the oven to 200°F. Line a baking sheet with paper towels. Heat 2 inches of oil to 350°F in a large deep skillet.

4. While the oil is heating, skewer each hot dog lengthwise, stopping about 1 inch from the top. When the oil is hot, dip a hot dog into the batter, using the stick to twirl the dog and coat it evenly; make sure the bottom end of the hot dog is sealed, but try not to get too much batter on the stick. Remove the dog from the batter and twirl it once to let excess batter drip back into the bowl, then holding the stick end, lower the corn dog into the oil, keeping it suspended about 5 seconds before letting go (this will prevent the corn dog from sticking to the bottom of the pan).

Dip 2 or 3 more hot dogs and add to the pan (do not fry more than 3 or 4 dogs at a time). Turn the dogs occasionally with tongs to make sure they cook evenly, and fry until the corn coating is a deep rich brown, 4 to 5 minutes. Lift them out of the oil one at a time with a Chinese wire-mesh skimmer and transfer to the lined baking sheet, and then into the oven. Dip and fry the remaining dogs, making sure to let the oil come back to 350°F between batches. (As you get near the end of the batter, you may need to spoon it over the dogs to coat them evenly.)

5. Serve the corn dogs hot with your favorite mustard and dill pickle spears.

MAKES 10 CORN DOGS

GREAT SANDWICHES

The following recipes are among the greatest sandwiches on the planet. Although it isn't fried, the renowned Lobster Roll is quintessential shack food—easy to make and exquisite to eat. Another definitive New England sandwich, the Clam Roll, is an out-of-body experience not to be missed. The Jersey Shore Tuna Sub is an indulgence from my childhood that I still find irresistible. Everyone who loves baseball (and even some who don't) loves a good hearty Sausage Sandwich, Loaded—"loaded" is slang in Boston for onions and peppers. Lastly, I'll share my ideas about the great American icon, the venerable hot dog and share a peculiar version, Jersey Shore Italian Hot Dogs, that is a must try for all hot dog lovers.

CLASSIC MAINE LOBSTER ROLL

Always a New England favorite, the Maine lobster roll is now becoming a favorite in other places as well. I never thought I'd see the day that the *New York Times* ran an article on the best lobster rolls in the city (NYC), but recently it did just that. It is only a matter of a time before lobster rolls become popular everywhere. The lobster roll, the king of clam shack offerings, is incredibly delicious, with its cool fresh lobster salad and warm crisp, buttery bun. It is humble, but don't be fooled by the garnish of pickles and potato chips. This dish is like a millionaire driving an old Chevy—understated, but still rich—typical of New England culture.

Making lobster rolls at home is easy, and they are a guaranteed hit with visitors and family alike. You will need to find real New England–style hot dog buns, which are top-sliced with cut sides so they can be buttered and griddled. If you can't find them, buy slightly oversized buns and trim the crust from the sides.

For equipment, you will need a 10-inch skillet, preferably cast iron. If you have paper bun holders, they are quite handy for holding the rolls when you stuff them and for serving.

- **4   New England–style hot dog buns**
- **4   tablespoons unsalted butter, softened**
- **4   Boston or Bibb lettuce leaves, washed and dried**
- **Lobster Salad (page 130)**
- **4   dill pickle spears**
- **Potato chips**

WORKING AHEAD

You can mix the lobster salad up to 4 hours ahead. Once the lobster salad is ready, this becomes a very easy and fast dish.

1. Heat a 10-inch skillet over medium heat. Spread the sides of the hot dog buns with the butter, using 1/2 tablespoon on each side. Place the buttered buns in the hot pan and toast, without moving, until golden brown on one side, about a minute. Turn and cook the other side, about 1 minute more. Remove from the heat.

2. Open the buns and place in paper bun holders or on small plates. Place a lettuce leave to the side of each bun. Divide the lobster salad evenly among them. Serve with the pickles and potato chips on the side.

MAKES 4 ROLLS

CLAM ROLL

The clam roll, like the lobster roll, is quintessential New England. It is a special treat, a rich indulgence—fried clams on a warm buttery bun served with tartar sauce—and it is worth every calorie. When you bite into a clam roll, you get the most astonishing burst of flavor. The warm soft bun and the crisp fried clams result in a textural contrast that is also terrific. This is true Yankee soul food.

For equipment, you will need a baking sheet, a 4-quart Dutch oven and a deep-frying thermometer or an electric deep fryer, a 10-inch skillet, a Chinese wire-mesh skimmer, and a pair of tongs.

About 6 cups peanut, canola, or other vegetable oil for deep-frying
4 New England–style hot dog buns
4 tablespoons unsalted butter, softened
1 cup buttermilk
1 pound whole belly (frying) clams
2 cups New England–Style Fry Mix (page 252)
4 dill pickle spears
Potato chips
1/2 cup Tartar Sauce (page 344)

1. Line a baking sheet with paper towels. Heat 3 inches of oil to 375°F in a 4-quart Dutch oven over medium heat or in a deep fryer.

2. Heat a 10-inch skillet over medium heat. Spread the sides of the hot dog buns with the butter, using 1/2 tablespoon on each side; set aside.

3. While the oil is heating and the skillet is heating up, pour the buttermilk into a large bowl. Although you will cook the clams in 2 batches, it is best to get all the clams ready to go before you start; that way you can cook the second batch right away, so all the clams will be

hot when you serve the clam rolls. Place all the clams in the buttermilk. Stir with a Chinese wire-mesh skimmer to coat, then lift one-quarter of the clams from the buttermilk, allowing the excess buttermilk to drip back into the bowl, and drop them into the fry mix. Rinse and dry the skimmer. Toss the clams in the bowl to coat evenly with the mix, then lift them out with the skimmer, gently shake off excess fry mix, and transfer to a plate. Repeat with the remaining clams, in 3 more batches.

4. About a minute before you are ready to start frying the clams, place the buttered buns into the hot pan and toast, without moving, until golden brown on one side, about a minute. Turn and toast the other side, about 1 minute more. Remove from the heat.

5. When the oil is hot, carefully drop half the clams into the oil. If any of the clams stick to the bottom of the pot, loosen them with tongs. Turn the clams, occasionally so they cook evenly: it will only take about 60 seconds until they are crisp and golden. Transfer the clams from the hot oil to the lined baking sheet. Cook the second batch of clams as soon as the oil returns to 375°F.

6. Open the buns and put on plates or a platter. Divide the fried clams evenly among them; some will fall over the sides of the buns—that's okay. Serve with the pickles, potato chips, and tartar sauce.

MAKES 4 ROLLS

JERSEY SHORE TUNA SUB

When you grow up on the Jersey Shore, you become spoiled regarding certain everyday foods, like pizza and subs. Some places are great, some are good, and very few are bad. Eating a great sub (short for submarine sandwich, also called a hoagie or grinder) is almost like a birthright, and places that don't make them well don't stay in business long. I'm sure I'm a little prejudiced, but when I want a really good sub that tastes the way they do at the Jersey Shore, I make them at home. Surprise your family and friends with big, beautiful homemade subs. With a little extra effort, a sub takes the concept of sandwich and makes it more festive, more special. I love Italian cold cuts, which is the classic filling, but my favorite is made with tuna fish salad. The tomatoes, lettuce, and onions should be sliced as thin as possible, and be sure to crisp up the bread in the oven before you make the subs.

1 French baguette or 4 submarine rolls
Tuna Salad (recipe follows)
2 to 3 three pickled hot cherry peppers, chopped (optional)
1/4 head iceberg lettuce, finely shredded (chiffonade; about 1 1/2 cups)
1/3 small red onion, cut into paper-thin rounds and separated into rings
1 to 1 1/2 tablespoons olive oil
2 teaspoons red wine vinegar
Kosher salt and freshly ground black pepper
1 medium ripe tomato (7 ounces), halved lengthwise and cut into very thin slices

WORKING AHEAD
The tuna salad can be made well ahead.

1. Preheat the oven to 375°F.

2. Split the baguette open with a serrated knife, cutting completely through it. Put the 2 halves back together and heat in the oven until toasty, with the crust well crisped. Or split the rolls and toast them. Let cool a few minutes before you assemble the sandwiches.

3. Spread the tuna evenly over the bottom half of the baguette (or rolls) with a tablespoon, pressing it down gently to cover the bread completely. Sprinkle the chopped hot peppers, if using, over the tuna to suit your taste; I use the full amount.

4. Spread the lettuce over the top half of the baguette (or rolls), sprinkle the onion rounds evenly over the lettuce, and drizzle with the olive oil. Tap the vinegar from a measuring

spoon over the lettuce. Sprinkle lightly with salt and pepper. Arrange the tomatoes over the lettuce. Lift the bottom half of the baguette carefully over the top half and then turn the sub right side up.

5. To cut the baguette, insert toothpicks along the length of the baguette, and cut into sandwiches with a serrated knife. Or, for a party snack, you can insert 16 toothpicks cut the sub into 1-inch sections.

MAKES 4 REGULAR SUBS OR 16 MINI SUBS

TUNA SALAD

The year-round staple of canned tuna turned into "tuna fish salad" with just a few ingredients is by far the most popular seafood salad in America. I have been eating it my whole life, and when I haven't had it for a while, I crave a creamy tuna salad sandwich on toast with crispy iceberg lettuce—or my very favorite, the South Jersey Tuna Sub. I love fresh tuna—hot, cold, raw, or cooked, but fresh tuna has little to do with canned tuna. It's a different experience; it might as well be a different fish.

Other than the unique flavor of canned tuna, it is the creamy mayonnaise and crisp celery that define this salad. To create a contrast between the smooth tuna and crunchy celery, it is important to break the fish up very well with the mayonnaise before you add the celery and other ingredients. I recommend dolphin-free solid white albacore tuna. The capers are optional because not everyone (read: some kids) likes them.

Two 6-ounce cans solid white tuna in oil or
    water
1/2 cup Hellmann's mayonnaise
  1 stalk celery, minced (1/2 cup)
  1 small dill pickle spear, cut into 1/8-inch
    dice (2 tablespoons)
  2 teaspoons fresh lemon juice
  2 teaspoons minced onion
  2 teaspoons capers, chopped (optional)
Kosher or sea salt
About 1/2 teaspoon freshly ground black
    pepper

1. Drain the tuna well and transfer to a mixing bowl. Add the mayonnaise and combine very well, using a large fork to mash and whip the tuna into a smooth mix. Add the celery, pickle, lemon juice, onion, and capers, if using. Stir to combine. Season with salt (not always needed) and pepper.

2. Transfer the salad to a plastic container with a lid and chill thoroughly. The salad keeps for 2 or 3 days in the refrigerator.

MAKES 2 CUPS, ENOUGH FOR 4 SANDWICHES

SAUSAGE SANDWICH, LOADED

If you live on the East Coast and you have been to a baseball game, a street festival, county fair, or sub shop, it is likely that you have had sausage and peppers served on a sandwich roll. My good friend Dave Littlefield, alias "the Sausage Guy," has been selling sausages outside of Boston's Fenway Park for many years. Almost every year, I work his cart for fun before the home opener. We sell hundreds of sandwiches in a very short time and are way too busy to fuss with them—and that is the key. Cooking the sausages, onions, and peppers together on a hot griddle, and not moving them around too much, means there are a lot of natural sugars that stick and caramelize, giving the sandwich its unique flavor. So when the recipe says "don't move too often," I mean it. It's also important to start with very good sweet Italian pork sausages flavored with fennel.

For equipment, you will need a 10- or 12-inch skillet with lid and a pair of tongs.

2   tablespoons olive oil
2   pounds sweet Italian sausages with fennel
2   medium onions (12 ounces), halved lengthwise and cut into 1/4-inch-wide strips (julienne)
2   medium green bell peppers (10 ounces each), halved, cored, seeded, and cut into 1/4-inch-wide strips (julienne)
Kosher salt and freshly ground black pepper
1   French baguette or 4 long sandwich rolls

1. Heat the olive oil in a 10- or 12-inch skillet over medium heat. Add the sausages and cook, turning every few minutes, until well browned on all sides but not cooked through, about 6 to 8 minutes. Transfer the sausages to a plate, leaving the fat in the skillet.

2. Increase the heat to high, add the onions and peppers to the pan, and sprinkle with salt and pepper. Toss occasionally, but don't move the vegetables too often—the idea is to caramelize the onions and peppers. Once they begin to caramelize, you may need to lower the heat just a bit to prevent burning. Cook until they are soft and nicely browned, about 6 to 8 minutes.

3. Preheat the oven to 375°F.

4. Return the sausages to the skillet, add 1/2 cup water, and partially cover the skillet. Cook, stirring once with tongs, until the peppers lose their color, the sausage shrinks a bit, and the water has evaporated, about 8 minutes. (You can test the doneness by slicing one sausage in half—it should not be pink in the center.) Season the sausage and peppers to taste with salt and pepper.

5. While the sausage and peppers cook together, using a serrated knife, cut the baguette into 4 portions, and split each piece (or split the rolls) open. Heat the baguette (or rolls) in the oven until toasty, about 10 minutes. Remove from the oven.

6. Stuff the bread (or rolls) with the sausages (generally 2 sausages per sandwich—there may be a couple left over), and then "load" them with the onions and peppers. Serve immediately.

MAKES 4 SANDWICHES

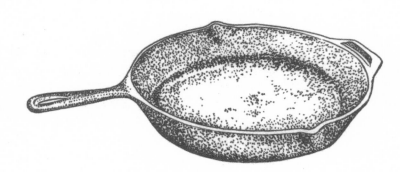

HOT DOGS

Humble though they are, hot dogs remain the topic of much debate, slander (sometimes warranted), and adoration (more often warranted). Enjoying hot dogs is a pursuit that is particularly well suited for summer, especially at the shore. They are quick, easy, and delicious. Don't worry about the fat—chances are you are very active with summer activities and will quickly burn off the calories.

Originally introduced to America as frankfurters, these sausages soon became known as hot dogs, for reasons unknown to me, but a great name. A frankfurter is a lightly smoked fine-textured cooked beef and/or pork sausage, often flavored with garlic and spices. Poor quality is not inherent, unless you buy cheap ones: you get what you pay for.

We have many fabulous dogs of impeccable quality on the East Coast. My favorite brand is Pearl Kountry Klub, an all-beef kosher-style dog with natural casings made in Roxbury, Massachusetts. They are very beefy—the taste of the meat isn't overpowered by the seasoning. We sell them exclusively in all the Summer Shacks. I also like kosher hot dogs—especially Sabrett's, Kayem, and Hebrew National. Two other brands of milder-style hot dogs that I have enjoyed are Saugy from Rhode Island and Maple Leaf from New York; both have natural casings that snap when you bite into them.

There are different theories and beliefs as to how the bun should relate to the dog. The one I like to follow is that the bun should be heated in the same fashion that you cook the dog. Grilled dog, grilled bun; griddled dog, griddled bun; steamed dog, steamed bun. It works, except in the case of a boiled hot dog—well, there are holes in every theory. Each has its own nuances and particular reason for being: The grilled dog and bun is an outdoor dish; I love the smoky flavor and the bits of crispy black on my dog and bun. The griddled or panfried version is an indoor dish, maybe for a rainy day—a bit richer than grilled because of the butter on the bun (yummy). Steamed is the commercial way of cooking hot dogs in ballparks and on the streets, where they remain in a gentle state of readiness that harsher cooking methods can't maintain. I like steamed dogs, but at home I prefer them cooked on a grill or griddle.

The single most important accompaniment for a good hot dog is mustard. I like spicy imported Dijon, smooth or whole-grain. Gulden's spicy brown mustard is very popular in my restaurants; it is perfect for hot dogs. Other popular accompaniments are sauerkraut, pickle relish, chopped raw onions, and melted cheese. Personally, I'm not a fan of cheese dogs. I used to like chili dogs in my school years, but now they are too much meat for this fish eater. My solution is to make a snappy Onion Chili especially for hot dogs; see page 287.

JERSEY SHORE ITALIAN HOT DOGS

It's not all play at the shore—many of us work for most of the summer, and this dish is a true workingman's lunch. The Italian hot dog is an American hybrid sandwich that evolved in the bars and gin mills along the Jersey Shore. Created well over fifty years ago by Italian-American bar owners for their hungry clientele, this delicious, hearty sandwich consists of a long crusty Italian- or Portuguese-style roll stuffed with a jumbo hot dog and topped with a stew of potatoes, peppers, onions, and tomatoes. It is a wonderful sight to behold and, although it is a little messy to eat, it delivers a full range of textures and bold flavors. Make this for your hungriest friends—they will love you for it.

For equipment, you will need a 10-inch skillet and a small saucepan.

4   large (6-inch) Portuguese or Italian rolls or four 6-inch lengths baguette
2   tablespoons unsalted butter
4   jumbo (4-ounce) hot dogs, preferably Pearl brand
2   cups Italian Pepper and Potato Stew (recipe follows)

WORKING AHEAD
If it is convenient, make the stew a day ahead. The flavors will develop overnight in your refrigerator.

1. Preheat the oven to 350°F.

2. Split the rolls open, and heat in the oven until nice and crisp.

3. Meanwhile, heat a 10-inch skillet over medium heat. Add the butter and hot dogs and cook for 8 to 10 minutes, turning occasionally so the hot dogs brown evenly.

4. While the hot dogs are cooking, reheat the stew.

5. When the dogs are heated through, place them in the toasted rolls and top with the stew.

MAKES 4 SANDWICHES

ITALIAN PEPPER AND POTATO STEW

1   large all-purpose potato (about 12 ounces), peeled, quartered lengthwise, and sliced 1/2 inch thick
1   tablespoon chopped garlic
3   tablespoon olive oil
1   onion, sliced about 1/2 inch thick
1   green bell pepper, cored, seeded, and sliced
1/2 teaspoon crushed red pepper flakes
1/2 teaspoon dried oregano
1   cup Red Sauce (page 349)
Kosher or sea salt and freshly ground black pepper

1. Place the potatoes in a pot of lightly salted water, bring to a gentle boil, and cook for about 15 minutes, until tender. Drain and set aside.

2. Meanwhile, in a 3-quart saucepan, sauté the garlic in the olive oil until light golden brown. Add the onion, bell pepper, red pepper flakes, and oregano and cook, stirring occasionally, for 10 minutes, or until the peppers are soft.

3. Add the red sauce and cooked potatoes and bring to a boil. Season to taste with salt and pepper. Turn off the heat and let the stew sit for at least an hour before serving.

MAKES ABOUT 3 CUPS, ENOUGH FOR 8 HOT DOGS

QUICK ONION CHILI

At the Sports Shack, the sports bar that is attached to the Summer Shack in Cambridge, we have a great following for Monday night football. We give out free hot dogs during the game and offer chopped onions, sauerkraut, pickle relish, and this special onion chili, which everyone loves. It is terrific on burgers as well as hot dogs.

2   tablespoons vegetable oil
2   medium onions (about 12 ounces), finely diced
1   tablespoon chili powder
1   teaspoon ground cumin
1/4 teaspoon cayenne pepper
2   teaspoons tomato paste
Kosher or sea salt and freshly ground black pepper

1. Heat the vegetable oil in a 10- to 12-inch sauté pan over high heat. Add the onions and cook, without stirring too often, until dark brown, about 12 minutes. Add the chili powder, cumin, and cayenne and cook, stirring often, for 1 minute.

2. Add the tomato paste, along with 1/2 cup water. Continue to cook over high heat until most of the water has evaporated and the onion chili is thick enough to coat a spoon, about 6 minutes. Season with salt and pepper, and serve at room temperature.

MAKES 1 HEAPING CUP

INSIDE THIS CHAPTER

Box: Salt	290
Skillet Corn Bread	291
Overnight Sandwich Bread	292
Boston Brown Bread	294
Strawberry Shortcake	296
Variation: Shortcake Derivatives	297
Shortcake Biscuits	297
Soft Whipped Cream	298

Angel Food Cake	299
Lemon Butter Cake	300
Nectarine Cobbler	302
Blueberry Buckle	303
Pie Dough	305
Food Processor Pie Dough	305
All-Butter Flaky Pie Dough	305
Blueberry Pie	307

Strawberry Pie	309
Apple Crunch	311
Whoopie Pies	313
Ice Cream Sundaes	315
Hot Fudge Sauce	317
Butterscotch Sauce	318
Raspberry Sauce	319

-9-

THE MORNING OVEN

Good morning—are you ready to bake? In our restaurants, all the baking is done in the morning. Of course at home the option is yours, but I believe that even at home, the morning is the right time to bake. Mixing sweet and savory foods in the same space can often lead to problems, like strawberries with a garlicky aftertaste. Best to take advantage of the clean work surfaces during the coolest part of the day and get your baking done early. The bread and pastry recipes in this chapter are either easy and reasonably time efficient to prepare or are set up to be made in stages. One example of the latter type is yeast bread proofed slowly in the refrigerator overnight to be baked the next morning. Another is the dough for shortcake biscuits, made in the morning to be baked after dinner for fresh, warm strawberry shortcake. At home, we often like to serve dessert an hour or two after dinner. After the effort that goes into a homemade dessert, I think serving it separately is a nice way to make it even more special.

I offer only a few bread recipes in this book, but each one is quite special. The skillet corn bread is terrific with simple summer dinners like grilled fish, and it only takes 30 minutes to make, start to finish. The Boston Brown Bread (page 294), Overnight Sandwich Bread (page 292), which require a bit more time and love, are for you serious bakers.

I think summer desserts ought to be based on fresh fruit. Simple shortcake (see page 296) is the perfect example of Summer Shack food. It is easy to make and features the freshest local berries and fruits, which can be rotated in and out as the season progresses. We make shortcake all summer, starting with strawberries in June, and it varies a little every week of the summer, ending with an apple version in September. In New England, pies are held in high esteem—as are people who bake great pies. A whole Blueberry Pie (page 307) is truly a thing of beauty, a dessert that says summer is here,

welcome to vacation. And don't miss my recipe for Strawberry Pie (page 309), a little-known but incredible pie. The Whoopie Pies (page 313), which are really cakes, are intended for kids, but I know adults can't resist them either.

Salt

Most of the recipes in this book call for kosher or sea salt. However, in this chapter the salt used for baking recipes is fine table salt, which can be measured more accurately. If you substitute kosher salt for table salt here, you will need to compensate by adding 1/8 teaspoon more for every 1 teaspoon called for.

If you don't want to bake, turn to the section on ice cream sundaes (page 315). Sauces that can be made ahead and kept in your refrigerator enable you, with very little effort, to transform ice cream into a special dessert that everyone will love. From an easy hot fudge sundae to a peach Melba with raspberries, you can't go wrong.

Lastly, traditional desserts are not always necessary to finish a shore dinner. Often fresh melon, tree fruits, or berries are the most appropriate finish to a meal. They help with digestion, they allow you to finish the meal with a little natural sweetness, and, best of all, they leave you feeling energetic enough to take a nice walk afterwards.

SKILLET CORN BREAD

Corn bread is a hallmark of Southern cuisine, but it is and always has been very popular in New England. At Summer Shack we serve corn bread and homemade potato rolls with every meal. Since we serve hundreds of people a day, we bake the corn bread in big sheet pans. But when I'm cooking at home, I prefer to make corn bread in a skillet, where it gets a crisp and tasty bottom crust. For authentic old-fashioned flavor, substitute bacon fat for the butter. Corn bread is best eaten freshly baked and warm, with a generous amount of butter and honey or apple butter, but it also reheats very nicely in a hot oven.

For equipment, you will need a well-seasoned 8- to 9-inch cast-iron skillet, a small saucepan, a whisk, and a cooling rack.

1 1/2 cups yellow cornmeal
1 1/2 cups all-purpose flour
1 tablespoon sugar
2 1/2 teaspoons baking powder
1 1/2 teaspoons salt
6 tablespoons unsalted butter or bacon fat
1 2/3 cups whole milk
3 large eggs, beaten
2 tablespoons vegetable oil

WORKING AHEAD

Since corn bread is easy to put together and quick to cook, I recommend you make it shortly before dinner. If you want to make it in the morning, wrap it in plastic wrap after it has cooled completely. Then reheat it whole or split to serve.

1. Adjust an oven rack to the middle position and preheat the oven to 425°F. Heat an 8- to 9-inch cast-iron skillet over medium heat for 10 minutes.

2. Meanwhile, place the cornmeal, flour, sugar, baking powder, and salt in a large bowl and whisk to combine.

3. Melt the butter in a small saucepan over low heat. Pour it into a medium bowl. Add the milk to the hot butter. Add the eggs and whisk until completely combined. Pour the wet ingredients into the dry and whisk lightly until well combined and smooth.

4. Add the vegetable oil to the hot skillet and tilt the skillet so that the oil covers the surface. Scrape the batter into the skillet with a rubber spatula—you will hear it sizzle. Immediately place the skillet in the oven and bake the corn bread until it is golden brown on top and a toothpick inserted in the center comes out clean, 20 to 25 minutes. Remove the skillet from the oven and cool the corn bread in the pan for 5 minutes.

5. Invert the corn bread onto a wire rack and cool for 5 minutes more before cutting into wedges.

MAKES ONE 8- OR 9-INCH ROUND BREAD

OVERNIGHT SANDWICH BREAD

In keeping with the spirit of the morning oven, this recipe takes advantage of an overnight fermentation, which imparts a particularly fine flavor. This pan loaf is light and moist without being sweet. You can slice the loaves to any thickness you like. When sliced a little thicker than commercial sandwich bread, this makes a great grilled cheese sandwich, which is very popular with our young customers at Summer Shack. It also make fabulous toast.

For equipment, you will need a 2- to 3-quart saucepan, a whisk, and two 9 by 5-inch loaf pans.

4   tablespoons unsalted butter
3   cups whole milk
1/4 cup sugar
5   teaspoons active dry yeast
7   cups all-purpose flour
1 1/2 tablespoons salt
Vegetable spray or butter for greasing the
    loaf pans

WORKING AHEAD

This recipe lets the dough proof (rise) very slowly overnight in the refrigerator: the slow fermentation truly improves the flavor of the bread. If you want to make this all in one day, let the loaves rise the third time at room temperature. Preheat the oven while they rise. Once they have risen to about an inch over the tops of the pans, bake as directed.

1. Melt the butter in a medium saucepan over low heat. Add the milk and sugar to the melted butter and stir well with a wooden spoon. Heat until the mixture is a little hotter than body temperature (100° to 110°F). Transfer to a large

mixing bowl and sprinkle the yeast over the top of the mixture. Whisk until the yeast is completely incorporated. Set aside for 10 minutes to let the yeast "bloom" and become frothy.

2. Combine the flour and salt in another large mixing bowl and mix well.

3. After the yeast has bloomed, make a well in the center of the flour and pour in the yeast mixture. Using your hands, slowly incorporate the flour into the liquid until it is all mixed in. Turn the dough onto a lightly floured surface. Clean the first bowl and lightly oil it (you will place the kneaded dough in there soon). Knead the dough until it forms a smooth ball, approximately 10 to 12 minutes; use as little extra flour as possible as you knead the dough, or it will become stiff.

4. Place the dough in the lightly oiled bowl and cover with a damp towel. Place the bowl in a warm place and let it rise until it doubles in size, approximately 1 hour.

5. Once the dough has doubled in size, punch it down so it deflates and transfer it to a clean surface. Cut the dough into 2 equal pieces, and shape each of them into a ball. Place the balls of dough on a baking sheet or large cutting board and drape a damp towel over them. Place in the warm place until they double once again about 30 to 40 minutes.

6. Lightly spray two 9 by 5-inch loaf pans with vegetable spray or lightly grease with butter. Once the dough has doubled for the second time, shape each ball of dough into a log to fit into a loaf pan. Place the dough in the loaf pans with the smoothest side facing up. Lightly spray the top of the bread with vegetable spray (or butter the plastic wrap) and lay a piece of plastic wrap loosely over each one.

7. Place the loaves in the refrigerator to rise slowly overnight. By morning, the dough should have risen to about 1 inch from the tops of the pans.

8. In the morning, pull the loaves out and set aside. Adjust an oven rack to the middle position and preheat the oven to 350°F.

9. Once the dough has risen to 1 inch over the tops of the pans, place in the oven and bake for 40 minutes, or until the tops are golden brown. When you flip the bread out of the pans, the sides and bottom should be light to medium brown. Place the bread on a cooling rack. Do not wrap the bread until it is completely cool. The loaves can be kept, tightly wrapped, at room temperature for 2 days or in the freezer for at least 2 weeks.

MAKES 2 LOAVES

BOSTON BROWN BREAD

oston brown bread is a venerable New England bread with roots in ancient English cooking, when puddings and breads were steamed because home kitchens had no ovens. You can still make this bread on top of the stove, but it is much easier to bake it, and it cooks more evenly in the oven.

This is everything you want in a brown bread. The rye flour keeps the batter really tender, the whole wheat zaps it with flavor, the cornmeal provides crunch, and the molasses makes it moist. This bread has a fine grain and is slightly sweet. It is outstanding when the round slices are buttered and toasted on a griddle or in a heavy pan, where they get crisp as they are heated through.

Save your coffee cans to make this bread (or ask someone who drinks canned coffee); if you don't have any, you can use 1-quart round pudding cylindrical molds, 4 to 5 inches in diameter.

For equipment, you will need a 2- to 3-quart saucepan, 2 12-ounce coffee cans, and a small roasting pan.

Softened butter for greasing the cans
2   cups whole milk
1/4 cup packed dark brown sugar
1/2 cup light molasses
1   teaspoon salt
1 1/4 cups rye flour
1 1/4 cups whole wheat flour
3/4 cup all-purpose flour
1/2 cup cornmeal
1   tablespoon baking soda
1   teaspoon baking powder
1   cup raisins

1. Adjust an oven rack to the lower position and preheat the oven to 350°F. Generously grease the two 12-ounce coffee cans with softened butter and set aside. Bring a kettle of water to a boil.

2. Combine the milk, brown sugar, molasses, and salt in a medium saucepan and heat over medium heat, stirring constantly, until the sugar dissolves and the molasses is fully incorporated, about 4 minutes. Remove from the heat and cool slightly.

3. Combine the rye, whole wheat, and all-purpose flours, the cornmeal, baking soda, and baking powder in a large mixing bowl and mix well. Slowly stir in the warm milk mixture and mix until smooth. Add the raisins and mix briefly to combine.

4. Divide the batter evenly between the two coffee cans, smoothing the tops. Cover each can with a piece of foil sprayed with vegetable spray.

Tie a piece of twine or wrap a rubber band around the foil to make the cans airtight.

5. Place the cans in a small roasting pan and pour enough hot water from the kettle into the roasting pan to come halfway up the sides of the cans. Place the pan in the oven and steam the breads until they have risen and are firm, about 2 hours. To test for doneness, remove the foil and stick a skewer into the loaves—it should come out clean. When the bread is done, transfer the cans to a cooling rack. Cool the bread in the cans for 5 minutes.

6. Run a thin metal spatula around the inside of each can to release the loaves, then ease each loaf out of the can. Cool the breads completely on a rack. Brown Bread will keep for up to 3 days if wrapped tightly in plastic wrap after it has completely cooled. After the first day, it is best griddled or toasted.

MAKES 2 ROUND LOAVES

STRAWBERRY SHORTCAKE

It is hard to imagine a better combination than this classic American dessert: hot, tender shortcake, split and filled with fresh local strawberries that have been sliced and macerated with a small amount of sugar, then topped with soft, lightly sweetened whipped cream. To me this dessert heralds the start of summer and exemplifies what summer cooking is all about—simplicity that depends on the high quality of local ingredients to create something that is extraordinary. Everything about this dessert is right; even the name rolls off the tongue with a certain sweetness.

1   quart local strawberries
1/4 cup sugar
Unbaked Shortcake Biscuits (recipe follows),
    at room temperature
Soft Whipped Cream (page 298)
Confectioners' sugar for dusting

WORKING AHEAD

The shortcake biscuits can be cut out in the morning and refrigerated on a baking sheet until ready to bake. The berries can be macerated for up to 1 hour before serving.

1. Wash and hull the strawberries. Depending on their size, slice them in half or cut into 1/2-inch-thick slices. Place them in a bowl with the sugar and let them macerate for at least 20 minutes, or up to 1 hour. Stir occasionally; the berries and sugar will make a natural syrup.

2. Preheat the oven to 425°F.

3. About 20 minutes before you are ready to serve, place the biscuits in the preheated oven and bake until they are risen and deeply browned, 10 to 12 minutes. (You can whip the cream while the biscuits are baking).

4. Pull the biscuits from the oven and allow them to cool for 5 minutes.

5. Split the warm biscuits and place the bottoms on individual plates. Spoon the macerated strawberries, with their juices over the biscuits. Put a large dollop of whipped cream over the strawberries on each biscuit and lean the top of

the biscuit against the berries and cream. Sprinkle the shortcakes generously with confectioners' sugar and serve immediately.

SERVES 6

Variation: Shortcake Derivatives

As perfect as real strawberry shortcake is, there are many variations that are close to or as good as the original. When strawberry season ends, or even before, this dessert can live on. You can make the dessert the same way as described above with a mixture of strawberries, raspberries, and even blueberries. Or you can make it with all raspberries—but not with all blueberries, because they don't create much syrup. You can slice peaches and macerate them in sugar for a peach shortcake or you can use nectarines, apricots, or figs. It is also wonderful to mix the tree fruits with berries to make, for example, a peach and berry shortcake or a raspberry and fig shortcake. I have even sautéed slices of apple in butter and sugar and served them with warm shortcake. There is a lot of room to play.

Another wonderful derivative of shortcake is to substitute Angel Food Cake (page 299) for the shortcake. Although the two are quite different, the result is equally delicious. Angel food cake is much lighter than shortcake and at times can be even more appealing. Simply put a wedge of angel food cake on a plate and top with the macerated berries and/or fruits, the soft whipped cream, and a sprinkling of confectioners' sugar.

SHORTCAKE BISCUITS

The "short" in shortcake refers to the high proportion of shortening (in this case butter), which makes this slightly sweet biscuit so tender. It is the basis for Strawberry Shortcake, a close second to apple pie in the all-American dessert category.

For equipment, you will need a rolling pin, a baking sheet, a 3-inch round biscuit cutter, and a pastry brush.

2 **cups all-purpose flour**
1/3 **cup sugar**
1 **tablespoon baking powder**
1/2 **teaspoon salt**
8 **tablespoons (1 stick) unsalted butter, cut into small pieces (hazelnut size), plus 3 tablespoons butter, melted**
1/3 **cup whole milk**
1 **large egg, lightly beaten**

WORKING AHEAD

You can make the dough and cut out the biscuits in the morning and keep refrigerated, covered. Pull them out 1 hour before you want to bake them and let them warm to room temperature. Bake the biscuits 15 minutes before you want to serve them so they are still hot when they reach the table.

1. Adjust a rack to the lower third of the oven and preheat the oven to 425°F. Line a baking sheet with parchment paper and set aside.

2. Place the flour, sugar, baking powder, and salt in a large bowl and mix to combine. Scatter the butter pieces over the top and rub the butter and flour mixture together until the butter is in

small pea-sized pieces and the flour has picked up a yellow tinge.

3. Combine the milk and egg in a glass measure or small bowl and stir lightly with a fork. Pour the liquid ingredients over the dry and toss with the fork to combine. Turn the dough out onto a floured work surface and knead it lightly just until it is smooth, about a minute.

4. Roll the dough out into a rectangle about 6 1/2 by 10 inches and 1 inch thick. Dip a 3-inch round biscuit cutter in flour and cut out 6 biscuits. Transfer the biscuits to the lined baking sheet and brush with the melted butter. Bake the biscuits until they are risen and deeply browned, 10 to 12 minutes. Serve warm.

MAKES 6 BISCUITS

SOFT WHIPPED CREAM

Besides vanilla ice cream, whipped cream's rich cousin, no other preparation can enhance as many different desserts as whipped cream. To my mind, whipped cream is a lot like a martini—it seems simple enough, only a couple of ingredients, but people rarely get it just right. Even in my restaurants some cooks who have little trouble with much more complex items will overwhip the cream. I battle this problem by forbidding the use of an electric mixer. I suggest that you too always whip cream by hand. It is very quick and there's less clean-up than with a mixer. All you need for equipment is a large, clean bowl, preferably stainless steel, and a fine whisk.

1   **cup heavy cream**
1 to 2 **tablespoons sugar**
1/2 **teaspoon vanilla extract**

1. Place the cream in a large bowl, preferably stainless steel, and begin whisking the cream, lifting the whisk out of the cream with each rotation. The science here is that you are bringing air into the fat molecules of the cream, which will hold the air in suspension. You can move the cream around all day, but it won't get thick without the air. Whisked properly, this small amount of cream will begin to thicken almost immediately. After about a minute or so, the cream will be thick enough that it will begin to adhere to the whip. Add the sugar: 1 tablespoon for sweet desserts, 2 for less sweet. Add the vanilla. Continue whipping until the cream is firm enough that it can be picked up with the whisk but soft enough that it falls off in seconds. The appearance should be silky smooth, with not a bit of graininess. Now you have whipped cream that will complement whatever you serve it with.

MAKES 2 CUPS

ANGEL FOOD CAKE

angel food is an apt name for this feather-light, puffy white cake. I am a big fan of angel food, especially as a lighter alternative to shortcake for fresh summer berries. Try the optional almond extract; it goes wonderfully with fruit.

Note: Take the eggs out of the refrigerator 30 minutes before you plan to begin making the cake and separate the whites from the yolks, so they can come to room temperature; reserve the yolks for another use. Make sure that the mixing bowl and whisk attachment, as well as the glass measuring cup and rubber spatula, are scrupulously clean and contain no traces of fat. Any fat could prevent the egg whites from reaching the full volume or cause the whipped white to deflate.

For equipment, you will need a 10-inch tube pan, a large fine strainer, a 2-cup glass measuring cup, a standing mixer or a handheld mixer and a large bowl, a large rubber spatula, and a long thin metal spatula.

1 **cup cake flour**
1 1/4 **cups superfine sugar**
1 1/2 **cups egg whites (from about 10 large eggs)**
1 **teaspoon cream of tartar**
1/2 **teaspoon salt**
1 **teaspoon vanilla extract**
1 **teaspoon almond extract (optional)**
Confectioners' sugar for dusting

1. Adjust a rack to the middle position and preheat the oven to 350°F. Have a 10-inch tube pan ready, but do not grease the pan.

2. Place the flour and 1/2 cup of the sugar in a fine sifter set on a piece of parchment or waxed paper, and have a medium bowl nearby. Sift the flour and sugar together three times—onto the parchment, then into the bowl, and back onto the parchment. Set aside.

3. Pour the egg whites into the bowl of a standing mixer or another large bowl and add the cream of tartar and salt. Beat the whites on medium speed with the whisk attachment until they are frothy, about 1 minute. Add 2 tablespoons of the remaining sugar and increase the speed to medium high. Continue beating, adding the sugar 2 tablespoons at a time at 30-second intervals, until all the remaining sugar (3/4 cup total) has been added. Pour in the vanilla extract and the almond extract, if using, and continue to whip the whites until they are glossy and stiff but not dry.

4. Sprinkle one-third of the sifted flour and sugar over the whites and fold in gently with a

rubber spatula. Add the remaining flour mixture in 2 more additions, folding gently but thoroughly. Scrape the batter into the tube pan, smooth the top, and tap the cake pan sharply on the counter to eliminate any air bubbles.

5. Bake until the cake is golden brown and a toothpick inserted in the center comes out clean, about 30 minutes. Remove from the oven and invert the cake pan onto a wine bottle or other long-necked bottle to keep the pan suspended above the counter. Cool the cake completely in the pan, about 2 hours.

6. To remove the cake from the pan, ease a long thin metal spatula between the pan sides and the cake, holding it flush against the sides of the pan and moving it around the pan in a smooth motion. Invert cake onto a serving platter (rap the top of the pan if necessary to unmold the cake). Sprinkle with confectioners' sugar just before serving, and cut into portions. Serve with berries and whipped cream.

SERVES 8

LEMON BUTTER CAKE

Fragrant, delicate, and moist beyond belief, this cake is perfect for afternoon tea or a late-night treat. You can serve small slices with a few strawberries and a dollop of whipped cream for a pretty fabulous dessert as well.

For equipment, you will need a 10-inch tube pan, a standing mixer or handheld mixer, and a cooling rack.

2 **cups sifted cake flour, plus more for flouring the pan**
2 **teaspoons baking powder**
1/4 **teaspoon salt**
3/4 **cup whole milk**
2 **teaspoons vanilla extract**
12 **tablespoons (1 1/2 sticks) unsalted butter, room temperature, plus more for greasing the pan**
Finely grated zest of 2 lemons
1 **cup sugar**
3 **large eggs, separated**
1/4 **teaspoon cream of tartar**

1. Adjust an oven rack to the middle position and preheat the oven to 350°F. Grease and flour a 10-inch tube pan.

2. Place the flour, baking powder, and salt in a mixing bowl and whisk to combine. Set aside. Pour the milk into a liquid measuring cup, add the vanilla, and set aside.

3. Beat the butter and lemon zest in the bowl of a standing mixer fitted with the paddle attachment, or in a large bowl with a handheld mixer, until fluffy, about 20 seconds. Add 3/4 cup sugar (set the remaining aside) and beat until the mixture is light and fluffy and the sugar has begun to dissolve, about 3 minutes more, stopping the machine to scrape down the bowl once or twice. Add the egg yolks one at a time, beating well after each addition. With the machine running on low speed, add the flour mixture and milk mixture alternately, beginning and ending with the dry ingredients. Mix until just combined, about 10 seconds. Using a rubber spatula, fold the batter once or twice by hand to complete the mixing.

4. Place the egg whites, cream of tartar, and a teaspoon of the remaining sugar in a clean bowl, and beat on medium speed with the whisk attachment until the egg whites are frothy, about 20 seconds. Increase the mixer speed to medium and continue beating until the egg whites form soft peaks, about 1 minute. With the mixer running, gradually sprinkle the remaining sugar over the egg whites and continue beating until the egg whites form stiff peaks—but no longer—about 30 seconds more.

5. Stir one-quarter of the egg whites into the batter, then fold in remaining egg whites until all traces of white have disappeared. Turn the batter into the prepared pan and smooth the top. Bake until the cake is well risen and golden-brown and a toothpick inserted in the center comes out clean, about 45 minutes.

6. Cool the cake in the pan on a rack for 5 minutes, then remove from the pan and cool right side up on the rack for at least 1 hour before slicing.

SERVES 8 TO 10

NECTARINE COBBLER

This old-fashioned dessert, made with ripe, in-season nectarines, uses shortcake biscuit dough as a topping. The dough is placed in small pieces over the top of the fruit and as it bakes, it creates an effect that is similar to cobblestones, hence the name. Cobbler can be and often is made with peaches, but because their skins are thick, they require peeling and that is a substantial amount of work—more than I care to do on a nice summer day. Nectarines work just as well in this dish.

For equipment, you will need a 2-quart glass baking dish or casserole and a pastry brush.

FOR THE FILLING

3 pounds ripe nectarines (about 8 baseball-sized nectarines)
Juice of 1 lemon
3/4 cup sugar
1/4 cup cornstarch
Pinch of ground cinnamon
Pinch of freshly grated nutmeg
1/4 teaspoon salt
4 tablespoons unsalted butter

Shortcake Biscuit dough (page 297)
Vanilla ice cream or Soft Whipped Cream (page 298)

WORKING AHEAD

The cobbler can be baked in the morning. Cover it with plastic wrap after it has cooled completely; to reheat, in a preheated 300°F oven for about 20 minutes before serving.

1. Adjust a rack to the middle position and preheat the oven to 425°F.

2. Make the filling: Cut the nectarines in half and remove the pits. Cut each half into 4 or 5 slices and drop the slices into a mixing bowl with the lemon juice, tossing them as you go to keep them from turning brown.

3. Combine the sugar, cornstarch, cinnamon, nutmeg, and salt, then sprinkle over the nectarines and stir gently with a rubber spatula to mix. Transfer the filling to 2-quart glass baking dish. Dot the top of the fruit with pea-sized pieces of the butter. Cover with aluminum foil and bake for 20 minutes, or until the juices start to bubble.

4. Once the nectarine filling is bubbling, remove the baking dish from the oven. Pinch off small pieces of the shortcake dough, about the size of a quarter, and scatter them over the fruit, leaving small spaces in between them to create a cobblestone effect.

5. Return the dish to the oven and bake until the biscuit topping is deep golden brown and

the filling is bubbling, about 10 to 15 minutes. Cool for 10 minutes, then scoop the cobbler into shallow bowls, with the crispy shortcake on top. Finish each serving with a scoop of vanilla ice cream or dollop of soft whipped cream.

SERVES 12

BLUEBERRY BUCKLE

Blueberry buckle, named after its uneven top, has roots in the South but is popular up and down the East Coast. This version is like the ultimate coffee cake: light, moist, absolutely creamy inside, crunchy on top, and bursting with blueberry flavor. It has admirable keeping properties because of the moist fruit and makes a splendid tea cake as well. You can make this with farmed or wild blueberries, fresh or frozen. Wild berries are my first choice because of their intense flavor. Even frozen, they taste better than the average cultivated blueberries when baked. This recipe calls for 2 1/2 pints blueberries, though you could make do with 2 pints. But I suggest you buy 3 pints and enjoy half a pint yourself.

For equipment, you will need a standing mixer or a handheld mixer and a large bowl, and a 9-inch round cake pan.

FOR THE STREUSEL TOPPING

- 6   tablespoons all-purpose flour
- 1/2 cup sugar
- 1/4 teaspoon ground cinnamon
- 1/8 teaspoon ground nutmeg
- 1/4 teaspoon salt
- 4   tablespoons unsalted butter, cut into small pieces (hazelnut size), at cool room temperature

FOR THE CAKE

- 1 3/4 cups all-purpose flour, plus more for flouring the pan
- 2   teaspoons baking powder
- 1/2 teaspoon salt
- 4   tablespoons unsalted butter, plus more for greasing the pan
- 1   cup sugar
- 1   large egg
- 2   teaspoons vanilla extract
- 1/3 cup whole milk
- 2 1/2 pints fresh blueberries, rinsed and picked over, or 1 pound frozen blueberries (not thawed)

1. Adjust a rack to the middle position and preheat the oven to 325°F. Grease and flour a 9-inch round cake pan.

2. To make the streusel: Combine the flour, sugar, spices, and salt in a small mixing bowl and stir with a fork until well combined. Add the butter pieces and rub into the flour mixture with your fingertips until the butter is well distributed and the topping is crumbly. Set aside.

3. To make the cake: Place the flour, baking powder, and salt in a bowl and mix to combine. Set aside.

4. Beat the butter in the bowl of a standing mixer fitted with the paddle attachment or in a large bowl with a hand mixer, until fluffy, about 2 minutes. Add the sugar and beat until the mixture is light and fluffy and the sugar has begun to dissolve, about 2 minutes more, stopping the machine to scrape down the bowl once or twice. Add the egg and vanilla and mix on medium speed until the mixture is smooth, about 1 more minute. Reduce the machine speed to low and add the flour in 3 additions and the milk in 2 additions, beginning and ending with flour. Using a rubber spatula, fold in the blueberries. If the blueberries are frozen, the batter will become heavier as you fold.

5. Scrape the batter into the prepared cake pan, and sprinkle the surface evenly with the streusel. Bake until the streusel is golden brown and a toothpick inserted in the cake comes out clean, about 40 minutes if using fresh blueberries, about 50 minutes if using frozen.

6. Cool the buckle in the pan on a rack for 20 minutes, then remove from the pan and cool streusel side up on the rack for at least 1 hour before slicing.

SERVES 8 TO 10

PIE DOUGH

Here are two pie doughs, both suitable for the fruit pies that follow. The first, made in a food processor, is a very tender, somewhat thicker crust; it uses 3 cups of flour. The second, made by hand, is an all-butter dough that makes a very crisp, flaky, thin crust; it uses 2 cups of flour. The choice is a matter of personal preference; both are very good.

FOOD PROCESSOR PIE DOUGH

This recipe is quick and easy and produces tender pie dough.

12 tablespoons (1 1/2 sticks) cold unsalted butter
6 tablespoons solid vegetable shortening
1 large egg
1/4 cup ice-cold water, or as needed
3 cups all-purpose flour
1 teaspoon salt

1. Cut the butter into small pieces, wrap it in plastic wrap, and place it in the freezer while you prepare the remaining ingredients. Cut the shortening into small pieces, wrap it in plastic, and place it in the freezer.

2. Beat the egg lightly with the 1/4 cup ice water in a glass measuring cup or small bowl; set aside. Place the flour and salt in a food processor and process briefly to combine. Add the chilled vegetable shortening and process to the texture of a fine meal, about 10 seconds. Scatter the chilled butter pieces over the flour and process in ten 1-second pulses, or until the butter pieces are small and uniform and the flour is yellowish in color.

3. Turn the flour mixture into a large mixing bowl and sprinkle it with the egg and water mixture. Fluff the dough with your fingertips to distribute the liquid evenly, and squeeze a bit in the palm of your hand. The dough should be moist enough to hold together and not crumble. If it feels dry, add an additional 1 to 2 tablespoons cold water and work it into the dough lightly with your fingertips.

4. Divide the dough into 2 pieces, one slightly larger than the other, and press them both into disks. Wrap each one tightly in plastic wrap. Refrigerate for at least 2 hours before rolling. The dough can be refrigerated for up to 2 days. It will keep frozen, tightly wrapped, for up to a month.

MAKES 1 THICK DOUBLE CRUST FOR A 9-INCH PIE

ALL-BUTTER FLAKY PIE DOUGH

This dough makes a thin, crisp, flaky crust that is terrific for fruit pies.

2 cups all-purpose flour
1/2 teaspoon salt
12 tablespoons (1 1/2 sticks) unsalted butter, cut into 12 pieces and chilled
About 6 to 8 tablespoons ice-cold water

1. Combine the flour and salt in a mixing bowl. Add the butter and, using your fingertips, mix

the flour and butter together until the butter begins to break up. When the flour has begun to pick up a a yellow tinge from the butter, add 6 tablespoons ice water a little bit at a time and mix until the dough just starts to come together.

2. Transfer the dough to a floured work surface and knead briefly, until the dough begins to become smooth. The dough should be moist enough to hold together and not crumble. If it feels dry, add an additional 1 to 2 tablespoons ice water and work it lightly into the dough with your fingertips. Divide the dough into 2 pieces, one slightly larger than the other, and press them both into disks. Wrap each piece tightly in plastic wrap. Refrigerate for at least 2 hours before rolling. The dough can be refrigerated for up to 2 days. It will keep frozen, tightly wrapped, for up to a month.

MAKES 1 DOUBLE CRUST FOR A 9-INCH PIE

BLUEBERRY PIE

Blueberry pie holds a place of honor in the food culture of New England. It is expected at certain events: to hold a clambake or lobster dinner and not serve blueberry pie is abnormal. It is more than a dessert—it is an icon. Serve blueberry pie, and the world is right; serve it warm with melting vanilla ice cream, and it is nirvana.

This recipe is for a classic double-crusted pie, with just enough cornstarch to keep the filling from being runny and tons of blueberry flavor. Half the blueberries are cooked in advance to make a thick compote; the rest are folded in, allowing their juices to enrich the filling while retaining some of their whole berry character.

For equipment, you will need a 3-quart saucepan, a rolling pin, a deep (but not deep-dish) 9-inch glass pie pan, and a pastry brush. If you have a pizza stone, baking the pie on a preheated stone ensures that the bottom crust bakes through and browns and prevents a soggy bottom.

FOR THE FILLING

- 4   **pints local blueberries, picked over and rinsed**
- 3/4 cup water
- 1   cup sugar
- 1/2 cup maple syrup
- 1   teaspoon grated lemon zest (optional)
- 1   tablespoon fresh lemon juice
- 1/8 teaspoon salt
- 1/3 cup cornstarch
- 2   tablespoons unsalted butter

Food Processor Pie Dough (page 305) or All-Butter Flaky Pie Dough (page 305)
- 1   tablespoon sugar

WORKING AHEAD

The pie dough can be made in advance and kept, well wrapped, in the refrigerator for a day or two or up to 1 month in the freezer. To thaw the frozen dough, transfer it to the refrigerator the night before you plan to make the pie.

1. To prepare the filling: Combine half the blueberries in a medium saucepan with 1/4 cup of the water, the sugar, maple syrup, lemon zest, if using, lemon juice, and salt and cook over very low heat stirring occasionally, until the berries begin to give off juice, about 5 minutes. Turn the heat up to medium and cook for 5 more minutes, or until the blueberries break apart.

2. Meanwhile, mix the the cornstarch with the remaining 1/2 cup cold water until smooth, to make a slurry. Gradually pour the slurry into the hot blueberry mixture, stirring until it thickens. Let the mixture bubble for 30 seconds

to cook the cornstarch, then remove the saucepan from the heat and stir in the butter. Add the remaining berries to the mixture and allow it to cool.

3. Remove the dough from the refrigerator and allow it to warm slightly at room temperature for 5 minutes. Lightly flour a work surface and roll out the larger piece of dough to a circle about 12 inches. Place it in a 9-inch glass pie dish and press it over the bottom and up the sides. Roll out the second piece of dough to an 11-inch circle.

4. Turn the filling into the pie shell. Drape the top crust over the filling. Trim the overhang and crimp the edges of the crusts together. Chill the pie while you preheat the oven. Position a rack in the lower third of the oven and preheat the oven to 375°F. If you are using a pizza stone, allow 30 minutes for it to heat up.

5. Remove the pie from the refrigerator. Brush the top crust lightly with water and sprinkle with the 1 tablespoon sugar. Make about 8 small incisions into the top crust to create steam vents. Bake the pie for about 45 minutes, until the top crust is brown and the filling is bubbling. Remove the pie from the oven and cool completely on a wire rack.

SERVES 8

STRAWBERRY PIE

For some reason, strawberry pie is not very common. But if it is made with deeply fragrant, ripe strawberries, like the ones we get in New England in June and July, it truly is glorious. If the berries are small, you can leave them whole. If they are a little larger, cut them in half. For the filling, some of the strawberries are sugared and crushed, then thickened with crushed tapioca, to make a thick compote, and the remaining strawberries are folded into the compote. This recipe is for a traditional double-crusted pie, but if you would prefer to make a lattice top, by all means do so.

For equipment, you will need a coffee or spice grinder, food processor, or mortar and pestle to crush the tapioca; a 3-quart saucepan; a rolling pin; a deep (but not deep-dish) 9-inch glass pie pan; and a pastry brush. If you have a pizza stone, baking the pie on a preheated stone ensures that the bottom crust bakes through and browns and prevents a soggy bottom.

FOR THE FILLING

1/2 cup Minute tapioca

1 1/4 cups sugar

2 quarts small ripe local strawberries (about 3 pounds), rinsed and hulled

1 tablespoon fresh lemon juice

1/8 teaspoon salt

2 tablespoons unsalted butter

Food Processor Pie Dough (page 305) or All-Butter Flaky Pie Dough (page 305)

1 tablespoon sugar

WORKING AHEAD

The pie dough can be made in advance and kept, well wrapped, in the refrigerator for a day or two or up to 1 month in the freezer. To thaw the frozen dough, transfer it to the refrigerator the night before you plan to make the pie.

1. To prepare the filling: Grind the tapioca in a clean coffee or spice grinder or a food processor, or using a mortar and pestle, until it resembles the texture of cornmeal.

2. Combine the 1 1/4 cups sugar, half of the strawberries (about 4 cups), and the lemon juice in a medium saucepan and cook over very low heat, stirring occasionally, until the berries begin to give off juice, about 10 minutes. Increase the heat to medium and cook until the strawberries have broken apart. Add the tapioca and stir until the filling thickens, about 5 minutes. Remove the saucepan from the heat and stir in the butter. Transfer to a large bowl.

3. Add the remaining strawberries to the cooked strawberry mixture and fold in gently with a rubber spatula. Allow to cool.

4. Remove the dough from the refrigerator and allow it to warm slightly at room temperature for 5 minutes. Lightly flour a work surface and roll out the larger piece of dough to a circle about 12 inches. Place it in a 9-inch glass pie dish and press it over the bottom and up the sides. Roll out the second piece of dough to an 11-inch circle.

5. Turn the filling into the pie shell. Drape the top crust over the filling. Trim the overhang and crimp the edges of the crusts together. Chill the pie while you preheat the oven. Position a rack in the lower third of the oven and preheat the oven to 375°F. If you are using a pizza stone, allow 30 minutes for it to heat up.

6. Remove the pie from the refrigerator. Brush the top crust lightly with water and sprinkle with the 1 tablespoon sugar. Make about 8 small incisions into the top crust to create steam vents. Bake the pie for 45 minutes, until the top crust is brown and the filling is bubbling. Remove the pie from the oven and cool completely on a wire rack.

SERVES 8

APPLE CRUNCH

Apple crunch is part of a family of hot apple desserts that are truly American. Take away the oatmeal, and you have an apple crisp. Take away the nuts, and you have a brown Betty. I love these types of desserts because they are as delicious as they are easy to make and, to a certain extent, they are foolproof. There is no real chemistry at work here, so you can take liberties such as substituting walnuts or almonds for the pecans. You could also substitute pears or quinces for some of the apples.

I like to mix different types of apples in this crunch to produce a range of textures and flavors. The green apples add tartness and a firm texture, the Macs turn to applesauce, and the Golden Delicious apples add sweetness and more flavor. I have fooled around with this dish for twenty years, but the recipe hasn't changed in the last four—this is my best version, the keeper.

For equipment, you will need an 8 by 11-inch baking dish and a baking sheet.

1 tablespoon softened butter for greasing the baking dish

FOR THE TOPPING

1 cup pecans, coarsely chopped
3/4 cup all-purpose flour
1 cup packed light brown sugar
1/2 cup rolled oats
1/2 teaspoon ground cinnamon
1/4 teaspoon salt
8 tablespoons (1 stick) unsalted butter, cut into 1/2-inch cubes and chilled

FOR THE FILLING

4 large Granny Smith or Greening apples
2 large McIntosh apples
2 large Golden Delicious, Gravenstein, Empire, Baldwin, or Macoun apples
1/4 cup sugar
Juice of 1/2 lemon
1/2 cup apple cider (or apple juice)
2 tablespoons all-purpose flour

Vanilla ice cream

WORKING AHEAD

You can make the crunch early in the day. Reheat it in a preheated 300°F oven for about 20 minutes before serving.

1. Adjust a rack to the middle position and preheat the oven to 350°F. Butter an 8 by 11-inch baking dish and set it aside.

2. Spread the pecans on a baking sheet and toast for 5 minutes. Remove from the oven and let cool.

3. To make the topping: Combine the flour, brown sugar, oats, cinnamon, salt, and nuts in a large mixing bowl and toss well. Add the chilled butter pieces and rub them into the dry ingredients with your fingertips until the mixture is crumbly. Set aside in a cool place.

4. To make the filling: Peel and core the apples, then slice them 1/2 inch thick. Place them in a large mixing bowl and toss them with the sugar, lemon juice, cider, and flour. Turn the apples into the baking dish and sprinkle the topping evenly over them.

5. Bake until the topping is brown and the filling is bubbly, about 1 hour. Remove from the oven and cool for 15 minutes.

6. Spoon the crunch into bowls, with the crunch topping on top, and serve with scoops of vanilla ice cream.

SERVES 6 TO 8

WHOOPIE PIES

 n this wonderful retro sweet concoction, intensely flavored dark chocolate "puffs" are used to sandwich gooey, marshmallowy buttercream. As with many of the dishes we cook at Summer Shack, retro feels natural. We started making whoopie pies with our young customers in mind, but the truth is just as many adults order them.

This is an easy food processor recipe that comes together fast. Lightly sweetened dark chocolate cakes complement the light, almost frothy filling. At Summer Shack, our pastry chef makes the filling with an Italian meringue, but for this home version, we have simply whipped Marshmallow Fluff together with confectioners' sugar and butter. Whoopie pies don't keep well and so are best eaten the day they are made— rarely a problem. If they will not be served right away, wrap them in plastic wrap and store at cool room temperature.

For equipment, you will need a 3-quart saucepan, a standing mixer or a handheld mixer and a large bowl, 2 baking sheets, a metal spatula, a pastry bag fitted with a large round tip, and a small icing spatula or a table knife.

FOR THE CAKES

1/2 **cup unsweetened cocoa powder**
1/2 **cup whole milk**
8 **tablespoons (1 stick) unsalted butter, cut into pieces**
1 **cup sugar**
1 **teaspoon light corn syrup**
2 **large eggs, lightly beaten**
1 1/2 **cups all-purpose flour**
1 **teaspoon baking powder**
1 **teaspoon baking soda**
1/4 **teaspoon salt**

FOR THE FILLING

12 **tablespoons (1 1/2 sticks) unsalted butter, softened**
1 1/2 **cups confectioners' sugar**
1 1/2 **cups Marshmallow Fluff**
2 **teaspoons vanilla extract**
Pinch of salt

WORKING AHEAD

You can make the filling up to 2 days ahead and keep it refrigerated, tightly covered. Bring it to room temperature before spreading it on the cakes.

1. Adjust the racks to the upper and lower thirds of the oven and preheat the oven to 350°F. Line two baking sheets with parchment paper.

2. To make the cakes: Combine the cocoa and milk in a medium saucepan, set over low heat, and whisk to create a smooth paste. Add the butter, sugar, and corn syrup and continue to

whisk until the mixture is smooth and glossy and the sugar has dissolved, about 3 minutes. Remove the saucepan from the heat and let cool.

3. Whisk the eggs into the cooled cocoa syrup.

4. Place the flour, baking powder, baking soda, and salt in the bowl of a standing mixer fitted with the paddle attachment or another large bowl. With the mixer on medium speed, or beating with a hand mixer, slowly pour the cocoa syrup into the flour mixture, mixing until combined.

5. Transfer the batter to a pastry bag fitted with a large plain tip and pipe out 2-inch rounds spaced 3 inches apart onto the baking sheets, 12 per pan. Place both pans in the oven and bake until the cakes puff and are set, about 10 minutes, rotating the pans top to bottom and back to front after 5 minutes.

6. Remove from the oven and slide the parchment sheets with the cookies onto a counter. Cool for 2 minutes, then transfer the cakes to a cooling rack with a metal spatula and cool completely.

7. To make the filling: Beat the butter in the bowl of the standing mixer, fitted with the paddle attachment, or in a large bowl with the handheld mixer, until fluffy, about 1 minute. Add the sugar and beat until the mixture is light and fluffy, about 2 minutes more. Add the Marshmallow Fluff, vanilla, and salt and beat to combine, about 30 seconds.

8. To assemble the whoopie pies, turn half the cakes onto their backs and spread each with a generous portion of filling. Place a second cake on the top of each to make a sandwich.

MAKES 12 WHOOPIE PIES

ICE CREAM SUNDAES

If you want a dessert that is sure to be a crowd pleaser, make ice cream sundaes. People, especially kids, love them. For those of us who like to bake, making sundaes can be a little humbling, because with only minimal effort, you are guaranteed to get the kind of smiles and compliments that you might not get with a dessert that took an hour or more to make. So next time you're not sure what to make for dessert, go easy on yourself. Buy some good-quality ice cream at your local store and stash it in the freezer. Hot Fudge Sauce (page 317), Butterscotch Sauce (page 318), and Raspberry Sauce (page 319) are all simple to make and keep well, so there is no excuse not to use your own homemade sauces for a very special sundae.

I won't insult you with recipes here, but I will give you a few ideas that work for me. A good sundae offers contrasts, usually in both temperature (hot and cold) and texture (soft and crunchy). A sundae can be as simple as two or three ingredients or as complex as a banana split. Just remember to temper your ice cream by taking it out of the freezer and putting it in the refrigerator at least 20 minutes before you make the sundaes. Also remember to chill your bowls in the freezer. Make the Soft Whipped Cream (page 298) right before you build the sundaes. These little details make a big difference. Oh, don't forget the cherry on top—try fresh Bing cherries in the summer. They are wonderful—although most kids like maraschino cherries better.

Hot Fudge Sundae: Vanilla and/or chocolate ice cream with Hot Fudge Sauce, soft whipped cream, toasted chopped walnuts or sliced almonds (optional), and a cherry on top.

Butterscotch Sundae: Vanilla and/or chocolate ice cream with warm Butterscotch Sauce, soft whipped cream, toasted chopped walnuts or sliced almonds (optional), and a cherry on top.

Mixed Berries Sundae: Vanilla, honey, and/or strawberry or other berry ice cream, fresh berries (your choice, depending on the berries in season), macerated with a little sugar, Raspberry Sauce, soft whipped cream, crumbled sugar cookies or crumbled sugar cones (optional), and a perfect berry on top.

Brownie Sundae: A brownie topped with your favorite ice cream (be sure some of the brownie is left exposed), Hot Fudge Sauce and/or Butterscotch Sauce, soft whipped cream, toasted chopped walnuts or sliced almonds (optional), and a cherry on top.

Ice Cream Cone Sundae: If you have kids, you probably buy the crisp sugar type of ice cream cones—and if you have cones, you will inevitably end up with broken ones. Save them up and coarsely chop them with a knife. Make Hot Fudge or Butterscotch Sundaes and sprinkle generously with the crumbled cones instead of chopped nuts.

Peach Melba: A fancy French classic, this is basically a sundae. It is best if you remove the skin from the peaches: cut an X in the bottom of each peach and blanch them in boiling water for a few seconds, until the skin blisters, then place in ice water to stop the cooking; the skins should peel away easily. Cut them in half and chill. Place a scoop of vanilla ice cream in each bowl and arrange 2 peach halves so they lean on the ice cream, drizzle some Raspberry Sauce around and over the ice cream and peaches, and top with a small dollop of soft whipped cream and a few fresh raspberries.

Nectarine and Blueberry Sundae:

If you like the idea of Peach Melba but don't want to bother peeling peaches, macerate sliced nectarines (which don't need to be peeled) with blueberries and sugar, then build the sundae with vanilla ice cream, the macerated fruit, Raspberry Sauce, soft whipped cream, and a few blueberries on top.

Honey and Fig Sundae: Honey or

vanilla ice cream drizzled with honey, quartered sweet ripe figs (1 or 2 per person, depending on the size), Raspberry Sauce, and toasted sliced almonds (skip the whipped cream on this one).

Banana Split: A classic, and rightfully so.

Split a ripe banana lengthwise and place in the center of an oval or round bowl. Put 2 or 3 small scoops of vanilla ice cream in between the banana halves. Top with sliced strawberries macerated with sugar or diced pineapple. Top with Hot Fudge Sauce, leaving some of the banana and strawberries showing, soft whipped cream, and a sliced strawberry; toasted coconut is also a nice garnish.

Cherries Jubilee: If you don't have a

cherry pitter, don't even consider this idea. Pit the cherries, at least 15 per person. Warm some butter and sugar together in a skillet, add the cherries, and stew them slowly in the butter and sugar until they begin to make a rich syrup. Add a little fruit juice, kirsh, or cherry liqueur. When the cherries are soft and the syrup is thick, spoon them over vanilla ice cream and top with a dollop of soft whipped cream.

Walk-Away Sundae: This is a great

concept that we use for every sundae at Summer Shack. Make the sundaes in disposable bowls with lids (optional) and use plastic spoons, so people can "walk away" with them as they please. If you have kids who want to leave the table, or if you want to take the sundaes to the beach or wherever you might want to enjoy them, you are free to do so. Make any of the above sundaes at home, "to go." Don't forget to slip a plastic bag in your pocket to bring home the trash.

HOT FUDGE SAUCE

I urge you to make this recipe. It's really easy and it gives you 4 cups of first-rate hot fudge sauce, cheaper and far better than any you can buy. The combination of bittersweet chocolate and corn syrup gives the sauce a super sheen, big dark chocolaty flavor, and irresistible chewiness. Try this over a scoop of ice cream or other confections; you won't regret it.

For equipment, you will need a 3-quart saucepan and a whisk.

1 1/2 cups sugar
1 cup light corn syrup
1 cup unsweetened cocoa powder
1 cup water
One 16-ounce bag bittersweet chocolate chips or 1 pound bittersweet chocolate, finely chopped

1. Place the sugar, corn syrup, cocoa, and water in a medium saucepan and whisk together until completely combined. Place the pan over medium heat and whisk constantly until the sugar has dissolved. Continue to cook, whisking every 30 seconds or so, until the mixture comes to a boil. Remove from the heat.

2. Add the chocolate chips to the cocoa mixture, being careful not to splash the hot liquid on yourself, and whisk until the chips are completely melted and combined.

3. Serve the sauce right away or cool and store in the refrigerator. The sauce will keep for well over a month if tightly sealed and refrigerated. To reheat, place the desired amount of sauce in a microwaveable container or a small saucepan and heat until warm or hot; it will take about 1 minute in the microwave, or just until it starts to boil on top of the stove.

MAKES 4 CUPS

BUTTERSCOTCH SAUCE

This sauce uses only a couple of teaspoons of corn syrup for smoothness, so it isn't as cloying and sweet as commercial butterscotch sauces. It has a rich, creamy texture and wonderful flavor of brown sugar and rum, perfect on ice cream.

For equipment, you will need a large saucepan, a wooden spoon, a whisk, a 4-cup glass measure, and a small fine strainer.

3 1/2 cups heavy cream
4 tablespoons unsalted butter
1 cup packed light brown sugar
2 teaspoons light corn syrup
1/4 teaspoon salt
1 teaspoon vanilla extract
2 teaspoons dark rum

1. Pour the heavy cream into a large saucepan and bring it to a simmer over low heat, then reduce the cream over the lowest heat possible, whisking frequently, until it has thickened and measures about 2 1/2 cups, about 30 minutes. Pour the hot cream into a 4-cup glass measure and set aside.

2. Heat the butter in the same saucepan over low heat until foamy. Add the sugar and corn syrup and stir with a wooden spoon until the mixture is bubbly, about 1 minute. Pour the hot cream into the saucepan, whisking constantly, and whisk until the sugar has completely dissolved and the sauce is smooth, about 1 minute. Remove the saucepan from the heat and add the salt, vanilla, and rum.

3. Place a small fine strainer over the glass measuring cup and pour the sauce through the strainer.

4. Serve the sauce warm, or cool and store in the refrigerator. Tightly sealed and refrigerated, the sauce will keep for up to 3 weeks. To reheat, warm in a saucepan over low heat, stirring constantly; do not boil. Add a tablespoon or two of cream if the sauce has become too thick.

MAKES 3 CUPS

RASPBERRY SAUCE

Raspberry sauce is excellent over peaches and ice cream, plain cakes, and morning pancakes, or even mixed with lime and soda for a Raspberry Lime Rickey (page 328). This recipe is easy and clean—just sugar, and berries. Raspberry sauce is almost as good made with frozen berries as it is with fresh.

For equipment, you will need a 3-quart saucepan and a fine strainer.

2 pints fresh raspberries or two 12-ounce bags frozen raspberries, defrosted
1 cup sugar
Pinch of salt

1. Combine the raspberries, sugar, and salt in a medium saucepan, cover (to keep splashing at a minimum), and cook over low heat, stirring once or twice, until the berries lose their shape, give up their juices, and begin to simmer, about 5 minutes for fresh raspberries, a little longer for frozen. Remove the saucepan from the heat.

2. Pour the raspberries and juice into a fine strainer set over a glass bowl or a 2-cup liquid measuring cup. Press on the berries firmly with a wooden spoon or heatproof spatula to extract all the juices and pulp; discard the seeds. Cover the sauce and chill it before serving. The sauce keeps refrigerated for up to 1 week.

MAKES 2 CUPS

INSIDE THIS CHAPTER

Fresh Lemonade 325

Muriel's Old-Fashioned
Cooked Lemonade 326

Fresh Watermelon Juice 327

Raspberry Lime Rickey 328

Grape and Ginger Punch 329

Sangria 330

Dark and Stormy 331

Shack Bloody Mary 332

Jasper's Sour Mix 333

Daiquiri 334

Variation: Sours 334

Tom Collins and Cousins 335

Watermelon Margarita 336

Silver Coin Margarita 337

Goombay Smash 338

Petite St. Vincent Rum
Punch 339

-10-

REFRESHMENTS

began my career in the restaurant business at a bar called O'Connor's, down on the Jersey Shore. I started as a "bar back" and soon became a bartender. It was as a bartender that I learned to combine flavors. The experience gave me confidence in my ability to make things taste great and inspired me to explore that talent in the kitchen. So, you see, I have a big soft spot for the subject at hand—and I still fancy myself to be a pretty good bartender.

I consider every part of a dining experience important. I would no more serve a second-rate beverage than I would a second-rate piece of fish. I think of beverages, whether lemonade, beer, wine, or cocktails, as food, and all the food that I serve to my friends, family, or guests at my restaurants as equally important.

Highballs and other cocktails, wine, punch and beer are festive, often colorful, even beautiful. They are a metaphor for great entertaining. Beverages should never be an afterthought, especially at a party where they can set the stage—remember they are often the first thing your guest will taste. A great cocktail, like a perfect margarita, creates its own excitement. I like to feature one or two special cocktails at my parties even when I have a full bar available. At my restaurants, we feature special cocktails every night.

Serving beer and wine is easy, but making cocktails is more like cooking. When you are planning on serving a substantial amount of the same drink, it is a good idea to make a base, as in the recipe for Shack Bloody Marys (page 332)—that way, you can just add the vodka and stir. The results will be consistent, and if the base is great, the drinks will be great. Another technique is to make a large batch of a particular drink complete with the booze added, as in the recipe for Petite St. Vincent Rum Punch (page 339). Then you only have to shake the premade drink with ice cubes.

Another way to handle a big crowd is to set up your bar for highballs—they are easy and quick and most people even enjoy making their own. *Old Mr. Boston Bartender's Guide* ("the cocktail bible") defines highballs as cocktails that are "all-time favorites and easy to make." It goes on to say, "Practically any liquor may be used, in combination with ice, soda, plain water, ginger ale, and a host of other carbonated liquids." A highball is served in a tall highball glass, usually 10 or 12 ounces. The wonderful thing about highballs is that with a moderately well stocked bar, you can offer a lot of different choices, usually making most of your guests quite happy. One person might like Scotch and soda, light on the Scotch; another, strong gin and tonic; another Cuba libre (rum and coke) with no lime. If you lay out all your offerings—liquors, carbonated beverages, and garnishes like lemon twists and lime wedges—your guests can make their own drinks.

Highballs are elementary: they all start with a tall glass filled with ice cubes. Usually the vodka, gin, rum, or whiskey is added first: 1 ounce is a light drink, 2 ounces is a fairly strong drink. Then the water or mixer is added until it comes close to the top of the glass. Depending on the drink, a garnish may be added and/or a tall straw or cocktail stirrer placed in the drink. The usual mixers are club soda, ginger ale, lemon-lime (7UP), tonic, Coke, and, nowadays, Diet Coke. For a special treat, try Schweppes Bitter Lemon with gin, vodka, or rum—it's a great alternative to tonic. Half & Half, an old-fashioned grapefruit and lemon soda, is also a wonderful mixer. It is not always easy to find anymore, so if you see it in the store, I suggest you buy a couple of bottles. For the under-thirty crowd, you may want to stock some Red Bull; it's a very popular mixer these days.

On other occasions, where time is not an issue, you can make individual cocktails, such as a Silver Coin Margarita (page 337) or a refreshing Tom Collins (page 335). Here are a few things to keep in mind: It is a good idea, especially in the summer, to keep all the ingredients for cocktails chilled—even the booze. This prevents the ice in the drinks from melting too fast and diluting them. Have at least two sets of cocktail shakers and strainers on hand if you are making more than one type of drink. For example, you could keep one for the margaritas and the other for the other drinks. And be sure to set up your bar as close to a sink as possible.

Ice is very important, but sometimes homemade ice cubes aren't very good. If this is true in your situation, purchase ice cubes from the store for parties—and for everyday use. Why pour your delicious homemade lemonade over bad ice? For that matter, when making lemonade or other drinks based on water, you might even want to use bottled water. Ice cubes come in different sizes. I like larger cubes rather then small cubes (which we call "cheater cubes" in the restaurant business), because larger cubes don't melt as fast—they keep drinks colder, and undiluted, longer. For drinks that are shaken in a cocktail shaker and meant to be served very cold, it is nice when some of the ice breaks up and forms little crystals on top of the drink. One trick to accomplish this is to crack the ice before

it goes into the shaker. An easy way to do this is to put it in a heavy freezer bag and bang it on a hard surface. It may sound silly, but it makes a difference.

You don't need a lot of equipment to make great drinks. A four-piece cocktail set is essential: a glass bottom shaker, a steel top shaker, a strainer, and a long spoon for stirring. After that, I think a citrus reamer, a little wooden tool that costs about $2, is indispensable for making good drinks with fresh juices. Blenders are also great because you can then easily turn most cocktails into frozen drinks. I'm not a huge fan of frozen drinks, but they are very popular. And kids love them: it is nice to make a batch of "virgin" frozen cocktails, like strawberry daiquiris, for the kids—it makes them feel important.

Beer is like ice cream: good all year round, but especially in the summer. An ice-cold beer goes perfectly with many shack-style foods. Steamers (see page 80) are terrific with beer. Not only do the two taste great together, but the process of getting messy and dipping the steamers, with a group of friends or family, almost requires that you wash them down with cold beer. A Chesapeake-style crab dinner (see Smashing Crabs, page 76) really requires pitchers or buckets of beer—no other beverage will suffice. Lobsters are good with wine or beer, but if you are outside at a picnic table, beer seems more appropriate. And beer is always a good choice at a barbecue with grilled foods like chicken, hamburgers, and hot dogs. (At the least, it should be offered along with wine.) It might appear that lighter lager-style beers are the most appropriate for sunny summer days, but in the Caribbean, where almost every day is beautiful, Guinness is very popular. This rich Irish stout is a wonderful match for raw oysters and littlenecks. When pairing beer and seafood, the style of the beer (light or rich) isn't as important as the taste. Beers that have a strong flavor of hops tend to clash with seafood—so when the menu is predominantly seafood, choose beers that are straightforward and clean tasting, with minimal hops.

I have been drinking wine for more than thirty-five years, and I have been involved in the business of selling wine for almost as long. However, although I have had many great wine experiences in California, Europe, and even in New England, I am not up to date on the countless wines available on the market today. I find European wines, especially French, to be the easiest to select because over the years, these winemakers have codified and stylized their wines. Although quality changes from year to year, the style doesn't. In California, several styles of wines can be made from the same grape, new vineyards seem to pop up weekly, and older vineyards make stylistic changes at will. And then there are wines from Australia, New Zealand, and South America. So, it is good to know the people at your wine shop, just as at the fish market. Then you can have their recommendations.

Here I will share some general thoughts on summer wines in terms of style, body, and taste. Matching wine, unlike beer, with summer foods is not totally subjective. Certain wines, especially big robust reds, are simply inappropriate for a summer dinner at the shore. Summer red wines should be young, light, and fruity. I would also go as far as to say they should be slightly chilled (40° to 50°F).

Truly the best wine for summer is a crisp, clean but fruity, light- or medium-bodied white wine, rosé, or sparkling wine. Summer is a great time to experiment with wines from around the world. Try a light fruity German Spätlese, an Alsatian Pinot Gris or Riesling, or a rosé from France or Portugal, or California and even New England, at your next picnic or dinner. I especially like chilled rosé as a summer wine. Portugal also produces a white wine, called *viñho verde*, that is a perfect summer wine—very young, clean, crisp, and effervescent.

As you choose different wines, think about the foods they might go with. A rich piece of bluefish grilled with garlic butter can stand up to a fairly hearty white wine, but if you are serving flounder, you will want to go with something lighter. Dinner will require a little more substantial wine than lunch might, but none of the summer wines you serve should be big, buttery, oaky, and/or cloying—keep your choices on the lighter side. And remember my favorite rule—when in doubt, Champagne (or a good sparkling wine) goes with just about anything at any time of day or year.

This chapter starts with a few of my favorite nonalcoholic libations, but the heart of the chapter deals with grown-up beverages. Drinking alcoholic beverages can be fun, but only when it is done in a safe and responsible way. Watch your guests and don't let them drink too much. And, of course, keep the booze away from the kids. Let the good times roll, but please be smart—and safe.

FRESH LEMONADE

*L*emonade is to summer drinks what corn and tomatoes are to summer vegetables. Where I spend my summers, kids still sell lemonade along the side of the road. These young capitalists are not just dispensing beverages, they are learning important life lessons, and for that reason, I always feel obligated to stop and have a drink. Since I have an unquenchable thirst, and I love lemonade, it usually works out well for me.

Fresh lemonade is easy to make. It tastes better and is much less expensive than store-bought. I like to put the juice of one orange in each batch—you can't taste it, but it improves the flavor. I also like to add a thinly sliced lemon, including the rind. The oils of the lemon rind add a bit of complexity to the flavor.

For equipment, you will need a citrus reamer or a juicer and a whisk. And if you don't have good tap water, use bottled water for the best-tasting lemonade.

9   **large lemons**
1   **navel orange (or 1/2 cup orange juice)**
2   **cups sugar**
2   **cups very hot or boiling water**
3   **cups cold water**
Thin lemon slices and fresh mint sprigs for garnish (optional)

WORKING AHEAD

Make lemonade in the morning for that afternoon. Although it will keep for a couple days, it is best on the first day.

1. Cut 8 of the lemons and the orange, if using, in half and juice them. There should be a little over 2 cups. Set the juice aside.

2. Place the sugar in a large mixing bowl, add the hot water, whisk until the sugar has completely dissolved. Add the lemon juice, orange juice, and 3 cups cold water.

3. Scrub the remaining lemon and cut it into thin slices. Add them to the lemonade and whisk well to bruise the lemon slices and release their oils. Refrigerate the lemonade for at least 2 hours.

4. To serve, add ice to individual glasses and pour the chilled lemonade over the cubes. Garnish with more lemon rounds and mint sprigs, if desired.

MAKES ABOUT 2 QUARTS

MURIEL'S OLD-FASHIONED COOKED LEMONADE

This is an amazing recipe, maybe worth the price of the book alone. It comes from my wife's mother, Muriel, and was beloved by our family. Since Muriel is no longer with us, I think it is time to share this recipe as a tribute to her. Everyone who has ever tasted it, including more than one famous chef, has asked how it is made. The recipe is based on a sugar syrup, with more than one surprising ingredient, that must be aged for a couple of days before diluting it into a refreshing beverage.

To make this lemonade will require a trip to a drugstore, preferably an old-fashioned one that will be sure to carry those odd items. For equipment, you will need a food processor, a 4-quart glass pitcher or jar, and a stainless steel strainer.

2   large lemons, well scrubbed
1   navel orange, well scrubbed
2 1/2 pounds (5 3/4 cups) sugar
2   tablespoons citric acid
1   tablespoon cream of tartar
1   tablespoon Epsom salts
3 1/2 cups boiling water

MAKING AHEAD

The lemonade syrup must be made ahead and allowed to stand at room temperature for 2 days before serving.

1. Cut the lemons and orange into quarters, and remove the seeds. Place the fruit in a food processor and pulse to chop.

2. Transfer the fruit and juices to a 4-quart glass pitcher or jar, add the sugar, citric acid, cream of tartar, and Epsom salts, and stir to combine. Pour the boiling water over the fruit. Stir well. Cover and let stand at room temperature for 2 days, stirring occasionally.

3. Strain the lemonade syrup into glass bottles. Refrigerate until ready to use. The syrup keeps indefinitely in the refrigerator.

4. The syrup must be diluted with water to make lemonade. This can be done right in a tall glass or glasses of ice for individual servings or in a pitcher for a large batch. The ratio of syrup to water is 1 part syrup to 4 or 5 parts water, depending on how strong you like it.

MAKES ABOUT 2 QUARTS SYRUP, ENOUGH FOR 8 TO 10 QUARTS OF LEMONADE

FRESH WATERMELON JUICE

atermelon juice is one of the most refreshing drinks I can think of. It is very popular in Southeast Asia, and I think it is only a matter of time before its popularity becomes worldwide. I love to serve it at my summer parties—straight up for some guests, and in Watermelon Margaritas (page 336) for others. Whenever I offer it, any other beverages available are soon forgotten.

The ideal tool for making watermelon juice is a handheld immersion blender, but if you don't have one, a standard blender or food processor will work; it will just take longer, because you will have to puree the watermelon in batches. Since the only ingredient needed is a watermelon, you can make as little or as much as you like. I highly recommend that you buy a seedless watermelon for the juice; you can use a regular one, but then you will have to remove all the dark seeds (the small white ones can be left in).

Simply remove all the red watermelon flesh from the rind, avoiding the white part of the rind. Cut the watermelon into large chunks, 2 to 3 inches each, and remove any visible black seeds (even a seedless melon will have a few). Place in a large stainless steel bowl and, using an immersion blender, blend the melon to a very fine puree, with no chunks. (Or puree the melon in a regular blender or food processor.) Pour the juice in glass jars and refrigerate.

To serve, stir the juice well and pour it into tall glasses filled with ice cubes.

RASPBERRY LIME RICKEY

Here is a blast from the past: lime rickeys are part of the roadside ice cream stand genre. They are not widely available these days, but they are easy to make. This is a very special treat, a very classy refreshment that just about everyone will adore. This recipe can easily be doubled or tripled.

For equipment, you will need a citrus reamer or a juicer, a stainless steel strainer, and a heavy 3-quart stainless saucepan.

4   limes, well scrubbed
3/4 cup water
1 1/2 cups sugar
6   cups sparkling water, club soda, or seltzer
1   cup Raspberry Sauce (page 319)
8   lime slices for garnish

WORKING AHEAD
The lime syrup can be made well in advance, and the raspberry sauce should be made ahead and chilled.

1. Cut the limes in half and juice them. There should be 1/2 cup juice. Quarter each of the juiced lime halves and set aside.

2. Pour the water into a medium heavy stainless steel saucepan, sprinkle the sugar over it, and bring to a simmer over medium heat, stirring to dissolve the sugar. Simmer until the syrup has reduced by half and turned straw-colored, about 5 minutes (it should register 210°F on an instant-read thermometer).

3. Remove the saucepan from the heat and add the quartered limes. Cover and let steep for 20 minutes.

4. Strain the syrup into a bowl; discard the limes. Add the lime juice to the syrup, and pour into a glass jar or other container. Cover tightly and refrigerate until ready to use. (The syrup can be refrigerated for up to 3 weeks.)

5. To make the lime rickeys, fill eight tall 10- to 12-ounce glasses with ice cubes. Pour 3/4 cup sparkling water into each glass. Add 1/4 cup of

the lime syrup to each glass and stir briskly. Drizzle 2 tablespoons raspberry sauce over the top of each drink and garnish with a lime slice. Add long straws and serve.

Note: To make plain lime rickeys, simply omit the raspberry sauce.

MAKES 8 DRINKS

GRAPE AND GINGER PUNCH

ere is a festive punch that the kids will love; adults like it too. It's great for parties and it makes the kids feel special to have their own punch. The color is unmistakable—and that is a good thing if the party has more than one type of punch. If you really like this combination, you can scale it down and make individual drinks—it's easy, because the grape juice and ginger ale are used in equal parts. And it's also easily doubled or tripled.

If you don't have a punch bowl, you can use any large bowl, with a regular ladle. Make a large "ice cube" by filling a container that will fit inside your bowl with water and freezing it overnight.

1   quart Concord grape juice, chilled
1   quart ginger ale, preferably Schweppes or Canada Dry, chilled
8   ounces seedless red grapes, stemmed and halved
A large "ice cube" (see headnote)

WORKING AHEAD

Make the large ice cube the day before. Chill the grape juice and the ginger ale in advance so they don't melt the ice too quickly.

1. Combine the grape juice, ginger ale, and grapes in a punch bowl. Add the large ice cube and let it chill the punch for 10 minutes before serving.

SERVES 8

SANGRIA

Sangria is a fabulous way to serve wine in the summer. This Spanish concoction is usually made with red wine, but you can make it with white, if you like. Choose a fruity wine that is not too expensive; a Spanish Rioja, California Zinfandel, or similar-style wine works very well. Adding a small amount of brandy is optional, but I recommend it.

For equipment, you will need a citrus reamer and a decorative large pitcher (glass or ceramic).

2   **large juice oranges, well scrubbed**
2   **large lemons, well scrubbed**
1   **lime, well scrubbed**
6   **tablespoons sugar**
1/4 **cup brandy (optional)**
One 750-ml bottle fruity red wine, such as Rioja
Club soda or seltzer

WORKING AHEAD
Sangria tastes better if it stands for at least 4 hours before serving. Make it in the morning and chill it for cocktails that afternoon.

1. Cut 1 orange and 1 lemon in half and juice them with a citrus reamer. Set the juice aside.

2. Cut the remaining fruit, including the lime, lengthwise in half, then cut crosswise into thin slices. Place the slices in a large pitcher, add the sugar, and bruise the fruit with a wooden spoon to release the aromatic oils. Add the citrus juice and stir to dissolve the sugar. Add the brandy, if desired, and stir to combine. Stir in the wine. Refrigerate for 4 and 8 hours to mellow the flavors.

3. To serve, add a few ice cubes each to individual glasses and pour in enough chilled sangria to fill the glasses about two-thirds full; try to get at least one piece of each fruit in each glass if you can. Top off with club soda or seltzer, stir, and serve.

SERVES 4 TO 6

DARK AND STORMY

This highball is the national drink of Bermuda; to be authentic, it should be made with Gosling's dark rum and Barrett's ginger beer, both produced on that beautiful island. It is one of my very favorite cocktails—complex and delicious, yet very refreshing, and it packs a kick, which is all you can ask of any cocktail. Ginger beer, which has a somewhat harsh raw ginger flavor, is very different from ginger ale—you cannot make a Dark and Stormy with ginger ale. Ginger beer is becoming more common these days, so chances are if you can find Gosling's rum, you will find ginger beer. Although I recommend Barrett's, any good ginger beer will be fine. But I strongly suggest you use Gosling's; without it, the drink will not be nearly as good. Unlike most highballs, the liquor in this one goes on top.

About 4 ounces ginger beer, preferably Barrett's
1 1/2 to 2 ounces dark rum, preferably Gosling's
A wedge of lime

1. Fill a highball glass with ice cubes, and pour in enough ginger beer to fill the glass a bit less then two-thirds full. Gently pour the rum over the top, so that the rum stays on top and the drink is two-toned. If you pour the rum over the back of a spoon, it will land gently on top. Add the lime wedge and a cocktail stirrer, but do not stir the drink. Serve immediately.

MAKES 1 DRINK

SHACK BLOODY MARY

This recipe is for people who like Bloody Marys enough to make a batch of mix to keep on hand. Once the mix is made, making a Bloody Mary or two, or more, is very quick and easy. And because the mix was made carefully to your taste, it will be nearly perfect. It's the way to go; making Bloody Marys one at a time is messy and the results inconsistent.

In our sports bar at the Cambridge Summer Shack, we make special cocktails for Monday night football, one for each team that is playing. One night, when the Baltimore Ravens were playing, my bartender, Frankie, added Old Bay seasoning to the Bloody Mary mix and called the drinks Old Bay Bloody Marys. Apparently this idea wasn't new, but it was new to us. The Old Bay was terrific with the spicy Bloody Mary mix, and we have kept it in our recipe ever since. The optional Vietnamese chile paste adds extra spice and a mild garlic flavor.

Bloody Marys are traditionally garnished with a celery stalk, which goes very well with the drink. I recommend that you use the tender light green stalks, with the leaves attached, from the heart of the celery. Other good garnishes are jumbo green olives, peperoncini (pickled peppers), and cucumber spears. Although a wedge of lemon or lime is traditional, I don't think this mix needs any more acidity. A jumbo shrimp (see Fabulous Retro Shrimp Cocktail, page 119) makes an unusual and welcome garnish. If you really like Old Bay seasoning, you can rim each glass with a wedge of lemon and then dip it into the spice—it gives a nice kick.

For equipment, you will need a citrus reamer or juicer.

OLD BAY BLOODY MARY MIX

2   limes
1   lemon
2   tablespoons Old Bay seasoning
1   tablespoon celery seeds
1/2   teaspoon Tabasco sauce
2   tablespoons Dijon mustard
1/4   cup grated fresh or prepared horseradish
3   tablespoons Worcestershire sauce
1   tablespoon Vietnamese chile-garlic paste (optional)
1   quart V-8 vegetable juice or tomato juice
About 2 teaspoons freshly ground black pepper

FOR EACH DRINK

2   ounces vodka
4   ounces Bloody Mary Mix

WORKING AHEAD

Since Bloody Marys are often served early in the day, make the mix the day before you need it.

1. To make the mix: juice the limes and lemon. Combine the juice in a large bowl with the Old Bay seasoning, celery seeds, Tabasco sauce, mustard, horseradish, Worcestershire sauce, and chile paste, if using, and whisk together well. Add the V-8 juice, season to taste with black pepper, and mix again.

2. Pour the mix into a glass jar (or jars). Keep refrigerated, tightly sealed, until ready to use. The mix keeps well up to a week in the refrigerator. Shake it well before using.

3. To serve, fill each tall glass (at least 12 ounces) about two-thirds full with ice cubes. Add the vodka and Bloody Mary mix. Stir well, and add a few more ice cubes to bring the liquid to the top. Garnish as desired.

MAKE 5 CUPS MIX, ENOUGH FOR 10 DRINKS

JASPER'S SOUR MIX

With a good sour mix—and this is a very good one—you can make dozens of different cocktails. I developed this recipe more than twenty years ago with my friend Max, the manager of my first restaurant, and I have never changed it. Make a daiquiri or Tom Collins with this mix (both recipes follow), and you will see why.

Superfine sugar dissolves much more easily and quickly than granulated sugar, but if you don't have it on hand, you can make this with regular sugar. Just whisk a bit longer and harder.

For equipment, you will need a citrus reamer or juicer, a whisk, and a small strainer.

1 large egg white
6 large limes
4 large lemons
2 1/2 cups superfine sugar
3/4 cup lukewarm water

WORKING AHEAD
Make this early in the day or the day before you need it.

1. Put the egg white into a medium stainless steel bowl and whisk until it becomes a little frothy. Now pour half of it away. (This is the best way that I know of to measure half an egg white.)

2. Cut the limes and lemons in half. Using a citrus reamer, juice them right into the bowl with the egg white; don't worry about seeds. (Or use a juicer and add the juice to the bowl.) Add the sugar and water and whisk, until the sugar has completely dissolved.

3. Strain the mix and pour into a glass bottle or jar. Keep refrigerated, tightly sealed, until ready to use. The mix will keep for at least 1 week refrigerated. Shake well before using.

MAKES ABOUT 4 CUPS, ENOUGH FOR ABOUT 16 DRINKS

DAIQUIRI

This classic cocktail, made with white rum and sour mix, was very popular (with adults) when I was a kid, back in the '50s and '60s. Over the years, it has morphed into a frozen concoction, most often flavored with strawberries or bananas. You can take this recipe and throw it in a blender with some fruit, and it will work well, but I urge you to try the original. Shaken with cracked ice and strained into a chilled small rocks glass or martini glass, this is an elegant cocktail for the evening—it is for sipping. On very hot days, you might want to serve a similar but more refreshing rum Collins (see page 335).

2 **ounces Bacardi or other good white rum**
2 **ounces Jasper's Sour Mix (page 333)**
A thin lemon slice for garnish

1. Fill a cocktail shaker about two-thirds full with ice, preferably cracked. Add the rum and sour mix and shake very hard, until you see small particles of ice in the drink.

2. Strain the daiquiri into a chilled rocks or martini glass. Hang the lemon slice over the side of the glass, and serve immediately.

MAKES 1 DRINK

Variation: Sours

Take this basic formula and technique, substitute whiskey, Scotch, vodka, or another liquor for the rum, and you have a sour, as in a whiskey sour. Sours can be served up (strained into a chilled glass) or on the rocks and are usually garnished with an orange slice and a maraschino cherry.

TOM COLLINS AND COUSINS

I wish I could tell you who Tom Collins was, but I don't know and don't know anyone who does, although there are plenty of different stories. I do know that this is, like the daiquiri, a retro drink that is worth taking another look at, or to be precise, taste of. When made with a great sour mix, it is delicious, elegant, and refreshing. A Tom collins is made with gin; substitute vodka, and it is a vodka collins, rum and it is, yes, a rum collins. A collins is always served in a collins glass (don't ask which came first), which is tall and narrow and holds about 12 ounces, and is traditionally frosted. I love these tall coolers served in frosted glasses—it just seems right.

1 1/2 ounces Bombay or other good gin
1 1/2 ounces Jasper's Sour Mix (page 333)
Club soda or seltzer
A maraschino cherry for garnish

1. Fill a cocktail shaker about half-full with ice, preferably cracked. Add the gin and sour mix and shake well.

2. Pour the mixture into a collins glass. Gently pour in club soda, filling the glass to the top. Garnish with the maraschino cherry and serve immediately.

MAKES 1 DRINK

WATERMELON MARGARITA

Watermelon is one of those foods that epitomize summer, and this luscious drink of iced cold watermelon juice laced with tequila and citrus is a brilliant way to consume this glorious fruit. If you serve these margaritas at a party, you had better make sure you have plenty, because everyone will want one or two. Find festive, colorful glasses and chill them if possible. Portions shouldn't be too big, because it is important that the margarita is icy cold for maximum enjoyment.

This cocktail was created years ago by my friend Mark Miller, who dubbed it a "Sunburnt Señorita," a reference to its color. I serve these at parties, small and large, every summer and have changed the recipe a little to make it my own. It is also featured at Summer Shack during the warm-weather months. You can multiply this recipe and make a very large batch ahead of time, but you still must shake each drink with a few ice cubes to obtain the very desirable foamy head.

2 ounces gold tequila
3/4 ounce Triple Sec or Cointreau
2 ounces Jasper's Sour Mix (page 333)
4 ounces Fresh Watermelon Juice (page 327; shake well before measuring), chilled
1 or 2 small watermelon wedges for garnish

1. Fill a cocktail shaker one-quarter full with ice cubes. Add the tequila, Triple Sec, sour mix, and watermelon juice and shake very well, until the margarita is foamy.

2. Pour it into a chilled margarita glass or glasses and garnish with the watermelon wedge(s).

MAKE 1 LARGE OR 2 SMALL DRINKS

SILVER COIN MARGARITA

This is my favorite margarita—"silver," as in Herradura silver tequila, and "coin," as in Cointreau. With fresh squeezed lime juice as the only other ingredient, this simple recipe demands high-quality tequila. It's a recipe for tequila lovers—use the tequila you love. I love Herradura silver, but Patron silver or any other great blue-agave silver tequila will more than suffice. Other "hybrid" margaritas that use sour mix or other flavorings and sweeteners, or that are frozen in a blender, can be made with less expensive tequila (see Watermelon Margarita, page 336).

Serve the Silver Coin straight up in a martini glass, very, very cold. A nice detail is to crack the ice cubes before you mix the drink and then shake it very hard before straining, so that there will be little ice crystals at the top of the margarita. This recipe doesn't call for any added sugar; the Cointreau contributes the only sweetness. You can add a teaspoon of superfine sugar if you prefer it a little sweeter. Be sure to chill the glass well ahead of time.

2 ounces Herradura silver tequila
1/2 ounce Cointreau
1/2 lime, cut into 4 wedges
Kosher salt

1. Fill a cocktail shaker about two-thirds full with ice, preferably cracked. Add the tequila and Cointreau, then squeeze the lime wedges into the shaker and add 3 of them. Use the last wedge of lime to wet the rim of a chilled margarita glass, and dip the rim of the glass in kosher salt.

2. Shake the drink very hard, until you see small particles of ice in the drink. Strain it into the salt-rimmed glass and serve immediately.

MAKES 1 DRINK

GOOMBAY SMASH

I really like the flavor of piña coladas, but I can only drink a few spoonfuls because they are so rich and sweet. This drink, from the Bahamas, Nassau in particular, has the same wonderful pineapple and coconut flavor but is lighter and more refreshing. A dangerous option is an additional shot of 151 rum (151 proof), which is where the name "smash" came from—I don't like it, but I'm compelled to mention it because it is authentic.

1 ounce gold rum, such as Mount Gay or Barbancourt
1 ounce coconut rum, such as Parrot Bay
3 ounces pineapple juice
2 dashes orange bitters
1/2 ounce 151-proof rum (optional)
A pineapple or orange wedge for garnish
A maraschino cherry for garnish

1. Fill a cocktail shaker about half-full with ice. Add the gold and coconut rums, pineapple juice, and bitters. Add the 151-proof rum if you must, and shake well.

2. Pour into a tall glass. Garnish with the pineapple wedge and maraschino cherry.

MAKES 1 DRINK

PETITE ST. VINCENT RUM PUNCH

There are many versions of rum punch found throughout the tropics. Years ago, when I was working at Petite St. Vincent Resort in the Grenadine Islands of the Caribbean, I fell in love with their special version of rum punch, which featured a very bold rum flavor with a wonderful combination of bitter and sweet, topped with lots of freshly grated nutmeg. To really appreciate this punch, you must buy a whole nutmeg and grate it over the drink—the spice makes it authentic and delicious. The brand name of the rum used at the resort I worked at was Very Strong, from St. Vincent. I guarantee you won't find it outside of the windward islands, but Barbancourt from Barbados exports some extra-strong (over 80 proof) rums. Because this punch is strong, I serve it in small (6- to 8-ounce) glasses. This punch is for sipping, not guzzling.

This recipe makes quite a lot—it can be cut in half, if desired.

1   **quart strong gold rum, chilled**
1   **cup grenadine**
1   **cup fresh lime juice (6 to 8 limes)**
2   **cups water**
1/2 **cup honey**
10 **dashes Angostura bitters**
Freshly grated nutmeg and lime wedges for garnish

WORKING AHEAD

This punch is usually served over ice, so you don't need to make a large ice cube, as described on page 329. I do recommend you make the punch earlier in the day and refrigerate it, ready to be poured over ice and served.

1. Combine the rum, grenadine, lime juice, water, honey, and bitters in a bowl and mix well. Transfer to glass bottles or jars and refrigerate.

2. To serve, fill rocks glasses with ice, pour the punch over the ice to fill the glasses, and grate nutmeg over each drink so it lightly coats the surface. Add a wedge of lime to each one and serve.

MAKES ABOUT 2 QUARTS

INSIDE THIS CHAPTER

All-Purpose Vinaigrette 342

Variation: Tomato Vinaigrette 342

Homemade Mayonnaise 343

Variation: Herb Mayonnaise 343

Jasper's Lobster Mayonnaise 344

Tartar Sauce 344

Summer Shack Rémoulade 345

Green Goddess Dressing 346

Cocktail Sauce 347

Soy-Ginger Sauce 348

Red Sauce 349

Variation: Fra Diavolo Sauce 350

White Wine Butter Sauce 351

Garlic Herb Butter 352

Stocks and Broths 353

Fish Stock 354

Crab Stock 355

Variation: Lobster Stock 356

Chicken Stock 356

- 11 -

BASIC RECIPES

eferred to often in other chapters of this book, these basic preparations are the workhorses in my seafood restaurants and my home kitchen. They have been time-tested over my thirty years in the kitchen, and many of them are my personal favorites. I hope you too will want to use them over and over.

ALL-PURPOSE VINAIGRETTE

Classic French-style vinaigrette is one of the most useful preparations you can make. This recipe makes a quart and keeps for up to 3 weeks, ready to use for tossed green salads or simple salads with chilled vegetables, like beets or potatoes (see New Potato Salad Vinaigrette, page 142) or as a dressing for grilled or roasted vegetables. It can also be used as a marinade for meat or poultry that is intended for the grill, or it can be brushed on shrimp, scallops, squid, fish, or vegetables before grilling. And you can easily make other vinaigrettes, like tomato, by adding an ingredient or two to the basic mixture. That said, the recipe is easily halved if you would prefer to make a smaller batch.

I like the flavor of red wine vinegar, but some versions can be extremely acidic. In vinaigrette, the vinegar gets the last word, so make sure yours is good quality. Look for vinegar with acidity between 5 and 6 percent—any higher, and the vinaigrette will be harsh.

You can make this by hand, using a whisk, but for best results, use a handheld mixer, blender, or food processor.

3 large shallots, minced (1/4 cup)
1 clove garlic, minced
2 tablespoons Dijon mustard
1 cup red wine vinegar (5 to 6 percent acidity)
1 cup extra virgin olive oil
2 cups vegetable oil
2 teaspoons kosher or sea salt
3/4 teaspoon freshly ground black pepper

1. Combine all the ingredients in a bowl and whisk very well. Or, if you have the technology, mix the vinaigrette with a handheld mixer; or place the mixture (in 2 batches) in a blender jar and combine on low speed for 10 seconds, or blend (in 2 batches) in a food processor.

2. Transfer to a quart jar with a tight-fitting lid and refrigerate until ready to use. The vinaigrette keeps refrigerated for up to 3 weeks; shake or stir before using.

MAKES ABOUT 4 CUPS

Variation: Tomato Vinaigrette
Cut 2 medium ripe tomatoes (12 ounces) lengthwise in half and use a small spoon to scoop the pulp and seeds into a coarse strainer set over a bowl. Push the juice through with a ladle or the back of a spoon. Dice the tomatoes into 1/3- to

1/2-inch pieces and add them to the juice. Stir in 1 1/4 cups vinaigrette and let sit for at least 30 minutes before serving. Tomato vinaigrette can be made a few hours in advance and refrigerated until ready to use.

MAKES 2 CUPS

HOMEMADE MAYONNAISE

Although I wouldn't bother to make it for everyday preparations like coleslaw or potato salad, mayonnaise is worth making for special sauces to pair with chilled lobster or seafood such as poached salmon (see the variation below and the recipe on page 344). If you have fresh local eggs from a nearby farm or can purchase organic eggs, the chances of a food-borne illness related to raw eggs is minimal. If your only option is commercial eggs, stick to store-bought mayonnaise (Hellmann's is my favorite). Commercial and homemade mayonnaise are interchangeable in all of the recipes in this book.

3   **large egg yolks**
1 1/2 **teaspoons Dijon mustard**
2   **cups grapeseed or canola oil**
1   **tablespoon ice water**
2   **teaspoons fresh lemon juice**
1/2 **teaspoon kosher or sea salt**
Small pinch of cayenne pepper
Freshly ground black pepper to taste

1. Whisk the egg yolks and mustard together in a small deep bowl until the yolks have thickened and lightened slightly. Whisking constantly, begin to add the oil drop by drop, to allow the yolks to absorb the oil, until an emulsion has formed. Once the mixture begins to thicken, you can add the oil a little faster, but be careful—if you add it too fast it might separate. When half the oil has been added, drizzle in the ice water and 1 teaspoon of the lemon juice to stabilize the emulsion. Continue adding the remaining oil in a steady stream. The mayonnaise should be thick and glossy. Add the remaining 1 teaspoon lemon juice along with the salt, cayenne, and black pepper.

2. Transfer to a bowl or other container, cover tightly, and refrigerate until ready to use. The mayonnaise will keep, refrigerated, for up to 3 days; check the seasoning before serving and add more salt, if you like.

MAKES ABOUT 2 CUPS

Variation: Herb Mayonnaise
This sauce is delicious over cold poached salmon, bass, or even lobster. Add 2 tablespoons finely chopped shallots, 1 tablespoon chopped fresh chives, 2 tablespoons chopped fresh Italian parsley, 2 teaspoons chopped fresh chervil, and 1 teaspoon chopped fresh tarragon to 2 cups mayonnaise (homemade or store-bought). Cover and keep refrigerated.

MAKES 2 CUPS

JASPER'S LOBSTER MAYONNAISE

Use this special mayonnaise for Lobster Salad (page 130) or as a sauce for Split Chilled Lobster (page 128). You can make it with homemade or store-bought mayonnaise. A hint of tarragon or chervil makes this very special, but too much will overpower the flavor of the lobster.

3/4 cup Homemade Mayonnaise (page 343) or Hellmann's mayonnaise
2 teaspoons Dijon mustard
Dash of Tabasco sauce
1 tablespoon ice water
1 teaspoon chopped fresh tarragon or 2 teaspoons chopped fresh chervil

1. Combine the mayonnaise, mustard, Tabasco, and ice water in a small bowl and whisk well to combine. Fold in the tarragon. Transfer to a bowl or other container, cover tightly, and refrigerate until ready to use. The mayonnaise will keep for up to 3 days in the refrigerator.

MAKES SCANT 1 CUP

TARTAR SAUCE

Tartar sauce is the most well known and popular of all seafood sauces. It has a special affinity for fried seafood, especially clams, scallops, and fish. This recipe is the Summer Shack tartar sauce. It's really good—we have served thousands of portions a week for years.

3 cups Hellmann's mayonnaise
Juice of 1/2 large lemon (2 tablespoons)
1/2 onion, minced (1/3 cup)
1/4 cup minced fresh Italian parsley
4 medium dill pickle spears, minced (1/2 cup)
2 tablespoons capers, rinsed and chopped
2 hard-boiled eggs, finely chopped
1/2 teaspoon kosher or sea salt
1/2 teaspoon freshly ground black pepper

1. Combine the mayonnaise, lemon juice, onion, parsley, pickles, capers, and eggs in a large bowl and whisk well to combine. Transfer to a bowl or other container, cover tightly, and refrigerate until ready to use. Tartar sauce keeps refrigerated for up to 1 week.

MAKES ABOUT 4 CUPS

SUMMER SHACK RÉMOULADE

This variation on mayonnaise is wonderful served with fried oysters and shrimp, chilled lobster, and peel 'n' eat shrimp, among many other cold and hot seafood dishes. For that matter, it is also tasty with cold roast chicken, turkey, pork, or veal. It is a French classic, straight out of Escoffier, but I have added my own touches to this to make it less refined, and more "shore." I use whole-grain, rather than smooth mustard, and add tomato paste, Old Bay, and other seasonings, as well as chopped scallions and shallots. This recipe was featured in *Gourmet* magazine where the sauce was served with warm steamed Stonington (CT) shrimp. *Gourmet* said, "The shrimp are seasonal, but you'll want to make this rémoulade year-round. It's that good."

1 cup Hellmann's mayonnaise
1 tablespoon whole-grained Dijon mustard
2 teaspoons tomato paste
1/2 teaspoon red wine vinegar
1/2 teaspoon Worcestershire sauce
1/2 teaspoon sugar
1 teaspoon Old Bay seasoning
1 medium shallot, minced (1 tablespoon)
2 dill pickle spears, minced (1/4 cup)
2 scallions, trimmed and minced
1 tablespoon minced fresh Italian parsley
1/2 teaspoon kosher or sea salt, or to taste
1/8 teaspoon cayenne pepper, or to taste
Freshly ground black pepper

1. Combine the mayonnaise, mustard, tomato paste, vinegar, Worcestershire sauce, sugar, and Old Bay in a medium bowl and whisk until smooth. Stir in the shallot, pickles, scallions, and parsley and mix well to combine. Season with the salt, cayenne, and black pepper. Transfer to a bowl or other container, cover tightly, and refrigerate until ready to use. The sauce keeps refrigerated for up to 2 weeks.

MAKES ABOUT 2 CUPS

GREEN GODDESS DRESSING

reen Goddess dressing is a retro salad dressing that has a fantastic and memorable name. To be honest, in my version the name and color are the only things that resemble the original. I use this sauce for chilled split lobster, fresh crabmeat, and sometimes for shrimp. I don't use it for salads, although it is good spooned over fresh cucumbers and tomatoes.

For equipment, you will need a blender or food processor.

1/2 ripe medium avocado, peeled and cut into chunks
Juice of 1 lemon, or to taste
4 big sprigs parsley, leaves removed and coarsely chopped (1/4 cup)
2 scallions, trimmed and finely chopped
1/3 cup extra virgin olive oil
1/4 cup water
Kosher or fine sea salt and freshly ground black pepper
Green Tabasco sauce

1. Combine the avocado, lemon juice, parsley, and scallions in a blender or food processor. Pulse the machine until the avocado is broken up.

2. With the machine running, slowly add the oil and then the water. Scrape down the container with a rubber spatula to be sure you have a very smooth puree.

3. Season to taste with salt, pepper, and Tabasco (green Tabasco sauce is mild, so be generous). Adjust the dressing with a bit more lemon juice if necessary. Scrape into a small bowl, cover, and refrigerate until needed. The dressing keeps refrigerated for up to 3 days.

MAKES 1 GENEROUS CUP

COCKTAIL SAUCE

Cocktail sauce is the darling of the raw bar. People love the combination of sweet tomato mixed with spicy horseradish. I use Heinz chili sauce, not ketchup, so the sauce isn't too sweet. Lemon juice and Worcestershire add a tartness that gives it some zing. I like to serve cocktail sauce on the side so people can take as little or as much as they like. A small drop (1/8 to 1/4 teaspoon) on a raw clam is quite nice, but more than that overpowers—I use even less on oysters. (It's not that I don't like the stuff, I often put a little on a cracker and eat it alone.) It is best suited, I think, for the dish that bears its name: Shrimp Cocktail (page 119).

One 24-ounce bottle Heinz chili sauce
2 tablespoons prepared horseradish
1 teaspoon Worcestershire sauce
1 tablespoon fresh lemon juice
1/4 teaspoon kosher or sea salt

1. Combine all the ingredients in a medium bowl and whisk very well so the flavor of the horse-radish permeates the chili sauce. Put in a small container, cover, and refrigerate until ready to use. The sauce keeps refrigerated for up to 3 weeks.

MAKES 1 HEAPING CUP

SOY-GINGER SAUCE

Here is a classic dipping sauce that is usually served with Asian dumplings. I like to use it as a sauce for rich fish like mackerel, bluefish, and tuna: serve the fish with rice and spoon a little bit of this sauce over the rice as well as the fish. It can also be used as a quick marinade for those same fish or even for poultry, pork, and steak.

1 cup light soy sauce, such as Kikkoman
1/2 cup rice wine vinegar
A large thumb-sized piece of fresh ginger, peeled and minced (1/4 cup)
1 tablespoon Asian sesame oil
5 tablespoons sugar
5 scallions, trimmed and finely chopped

1. Combine all the ingredients in a medium bowl and whisk well. Transfer to a bowl or other container and cover tightly. Refrigerate if not using within a couple of hours. The sauce keeps refrigerated for up to 3 weeks.

MAKES ABOUT 2 CUPS

RED SAUCE

I know my red sauce. My credentials? I grew up at the Jersey Shore, I had an Italian grandmother, and I worked as a cook at Marenzi Restaurant in North Beach, San Francisco, back in the 1970s. This recipe is one for you to keep. It's a Neapolitan red sauce that is a great building block for all sorts of dishes. Use it for a quick pasta dinner or for simmering squash and/or bell peppers and onion. Or use the sauce as the base for a "fra diavolo" with mussels, lobster, or other seafood (even leftovers) and serve with rice or pasta, or drizzle it over grilled squid or other seafood see the variation that follows.

The most important part of making this sauce is to really caramelize (brown) the onions and carrots, creating a natural sweetness that balances well with the acidic tomatoes.

For equipment, you will need a 5-quart Dutch oven or other heavy pot.

Two 35-ounce cans whole tomatoes in juice
6 tablespoons olive oil
2 dried bay leaves
1 head garlic (about 12 medium cloves), separated into cloves, peeled, and finely chopped
2 medium onions (12 ounces), cut into 1/4-inch dice
2 medium carrots (8 ounces), peeled and cut into 1/4-inch dice
1 1/2 teaspoons dried oregano
2 tablespoons tomato paste
1 teaspoon kosher or sea salt
1 teaspoon freshly ground black pepper
1 1/2 cups water (or substitute dry white wine or clam juice, depending on the intended use)

1. Place the tomatoes in a large bowl and crush them with your hands so they break up into a range of smaller pieces.

2. Heat the olive oil in a 5-quart Dutch oven or other heavy pot over medium heat until fragrant but not smoking, about 40 seconds. Add the bay leaves and stir them until they begin to brown, about 10 seconds. Add the garlic and cook for 1 minute, or until it starts to turn golden. Add the onions, carrots, and oregano and cook until the onions are very brown, about 15 to 20 minutes. Stir infrequently—just enough to prevent them from scorching.

3. Add the crushed tomatoes, with their juice, the tomato paste, salt, pepper, and water and bring to a boil. Lower the heat, partially cover, and simmer, stirring occasionally so the sauce

doesn't stick, until the sauce has reduced by 2 or 3 inches and is thick enough to coat the back of a spoon, about 1 hour. Remove from the heat and let cool to room temperature.

4. Transfer the sauce to a bowl or other container, cover tightly, and refrigerate until ready to use. The sauce will keep refrigerated for up to 10 days. It can also be frozen for up to 1 month.

MAKES ABOUT 2 QUARTS

Variation: Fra Diavolo Sauce

For equipment, you will need a 3-quart saucepan.

3 **tablespoons olive oil**
4 **large cloves garlic, chopped (1/4 cup)**
1 1/2 **teaspoons crushed red pepper flakes**
2 **cups Red Sauce (above)**
One 8-ounce bottle clam juice
Kosher or sea salt

1. Heat the olive oil in a 3-quart saucepan over medium heat. Add the garlic and crushed red pepper and sauté until the garlic is fragrant and beginning to brown, about 40 seconds. Add the red sauce and clam juice and bring to a simmer. Reduce the heat and simmer gently, stirring occasionally, until the sauce returns to the thickness of the red sauce, about 15 minutes. Let cool, then cover and refrigerate until ready to use. The sauce keeps refrigerated for up to 5 days.

MAKES 2 CUPS

WHITE WINE BUTTER SAUCE

Butter sauce, or white butter sauce, is widely used in restaurants, but it is not common in home cooking. It originated in France, where it is called *beurre blanc*. It is a rich sauce with a lovely mild flavor, which makes it perfect for lean white fish such as cod, halibut, and flounder. It is very easy to make, so I urge you to add it to your seafood repertoire.

For equipment, you will need a small saucepan.

WORKING AHEAD

You can make the butter sauce an hour before you use it, but be sure to keep it in a warm place or in a double boiler over warm water so it doesn't separate. The sauce cannot be reheated.

1/2 **cup dry white wine**
2 **shallots, minced**
2 **tablespoons heavy cream**
6 **tablespoons cold unsalted butter, cut into small pieces**
1 **tablespoon white wine vinegar or fresh lemon juice**
Kosher or sea salt and freshly ground black pepper

1. Combine the white wine and shallots in a small saucepan and bring to a boil over medium heat. Reduce the liquid to about 2 tablespoons (the pan will look almost dry), about 10 minutes.

2. Add the cream and bring to a boil. Reduce the heat slightly and simmer until the cream has thickened and looks buttery, about 3 to 4 minutes. Reduce the heat to low and add the butter one piece at a time, stirring with a wooden spoon or whisking constantly, until the sauce is smooth and creamy. Remove the saucepan from the heat and stir in the vinegar. Add salt and pepper to taste. Keep the sauce warm until ready to serve.

MAKES ABOUT 1/2 CUP

GARLIC HERB BUTTER

This savory green compound butter is exquisite melted over broiled or grilled bluefish (see page 161). It also goes well with clams, mussels, and full-flavored fish such as bass, snapper, mackerel, and tuna. It is similar to the butter used for the famous *escargots bourguignonne*. At my restaurants we sometimes serve whelks (sea snails) stuffed with this butter and baked. Try a thin slice of the butter over grilled steaks and chops, letting it melt as it comes to the table—it's a knockout.

The trick to the beautiful green color of this butter is to chop the parsley when it is still wet from washing. The extra liquid helps to extract the juice from the parsley.

This recipe makes one cylinder of butter that weighs about half a pound, but the butter is extremely versatile and can be kept in tip-top condition for 2 months in the freezer, so there is no reason to make a small amount. In fact, you might want to double the recipe.

This is best made in a food processor. The butter can be made by hand, if you chop everything really fine, but it won't have the same brilliant green color.

12 to 15 large sprigs fresh Italian parsley
15 fresh chives, chopped
4 cloves garlic, chopped
1 large shallot, chopped (2 tablespoons)
3/4 teaspoon kosher or sea salt
1/4 teaspoon freshly ground black pepper
Pinch of cayenne pepper
1/2 pound (2 sticks) unsalted butter, softened

1. Remove the thick stems from the parsley. Don't worry about the small stems attached to the leaves—they will dissolve into the butter. Wash the parsley and coarsely chop it while it is still wet.

2. Place the parsley, chives, garlic, and shallot in a food processor and pulse to start breaking down the ingredients. Add the salt and both peppers and pulse to mix, then add the butter and process for 1 minute. Using a rubber spatula, scrape down the sides and bottom of the bowl and then process the butter for another minute, or until it is light and fluffy and has turned green.

3. Place a sheet of plastic wrap about 14 inches long on the counter, with a long side parallel to the counter edge. Using a rubber spatula, place the butter, in dabs, across the lower edge of the plastic wrap, to make a log ending 2 inches short of either end. Using the plastic wrap for support, roll the butter up into a tight cylinder about 10 inches long and 1 1/4 inches in diameter, then twist the ends in opposite directions to secure the plastic. Roll the cylinder up in aluminum foil and refrigerate.

4. Once it has completely chilled, you can cut the log into 4 smaller sections for storage and then rewrap. Refrigerate for immediate use, or freeze for future use—the butter can be frozen for 2 months.

5. To serve, take the butter out of the refrigerator and let it soften for 10 minutes. Slice the butter into rounds to place on top of grilled seafood or meat.

MAKES ABOUT 8 OUNCES, ENOUGH FOR 10 SERVINGS

STOCKS AND BROTHS

In the spirit of simple cooking at the shore, I want to preface the following recipes for stock (fish, crab, lobster, and chicken) by saying that it really isn't necessary to make stock for the recipes in this book. Although making stock really isn't much work—it takes more time than effort—it does require a simmering pot, and that might be too steamy or hot for your kitchen on a summer day. Without question, a homemade stock is the first choice, but even I don't cook with fresh stocks at the shore—I'd rather fish or golf than watch a stockpot. So in every recipe that calls for stock, I list, in order of preference if there is more than one choice, the appropriate substitute, usually canned chicken broth, bottled clam juice, or water. The exception is for the crab and lobster soups. Because these use very little of the actual crab or lobster meat for garnish, the small amount of meat alone cannot add enough flavor to the soups—they depend on the flavor of the simmered carcasses in the homemade stock.

The mild flavor of chicken stock is such that it both enhances dishes and carries other flavors, letting them take over the flavor profile of the dish. For example, a fish stew or chowder made with chicken stock will taste richer and better than one made with water, but it won't taste like chicken—it will taste like fish. I recommend you purchase a low-sodium canned chicken broth; these are higher quality and tend to be better then the heavily salted commercial broths.

Bottled clam broth is more assertive then chicken broth. In some cases, it works beautifully as a substitute for fish stock, but in others, chicken broth is actually a better choice. Again, my preference is stated in the individual recipe. If you cook steamers at home and you wind up with extra clam broth, freeze it to use later—it's the same as bottled broth. The best-quality bottled clam broths have only one ingredient: the juice of fresh clams. The clam juice has enough natural salt to preserve the broth.

FISH STOCK

f you catch fish, you will certainly have no shortage of heads and frames, which make a wonderful stock, and a very inexpensive one. You can make large quantities and freeze some of the stock; it is useful to have on hand for fish soups, chowders, and stews. Strong fish like salmon, bluefish, and mackerel make a stock that is very assertive and is restricted to dishes made with those species. Mild-flavored fish, such as flounder, halibut, cod, and sea bass, are best for stock. Heads make the stock very rich, but be sure to remove the gills before using them in stock.

For equipment, you will need a 7- to 8-quart stockpot, a ladle, and a large fine strainer.

4 pound fish frames (bones) and split heads from mild white fish such as sole, flounder, fluke, halibut, haddock, and/or cod, cut into 2-inch pieces and rinsed clean of any blood
1/2 cup dry white wine
About 2 quarts water
2 medium onions, very thinly sliced
4 stalks celery, very thinly sliced
2 medium carrots, peeled and very thinly sliced
2 small dried bay leaves
1/4 cup roughly chopped fresh Italian parsley leaves and stems
6 to 8 sprigs fresh thyme
1 tablespoon whole black peppercorns
Kosher or sea salt

1. Combine the fish bones, white wine, and just enough water to cover the bones in a 7- to 8-quart stockpot and bring to a boil over high heat, skimming off the white foam from the top as the stock approaches the boil. (Using a ladle and a circular motion, push the foam from the center to the edge of the pot, where it is easy to remove.) Reduce the heat to a simmer. Add the onions, celery, carrots, bay leaves, parsley, thyme, and peppercorns and stir them into the liquid. If the ingredients are not covered by liquid, add a little more water. Allow the stock to simmer gently for 20 minutes.

2. Remove the stock from the stove, stir it again, and allow it to steep for 10 minutes.

3. Strain the stock through a fine strainer into a bowl or other container and season lightly

with salt. If you are not going to use the stock within an hour, chill it as quickly as possible: Place the bowl in the sink and fill the sink with enough very cold water to come halfway up the sides of the bowl, taking care not to let water splash into the stock. Cool for 30 minutes. Cover the stock only after it has cooled completely. Refrigerate for up 3 days, or freeze for up to 2 months.

MAKES ABOUT 2 QUARTS

CRAB STOCK

Crab stock is essential for making aromatic crab soups and other crab dishes. My recipe starts with the cooked carcasses of Jonah or rock crabs. Cook the whole crabs (see page 123) and pick the claw and body meat for the soup garnish. From 2 pounds of crabs, you will get about 6 to 8 ounces of meat. If you live in an area that has fresh blue crabs, you can purchase inexpensive "soup crabs" and substitute them for the crabs called for in this recipe. There is no need to cook the soup crabs in advance—just coarsely chop them and follow the recipe.

This recipe can easily be doubled.

For equipment, you will need a 7- to 8-quart stockpot, a ladle, and a large fine strainer.

2   **pounds carcasses from steamed or boiled Jonah or rock crabs or 2 pounds soup crabs**

About 2 quarts water

1   **small onion, very thinly sliced**
1   **stalk celery, very thinly sliced**
1   **medium carrot, peeled and very thinly sliced**
1   **small dried bay leaf**
4   **sprigs fresh Italian parsley, leaves and stems coarsely chopped**
2   **sprigs fresh thyme**
1   **tablespoon whole black peppercorns**
1   **tablespoon kosher or sea salt**

1. Place the crab carcasses in a 7- or 8-quart stockpot and add enough water to cover. Bring to a boil over high heat, skimming off the white foam from the top as the stock approaches a boil. (Using a ladle and a circular motion, push the foam from the center to the edge of the pot, where it is easy to remove.) Reduce the heat to a simmer. Add the onion, celery, carrot, bay leaf, parsley, thyme, and peppercorns and stir them into the liquid; add more water if necessary to cover. Allow the stock to simmer gently for 1 hour.

2. Remove the stock from the stove, stir it again, and allow it to steep for 10 minutes.

3. Strain the stock through a fine-strainer into a bowl or other container and season with the salt. If you are not going to use the stock within an hour, chill it as quickly as possible: Place the bowl in the sink and fill the sink with enough very cold water to come halfway up the sides of the bowl, taking care not to let water splash into the stock. Cool for 30 minutes. Cover the stock only after it has cooled completely. Refrigerate for up 3 days, or freeze for up to 2 months.

MAKES ABOUT 6 CUPS

Variation: Lobster Stock

Substitute 2 pounds cooked lobster bodies, with the head sacs removed. Cut each into a few pieces. Follow the directions for the crab stock, but add 2 cups canned tomatoes with their juice when you add the other vegetables.

CHICKEN STOCK

This recipe calls for a carcass left over from roast chicken. Whenever I have leftover carcasses from roast chicken (which is often), they go into the freezer, along with the necks and giblets, for stock. But if I don't have any stashed away, I use canned broth—I just can't be bothered to buy chicken bones to make stock. This recipe uses one chicken carcass. I usually wait until I have two or more, and then increase the recipe accordingly. The stock keeps very well in the freezer.

For equipment, you will need a 7- to 8-quart stockpot, a ladle, and a large fine strainer.

A leftover roast chicken carcass, plus the raw giblets and neck from the chicken
2   **medium onions, diced**
1   **large carrot, peeled and chopped**
1   **large stalk celery, chopped**
3   **large cloves garlic**
4   **large sprigs fresh thyme**
1   **small dried bay leaf**
1   **tablespoon whole black peppercorns**
2   **quarts water, or enough to cover**

1. Combine all the ingredients in a large stockpot and bring to a boil over high heat, skimming off the foam from the top as the stock approaches a boil. (Using a ladle and a circular motion, push the foam from the center to the edge of the pot, where it is easy to remove.) Reduce the heat to a simmer, partially cover the pot, and simmer until the stock is full-flavored and has reduced to 5 to 6 cups, 1 to 1 1/2 hours. If the liquid goes below the level of the ingredients as the stock simmers, add more water.

2. Remove the pot from the stove and cool slightly.

3. Strain the stock through a large fine strainer into a bowl. If you are not going to use the stock within 30 minutes, place the bowl in the sink and fill the sink with enough very cold water to come halfway up the sides of the bowl, taking care not to let water splash into the stock. Cool for 30 minutes. Cover the stock only after it has cooled completely. Refrigerate for up to 5 days, or freeze for up to 2 months.

MAKES 5 TO 6 CUPS

INDEX

Ají Verde (Yucatán Green Sauce), 154, 161, **192**

albacore tuna, grilling times for, 151

All-Butter Flaky Pie Dough, **305–6,** 307, 309

All-Purpose Vinaigrette, 23, 137, 142, 154, 167, 187, 194, 199, **342**

almond(s)

Almond and Parmesan Bread Crumbs, **216**

Almond and Parmesan Bread Crumbs, **216**

anchovies

canned, 34

Tuna (or Salmon) Tartare, **64–65**

andouille

Indoor Clambake, **77–78**

Angel Food Cake, 297, **299–300**

appetizers

Baked Oysters "Casino," **232–33**

Broiled Butterfish with Mirin Glaze, **228–29**

Cherrystone Seviche, 46, **60–61**

Chilled Crab Claws, **125**

Chilled Maine Shrimp with Cabbage and Peanuts, Vietnamese-Style, **121–22**

Chilled Mussels with Curry Mayonnaise, **132–33**

Chilled Whole Crab, **125**

Clam Cakes (Fritters), **270–71**

Clam Soup That Cures, **95–96**

Conch Salad Bahamian-Style, 46, **62–63**

Coney Island Red Clam Chowder, **99–100**

Crab, Tomato, and Vegetable Soup, **106–7**

Crabmeat Cocktail, **126**

Creamy Cape Cod Clam Chowder, **97–98**

Fabulous Retro Shrimp Cocktail, **119–20,** 332, 347

Grilled Clams with Garlic Butter, **186–87**

Grilled Oysters with Lemon Butter, **185–86**

Home-Style Lobster Stew, **104–5**

Key West Shrimp Boil, 31, 68, **79**

Little Neck Steamers, **81**

Marinated and Grilled Calamari Accordion-Style, **187–88**

Mostly Crab Crab Cakes with English Mustard Sauce, **211–12**

Mussels in Spicy Red Sauce, **87**

Mussels with White Wine, Garlic, and Herbs, **86**

Oyster Shooters, **55**

Quick and Tasty Oyster Stew, **103–4**

Scallop and Bacon Hors d'Oeuvres, **231–32**

Scorch, **63**

Seafood Seviche with Citrus, **61–62**

Spicy and Greasy Rhode Island Calamari, **262–64**

Split Chilled Lobster, **128–29,** 344

Steamers Cooked in Beer, **82–83**

Steamers with Drawn Butter, **80–81**

Tuna (or Salmon) Tartare, **64–65**

Wild Mussels Cooked Like Steamers, **84**

apple(s)

Apple Crunch, **311–12**

in shortcake derivative, 297

Apple Crunch, **311–12**

apricots, in shortcake derivative, 297

avocado(s)

Ají Verde (Yucatán Green Sauce), 154, 161, **192**

Avocado or Papaya Hot Pepper Oil, **181**

Green Goddess Dressing, 128, 134, 158, **346**

Avocado or Papaya Hot Pepper Oil, **181**

bacon

Scallop and Bacon Hors d'Oeuvres, **231–32**

Baked Oysters "Casino," **232–33**

Baked Plum Tomatoes Gratinée, 208, 235, **244–45**

Baked Stuffed Rock Lobster Tails, **242–43**
banana splits, **128–29,** 344
beef
 flank steaks, 199
 Grilled Long Burgers, **195–96**
 grilling steaks, 198–200
 porterhouse steaks, 198
 rib-eye steaks, 199
 sirloin steaks, 198–99
 skirt steaks, 199
 steak tips, 199–200
 T-bone steaks, 198
 tenderloin/filet mignon, 199
beer
 Beer-Battered Fish and Chips, 165
 Smashing Crabs, 31, 32, **76,** 123, 323
 Steamers Cooked in Beer, **82–83**
Beer-Battered Fish and Chips, 165, 257, **266–67**
bell peppers
 Brazilian Relish, 154, 155, 161, 164, **183**
 Corn Relish, 152, 157, 158, 165, **173–74**
 grilling, 202
 Italian Pepper and Potato Stew, 286, **287**
 Portuguese Salad, **135–36,** 216, 257
 Red Pepper Aïoli (Rouille), **115**
 Sausage Sandwich, Loaded, **283–84**
 Tapenade, 155, 156, 161, 162, **174**
berry sundaes, 315
beverages
 Daiquiri, **334**
 Dark and Stormy, **331**
 Fresh Lemonade, **325**
 Fresh Watermelon Juice, **327,** 336
 Goombay Smash, **338**
 Grape and Ginger Punch, **329**
 Jasper's Sour Mix, **333,** 336
 Muriel's Old-Fashioned Cooked Lemonade,
  326
 Oyster Shooters, **55**
 Petite St. Vincent Rum Punch, 240, 322, **339**

 Raspberry Lime Rickey, 319, **328–29**
 Sangria, **330**
 Shack Bloody Mary, 322, **332–33**
 Silver Coin Margarita, 323, **337**
 Tom Collins and Cousins, 323, **335**
 Watermelon Margarita, 30, 327, **336,** 337
Black Beans and Rice, 166, 167, 180, 190,
  222–23, 240, 259
blackfish. *See* tautog
black olives
 Green Beans, Red Onions, Black Olives, and
  Blue Cheese with Romaine, **137**
 Tapenade, 155, 156, 161, 162, **174**
black sea bass. *See* sea bass
blenders, 30
blueberries
 Blueberry Buckle, **303–4**
 Blueberry Pie, 290, **307–8**
 nectarine and blueberry sundaes, 316
 in shortcake derivative, 297
Blueberry Buckle, **303–4**
Blueberry Pie, 290, **307–8**
blue cheese
 Green Beans, Red Onions, Black Olives, and
  Blue Cheese with Romaine, **137**
bluefish
 about, 161
 Broiled Bluefish with Garlic Butter, **230**
 grilling, 161–62
  times for, 151
 Plank-Roasted Salmon (or Bluefish),
  236–37
 Portuguese Fisherman's Stew, **109–10**
 raw, eating, 47
 serving, 162
 Slow-Roasted Whole Fish with Onion and
  Fennel Stuffing, **238–39**
Boardwalk French Fries, 82, 266, **268–69**
Boston Baked Scrod, **234**
Boston Brown Bread, 290, **294–95**

brandy
    Sangria, **330**
Brazilian Relish, 154, 155, 161, 164, **183**
bread(s)
    Almond and Parmesan Bread Crumbs, **216**
    Boston Brown Bread, 290, **294–95**
    Croûtes, **115**
    Overnight Sandwich Bread, 290, **292–93**
    Shortcake Biscuits, 296, **297–98,** 302
    Skillet Corn Bread, **291–92**
breading foods, 249
Broiled Bluefish with Garlic Butter, **230**
Broiled Butterfish with Mirin Glaze, **228–29**
broths, about, 34, 353
brownie sundaes, 315
Busha Browne's jerk seasoning, 170
butter(s)
    about, 34
    clarified, 207–8
    Drawn Butter, **75,** 78, 79
    Garlic Butter Sauce, 152, 154, **186**
    Garlic Herb Butter, 160, 172, 188, 189, 193,
        230, **352–53**
    Grilled Clams with Garlic Butter, **186–87**
    Grilled Oysters with Lemon Butter, **185–86**
    Lemon Herb Butter, 158, 160, 162, 164, 167,
        172–73, 190
    White Wine Butter Sauce, 152, 154, 158, 164,
        351
butter beans
    Succotash Salad, 20, 23, **138–39,** 234, 257, 260
butterfish
    Broiled Butterfish with Mirin Glaze, **228–29**
Butterscotch Sauce, 315, **318**
butterscotch sundaes, 315
Buttery Crumbs, **235,** 244

cabbage
    Chinese or Napa
        Chilled Maine Shrimp with Cabbage and
            Peanuts, Vietnamese-Style, **121–22**

    Savoy
        Crab, Tomato, and Vegetable Soup, **106–7**
    white
        Summer Shack Coleslaw, 21, 23, 76, **140,**
            234, 254, 256, 257, 258, 260, 261, 266
cakes
    Angel Food Cake, 297, **299–300**
    Blueberry Buckle, **303–4**
    Lemon Butter Cake, **300–301**
calamari. *See* squid
Callaloo, **108–9**
canola oil, 33, 207, 249
capers
    Pan-Roasted Whole Flounder or Fluke with
        Brown Butter, Lemon, and Capers,
        224–25
Caribbean Hot Pepper Oil, 154, 155, 156, 162,
    166, 167, **181,** 188, 190
Caribbean "Jammed" Crabs, **240–41**
Caribbean Spiced Salt, 32, 160, 162, 165, 166,
    167, **169,** 178, 240, 259
carrots
    Summer Shack Coleslaw, 21, 23, 76, **140,** 234,
        254, 256, 257, 258, 260, 261, 266
cast-iron pans, 28, 206
Cataplana, **101–2**
Cataplana with Mussels, **102**
charcoal, wood, 147–48
charcoal briquettes, 148
charcoal grills, 30
cheese
    about, 34
    Almond and Parmesan Bread Crumbs, **216**
    Green Beans, Red Onions, Black Olives, and
        Blue Cheese with Romaine, **137**
chef's knives, 26
cherries jubilee, 316
cherrystone clams, 37
Cherrystone Seviche, 46, **60–61**
cherry tomatoes, grilling, 203
chicken

Chicken Stock, 99, 106, 108, 109, **356–57**
cutting up, 274–75
Grilled Marinated Chicken, **194–95**
Jasper's Fried Chicken, **272–73**
Chicken Stock, 99, 106, 108, 109, **356–57**
chiffonade, 108
chili
Quick Onion Chili, 285, **287**
chili peppers
Avocado or Papaya Hot Pepper Oil, **181**
Caribbean Hot Pepper Oil, 154, 155, 156, 162,
166, 167, **181,** 188, 190
Scorch, **63**
Chilled Crab Claws, **125**
Chilled Maine Shrimp with Cabbage and
Peanuts, Vietnamese-Style, **121–22**
Chilled Mussels with Curry Mayonnaise, **132–33**
Chilled Whole Crab, **125**
chilling
for handling seafood, 38–39
of seafood to be grilled, 149–50
chimneys, for grilling, 29
Chinese cabbage
Chilled Maine Shrimp with Cabbage and
Peanuts, Vietnamese-Style, **121–22**
Chinese cleavers, 27
Chinese wire-mesh skimmers, 27
chocolate
Hot Fudge Sauce, 315, **317**
Whoopie Pies, 290, **313–14**
chouriço
Cataplana, **101–2**
Cataplana with Mussels, **102**
Indoor Clambake, **77–78**
Portuguese Fisherman's Stew, **109–10**
Slow-Roasted Whole Fish with Onion and
Fennel Stuffing, **238–39**
chowders
Coney Island Red Clam Chowder, **99–100**
Creamy Cape Cod Clam Chowder, **97–98**
citrus reamers, 26

clam(s)
about, 58
belly, 254
Cataplana, **101–2**
Cherrystone Seviche, 46, **60–61**
Clam Cakes (Fritters), **270–71**
Clam Roll, **279–80**
Clam Soup That Cures, **95–96**
Coney Island Red Clam Chowder, **99–100**
Creamy Cape Cod Clam Chowder, **97–98**
deep-frying, cooking time for, 253
digging for, 36–37
fried
about, 254
serving, 254
Grilled Clams with Garlic Butter, **186–87**
hard-shell
about, 56
gathering, 37
Indoor Clambake, **77–78**
Little Neck Steamers, **81**
Pork Stew with Clams and Garlic Sauce,
111–12
Portuguese Fisherman's Stew, **109–10**
purchasing, 58
raw, eating, 39, 47, 59
regional, 57
Shack Bouillabaisse, **113–14**
shucking, 58–59
soft-shell
about, 56
gathering, 37
steamers, how to eat, 81
Steamers Cooked in Beer, **82–83**
Steamers with Drawn Butter, **80–81**
storing, 39, 58
Clam Cakes (Fritters), **270–71**
clam hoes, 38
clam knives, 27
Clam Roll, **279–80**
Clam Soup That Cures, **95–96**

clarified butter, 207–8

Classic Maine Lobster Roll, **278–79**

cleaning mussels, 85

cleaning oysters, 50

cleaning squid, 265

cleavers, 27

cobbler

    Nectarine Cobbler, **302–3**

Cocktail Sauce, 50, 55, 79, 119, **347**

coconut milk

    Callaloo, **108–9**

cod

    Beer-Battered Fish and Chips, 165, 257,
        266–67

    Boston Baked Scrod, **234**

    Fish Stock, 99, 109, 113, **354–55**

    Perfect Panfried Breaded Fish, **215–16**

    Portuguese Fisherman's Stew, **109–10**

    salt, 34

        Salt Cod Cakes, **213–14**

    Slow-Roasted Whole Fish with Onion and
        Fennel Stuffing, **238–39**

Cointreau

    Silver Coin Margarita, 323, **337**

    Watermelon Margarita, 30, 327, **336,** 337

Cold Cucumber Sauce, 22, 157, 159, 162, 164,
    180

Cold Poached Salmon, **134–35**

common crackers, 99

conch

    Conch Salad Bahamian-Style, 46, **62–63**

    cracking, 63

    raw, eating, 39, 47

    Scorch, **63**

Conch Salad Bahamian-Style, 46, **62–63**

condiments. *See also* relishes; savory sauces

    about, 33–34

    Curry Paste, **171**

Coney Island Red Clam Chowder, **99–100**

cooking utensils, 26–27, 29

coolers, 31

corn

    on the cob, 90–91

        boiling, 90–91

        etiquette for eating, 91

        grilling, 201

        serving, 91

        shucking, 90

    Corn Relish, 152, 157, 158, 165, **173–74**

    Crab, Tomato, and Vegetable Soup, **106–7**

    Indoor Clambake, **77–78**

corn bread

    Skillet Corn Bread, **291–92**

corn oil, 249

Corn Relish, 152, 157, 158, 165, **173–74**

Crab, Tomato, and Vegetable Soup, **106–7**

crab(s) and crabmeat

    blue crabmeat, 123

    Callaloo, **108–9**

    Caribbean "Jammed" Crabs, **240–41**

    Chilled Crab Claws, **125**

    Chilled Whole Crab, **125**

    chilling, 124

    cleaning whole crabs, 124

    cooked, storing, 124

    cooking crabs, 123–24

    Crab, Tomato, and Vegetable Soup, **106–7**

    Crabmeat Cocktail, **126**

    Crab Stock, **355–56**

    cracking crabs, 125

    deep-frying, cooking time for, 253

    handling live crabs, 40

    Jonah crab claws, 123

    Maine rock crabmeat (peekytoe), 122–23

    Mostly Crab Crab Cakes with English Mus-
        tard Sauce, **211–12**

    serving, 125

    Smashing Crabs, 31, 32, **76,** 123, 323

    snow crabmeat, 122

    soft-shell crabs, 122, 209

        cleaning, 210

        fried, about, 260

Sautéed Soft-Shell Crabs with Garlic and
Parsley, **208–9**
serving, 260
sizes of, 209
steaming times for crabs, 69
stone crab claws, 123
storing, 39
whole snow crabs, 122
Crabmeat Cocktail, **126**
Crab Stock, **355–56**
crackers
Buttery Crumbs, **235,** 244
common crackers, 99
Pilot crackers, 99
Slow-Roasted Whole Fish with Onion and
Fennel Stuffing, **238–39**
cracking conch, 63
cranberry beans
Succotash Salad, 20, 23, **138–39,** 234, 257,
260
cream
Butterscotch Sauce, 315, **318**
Creamy Cape Cod Clam Chowder,
97–98
Quick and Tasty Oyster Stew, **103–4**
Soft Whipped Cream, 296, **298,** 302, 315
Creamy Cape Cod Clam Chowder, **97–98**
Creamy Mustard Sauce, 123, 125, 126, **127,** 212,
260
Creamy Potato Salad, 20, **141–42**
Crispy Fried Seafood (master recipe), **250–51**
Croûtes, **115**
cucumbers
Brazilian Relish, 154, 155, 161, 164, **183**
Cold Cucumber Sauce, 22, 157, 159, 162, 164,
180
Portuguese Salad, **135–36**
Curry Mayonnaise, 132, **133,** 259
Curry Paste, 108, 152, 154, 167, **171**
cutting fish, 42–43
cutting up chicken, 274–75

Daiquiri, **334**
dairy products. *See also specific dairy products*
about, 34
purchasing, 25
Dark and Stormy, **331**
dasheen, 108
debearding mussels, 85
deep-fat fryers, 28, 30
deep-frying. *See also specific foods*
basics of, 249–50
desserts. *See also* cakes; pie(s)
Apple Crunch, **311–12**
Blueberry Buckle, **303–4**
ice cream sundaes, 315–19
Nectarine Cobbler, **302–3**
Strawberry Shortcake, **296–97**
Whoopie Pies, 290, **313–14**
dill pickles
Summer Shack Rémoulade, 79, 119, 134, 212,
255, 256, 257, 259, 260, 261, **345**
Tartar Sauce, 212, 213, 254, 256, 259, 261,
266, 279, **344**
dipping sauces
Soy-Mirin Dipping Sauce, **127**
Wasabi, Lime, and Soy Dipping Sauce, 50, **59**
diver scallops, 152
dockside shopping, 24–25
dolphinfish. *See* mahimahi
double-dipping steamers, 81
Drawn Butter, **75,** 78, 79
dressings. *See also* mayonnaise; vinaigrettes
Green Goddess Dressing, 128, 134, 158, **346**
dried beans
Succotash Salad, 20, 23, **138–39,** 234, 257,
260
drinks. *See* beverages
dry fry mixes
New England-Style Fry Mix, 250, **252,** 254,
256, 257, 258, 259, 260, 261, 272, 279
Southern-Style Fry Mix, 250, **253,** 255, 256,
257, 259, 272

"dry" scallops, 152
Dutch ovens, 28

eggplant, grilling, 202
eggs
    Ají Verde (Yucatán Green Sauce), 154, 161,
        192
    Indoor Clambake, **77–78**
egg whites
    Angel Food Cake, 297, **299–300**
egg yolks
    Herb Mayonnaise, **343**
    Homemade Mayonnaise, 127, 133, 140, 171,
        343, 344
    Jasper's Lobster Mayonnaise, 128, 130, 134,
        344
    Red Pepper Aïoli (Rouille), **115**
electric deep-fat fryers, 30
English Mustard Sauce, **212**
equipment, 26–31

Fabulous Retro Shrimp Cocktail, **119–20,** 332,
        347
farmers' markets, 25
farm stands, 25
fennel
    Fennel Slaw, 152, 157, 165, **184**
    Shack Bouillabaisse, **113–14**
Fennel Slaw, 152, 157, 165, **184**
figs, in shortcake derivative, 297
filleting fish
    flatfish, 41
    round fish, 42
fish
    Beer-Battered Fish and Chips, 165, 257,
        266–67
    bleeding, 38
    Boston Baked Scrod, **234**
    Broiled Bluefish with Garlic Butter, **230**
    Broiled Butterfish with Mirin Glaze, **228–29**
    cutting, 42

deep-frying, cooking time for, 253
filleting, 41, 42
Fish Stock, 99, 109, 113, **354–55**
flat, skinning and filleting, 41
freezing, 39
fried
    about, 257
    serving, 257
gutting, 40
Pan-Roasted Whole Flounder or Fluke with
        Brown Butter, Lemon, and Capers,
        224–25
Perfect Panfried Breaded Fish, **215–16**
Plank-Roasted Salmon (or Bluefish),
        236–37
portioning, 42–43
Portuguese Fisherman's Stew, **109–10**
Portuguese-Style Panfried Hake, **217–18**
raw, eating, 39–40, 47
round, skinning and filleting, 42
salt and pepper fish, 149
Salt Cod Cakes, **213–14**
scaling, 40–41
Seafood Seviche with Citrus, **61–62**
Slow-Roasted Whole Fish with Onion and
        Fennel Stuffing, **238–39**
Tuna (or Salmon) Tartare, **64–65**
fish fillet knives, 27
Fish Stock, 99, 109, 113, **354–55**
fish tweezers, 27
flounder
    Beer-Battered Fish and Chips, 165, 257,
        266–67
    Fish Stock, 99, 109, 113, **354–55**
    Pan-Roasted Whole Flounder or Fluke with
        Brown Butter, Lemon, and Capers, **224–25**
    Perfect Panfried Breaded Fish, **215–16**
flours, at the beach, 33
fluke
    Beer-Battered Fish and Chips, 165, 257,
        266–67

Fish Stock, 99, 109, 113, **354–55**

Pan-Roasted Whole Flounder or Fluke with Brown Butter, Lemon, and Capers, **224–25**

Perfect Panfried Breaded Fish, **215–16**

food processor(s), 30

Food Processor Pie Dough, **305,** 307, 309

Fra Diavolo Sauce, **350**

freezing seafood, 39

French knives, 26

Fresh Horseradish Sauce, 50, **54,** 55, 134

Fresh Lemonade, **325**

fresh shell beans

Succotash Salad, 20, 23, **138–39,** 234, 257, 260

Fresh Watermelon Juice, **327,** 336

fried foods. *See* deep-frying; *specific foods*

Fried Peppers with Garlic and Olive Oil, **219–20**

fritters

Clam Cakes (Fritters), **270–71**

fruit(s). *See also specific fruits*

about, 35

purchasing, 25

in shortcake derivative, 297

Tropical Fruit Salsa, 154, 160, 162, 166, 167, **178**

Fry Daddy, 30

frying peppers

Fried Peppers with Garlic and Olive Oil, **219–20**

fry mixes

New England-Style Fry Mix, 250, **252,** 254, 256, 257, 258, 259, 260, 261, 272, 279

Southern-Style Fry Mix, 250, **253,** 255, 256, 257, 259, 272

garlic

Fried Peppers with Garlic and Olive Oil, **219–20**

Garlic Butter Sauce, 154, **186**

Garlic Herb Butter, 160, 172, 188, 189, 193, 230, **352–53**

Grilled Clams with Garlic Butter, **186–87**

Pork Stew with Clams and Garlic Sauce, **111–12**

Roasted Garlic and Mustard Glaze, 154, 156, 162, **175,** 200

Sautéed Soft-Shell Crabs with Garlic and Parsley, **208–9**

Garlic Butter Sauce, 154, **186**

Garlic Herb Butter, 160, 172, 188, 189, 193, 230, **352–53**

gas grills, 30, 148

gin

Tom Collins and Cousins, 323, **335**

ginger

Soy-Ginger Sauce, 88, 156, 161, 162, 199, 207, **348**

Steamed Black Sea Bass with Ginger and Scallions, **88–89**

ginger ale

Grape and Ginger Punch, **329**

ginger beer

Dark and Stormy, **331**

glazes

Maple Lemon Glaze, 152, 154, 164, **179,** 200, 228

Roasted Garlic and Mustard Glaze, 154, 156, 162, **175,** 200

Goombay Smash, **338**

grains, at the beach, 33

Grape and Ginger Punch, **329**

grape(s) and grape juice

Grape and Ginger Punch, **329**

grapefruit

Seafood Seviche with Citrus, **61–62**

grapeseed oil, 33, 207, 249

grape tomatoes, grilling, 203

GreatGrate, 185, 186

green beans

Crab, Tomato, and Vegetable Soup, **106–7**

Green Beans, Red Onions, Black Olives, and Blue Cheese with Romaine, **137**

Green Beans, Red Onions, Black Olives, and
	Blue Cheese with Romaine, **137**
Green Goddess Dressing, 128, 134, 158, **346**
grenadine
	Petite St. Vincent Rum Punch, 240, 322,
		339
Grilled American Lobster Tails, **191**
Grilled Clams with Garlic Butter, **186–87**
Grilled King Mackerel with Lime Marinade and
	Garlic Butter, **188–89**
Grilled Long Burgers, **195–96**
Grilled Marinated Chicken, **194–95**
Grilled Oysters with Lemon Butter, **185–86**
Grilled Rock Lobster Tails with Ají Verde,
		190–92
grilling, 146–203. *See also specific foods*
	building fire for, 148
	grills for, 147, 148
	of meat, 193
		sausages, 197
		steaks and chops, 198–200
	of poultry, 193
	sauces, butters, garnishes, and accompani-
		ments for, 172–83
	of seafood. *See* seafood, grilling
	seasoned salts and spice rubs for, 167–72
	setting up for, 147, 148
	of vegetables, 201–3
	wood charcoal and charcoal briquettes for,
		147–48
grilling tools, 29
Griswold pans, 28, 206
grouper
	deep-frying, cooking time for, 253
	fried
		about, 259
		serving, 259
	Perfect Panfried Breaded Fish, **215–16**
	Seafood Seviche with Citrus, **61–62**
gutting fish, 40

haddock
	Beer-Battered Fish and Chips, 165, 257,
		266–67
	Boston Baked Scrod, **234**
	Fish Stock, 99, 109, 113, **354–55**
	Perfect Panfried Breaded Fish, **215–16**
hake
	Beer-Battered Fish and Chips, 165, 257,
		266–67
	Perfect Panfried Breaded Fish, **215–16**
	Portuguese Fisherman's Stew, **109–10**
	Portuguese-Style Panfried Hake, **217–18**
halibut
	about, 158
	Fish Stock, 99, 109, 113, **354–55**
	grilling, 158
		times for, 151
	Perfect Panfried Breaded Fish, **215–16**
	Portuguese Fisherman's Stew, **109–10**
	serving, 158
handheld blenders, 30
"hard bread," 99
hard-shell clams, 37, 56
herb(s)
	dried, 32
	fresh, 32
Herb Mayonnaise, **343**
Herb Rub for Planked Fish, **237**
herring, eating raw, 39
Home Fries, 23, 217, **221–22,** 238, 257
Homemade Mayonnaise, 127, 133, 140, 171,
		343, 344
Home-Style Lobster Stew, **104–5**
honey and fig sundaes, 316
hors d'oeuvres. *See* appetizers
horseradish
	Cocktail Sauce, 50, 55, 79, 119, **347**
	Fresh Horseradish Sauce, 50, **54,** 55, 134
	Shack Bloody Mary, 322, **332–33**
horticultural beans

Succotash Salad, 20, 23, **138–39,** 234, 257, 260

hot dogs, 285–87

    Jersey Shore Italian Hot Dogs, **286**

    Summer Shack Corn Dogs, **276–77**

Hot Fudge Sauce, 315, **317**

hot fudge sundaes, 315

ice

    for serving oysters, 50

    for storing seafood, 38–39

ice cream cone sundaes, 315

ice cream sundaes, 315–19

Indoor Clambake, **77–78**

ingredients. *See also specific ingredients*

    at the beach, 32–35

    shopping for, 24–25

Italian Pepper and Potato Stew, 286, **287**

Jamaican Jerk Seasoning, 154, 162, 166, **170–71**

Japanese fish tweezers, 27

Japanese-style knives, 26

Jasper's Fried Chicken, **272–73**

Jasper's Lobster Mayonnaise, 128, 130, 134, **344**

Jasper's Sour Mix, **333,** 336

Jersey Shore Italian Hot Dogs, **286**

Jersey Shore Tuna Sub, **281–82**

Key West Shrimp Boil, 31, 68, **79**

kielbasa

    Indoor Clambake, **77–78**

kingfish

    Grilled King Mackerel with Lime Marinade and Garlic Butter, **188–89**

kitchen appliances, 30

knives

    chef's, 26

    clam, 27

    cleavers, 27

    fish fillet, 27

    French, 26

    Japanese-style, 26

    oyster, 27

lamb chops, grilling, 200

lemon(s) and lemon juice, **63**

    about, 35

    Conch Salad Bahamian-Style, 46, **62–63**

    Fresh Lemonade, **325**

    Green Goddess Dressing, 128, 134, 158, **346**

    Grilled Oysters with Lemon Butter, **185–86**

    Jasper's Sour Mix, **333,** 336

    Lemon Butter Cake, **300–301**

    Lemon Herb Butter, 158, 160, 162, 164, 167, **172–73,** 190

    Maple Lemon Glaze, 152, 154, 164, **179,** 200, 228

    Muriel's Old-Fashioned Cooked Lemonade, **326**

    with oysters, 53

    Pan-Roasted Whole Flounder or Fluke with Brown Butter, Lemon, and Capers, **224–25**

    Sangria, **330**

    Shack Bloody Mary, 322, **332–33**

    Tartar Sauce, 212, 213, 254, 256, 259, 261, 266, 279, **344**

Lemon Butter Cake, **300–301**

Lemon Herb Butter, 158, 160, 162, 164, 167, **172–73,** 190

lima beans

    Succotash Salad, 20, 23, **138–39,** 234, 257, 260

limes and lime juice

    about, 35

    Cherrystone Seviche, 46, **60–61**

    Grilled King Mackerel with Lime Marinade and Garlic Butter, **188–89**

limes and lime juice (*continued*)

Jamaican Jerk Seasoning, 154, 162, 166,
170–71

Jasper's Sour Mix, **333**, 336

Petite St. Vincent Rum Punch, 240, 322, **339**

Raspberry Lime Rickey, 319, **328–29**

Seafood Seviche with Citrus, **61–62**

Shack Bloody Mary, 322, **332–33**

Tropical Fruit Salsa, 154, 160, 162, 166, 167,
178

Wasabi, Lime, and Soy Dipping Sauce,
50, **59**

Wasabi Lime Vinaigrette, 156, 161, 162, **177,**
188, 207

linguiça

Indoor Clambake, **77–78**

Portuguese Fisherman's Stew, **109–10**

Slow-Roasted Whole Fish with Onion and
Fennel Stuffing, **238–39**

little neck clams, 37

Little Neck Steamers, **81**

lobsters

Baked Stuffed Rock Lobster Tails, **242–43**

Classic Maine Lobster Roll, **278–79**

cooking for a large group, 72

cutting up, 71–72

eating

raw, 39

technique for, 72–74

Grilled American Lobster Tails, **191**

Grilled Rock Lobster Tails with Ají Verde,
190–92

Indoor Clambake, **77–78**

live, handling, 40

Lobster Salad, **130,** 278, 344

Lobster Stock, 113, **356**

Pan-Roasted Lobster with Tomatoes, Butter,
and Herbs, **226–27**

in the rough, 31, 71–72

Shack Bouillabaisse, **113–14**

Split Chilled Lobster, **128–29,** 344

steaming, 69, 71

storing, 39

Lobster Salad, **130,** 278, 344

Lobster Stock, 113, **356**

mackerel

about, 155

Grilled King Mackerel with Lime Marinade
and Garlic Butter, **188–89**

grilling, 155–56

times for, 151

Portuguese Fisherman's Stew, **109–10**

raw, eating, 39, 47

Seafood Seviche with Citrus, **61–62**

serving, 156

mahimahi

about, 166

grilling, 166

times for, 151

serving, 167

main courses. *See also* chowders; soups; stews

Baked Stuffed Rock Lobster Tails, **242–43**

Beer-Battered Fish and Chips, 165, 257,
266–67

Boston Baked Scrod, **234**

Broiled Bluefish with Garlic Butter, **230**

Caribbean "Jammed" Crabs, **240–41**

Chilled Maine Shrimp with Cabbage and
Peanuts, Vietnamese-Style, **121–22**

Cold Poached Salmon, **134–35**

Green Beans, Red Onions, Black Olives, and
Blue Cheese with Romaine, **137**

Grilled American Lobster Tails, **191**

Grilled King Mackerel with Lime Marinade
and Garlic Butter, **188–89**

Grilled Marinated Chicken, **194–95**

Grilled Rock Lobster Tails with Ají Verde,
190–92

Indoor Clambake, **77–78**

Jasper's Fried Chicken, **272–73**

Lobster Salad, **130,** 278, 344

Marinated and Grilled Calamari Accordion-Style, **187–88**

Mostly Crab Crab Cakes with English Mustard Sauce, **211–12**

Pan-Roasted Lobster with Tomatoes, Butter, and Herbs, **226–27**

Pan-Roasted Whole Flounder or Fluke with Brown Butter, Lemon, and Capers, **224–25**

Pan-Seared Tuna with Japanese Flavors, **207–8**

Perfect Panfried Breaded Fish, **215–16**

Plank-Roasted Salmon (or Bluefish), **236–37**

Portuguese-Style Panfried Hake, **217–18**

Salt Cod Cakes, **213–14**

Sautéed Soft-Shell Crabs with Garlic and Parsley, **208–9**

Slow-Roasted Whole Fish with Onion and Fennel Stuffing, **238–39**

Smashing Crabs, 31, 32, **76,** 123, 323

Steamed Black Sea Bass with Ginger and Scallions, **88–89**

Wild Mussels Cooked Like Steamers, **84**

managing time, 22–23

Maple Lemon Glaze, 152, 154, 164, **179,** 200, 228

maple syrup

    Blueberry Pie, 290, **307–8**

    Maple Lemon Glaze, 152, 154, 164, **179,** 200, 228

margaritas

    Silver Coin Margarita, 323, **337**

    Watermelon Margarita, 30, 327, **336,** 337

Marinated and Grilled Calamari Accordion-Style, **187–88**

Marshmallow Fluff

    Whoopie Pies, 290, **313–14**

Mason jars, 29

mayonnaise

    Creamy Mustard Sauce, 123, 125, 126, **127,** 212, 260

    Curry Mayonnaise, 132, **133,** 259

    Herb Mayonnaise, **343**

    Homemade Mayonnaise, 127, 133, 140, 171, **343,** 344

    homemade versus purchased, 33

    Jasper's Lobster Mayonnaise, 128, 130, 134, **344**

    Red Pepper Aïoli (Rouille), **115**

    Summer Shack Coleslaw, 21, 23, 76, **140,** 234, 254, 256, 257, 258, 260, 261, 266

    Summer Shack Rémoulade, 79, 119, 134, 212, 255, 256, 257, 259, 260, 261, **345**

    Tartar Sauce, 212, 213, 254, 256, 259, 261, 266, 279, **344**

meats. *See also specific meats*

    purchasing, 25

Mignonette Sauce, 50, **53**

milk

    Home-Style Lobster Stew, **104–5**

    Quick and Tasty Oyster Stew, **103–4**

mirin

    Broiled Butterfish with Mirin Glaze, **228–29**

    Soy-Mirin Dipping Sauce, 125, **127**

mixed berries sundaes, 315

Mostly Crab Crab Cakes with English Mustard Sauce, **211–12**

Muriel's Old-Fashioned Cooked Lemonade, **326**

mushrooms, grilling, 201

mussels

    Cataplana with Mussels, **102**

    Chilled Mussels with Curry Mayonnaise, **132–33**

    cleaning, 85

    debearding, 85

    Indoor Clambake, **77–78**

    Mussels in Spicy Red Sauce, **87**

    Mussels with White Wine, Garlic, and Herbs, **86**

mussels (*continued*)

    picking, 36, 38

    Portuguese Fisherman's Stew, **109–10,** 216, 257

    raw, eating, 39

    Shack Bouillabaisse, **113–14**

    storing, 39

    Wild Mussels Cooked Like Steamers, **84**

Mussels in Spicy Red Sauce, **87**

Mussels with White Wine, Garlic, and Herbs, **86**

mustard

    English Mustard Sauce, **212**

    Roasted Garlic and Mustard Glaze, 154, 156, 162, **175,** 200

Napa cabbage

    Chilled Maine Shrimp with Cabbage and Peanuts, Vietnamese-Style, **121–22**

nectarine(s)

    nectarine and blueberry sundaes, 316

    Nectarine Cobbler, **302–3**

    in shortcake derivative, 297

Nectarine Cobbler, **302–3**

needle-nose pliers, 27

New England-Style Fry Mix, 250, **252,** 254, 256, 257, 258, 259, 260, 261, 272, 279

New Potato Salad Vinaigrette, **142–43,** 257, 342

nuts

    Almond and Parmesan Bread Crumbs, **216**

    Apple Crunch, **311–12**

    Chilled Maine Shrimp with Cabbage and Peanuts, Vietnamese-Style, **121–22**

ocean perch

    Beer-Battered Fish and Chips, 165, 257, **266–67**

oils

    about, 33, 207

    Avocado or Papaya Hot Pepper Oil, **181**

    Caribbean Hot Pepper Oil, 154, 155, 156, 162, 166, 167, **181,** 188, 190

    for deep-frying, 249

okra

    Callaloo, **108–9**

Old Bay seasoning, 14, 32, 68, 76, 167, 332, 345

olive oil, 33, 207

onions

    Green Beans, Red Onions, Black Olives, and Blue Cheese with Romaine, **137**

    grilling, 202

    Quick Onion Chili, 285, **287**

    Red Onion Vinaigrette, 156, 157, 158, 161, 162, **182,** 188

    Sausage Sandwich, Loaded, **283–84**

oranges and orange juice

    Conch Salad Bahamian-Style, 46, **62–63**

    Fresh Lemonade, **325**

    Muriel's Old-Fashioned Cooked Lemonade, **326**

    Sangria, **330**

    Scorch, **63**

    Seafood Seviche with Citrus, **61–62**

    Tropical Fruit Salsa, 154, 160, 162, 166, 167, **178**

outdoor grills, 30

outdoor propane burners, 30–31

ovens, 30

Overnight Sandwich Bread, 290, **292–93**

oyster(s)

    Baked Oysters "Casino," **232–33**

    cleaning, 50

    condiments for, 53–54

    deep-frying, cooking time for, 253

    fried

        about, 255

        serving, 255

    Grilled Oysters with Lemon Butter, **185–86**

    purchasing, 49

    Quick and Tasty Oyster Stew, **103–4**

    raw

        about, 48–49

        eating, 39, 47, 49, 59

Oyster Shooters, **55**
  serving, 50
 shucking, 50–51
 storing, 39, 49–50
 varieties of, 52–53
oyster knives, 27
Oyster Shooters, **55**

Pan-Roasted Lobster with Tomatoes, Butter, and
  Herbs, **226–27**
Pan-Roasted Whole Flounder or Fluke with Brown
  Butter, Lemon, and Capers, **224–25**
pans, 27–29
Pan-Seared Tuna with Japanese Flavors,
  207–8
papayas
  Avocado or Papaya Hot Pepper Oil, **181**
  Tropical Fruit Salsa, 154, 160, 162, 166, 167,
   178
Parmigiano-Reggiano cheese
  Almond and Parmesan Bread Crumbs, **216**
Parsley Salad, **139,** 155, 156
peaches
  peach Melba, 315–16
  in shortcake derivative, 297
peanut(s)
  Chilled Maine Shrimp with Cabbage and
   Peanuts, Vietnamese-Style, **121–22**
peanut oil, 33, 207, 249
pecans
  Apple Crunch, **311–12**
peeling shrimp, 120
pepper, black
  with oysters, 53
peppers. *See* bell peppers; chili peppers; frying
  peppers
Perfect Panfried Breaded Fish, **215–16**
Petite St. Vincent Rum Punch, 240, 322, **339**
pickles
  Summer Shack Rémoulade, 79, 119, 134, 212,
   255, 256, 257, 259, 260, 261, **345**

Tartar Sauce, 212, 213, 254, 256, 259, 261,
   266, 279, **344**
pie(s)
  Blueberry Pie, 290, **307–8**
  Strawberry Pie, 290, **309–10**
pie dough
  All-Butter Flaky Pie Dough, **305–6,** 307, 309
  Food Processor Pie Dough, **305,** 307, 309
pie pans, 29
Pilot crackers, 99
pineapples and pineapple juice
  Goombay Smash, **338**
  Tropical Fruit Salsa, 154, 160, 162, 166, 167,
   178
Plank-Roasted Salmon (or Bluefish), **236–37**
plastic ware, 29
pliers, needle-nose, 27
pollock
  Beer-Battered Fish and Chips, 165, 257,
   266–67
pork
  chops, grilling, 200
  Pork Stew with Clams and Garlic Sauce,
   111–12
Pork Stew with Clams and Garlic Sauce, **111–12**
portioning fish, 42–43
Portuguese Fisherman's Stew, **109–10**
Portuguese Salad, **135–36,** 216, 257
Portuguese-Style Panfried Hake, **217–18**
potatoes
  Boardwalk French Fries, 82, 266, **268–69**
  Coney Island Red Clam Chowder, **99–100**
  Creamy Cape Cod Clam Chowder, **97–98**
  Creamy Potato Salad, 20, **141–42**
  grilling, 201–2
  Home Fries, 23, 217, **221–22,** 238, 257
  hot or warm potato salad, 143
  Indoor Clambake, **77–78**
  Italian Pepper and Potato Stew, 286, **287**
  New Potato Salad Vinaigrette, **142–43,** 257,
   342

potatoes (*continued*)

    Salt Cod Cakes, **213–14**

punch

    Grape and Ginger Punch, **329**

    Petite St. Vincent Rum Punch, 240, 322, **339**

quahogs, 37

quahog scratchers, 37

Quick and Tasty Oyster Stew, **103–4**

Quick Onion Chili, 285, **287**

ranges, 30

raspberries

    Raspberry Lime Rickey, 319, **328–29**

    Raspberry Sauce, 315, **319,** 328

    in shortcake derivative, 297

Raspberry Lime Rickey, 319, **328–29**

Raspberry Sauce, 315, **319,** 328

raw seafood, eating, 39–40, 47, 59

red onions

    Green Beans, Red Onions, Black Olives, and
        Blue Cheese with Romaine, **137**

    Red Onion Vinaigrette, 156, 157, 158, 161,
        162, **182,** 188

Red Onion Vinaigrette, 156, 157, 158, 161, 162,
    182, 188

Red Pepper Aïoli (Rouille), **115**

Red Sauce, 87, 287, **349–50**

red snapper. *See* snapper

red wine

    Sangria, **330**

relishes

    Brazilian Relish, 154, 155, 161, 164, **183**

    Corn Relish, 152, 157, 158, 165, **173–74**

    Tapenade, 155, 156, 161, 162, **174**

rice

    Black Beans and Rice, 166, 167, 180, 190,
        222–23, 240, 259

roadside stands, 24–25

Roasted Garlic and Mustard Glaze, 154, 156,
    162, **175,** 200

roasting pans, 28–29

rolling pins, 29

romaine

    Green Beans, Red Onions, Black Olives, and
        Blue Cheese with Romaine, **137**

rouille. *See* Red Pepper Aïoli (Rouille)

rubs

    Herb Rub for Planked Fish, **237**

    Jamaican Jerk Seasoning, 154, 162, 166,
        170–71

rum

    Daiquiri, **334**

    Dark and Stormy, **331**

    Goombay Smash, **338**

    Petite St. Vincent Rum Punch, 240, 322, **339**

Saffron Stewed Tomatoes, 154, 157, 161, 162,
    176–77

salads

    Chilled Maine Shrimp with Cabbage and
        Peanuts, Vietnamese-Style, **121–22**

    Conch Salad Bahamian-Style, **62–63**

    Creamy Potato Salad, 20, **141–42**

    Fennel Slaw, 152, 157, 165, **184**

    Green Beans, Red Onions, Black Olives, and
        Blue Cheese with Romaine, **137**

    Lobster Salad, **130,** 278, 344

    New Potato Salad Vinaigrette, **142–43,** 257,
        342

    Parsley Salad, **139,** 155, 156

    Portuguese Salad, **135–36,** 216, 257

    potato, hot or warm, 143

    Shrimp Salad, **131**

    Succotash Salad, 20, 23, **138–39,** 234, 257,
        260

    Summer Shack Coleslaw, 21, 23, 76, **140,** 234,
        254, 256, 257, 258, 260, 261, 266

    Tuna Salad, 281, **282–83**

salad spinners, 29

salmon

    about, 163

Cold Poached Salmon, **134–35**

cold-smoked, 34

grilling, 163–64

   times for, 151

Plank-Roasted Salmon (or Bluefish), **236–37**

raw, eating, 39, 47

Salmon Tartare, **64–65**

Seafood Seviche with Citrus, **61–62**

serving, 164

Slow-Roasted Whole Fish with Onion and
Fennel Stuffing, **238–39**

Salmon Tartare, **64–65**

salt

   for baking recipes, 290

   at the beach, 33

   Caribbean Spiced Salt, 32, 160, 162, 165, 166,
167, **169,** 178, 240, 259

   Seasoned Salt for Chicken, 194, **273**

   Spiced Seafood Salt, 32, 78, **168,** 207, 215,
257, 266

salt and pepper fish, 149

salt cod, 34

   Salt Cod Cakes, **213–14**

Salt Cod Cakes, **213–14**

sandwiches, 278–84

   Clam Roll, **279–80**

   Classic Maine Lobster Roll, **278–79**

   Grilled Long Burgers, **195–96**

   Jersey Shore Tuna Sub, **281–82**

   Lobster Salad, **130,** 278, 344

   Sausage Sandwich, Loaded, **283–84**

   Shrimp Salad, **131**

   Summer Shack Corn Dogs, **276–77**

Sangria, **330**

sardines

   about, 154

   canned, 34

   grilling, 154–55

      times for, 151

   raw, eating, 39

   serving, 155

sauces. *See* savory sauces; sweet sauces

sausage(s). *See also* hot dogs

   Cataplana, **101–2**

   grilling, 197

   Indoor Clambake, **77–78**

   Portuguese Fisherman's Stew, **109–10**

   Sausage Sandwich, Loaded, **283–84**

   Slow-Roasted Whole Fish with Onion and
Fennel Stuffing, **238–39**

Sausage Sandwich, Loaded, **283–84**

Sautéed Soft-Shell Crabs with Garlic and
Parsley, **208–9**

sauté pans, 27

savory sauces

   Ají Verde (Yucatán Green Sauce), 154, 161,
192

   Cocktail Sauce, 50, 55, 79, 119, **347**

   Cold Cucumber Sauce, 22, 157, 159, 162, 164,
180

   Creamy Mustard Sauce, 123, 125, 126, **127,**
212, 260

   English Mustard Sauce, **212**

   Fra Diavolo Sauce, **350**

   Fresh Horseradish Sauce, 50, **54,** 55, 134

   Italian Pepper and Potato Stew, 286, **287**

   Mignonette Sauce, 50, **53**

   Quick Onion Chili, 285, **287**

   Red Sauce, 87, 287, **349–50**

   Saffron Stewed Tomatoes, 154, 157, 161, 162,
176–77

   Soy-Ginger Sauce, 88, 156, 161, 162, 199,
207, **348**

   Soy-Mirin Dipping Sauce, 125, **127**

   Tartar Sauce, 212, 213, 254, 256, 259, 261,
266, 279, **344**

   Tropical Fruit Salsa, 154, 160, 162, 166, 167,
178

   Wasabi, Lime, and Soy Dipping Sauce, 50,
59

   White Wine Butter Sauce, 152, 154, 158, 164,
351

Savoy cabbage
    Crab, Tomato, and Vegetable Soup, **106–7**
scaling fish, 40–41
scallions
    Callaloo, **108–9**
    Steamed Black Sea Bass with Ginger and
        Scallions, **88–89**
scallop(s)
    about, 152
    deep-frying, cooking time for, 253
    diver, 152
    "dry," 152
    freezing, 39
    fried
        about, 256
        serving, 256
    grilling, 152
        times for, 151
    raw, eating, 39, 47
    Scallop and Bacon Hors d'Oeuvres, **231–32**
    Seafood Seviche with Citrus, **61–62**
    serving, 152
    Shack Bouillabaisse, **113–14**
    "soaked" or "treated," 152
    storing, 39
Scallop and Bacon Hors d'Oeuvres, **231–32**
Scorch, **63**
sea bass
    raw, eating, 47
    Seafood Seviche with Citrus, **61–62**
    Slow-Roasted Whole Fish with Onion and
        Fennel Stuffing, **238–39**
    Steamed Black Sea Bass with Ginger and
        Scallions, **88–89**
seafood. *See also* fish; shellfish; *specific types of
    seafood*
    canned, 34
    contaminants on, 40
    cured, 34
    deep-frying
        cooking times for, 253

Crispy Fried Seafood (master recipe),
    250–51
    fry mixes for, 252–53
    times for, 253
dried, 34–35
freshness of, judging, 36
grilling
    chilling seafood for, 149–50
    cooking times for, 151
    method for, 148–49, 150
    salt and pepper fish, 149
    seafood combinations for, 149
handling of, 38–40
purchasing, 24–25, 36
raw, eating, 39–40, 47
smoked, 34–35
Seafood Seviche with Citrus, **61–62**
sea scallops. *See* scallop(s)
seasoned salt(s)
    Caribbean Spiced Salt, 32, 160, 162, 165, 166,
        167, **169,** 178, 240, 259
    Seasoned Salt for Chicken, 194, **273**
    Spiced Seafood Salt, 32, 78, **168,** 207, 215,
        257, 266
Seasoned Salt for Chicken, 194, **273**
seviche
    Cherrystone Seviche, 46, **60–61**
    Seafood Seviche with Citrus, **61–62**
Shack Bloody Mary, 322, **332–33**
Shack Bouillabaisse, **113–14**
shell beans, fresh
    Succotash Salad, 20, 23, **138–39,** 234, 257,
        260
shellfish. *See also specific types of shellfish*
    freezing, 39
    freshness of, judging, 36
    gathering, 36–38
    raw, eating, 39, 47, 59
    storing, 39
sherry
    Quick and Tasty Oyster Stew, **103–4**

Shortcake Biscuits, 296, **297–98,** 302

shrimp

about, 153

Chilled Maine Shrimp with Cabbage and Peanuts, Vietnamese-Style, **121–22**

deep-frying, cooking time for, 253

Fabulous Retro Shrimp Cocktail, **119–20,** 332, 347

fried

about, 261

serving, 261

grilling, 153

times for, 151

Key West Shrimp Boil, 31, 68, **79**

peeling, 120

raw, eating, 39

serving, 154

Shack Bouillabaisse, **113–14**

Shrimp Salad, **131**

steaming times for, 69

storing, 39

Shrimp Salad, **131**

shucking clams, 58–59

shucking corn, 90

shucking oysters, 50–51

side dishes. *See also* salads

Baked Plum Tomatoes Gratinée, 208, 235, **244–45**

Black Beans and Rice, 166, 167, 180, 190, **222–23,** 240, 259

Boardwalk French Fries, 82, 266, **268–69**

Clam Cakes (Fritters), **270–71**

Fried Peppers with Garlic and Olive Oil, **219–20**

Green Beans, Red Onions, Black Olives, and Blue Cheese with Romaine, **137**

Home Fries, 23, 217, **221–22,** 238, 257

Parsley Salad, **139,** 155, 156

Portuguese Salad, **135–36,** 216, 257

Saffron Stewed Tomatoes, 154, 157, 161, 162, **176–77**

Succotash Salad, 20, 23, **138–39,** 234, 257, 260

Silver Coin Margarita, 323, **337**

silver hake. *See* hake

Skillet Corn Bread, **291–92**

skinning fish

flatfish, 41

round fish, 42

slaws

Fennel Slaw, 152, 157, 165, **184**

Summer Shack Coleslaw, 21, 23, 76, **140,** 234, 254, 256, 257, 258, 260, 261, 266

Slow-Roasted Whole Fish with Onion and Fennel Stuffing, **238–39**

Smashing Crabs, 31, 32, **76,** 123, 323

smelts

deep-frying, cooking time for, 253

fried

about, 258

serving, 258

snapper

about, 165

grilling, 165–66

times for, 151

Perfect Panfried Breaded Fish, **215–16**

Seafood Seviche with Citrus, **61–62**

serving, 166

Slow-Roasted Whole Fish with Onion and Fennel Stuffing, **238–39**

soft-shell clams, 37

soft-shell crabs. *See* crab(s) and crabmeat, soft-shell

Soft Whipped Cream, 296, **298,** 302, 315

sole

Fish Stock, 99, 109, 113, **354–55**

soups

Callaloo, **108–9**

Clam Soup That Cures, **95–96**

Coney Island Red Clam Chowder, **99–100**

Crab, Tomato, and Vegetable Soup, **106–7**

Creamy Cape Cod Clam Chowder, **97–98**

sour cream
  Cold Cucumber Sauce, 22, 157, 159, 162, 164, **180**
  Creamy Mustard Sauce, 123, 125, 126, **127,** 212, 260
Southern-Style Fry Mix, 250, **253,** 255, 256, 257, 259, 272
Soy-Ginger Sauce, 88, 156, 161, 162, 199, 207, **348**
Soy-Mirin Dipping Sauce, 125, **127**
soy sauce
  Soy-Ginger Sauce, 88, 156, 161, 162, 199, 207, **348**
  Soy-Mirin Dipping Sauce, 125, **127**
  Wasabi, Lime, and Soy Dipping Sauce, 50, **59**
Spanish mackerel. *See* mackerel
spice(s), dried, 32
Spiced Seafood Salt, 32, 78, **168,** 207, 215, 257, 266
spice mixes, 32–33
Spicy and Greasy Rhode Island Calamari, **262–64**
spinach
  Callaloo, **108–9**
Split Chilled Lobster, **128–29,** 344
spoons, wooden, 26
squash, grilling, 202
squid
  cleaning, 265
  deep-frying, cooking time for, 253
  Marinated and Grilled Calamari Accordion-Style, **187–88**
  Portuguese Fisherman's Stew, **109–10**
  raw, eating, 39
  Spicy and Greasy Rhode Island Calamari, **262–64**
staying cool, 20–21
Steamed Black Sea Bass with Ginger and Scallions, **88–89**
steamer(s), 37
  how to eat, 81

Steamers Cooked in Beer, **82–83**
Steamers with Drawn Butter, **80–81**
steamer pots, 28, 70
Steamers Cooked in Beer, **82–83**
Steamers with Drawn Butter, **80–81**
stews
  Cataplana, **101–2**
  Cataplana with Mussels, **102**
  Home-Style Lobster Stew, **104–5**
  Italian Pepper and Potato Stew, 286, **287**
  Pork Stew with Clams and Garlic Sauce, **111–12**
  Portuguese Fisherman's Stew, **109–10**
  Quick and Tasty Oyster Stew, **103–4**
  Shack Bouillabaisse, **113–14**
stocks
  about, 34, 353
  Chicken Stock, 99, 106, 108, 109, **356–57**
  Crab Stock, **355–56**
  Fish Stock, 99, 109, 113, **354–55**
  Lobster Stock, 113, **356**
strawberries
  Strawberry Pie, 290, **309–10**
  Strawberry Shortcake, **296–97**
Strawberry Pie, 290, **309–10**
Strawberry Shortcake, **296–97**
striped bass
  about, 157
  grilling, 157
    times for, 151
  Perfect Panfried Breaded Fish, **215–16**
  Portuguese Fisherman's Stew, **109–10**
  raw, eating, 39, 47
  Seafood Seviche with Citrus, **61–62**
  serving, 157
  Slow-Roasted Whole Fish with Onion and Fennel Stuffing, **238–39**
Succotash Salad, 20, 23, **138–39,** 234, 257, 260
sugar, at the beach, 33
Summer Shack Coleslaw, 21, 23, 76, **140,** 234, 254, 256, 257, 258, 260, 261, 266

Summer Shack Corn Dogs, **276–77**

Summer Shack Rémoulade, 79, 119, 134, 212, 255, 256, 257, 259, 260, 261, **345**

summer squash, grilling, 202

sweet sauces

Butterscotch Sauce, 315, **318**

Hot Fudge Sauce, 315, **317**

Raspberry Sauce, 315, **319,** 328

swordfish

about, 159

grilling, 159

times for, 151

raw, eating, 40

serving, 159–60

Tapenade, 155, 156, 161, 162, **174**

Tartar Sauce, 212, 213, 254, 256, 259, 261, 266, **344**

tautog

about, 164

Beer-Battered Fish and Chips, 165, 257, **266–67**

grilling, 164–65

times for, 151

serving, 165

tequila

Silver Coin Margarita, 323, **337**

Watermelon Margarita, 30, 327, **336,** 337

thermal coolers and boxes, 31

time management, 22–23

tinker mac, grilling times for, 151

tomatoes

about, 35

Ají Verde (Yucatán Green Sauce), 154, 161, **192**

Baked Plum Tomatoes Gratinée, 208, 235, **244–45**

Brazilian Relish, 154, 155, 161, 164, **183**

Cataplana, **101–2**

Cataplana with Mussels, **102**

Coney Island Red Clam Chowder, **99–100**

Crab, Tomato, and Vegetable Soup, **106–7**

Fra Diavolo Sauce, **350**

grilling, 203

Pan-Roasted Lobster with Tomatoes, Butter, and Herbs, **226–27**

Pork Stew with Clams and Garlic Sauce, **111–12**

Portuguese Fisherman's Stew, **109–10**

Portuguese Salad, **135–36,** 216, 257

Portuguese-Style Panfried Hake, **217–18**

Red Sauce, 87, 287, **349–50**

Saffron Stewed Tomatoes, 154, 157, 161, 162, **176–77**

Shack Bouillabaisse, **113–14**

Tomato Vinaigrette, 154, 155, 156, 157, 165, 187, **342–43**

tomato juice

Shack Bloody Mary, 322, **332–33**

Tomato Vinaigrette, 154, 155, 156, 157, 165, 187, **342–43**

Tom Collins and Cousins, 323, **335**

tongs, 29

top neck clams, 37

Triple Sec

Watermelon Margarita, 30, 327, **336,** 337

Tropical Fruit Salsa, 154, 160, 162, 166, 167, **178**

tuna

about, 160, 208

canned, 34

grilling, 160

times for, 151

Jersey Shore Tuna Sub, **281–82**

Pan-Seared Tuna with Japanese Flavors, **207–8**

raw, eating, 39, 47

Seafood Seviche with Citrus, **61–62**

serving, 161

Tuna Salad, 281, **282–83**

Tuna Tartare, **64–65**

Tuna Salad, 281, **282–83**

Tuna (or Salmon) Tartare, **64–65**

utensils, 26–27, 29

vegetable(s). *See also specific vegetables*
   grilling, 201–3
   purchasing, 25
vegetable juice
   Shack Bloody Mary, 322, **332–33**
vegetable oils. *See* oils
vegetable oil sprays, 33
vinaigrettes
   All-Purpose Vinaigrette, 23, 137, 142, 154,
      167, 187, 194, 199, **342**
   Red Onion Vinaigrette, 156, 157, 158, 161,
      162, **182,** 188
   Tomato Vinaigrette, 154, 155, 156, 157, 165,
      187, **342–43**
   Wasabi Lime Vinaigrette, 156, 161, 162, **177,**
      188, 207
vodka
   freezing, 55
   Oyster Shooters, **55**
   Shack Bloody Mary, 322, **332–33**

walk-away sundaes, 316
Walkerswood jerk seasoning, 170
wasabi
   Wasabi, Lime, and Soy Dipping Sauce, 50, **59**
   Wasabi Lime Vinaigrette, 156, 161, 162, **177,**
      188, 207
Wasabi, Lime, and Soy Dipping Sauce, 50, **59**
Wasabi Lime Vinaigrette, 156, 161, 162, **177,**
   188, 207
watermelon
   Fresh Watermelon Juice, **327**
   Watermelon Margarita, 30, 327, **336,** 337

Watermelon Margarita, 30, 327, **336,** 337
whipped cream
   Soft Whipped Cream, 296, **298,** 302, 315
white cabbage
   Summer Shack Coleslaw, 21, 23, 76, **140,** 234,
      254, 256, 257, 258, 260, 261, 266
white wine
   Cataplana, **101–2**
   Cataplana with Mussels, **102**
   Cold Poached Salmon, **134–35**
   Mussels in Spicy Red Sauce, **87**
   Mussels with White Wine, Garlic, and Herbs,
      86
   Pork Stew with Clams and Garlic Sauce,
      111–12
   White Wine Butter Sauce, 152, 154, 158, 164,
      351
White Wine Butter Sauce, 152, 154, 158, 164,
   351
Whoopie Pies, 290, **313–14**
Wild Mussels Cooked Like Steamers, **84**
wine. *See* red wine; sherry; white wine
wire grill brushes, 29
wire-mesh skimmers, 27
wood charcoal, 147–48
wooden citrus reamers, 26
wooden spoons, 26
working ahead, 22–23

yellowtail
   Seafood Seviche with Citrus, **61–62**
yogurt
   Cold Cucumber Sauce, 22, 157, 159, 162, 164,
      180

Zatarains, 32
zucchini, grilling, 202

A NOTE ABOUT THE AUTHOR

Jasper White is the chef and owner of the Summer Shack restaurants and the author of *50 Chowders*, *Lobster at Home*, and *Cooking from New England*. Born and raised at the Jersey Shore, White graduated from the Culinary Institute of America in Hyde Park, New York. He was the chef at a variety of Boston restaurants, including the Parker House, before opening his own restaurant, Jasper's, in 1983. After twelve years, White closed Jasper's, and in 2000 he opened his first Summer Shack restaurant in Fresh Pond, Cambridge. Locations in Boston, Mohegan Sun Casino in Uncasville, Connecticut, and Logan Airport followed. White lives outside of Boston with his family.